Christianity: A Successful Failure

Finding Faith in an Age of Fear and Falsehood

Tim Spiess

DEDICATION

This book it dedicated to my life companion who is faithful and who sticks with me though most forsake me. And to all who yearn for what is true and right and long to see meaning and beauty in the lives that we are given—who want to live out true love with others, and who work to bring this to pass, "Your kingdom come. Your will be done, on earth as it is in heaven" A kingdom of Light, Life and Love.

CONTENTS

ACKNOWLEDGMENTS

Without my best friend on this side – which friend supports me with all her heart – this book would most likely not exist.

All it takes is for someone to show the way . . .

PREFACE

This book is first and foremost an existential adventure and challenge, meaning it will encourage and enable the reader to question basic life-views that we all hold and that most of us have been taught to believe, or assume, are true. *Trying to find the best answers to life's most important questions is required if you want to live a complete life and find deeper meaning and truth in this life.* Seeking answers to questions like:

- Is it reasonable to believe I evolved from hydrogen gas which is what naturalistic evolution teaches?
- Can mere physical chemicals reasonably account for my ability to know right from wrong, or to know and experience forgiveness?
- Is love merely an emotion?
- What is the purpose of human life?
- What is the purpose of my life?
- What is truly important in life?
- What am I as a human being?
- How do I value things and why?
- What am I truly living for and is it valuable?
- Is there is a higher form of love and can I experience a life where I give and receive that love with others on a daily basis?
- Does Christianity genuinely represent God well?
- If Christianity is wrong, what do I do about my guilt?

In sum, this book is about answering the question, "what view makes the best sense of the reality that I experience and answers best the question about what I am and what is truly valuable?" You might ask why I need to address Christianity to answer that question, and the book will make that clear. In short, Christianity claims to provide the best answer to that essential question.

The simple truth is that the vast majorities of people merely go along with "the program" given to them by others (parents, religious leaders, etc.) and complain when it doesn't go their way. Sadly, they never ask those questions, or if they do, they give up quickly and never diligently pursue satisfying answers—answers that pass the test of reason and logic—answers that lead to good and positive change.

As one might be able to tell from the title I am not a Christian, although I was one for years. If you have not been exposed to Christian concepts, you are fortunate, although you would be very unusual indeed since Christians and their God beliefs have been spread all over the earth. This book is not coming from, nor defending, a Christian worldview. In fact, it is challenging many of the beliefs that Christians say are true—it is challenging Christianity itself as its contemporary religious leaders and authorities define Christianity.

The book could be entitled, "Religion: A Successful Failure," since Christianity is not unique in its failures but mirrors the other major world religions like Islam or Judaism, etc. However, since I was both raised as a Christian and then after a genuine conversion experience as an adult spent many years involved in and committed to the Christian religious system, it is appropriate I focus specifically on the Christian religion. In other words, the criticism of, "oh, well, he doesn't have any practical knowledge or experience with Christianity'" would be false. (As we shall see, that criticism is fallacious anyway since I don't need experience to judge whether most non-experiential things are true or false.)

Reading this book will take some courage *if* you do so sincerely with a willingness to learn or change. If you read this book with a defensive shield on, then no courage is required, and you are wasting your time.

If you are a Christian, this book will be very challenging. I hope you will discover that I am not unfair or mean-spirited in my corrections and in identifying the things that are wrong with Christianity. My approach in this respect should remove the temptation to make the unfair accusation that it is my bitterness or bad experiences with Christians or "the church," or some other such incorrect thing that is the motivation for this book. *The fact is that the motivation for this book is to bring desperately needed and beneficial change to many people, including Christians who see their need.*

There are many excellent and well-intentioned Christians who spend time sincerely helping people. This book takes nothing away from their efforts to help other people, unless, of course, the primary way they view helping others is to get them to believe wrong Christian doctrine or participate in religious rituals or the foolish expenditure of resources.

If you are an atheist, non-theist or agnostic, this book should be of particular interest to you. Many non-theists and agnostics have legitimate gripes against Christianity and Christians and have correctly identified wrong beliefs and practices. However, if you are going to try and use this book as fodder for your cannon against the existence of God, you should be surprised how that will not work *if* you use reason and observation well, the tools you properly extol. I urge you to evaluate all possibilities of what can be true about human life and not filter out possibilities that you don't like or don't currently fit your life or worldview.

Hopefully, we can agree that one characteristic of a good person is one who will try and be fair and as objective as possible. The critical term "objective" is defined as follows:

- "Expressing or dealing with facts or conditions as perceived without distortion by personal feelings, prejudices, or interpretations" [1];
- "Not influenced by personal beliefs or feelings; fair or real" [2]; or,
- "Of a person or their judgment; not influenced by personal feelings or opinions in considering and representing facts." [3]

Being as objective as possible is extremely important in evaluating anything. If the reader has noticed, people's concern with being objective is becoming an increasingly rare thing so you will have to be different and thus be concerned about being objective.

Equally crucial to trying to be as objective as possible is that we acknowledge that *we all have a world or existential view that has components of personal beliefs, feelings, bias, prejudices, opinions, etc.*; and that world or existential view will usually cause us to have a bias against other views. Part of this author's job in writing this book is to attempt to put aside my personal bias, feelings, etc. in as much as that is possible, and thus to be as objective and fair as possible.

Ultimate or absolute reality does exist and the more objective we are, the more we will not be afraid to apply the valuable tools of observation, reason, and logic to the worthwhile pursuit of finding, discovering, clarifying and understanding that reality.

A word about science - many believe that "science" is the sure and sole realm of truth and that it provides the best worldview and that it that will

---

[1] Merriam-Webster Dictionary, www.merriam-webster.com, April 2018

[2] Cambridge Dictionary, www.dictionary.cambridge.org, April 2018

[3] Oxford Living Dictionary, www.en.oxforddictionaries.com, April 2018

solve humankind's problems. That perspective is an erroneous view as we shall see. Science – empirical science – deals with the physical realm and is practiced in the present. Some of the most important concepts regarding human existence are outside the physical realm, namely love, forgiveness, compassion, justice, etc. Science is a valuable tool/practice and practicing science well can solve many human problems. However, it is inadequate and impotent to address the most critical human issues that exist, which problems cause human conflict, abuse and neglect and all the evils associated with those things.

I will close the preface with a few comments about the book format and style.

I have endeavored to keep the content of this book as simple as possible. I have concluded that simplicity conveys truth in the fullest and clearest manner possible. To help the reader get what I am trying to convey, I have included both *Opening Chapter Questions* as well as *Chapter Summaries*. The purpose of the *Opening Chapter Questions* is to help the reader begin considering what the Chapter addresses and to bring their attention and focus to those ideas. The purpose of the *Chapter Summaries* is to repeat in a clear and concise way the central concepts conveyed in the chapters. One of the benefits of having these *Opening Questions* and *Chapter Summaries* is if a particular chapter does not interest you, you can still follow the flow of the book by just reading the *Opening Questions* and *Chapter Summary*.

The Purpose of this Book

I hope the reader likes illustrations because I am going to use quite a few of them.

The purpose of my previous book was to take the lamp out of the closet and put the lamp on the table in the room so people could see by it. However, people are not making it into the room to see the lamp and the things in the room, but instead, are being kept in or led into the house next door because the house next door has a cool light that is very attractive. The lamp in the first house – the life-giving one that can help people see clearly – is a pure, bright, clear, warm light. Also, the first house has many mirrors in it, and the bright clear light helps people see what is in the mirrors. It can be a bit disconcerting since it shows things in the room – including the people - as we are. People who stay in this house get pruned, grow and blossom just like plants and flowers exposed to care and the sun.

The light in the house next door, however, is made of many colors and flashes and pulses—a lot like the lights in Las Vegas! The house was built on purpose right next to the house with the bright, clear light. People who are in this house get little attention, stagnate, don't grow and slowly whither, just like plants that don't get any care or enough sun.

Next to both houses is a lot of darkness— cold, chilling darkness. Many are standing in that cold dark lot because they went into the house with multi-colored lights and experienced the hypocrisy and lovelessness of those who dwell there, and they rightfully ran out. Now they are understandably frightened of houses with lights and so they are not willing to go into the house with the pure, bright, clear, warm light. So, they stay in the dark, cold lot which causes their spirits and hearts to get cold as well.

The purpose of the house with the many colored lights is to draw people away from the house with the bright clear, warm light. The lights in the Las Vegas house distorts things and makes things in the room somewhat difficult to see – fuzzy and unclear. There are very few mirrors in this house, and the ones that are there distort favorably the image of the people looking into it. This favorable distortion is desirable to people so as they journey towards the house with the bright clear light – which light can really help them but which light shows them things they don't or may not want to see – they are easily distracted and drawn by the cool, multi-colored, entertainment luring alternative. The vast majority end up on the house with the flashy lights and stay there. Unfortunately, one of the effects of staying in this house is that people's spirits wither and die there.

This book is about the house with the flashy, cold lights and how it is different than the house with the bright, clear, warm Light. Thus, the purpose of the book is to describe the flashy-lighted house fairly fully and to expose its true nature; and by revealing its nature and purpose, to encourage people to go over to the house with the bright clear, warm light.

This author spent many years in the flashy-lighted house before I made my way out and so is very familiar with it. This author hopes that as people use reason well to understand and acknowledge the nature of the flashy-lighted house, that they might leave the house with the flashy, cold, radioactive, disorienting light and enter the house with the pure, bright, warm, clear, Life-giving light.

In addition to drawing people away from the multi-colored lights house, this book is intended to bring people out of the dark, cold, empty lot that many are standing in next to the two houses. You will find every precious thing you are looking for if you are willing to step inside the house with the pure, bright, warm, clear, Life-giving light. In other words, we don't have to wander about life like Bono's song which proclaims, "But I still haven't found, what I "m looking for."

INTRODUCTION: A SUCCESSFUL FAILURE?

The phrase "successful failure" has been used before, perhaps most recently and most popularly in the story about the Apollo 13 moon mission. If you have seen the movie/story, it is about NASA's attempt to land yet another manned space mission on the moon. As the story goes, there is a large failure with an oxygen tank on the way to the moon, which failure not only makes a landing on the moon impossible but getting the astronauts back to the earth improbable. With much effort, they manage to get those three astronauts back to earth safely. Thus, it was called NASA's most successful failure mission, meaning the mission to land on the moon was a failure, but getting the three men back safely was a success.

So, you might be wondering about what a "successful failure" is especially in the context of a major world religion. How can a world religion be a success or a failure? Let's refer back to the Apollo 13 mission. There were two perspectives which account for the two terms "successful" and "failure." From NASA's perspective, the mission was a failure—it did not accomplish its objective of landing on the moon. From the perspective of the wives and children and friends of the astronauts, the mission was a success — their loved one returned to them.

Now, what if there were a space exploration organization higher than NASA and with more knowledge and information than NASA, and who said, "we don't want you to send a mission to the moon, for that is largely a waste of time and resources." What if NASA didn't listen and sent the moon mission anyway? Assuming it is true that the higher space organization knew what is best for NASA and told NASA that their planned mission would be a waste; in what way could it be considered a "success" even NASA accomplished the lower mission objectives? The people at NASA would be high-fiving one another yelling, "success," while the wiser ones who asked NASA not to send the mission at all would be despondent knowing the mission was a waste and failure.

It is about different perspectives and what is ultimately valuable.

The "Christianity mission" is a successful failure, but the success and failure aspects of it are due to the view of two different people with very different perspectives.

The two perspectives are Christian leadership versus Joshua of Nazareth.[4]

The term "successful" in the title, "Christianity: A Successful Failure," is being judged by normal world standards. The concept of "success" is normally defined by the vast majority of people of the earth as involving the gaining, possessing or controlling of money or wealth and having many people backing the work and the leaders exercising authority or power or control over those many people. Would you not agree? Entities judged as "successful" can range from individuals to organizations to businesses to governments, etc.

The term "failure" according to normal world standards would be the opposite of "successful." So, a person or entity who/which does not accumulate, possess nor control material wealth; nor does that person or entity exercise authority or control over others; would be judged as a "failure" or a "nobody." If the person or entity is exceptional or very capable of accomplishing "success," then their failure is considered all the worse.

From a pure principle standpoint, "failure" is defined as the lack of accomplishing stated goals or objectives.

Is the reader with me so far? The book deals with two different perspectives: the perspective of Christian leadership and Christians versus the perspective of the real, historical person of Joshua of Nazareth.

This book will, in part, explain why the real, historical person of Joshua of Nazareth would judge contemporary Christian and bible religion as a failure and those who practice it as failing.[5]

---

[4] I will be referring to the historical person of Jesus of Nazareth as Joshua of Nazareth in this book for the following reasons. First, it is a better English transliteration of the Hebrew name of the historical person than "Jesus" - the name "Jesus" is the result of a Hebrew to Greek to English translation. The name "Joshua" is the result of a Hebrew to English translation. Second, because the term "Jesus" or phrase "Jesus Christ" carries with it an inordinate amount of erroneous religious baggage and I would prefer not to encourage that baggage to "download" into the minds of those who read this book. In other words, when I say the word "Jesus" to a religious person - depending upon which of the thousands of sects they belong to – they will bring to their mind the "jesus" that their denomination created and indoctrinated them into instead of the real and historical person of Joshua of Nazareth.

[5] For the readers who don't believe it is possible to know what the perspective is of the

A "successful failure" means that two standards or authorities disagree on the outcome of the effort. One standard - the average person on the earth including Christian leaders and the vast majority of religious people - sees or judges something as "successful"; while another standard – the person of Joshua of Nazareth and those who agree with him – sees or judges the same thing as a "failure." That something, of course, is the religion of Christianity, or the religious efforts of people who claim to be some flavor of "Christian" or who claim to make up or be part of "the church."

Some will yell, "divisiveness" at the previous statements. I counter that some division is necessary while most division is unnecessary and destructive. For example, if you have one-hundred people and some believe that violence is acceptable to get their way; while others think that reason and non-violent means are the only right way to accomplish something; there needs to be a division among those people, and that division would be proper and necessary.

The "successful mission" of that which calls itself "the church" is to have larger, more powerful congregations of people and thus become a force (gaining wealth and controlling more people) in a community, society, culture or nation—voices proclaiming a religious, moral or political agenda that people adopt. While many if not most religious leaders will deny this claim and instead claim something like, "our main goal is to bring people to Christ," their actions and words betray their claim as false. As this book will demonstrate, they are not looking to the historical person of Joshua of Nazareth as their Leader. Instead, their "christs" are ever-changing talisman which Christians create and whose purpose is, in general, to give the people what they want, not what they need.

The "successful mission" of Joshua of Nazareth for his followers is to transform individual people's lives for the better, and thus we become the collective model for how human beings are supposed to live—together by love, for truth and rightness. Even at this early stage of the book, the reader should be able to see some contrast between the two goals or "missions" of Christianity versus Joshua of Nazareth.

There is no doubt that Christianity is successful from the perspective of what people, in general, consider success. It has about two and a quarter billion human beings (or about 31% of the earth's population) who somehow identify with it or take some Christian label or are a member in one of its thousands of divisions/sects. Those who call themselves Christians and who control the organizations and resources of "the church"

---

real, historical person of Jesus of Nazareth; or that it is not likely that his deeds and words were accurately captured and preserved in the four small books called "the gospels,' please see *Section 6, Objections to the Solution.*

have many billions of dollars at their disposal and hundreds of millions of people they control or heavily influence. From the world's perspective of money and control over people, "the church" is hugely successful. Furthermore, the United States of America - the most powerful and influential nation in the past century - was influenced by Christians and their beliefs as is also true with most European countries, including the U.K. Clearly the leaders of those nations are currently turning away from even Christian ethics let alone Christian existential beliefs.

The question, however, for those who care is, how does Joshua of Nazareth define "successful"?

This book will look at and contrast what the world (including the religious world) considers successful versus what Joshua of Nazareth considers successful. In doing this, we will support the proposition that Christianity (and by inference its adherents) is a successful failure.

Some would say it is impossible to evaluate a world religion objectively or from a perspective of successfulness or failure. My response is, why?

If we have a standard that we can agree on, then anything can be evaluated with conclusions drawn as to true or false, right or wrong, success or failure based on that standard. Whether it be a standard of measure (e.g., Metric or English), or standard of performance (e.g., a time for running a marathon), or the claims of a religion (e.g., God is in control), we can draw correct conclusions by comparing things to the standard. We can successfully assess religious claims and practices because our tools of observation, reason, and logic enable this.

If Christianity claims that believing in its God will lead to something important like lives better lived or "blessed" lives, then all we need do is look at the Christians to see if their claims are valid. More fundamentally, if Christians claim that their God-beliefs are based on the person they call "Jesus Christ," then it is a relatively simple task to compare the Christian beliefs and practices against the teachings of Joshua of Nazareth as preserved in the four gospel books. This book will focus primarily on the latter evaluation although the former evaluation will be touched upon as well.

Some would seek to deny that Christian religion is successful. I would ask the reader to look at the wealth of the Roman Catholic Church and according to the world's definition of "successful" make the case that it is not. Look at the Vatican property with the Sistine Chapel etc. and the worldwide properties just the Roman Catholic religion controls, and then conclude, "oh, they don't control much wealth." I would ask the reader to look at the control and power the Roman Catholic wields over people and then find people who will conclude, "oh, that is not a successful organization." Look at the wealth and power the Roman Catholic religious system wields in the U.S. – the expensive religious buildings and the health systems they control and gain money from – and make a case it is not "successful.'

Look at the wealth of all of the Eastern Orthodox or Anglican organizations. Look at the wealth of all of the other Bible-based Christian divisions sects on the earth and the money they have invested in their buildings (crystal cathedrals et al.) and property and programs and businesses and media empires (TBN for example). The Protestants in the U.S. also own their share of expensive health systems from which they gain many millions of dollars!

Christians who are not part of these larger organizations will object saying, "we are not like them, and we are just a small local church." Well, the fact is that the small religious organizations are just like the large ones with few significant differences. The beliefs, routines, rituals, and most importantly, people's lifestyles are the same. The only difference is the size of the organization. It is much the same as Lowes or Home Depot versus the local Ace Hardware. The operation and purpose are the same no matter if you are Lowes or Ace Hardware, with just a few minor differences separating the two.

Collectively, large or small, look at the power that the leaders of the Bible-based Christian sects wield over hundreds of millions of people—can you look at them and then conclude, "oh no, they are not successful organizations" according to how the world defines successful? There are Christian religious organizations (what people call "churches") near this author who take in millions of dollars of people's money each *month* with an income of over $50 million per year. You may not like what they stand for, but not liking what they stand for does not nullify the objective truth that they are successful according to the world's definition of success. The vast majority of small businesses and some middle-sized companies in the U.S. do not generate millions of dollars of revenue like many hundreds of Christian religious organizations in the U.S. do, and that statement excludes the U.S. Roman Catholic system! The simple fact is "the church" is powerful and successful according to the world's standards.

In great contrast, look at the Man who, some two thousand years ago, walked the earth and accumulated no material wealth and did not hold any positions of earthly power or earthly authority. This Man did not seek to control material wealth nor to take from people, but only to give to them and help them in the deepest most meaningful ways possible. For doing that publically for about three years, he was rejected and killed by the people. That is his success story which most people would call a failure.

The contrast could not be any sharper.

This book will clarify that simple contrast.

Religion-Based Morality Versus Existential Truth

History has reached a point in the U.S. where there are no obvious group-related moral injustices against distinct groups of people. That makes it hard to find good fights to join like the civil rights movement in the sixties. The enemy is no longer primarily in the seats of government power, or even in the corporate offices. Rather, the enemy is the individual and the turning away from a common ethic to irrational, selfish emotionalism instead—turning away from an accurate absolute view of reality to an erroneous relativistic view of reality.

Please understand that this book does not condemn Christians or Biblians. Instead, it seeks to correct them using the best standard possible. This author is well aware of the following simple truth and hopes others will come to this awareness as well—*that God condemns no one, instead, we condemn ourselves.* Please read that again and understand the truth it conveys. Our heavenly Father *condemns no one*; instead, *we condemn ourselves.* God merely created the organisms/beings and the system/rules to allow us to choose our after death destiny.

A significant weakness of the non-theistic existential worldview is the lack of ultimate justice. For example, it should be offensive to the reader that Hitler and Mother Teresa would have the same after death experience, even if that experience is merely the annihilation of their soul. Our conscience should be repulsed at the thought that Adolf Hitler and Mother Teresa would have the same ultimate destiny—our conscience should choke at that possibility. Why is that? Is there some physical aspect of human nature that accounts for that?

The concept of condemning ourselves is much like the U.S. legal system, at least how it is supposed to be. Legislators create the laws that people are to obey. A judge's role is to determine whether an individual broke the law or not. If the judge finds that the person broke the law, the punishment is often also prescribed by rules, regulation or guidelines.

Therefore, in a perfect system, the only people receiving a consequence/ramification/punishment for their wrong behaviors are those who did something wrong...they broke a law, rule, policy, etc. The person is not before the judge because the judge didn't like them and wanted them to be there; instead, the person who committed the wrong called for the consequence. As an example, the person who murdered another person deserves a consequence including being accountable for the life they wrongly took.

And so it is with God and the system He created for we human beings.

God does not "look down" and say, "I don't like you, you are going to be punished" – in fact, it is just the opposite. He looks down and says,

"Please stop destroying yourselves – don't you know I love you?!" When a person rejects trying to live by love and thus practices wrong, the person who committed the wrong will stand before The Judge, and God will merely validate the facts surrounding the choices made and the wrongs committed. We will address further aspects of this line of thought later in the book.

Many good, decent, moral people are Christians. However, many good, fair, moral people are agnostics or non-theists or Muslims or Jews or Buddhists, etc. In fact, my experience has been that in general religious people, including Christians, want what is good and right according to some religious moral standard. Having some moral standard is better than having no moral standard (unless of course you ignore it or use it to benefit one's self) since human beings are not naturally predisposed to exemplary behavior and in fact, are naturally predisposed to selfish and destructive behavior. Thus, having a moral standard does help restrain and constrain bad behavior. To deny this is irrational.

Furthermore and by definition, a religious moral standard includes the concept that God is the Giver of the moral standard and that God will hold people accountable to that moral standard. Stated another way, people who hold to a religious moral standard believe that there will be after-physical-life consequences for our behavior and that God will be the Judge helping us see the effects of our choices.

The conclusion is that some religious moral standards *within the group that holds to them* have played an important role in constraining harmful, destructive or evil behavior. Some rules of conduct (ethics) are necessary, and religion in no small measure has provided them. Religion becomes particularly destructive – and religious moral standards are tossed aside, or negatively modified to conform to the desire of the group - when separate groups with competing or different God-claims enter into conflict with one another. This conflict happens because the one people group says to the other, "God is on OUR side, and so it is right to use any means necessary to make you guys submit to our true God." In other words, the God-rules only apply to "us," not "them" because "they don't believe in our god."

Some examples of inter-religious conflict would include the Crusades between Christians and Muslims or the current conflict between Buddhists and Muslims in Indonesia. A recent case of intra-religious strife would be the deadly conflict between the Protestants and Catholics in Ireland or between the Shite and Sunni Muslims. However, one does not have to reach the point of violence to lack true peace—we humans are only too good at hating one another long before we raise our fist.

For example, the thousands of bible-Christian sects who excommunicated each other and thus account for many of those thousands of sects/divisions/denominations are hardly at peace and unity! While it is true that they no longer kill each other regularly as "heretics" in most places, that hardly amounts to unity. And while there no longer is large scale open animosity between the sects, it is equally valid that they are *not* unified and certainly their members *do not love one another* (unless you wrongly re-define love as mere civility or cold politeness, as we shall see later).

If it is true that human beings are predisposed to harmful beliefs and behavior – and taking into consideration the facts of history, it is the most reasonable belief – then how do you think people are going to do with *no* higher moral standard and no concept of accountability for one's behavior in this life? All one has to do is to look at the people of the United States here in the early twenty-first century, for example, and the conclusion should be obvious. As the people of the U.S. move away from a belief that God exists and will hold people accountable for how they live their lives, the following is happening:

- Expanding racial conflict;
- Political tension, conflict, and violence;
- Harmful drug usage increasing every year;
- Suicide increasing every year;
- Government corruption and waste increasing each year;
- The wealthy becoming more wealthy and powerful and the common man's wealth and power diminishing;
- Corporate greed is rising each year…

And the list goes on and on. Those things are the fruit of a people group – in this example, the U.S. citizens – throwing away a universal moral standard upon which they agreed to live by or respect to some degree in times past (which standard was derived from religion).

Is there a correlation between the increase in immorality in the United States and the passing away of a religious derived or absolute moral standard? Of course, there is, and it does not take some million dollar government study or some think tank research to judge that rightly. Most of the animosity between the two primary political ideologies of "liberal" and "conservative" is due to ethics based differences or what they label as "social" issues, code language for ethical or moral differences.

However, this book is not going to make a case for why nations or societies need some religiously based moral standard or order to function well! For a religious person or a primarily morally concerned person, that is probably a sacrilegious statement, but therein lays a fundamental error of religious people! The simple fact is that a moral standard – including religious-based ones (like Mosaic) – *only works to constrain evil, it does not produce love and the critically important things associated with love.* Nor does a moral standard deliver hope or a good reason or purpose for living one's life. Those things require something else—something higher.

The people of the U.S. desperately need some universal moral or ethical standard to reduce conflict and find unity again. I will address in this book the fact that the root problems of conflict in this nation are not political ideologies but something more profound—a changing existential view of human existence.

Christianity and by extension Christians are significantly wrong about many things about God, but that does not mean that Christians are going to hell because of their false beliefs! Let's get that out right at the beginning. Sadly, for many Christians, a person having wrong ideas about God is generally considered to be worthy of hell, *but that "heaven or hell based on merely religious beliefs" thinking is one of THE MOST harmful and wrong beliefs that Christian's teach and hold!* In fact, it has been one of the most powerful fear motivating beliefs in all of history, capturing billions of souls to do the will of the religious leadership. Today, it still serves as a powerful fear motivator to dissuade or prevent discussing different views of God or our soul's destiny or the purpose of one's life.

Neither this author nor this book condemns anyone! Instead, we often condemn ourselves and then often wrongly!

People who have wrong beliefs about things, including about God, are not sent to hell for that. Instead, beliefs are only one factor in determining one's destiny. Some views are more important than others because they either guide or drive our behavior and lifestyle. Some ideas do not affect our daily conduct much at all. Beliefs about the extent of universe or opinions about the soil composition of Mars or how many angels can fit on the head of a pin have little to no power to shape our behavior. The same is true for many God beliefs. Many God beliefs have no bearing on how we live our lives, such as where God exists or the exact process of our soul's journey from our body to God or how many angels attend God, etc.

However, some God beliefs *do* have a bearing on how we conduct ourselves each day and have a more significant impact on our eternal destiny.

The most basic God belief is to answer the question, does God exist? If that question is answered "yes" by an individual, perhaps the next most important God-related questions are *who is God and what is God like and what does he want of me/us. Other important questions are how am I to live my life and will I be accountable for how I live my life? Is there something better than fear to lift me above the accountability concern?* Aside from whether God exists or not - which is a more fundamental level question – if we believe God does exist, then certainly what God is like and what he wants of us are paramount especially if God has set up a system that allows us to determine our after physical-death destiny. (Beliefs, faith, and religion are not the same, and we shall cover that important distinction later.)

People of all time and all races and cultures and religions have asked the reasonable questions, "who created me; what is he/she like and what does he/she want of me." Religious leaders then race in to try and answer those questions, and the average person is only too quick to listen to them and even pay them for their opinions. The religious leaders and their followers then build impressive institutions or organizations to hide the fact that many of their God beliefs are often merely opinions that do not stand the test of reason, logic or observation.

And what is the typical reason given as to why the people should consider the religious leader as an authority about God? They include, "he/she is called of God"; or "they have a degree from seminary"; or "they are anointed of God"; or "he/she graduated Magna Cum Laude from Best Theological college"; or "the Holy Spirit called them"; or "he is a really good, godly man"; or "he/she is so-and-so religious leaders son/daughter"; or other such things. A critical question in this regard is, *are these valid reasons to believe that religious leaders know God?* This point about qualifications of religious leaders is, and we shall look at that later.

Given the division among the bible-Christian religious sects - by some estimates, tens of thousands of divisions/sects - I would suggest that those leaders are not doing a good job. "But," you should ask, "what is your standard for making that judgment?" Good question!

In my "Finding Life" video series, I make the case that the best person in history to tell us about God is the one who defeated death to prove that all he said was true (https://www.youtube.com/channel/UCG4n6QnuLUsVvImWjG9fAhQ). That person is Joshua of Nazareth, and you can read his story and teachings in my book "The Light of the World: The Life and Teachings of Jesus of Nazareth" (http://www.amazon.com/Light-World-Teachings-Jesus-Nazareth/dp/0692300481); or in the four gospels in any bible.

That historical person, Jesus (Joshua) of Nazareth says regarding his follower's unity, "Father, I pray that they may be one as we are one" (John 17). The will of Joshua and the one he calls "Father" is for his followers to be unified, "as one." Equally clear is the fact that the thousands of divided, largely loveless, divided, bickering, utterly unconnected groups of people who do not live significantly different than those they judge as "unsaved" or "un-churched" does not represent Joshua's teaching on unity. And yet this is precisely what exists on the earth today representing Christianity.

So, there you have it. This author's standard to be able to make a correct judgment about the state of Christianity's unity is the one whom all Christian sects point to as their supposed god and expert about God. I will use that same standard to reveal how Christianity is a successful failure.

There is another teaching of Joshua of Nazareth that serves to prove the claim of this book is true. In fact, of all the instructions he gave, he only gave one he labeled as a "command," meaning it is of paramount importance. As we shall see, that command plays a significant role in the successful failure that is Christianity.

Again, this book is not about condemning anyone—we do that to ourselves well enough. This book is about people finding truth and thus hope, and becoming change agents in this sad, dark world which desperately needs positive change. Therefore, this book will not be a scary experience for those who can overcome their fear or self-pride regarding exploring God beliefs or fundamental existential beliefs. If you don't have self-pride or fear as your shield against truth – that is you are willing to go where reason and logic take you - then this book can provide an extremely beneficial and possibly life-changing experience.

Let us begin this journey with getting a grip on reality.

SECTION 1:
MY EXISTENCE, THE STATE OF THINGS AND FUNDAMENTAL PROBLEMS

Section Theme:

- Establishing or setting a foundation of reality.
  - I exist;
  - Other people exist;
  - Essential, real things like truth, reason, logic, and forgiveness exist and are not physical;
  - People do a lot of wrong things each day causing much conflict, neglect, hurt, pain and suffering. Thus, our (my) existence could be much better.

Section Introduction

There are some things about our existence that are undeniable. The fact that you and I exist is undeniable. The fact that we human beings are reasoning, sentient beings programmed with a moral conscience is undeniable. The fact that many people do evil, wrong, harmful things to each other each day is undeniable. The fact that we as human beings can conceive of utopic or paradise type conditions is undeniable. Finally, the fact that while we human beings can imagine how things ought to be, yet they are not and have never been on a large scale, is undeniable.

For those of you who have seen the movie, The Matrix, this section is accomplishing what was accomplished by Morpheus for Neo in the first movie. This section's chapters will establish how things really are and why people are the way we are.

1

A REASONABLE BASIS FOR RELIGIOUS AND SPIRITUAL BELIEFS

Opening Questions:

- Is it reasonable to believe that a creator of the human race exists?
- Why are there so many religious people on the planet?
- What is the most reasonable answer to account for my existence?
- Can atoms, molecules, acids, proteins, cells, tissues, organs and organ systems adequately account for my capabilities and what I experience as a human being?
- Does science have the tools to adequately explain certain aspects of human nature, the human experience and origin questions?

A book of this title is likely to attract readers of many different beliefs. It is reasonable to think that some who are hostile towards, or at least very skeptical of, Christian religion would be interested in reading this book. That is a good thing, and I hope they do —there is *much* to be upset about Christianity and Christians – especially their wrong beliefs about God and the hypocrisy that many practice. However, just because Christians have many incorrect beliefs and practices, it does not mean that they are wrong about everything. Stated another way, just because the Christians poison the well, it does not mean the well does not exist. Furthermore, just because many Christians are hypocrites, it does not mean that all are or that their hypocrisy nullifies certain truths about God. There are sincere, loving people who are Christians and to deny such indicates that you will benefit from reading this book and learn from it!

3

When dealing with people with whom you have fundamental disagreements, it is a common practice to reject almost everything they say or believe. Not only is this a harmful and destructive practice and one which prevents communication from taking place, but it is erroneous. This negative dynamic is typical among people who hold sincere political or religious beliefs. *For those who can receive it, to be a truly exceptional human being means you will listen to the other side and use reason in a compassionate and empathetic way to try and arrive at truth.* Imagine how much the communication would improve between the political "left" and "right" in the United States, for example, if they strove to practice that principle! We will look to see how genuinely tolerant we are of other people in a later chapter.

The beliefs that are the source of disagreement frequently prevent the people from getting to know each other even in a cursory way. For people to understand each other communication must take place, and when it does not, people remain ignorant of each other's essential views. When we are unaware of each other's views, we cannot build bridges to the other side—people will remain fearful and will tend to judge too quickly or to stereotype and reject. If left to ourselves we naturally withdraw and build walls and defenses due to our nature, as we will see.

The simple truth is that we as human beings, in general, *are insecure in our fundamental beliefs about reality;* or stated another way, *we are insecure in exploring our existential beliefs.* The word "existential" means "of existence," or it refers to attempts to understand our existence. This insecurity is an aspect of fear and is manifest when we get defensive when talking about something. We will take a closer look at why that is true later on.

Before we take a close look at why Christianity is a successful failure, we need first to establish some framework to make judgments about the world in general as well as about Christian beliefs or practices that exist within that world. In other words, we must have some high-level grasp on reality and be able to understand and accurately describe it to make sound judgments of beliefs or practices that interact or intersect with that reality. If I stay within a Christian world-view, I will not be able to accurately and effectively evaluate Christianity. We must come from a higher, more objective perspective to assess Christianity objectively.

This perspective or framework is essential especially for the people who are reading this book with the purpose of affirming that their judgments about Christianity or Christians are correct. To do that well we have to establish some facts regarding a world-view since Christianity is a worldview. In other words, we cannot make judgments well in a vacuum—with no points of reference or no larger context; nothing can be properly understood. We need facts to establish some framework to make sound judgments.

For example, before you could find your way to some destination, you need geographical facts to do so. So if you were trying to find your way to Chicago after someone left you in the middle of a forest in Central Canada — and you had no idea where you were on the earth and no directional tools to help you —that would be a challenging endeavor.

Or, as another example, before you could place a hospital well in a city, you would first need to know the existing layout of the city. If you did not understand the entire layout, you might well place the hospital where it would not be easily accessed or utilized optimally by the majority of the population. *So it is with determining exactly why and how Christianity and Christians are a successful failure.* We must build a framework to account for reality; we must have some basic understanding of the larger world of which Christianity and its adherents are a part.

As noted above and in general, when someone does not like something (has a preexisting bias), then it is common to make the mistake of "throwing the baby out with the bathwater," also known as the Hasty Generalization fallacy. That fallacy is given illustration by the expression about the baby and bathwater. If you have ever washed a dirty baby whom you love, the saying will make perfect sense—that you don't throw the valuable thing out (the baby) with that which is worthless (the dirty bathwater). Instead, we should only throw out that which is worthless. In the case of concepts or beliefs and using reason to understand those concepts or ideas, we should not dismiss or ignore that which is true (the baby) because we don't like the wrong or incorrect things surrounding it or associated with it (the dirty bathwater).

For example, a person might observe Christians behaving hypocritically (the bathwater) and as a result rejects, dismisses or will not consider the possibility that Joshua of Nazareth is accurately represented in the four gospel books (the baby). That is a rejection based on fallacious reasoning with a wrong conclusion. The only right conclusion from looking at Christianity's dirty bathwater is to rightly judge that the bathwater is dirty and unworthy of partaking in. However, if you are a truly exceptional person, then perhaps helping those who hold to the beliefs and practices of the dirty bathwater to see the error of their ways would be the right and noble thing to do even if nothing comes of it?

So let us start in on this adventure and spend a bit of time building this framework to gain the broader perspective that best represents reality, and thus be in an excellent position to judge Christianity as a successful failure.

This chapter will be about finding the answer to the questions – What is religion and is it reasonable for people to have religious beliefs and practices?

Simple, Undeniable Existential Truths: The Basics of Reality

Certain facts about reality are undeniable and human existence is quite simple. We exist and interact with other people and things of this planet. We have basic biological needs that we must meet for our bodies to remain alive—food, clothing, and shelter. We have a compelling social need to be accepted, affirmed and involved with others. We have a strong urge to express our sexuality. We have a spiritual need to have a clear conscience and to be forgiven of our wrongs and free from guilt.

Furthermore, we are self-aware beings with the ability to evaluate our surroundings, interactions, and experiences with a rational mind. We can know truth and rightness, and we do in fact apply those judgments in living out our daily experiences. For example, when we determine someone is lying to us, we have made a judgment about what is true versus what is false. Or, if someone calls us an idiot, we decide as to whether that was a right or wrong thing to say. When we make a mathematical calculation, we determine whether or not we believe the calculation creates an accurate result. If we see a man in a park harming a young child, we make a judgment and hopefully intervene.

More facts that are undeniable include that we human beings will physically die. That is to say; our bodies will fail and cease to function. Equally undeniable is that we are more than atoms, molecules, acids, proteins, cells, organs, organ systems and a bit of biochemical energy. Just as it is unreasonable and irrational to believe that a computer's hardware created or accounts for a computer's software and its application's abilities, in the same way, it is silly to say that our bodies somehow account for our personality, soul or spirit.

It is irrational to believe that our personality; our ability to reason; our ability to have complex abstract thoughts; our knowing right from wrong; our ability to see ourselves and ponder existential questions; and our ability to love and to forgive; are all caused by merely physical things.

To believe that all things are merely physical is no different than a sibling exclaiming to his mother as they entered the theatre to watch his sister's high school play, "look, mom, the bricks of the building and wood of the stage created and communicated the content of the play we are watching!"

This book will not make a protracted defense of these simple realities for they are self-evident, but the reader is free to try and use reason and logic to prove them wrong. For those who disagree with my assertions above, I ask you at least allow for the possibility that they are correct and thus move forward.

So, where did we come from and what happens to us when our bodies die? These are entirely reasonable questions. In fact, for reasoning, self-aware, sentient being and a being that can love – they are *the* questions of life! And yet how many people seriously ponder those questions? I have observed that very few are willing to ponder those questions seriously. Some of the reasons people don't consider those questions are as follows.

Some are afraid to ponder the questions. They like existing – they love their life in this world and fear causes them to stay away from the questions. They would much prefer to pretend death will not happen to them, or if it does, it is a long way off.

Some have believed the falsehood that they are just atoms and molecules and so they think their lives are merely physical existence, and when their bodies die, they cease to exist. As such, fear would also keep many of them away from pondering that end. I assert that this is untenable to regularly contemplate the end of our existence for both a reasoning being as well as a being who knows real love.

A physicalist (a person who believes all aspects of human life can be accounted for by matter or physical things) must deny certain capacities, abilities, and traits of both our persons and our experiences to hold to that view. For example, the concept of forgiveness between two people is a spiritual or metaphysical concept that cannot rationally be reduced to a chemical cause; and just because it is not a chemical does not mean it is not real. That claim would commit the fallacy of begging the question. Having a physicalist worldview does not prove that physicalism is a correct understanding of reality. In fact and as we shall see, physicalism is severely lacking as a worldview or existential belief.

For many, perhaps for the majority, religion comes in to provide what they believe are reliable answers to the question, "what happens to me when my body dies?" Many religious leaders have been taught the answers from their teachers, and they were taught by their teachers, etc. over the generations. So what is this thing called "religion"? Before we can have a rational and meaningful discussion about something, we need to define it correctly, or else we are wasting our time. We will define many terms in this book.

The popular definition of "religion" is the things people believe and the behavior they engage in regarding God; gods; things spiritual or metaphysical; after death existence; or morality. This understanding of religion is the commonly held definition that the people of the world believe. This view or definition of religion has millions of voices (the religious leaders) informing the billions who inquire about God and his role in human life. There are many different religions and spiritual beliefs many of which contradict each other and lead to conflict.

The definition that Jesus (or Joshua) of Nazareth gives to "religion" is *the things people believe and do concerning God, spiritual or metaphysical things, human life, and death - that have no basis in my teachings or which nullify or work against my teachings.* [6] This view or definition of religion has one voice informing those who inquire about God and His role in human life.

This distinction is critical – between the conventional definition of religion and Joshua of Nazareth's definition of religion.

The term "religious" means *people who believe some God, gods or a spiritual reality exists and who have practices around those God or spiritual beliefs which beliefs or practices have no reasonable basis in Joshua of Nazareth's teachings.* Please read that again and understand the distinction between that definition and the term used by agnostics and atheists against people who believe God exists.

The prior definitions do not mean that all religious people are wrong about all things God; nor does it mean that all of their practices are meaningless or harmful. As I said, it merely means *they have no basis in Joshua of Nazareth's teachings.* Most people who hold God beliefs which cancel out or nullify Joshua's teachings are "religious" people, but that does not mean that all religious people have beliefs or practices which cancel out or invalidate Joshua's instructions. For example, many non-Christian religious people have views that happen to align with some of Joshua's ethical teachings.

It is imperative that the reader understand that I am using *the historical person of Joshua of Nazareth as he reveals himself through his own words in the four gospel books as my Standard to make points, distinctions and judgments about religion, Christianity, and God.* This definition is proved correct by comparing what a religious person believes, says or does against the teachings of Joshua of Nazareth. It is just as important to consider what Joshua of Nazareth *did not say* as it is to consider what he did say as we shall see.

Many atheists, non-theists and others hostile to the belief that God exists often use the term "religious" to describe *any* person who believes a God or gods exist. Their definition of "religious" is significantly different to the way I am defining it in this book. Do you see the distinction? Both views – that of the followers of Joshua of Nazareth, and that of non-theists and others of their ilk – have in common that religious people are in error about something. Joshua says that people who hold beliefs and practices

---

[6] See Mark 7. The term "religion" is synonymous with the term "tradition" in that passage. Here is the passage, "And Jesus said to them, "Rightly did Isaiah prophesy of you hypocrites, as it is written (in the Hebrew scripture), "This people honors me with their lips, but their heart is far away from me. But in vain do they worship me, teaching as doctrines (truths from God) the precepts of men.' Neglecting the commandment of God, you hold to the **tradition (religion) of men**." Jesus was also saying to them, "You are experts at setting aside the commandment of God to keep your **tradition (religion)**."

which hide, contradict, substitute for, cancel out or nullify HIS teachings are in great error.

Non-theists and those who hold similar beliefs say that any person who believes a God or god's exist and expresses or communicates that idea in some way is religious and in error about all their God beliefs. That belief is not a reasonable or valid belief or judgment, or at least it cannot be proven to be true.

My definition or meaning of the term "religious" is defensible using the standard of Joshua of Nazareth and his teachings in the four gospel books. Non-theists have no standard to defend their definition of "religious" although most would say "science." Science cannot prove that God does not exist and in fact, the physical evidence points to a creator/designer. Furthermore, science is lost regarding its ability to address some of the most important concepts that we deal with as human beings like love, forgiveness, justice, etc. (Which real and vital ideas are metaphysical by the way!)

The simple truth is that all people have some beliefs about the reality they experience each day; what is important what is not; what is worth pursuing and what is not; what is valuable and what is not; why am I getting out of bed today. People reasonably wonder about the creation of the earth and its life. If people reject the irrational view that all the fantastic, diverse, genetic code-based, complex organic machines we call organisms on the planet had no designer (see the Intelligent Design books for a robust defense of this simple reality), then they reasonably wonder about the designer/creator.

People have beliefs about their nature and human nature in general. If people reject the irrational view that mere physical particles (atoms, molecules, acids, proteins, cells, tissues, organs and the organ systems of our body) can account for all aspects of our existence including:

- Our ability to reason;
- Our ability to know right from wrong;
- Our sentience (to have emotions caused by perceptions);
- Our love ("love" as defined by Joshua of Nazareth is selfless behavior motivated by compassion, the opposite principle to evolution's supposed mechanism of survival of the fittest).

…then they reasonably wonder what their soul is as well as their mind or spirit. Furthermore, it is entirely reasonable that they will wonder what will happen to those metaphysical components – what will happen to *them* — when their body dies.

If non-theists were honest with themselves and others when asked what happens to them when they die, they would say something to this effect:

- "I cease to exist—all my experiences and memories and important relationships I had in life are gone, lost to an empty void of nothingness;
- No love will endure;
- No cherished events or memories or people will endure;
- Every valuable and meaningful thing I experienced in life will be gone, wiped out, erased;
- Everyone I loved will be lost in an empty black void of nothingness".

If we, as human beings, are doing a half-way decent job at questioning those fundamental things about human existence—about our existence—about *my* existence; then we are doing well. If we are not exploring the most important questions of life, then we are not living a full life but rather a half-life, a delusional life. If we redefine or ignore love's true nature and meaning, then we are living a half-life. However, when we turn to religion for those answers and deny reason when doing so, we do not do well.

Religion is essential to billions of people. It is fair to say that we human being tend to be religious or spiritual beings. In fact, over ninety percent of the human beings on the planet if asked, "how or why do you exist" would have some answer that is "religious" or "spiritual" in nature. While that does not prove anything regarding God claims, it does show that the human mind has a reasonable default view most likely based on simple observations and deductions like complicated things require a designer; or beings which have spiritual or metaphysical components must have a sufficient cause of those components.

The Reasonableness of the Existence of God

It is only reasonable for people to be religious or spiritual since believing that we are merely a physical entity is not rational. Nor is it reasonable to think that non-organic machines like an automobile just happened through natural forces. We know, based on the mind we have, that a designer *must* exist to account for even merely the physical, complex organic machines that are our bodies.

I would say that to believe that all things evolved from nothing or hydrogen gas or a giant explosion is irrational, and yet that is the basic premise of naturalistic evolutionary doctrine.

The fact is that well over ninety percent of the human's on the earth believe a creator or creators exist and are reasonable for doing so. For example, it is unreasonable to think that a computer created itself and further that the hardware somehow created the software or the software was integrated into the hardware by natural forces. And yet this is the underlying belief of those people who deny the requirement of a designer to account for complex machines with inter-dependent subsystems or who deny the spiritual or metaphysical realities of human nature.

- Our abilities of:
- Self-awareness;
- Sentience (the ability to experience emotions based on and connected to thoughts, perceptions, and experiences);
- Internally knowing what is right from wrong;
- Being able to reason abstractly with no physical things to support that reasoning.

All these abilities of human beings cannot reasonably be accounted for by mere physical matter. *Atoms, molecules, acids, proteins, cells, tissues, organs, organ systems and a bit of biochemical energy cannot adequately account for our human abilities or our experiences.* To believe that mere physical objects can somehow account for our abilities and experiences is to think that the bricks, mortar, wood, metal, and plastic of the theatre can account for the concepts conveyed in the Shakespeare play in that theatre. Or, it is similar to believing that a computer's hardware created or can account for the computer's software.

The Bicycle Illustration

As I have stated, our physical aspect alone clearly requires a designer. That our bodies need a designer is self-evident since things (inorganic or organic) with relatively complex inter-related systems or subsystems that work together to make the whole work, in no way could have come together by chance but instead require a designer. *That is to say that the probability is zero that those interdependent sub-systems – or the forces that built them - "knew" how to integrate with each other to accomplish the purpose of the machine.* Furthermore, the probability is zero that those interdependent sub-systems just integrated themselves through random chance. Let's explore and explain this important concept using a relatively simple inorganic machine - a bicycle - as an example.

A bicycle has several component systems. The frame needs to be designed to be able to bear the load of the rider and the forces they will experience using the whole machine. The frame is made up of various pieces of material joined in such a way as to both bear the load of the rider as well as connect/integrate the other component systems to the machine and it also includes a seat for the passenger to rest their body on while on the machine. The device needs a steering system to enable the rider to direct the bike. The steering system is made up of several tubes that need to rotate while staying firmly attached to the frame as well as handlebars the rider can use to direct the front wheel. The machine needs a braking system to allow the rider to stop the bike safely. The braking system is made up of cables, springs, clamps, and pads, all working together to enable the rider to apply different amounts of friction against the wheels to slow the rotation of the wheels.

The machine needs a way to move across the ground so that the rider can travel faster than just walking or running. The motion system is made up of wheel rims, rubber tires, spokes, axles and bearing to hold the wheels to the frame while still enabling the wheels to rotate freely. The machine will need an engine – in this case, the rider's muscles – and a way to transfer the power the engine produces to the means the machine will use to move forward – a drive system. This system is comprised of pedals which take the power of the engine and transfer it to round gears which connect to a chain which transfers the engine's force to the rear wheel to spin the wheel.

Can you see that a relatively simple machine like a bicycle is made up of several subsystems and that the whole machine would not work without each of the subsystems integrating into the other subsystems? Please remember that in the case of the bicycle, even the subcomponents – like the brake system or the propulsion or drive system – have multiple parts that also reasonably require a designer.

Here are some fundamental questions that reveal that the simple machine – the bicycle – requires a designer. How would the drive system come together and know how to orient itself on the frame? How would the braking system create itself and know how to orient itself to the propulsion system and the frame? How would the steering system create itself and know where and how to attach to the load-bearing system? Hundreds of other such questions could be asked, and each one deserves a reasonable answer.

Is it not unreasonable to believe that a simple machine like a bicycle could somehow arise and exist without a mind designing it? The mathematical probability is virtually zero. That is to say, that even with billions of years of trial and error, a bicycle forming itself without a mind designing it is as likely as the following. Imagine having a can at the bottom of the Pacific Ocean, and you flying over the ocean in a plane not knowing where the can is, and having to drop a ball into the can of the same diameter, tens of thousands of times in a row! That probability picture is similar to what we are talking about regarding complex machines with inter-related subsystems forming themselves.

The idea that natural forces over time could somehow reasonably account for the existence of even a simple machine, like a bicycle, is *untenable or irrational*. The problem some people have with this line of reasoning is organic versus the inorganic aspects of the argument. In other words, they claim there is some logical error or gulf over trying to compare the organic and the inorganic. My question is why? Why are cellular structures that provide identical functionality to metal or plastic molecular structures not legitimately comparable?

That fact is that organic machines – particularly the bodies of creatures like mammals, on this planet – exist, and those machines/bodies are far more complicated than the most complex machine that man has so far been able to create.

So, the question is, how could even a simple machine like a bicycle exist without a mind designing both the subsystems as well as how those subsystems have to integrate or connect for the whole machine to exist and accomplish its purpose? Given a few billion years and the forces of nature, will even a simple device with just a few inter-dependent subsystems arise without a designer directing its creation?

The laws of thermodynamics are well established physical laws that no reasonable scientist questions. The second law of thermodynamics states that the total entropy (disorganization) of an isolated system can only increase over time. Here is a fuller definition of entropy: "the degradation of the matter and energy in the universe to an ultimate state of inert uniformity; a process of degradation or running down or a *trend to disorder*." [7]

In other, simpler words, the second law of thermodynamics states that physical matter will become *less organized or ordered* over time…particles will disperse or degrade into their simplest form. That dear reader is the exact opposite of what naturalistic evolutionists claim—evolutions claim that matter naturally become more complex and ordered over time.

The reasonable view is that the natural forces of nature will not produce biomechanical machines of even simple complexity. It requires the creative conceptualization of a reasoning mind to order the components of even a simple machine. And it needs specifically directed and controlled energy and physical manipulation/shaping to bring the machine into existence.

If it is not reasonable for a simple machine to form itself, how much more unreasonable for a complicated machine with many complex interrelated and inter-dependent sub-systems to design and create itself! For more complicated inorganic machines consider some manufacturing plants or an automobile or space shuttle.

Do not be misled by the lottery fallacy. That is the argument that improbable things happen regularly, like someone winning the lottery. The lottery is a chance-based game of guessing the same number – a number of a fixed length - drawn randomly. As more and more people play the lottery, the probability that *someone* will win is quite high; thus someone regularly wins the lottery. In other words, the probability is quite high or very likely that someone will win the lottery as more and more people guess the six digit number.

---

[7] Merriam-Webster Dictionary, www.merriam-webster.com, April 2018

However, the argument that a bicycle and its related sub-systems would form over time by natural forces is like saying that *a particular person* will win the lottery, and in fact is has a *much lower* probability than a bicycle just happening through natural forces. In other words, it is like saying that the person "Jack Goodluck" will win the next lottery. So, for example, let us say a lottery is held in a six-state area in the US. Let us also assume that the six-state area has twenty-five million people in it. What would be the probability that the individual Jack Goodluck who lives in Smalltown in one of those six states will pick the winning number of that lottery? It is a similar probability that the bicycle's steering system will randomly happen by itself. [8]

The simple truth is that unlikely things do NOT happen regularly! An intelligence design proponent, Dr. Hugh Ross, calculated the probability of life occurring on the earth at one in less than ten to the two-hundred and eighty-second power, or less than 1 in 10^{282} [9]. For comparison's sake, a widely accepted estimate of the number of atoms in the known universe is approximately 10^{80}. Therefore, the probability of life occurring purely naturally and randomly on the earth is for all practical purposes, zero.

To argue that since life exists, it proves that the probability arguments like Mr. Ross are wrong is *far less reasonable* than to theorize that a designer must exist to account for those machines. In other words, throwing away the science of probability theory because you don't like where it takes you is far less reasonable than theorizing that a highly advanced Being created life on this planet.

Now take the next step. Consider biological or organic machines or organisms that can self-replicate self-heal or have automated systems that defend against harmful agents. Can you imagine a bicycle that could fix itself without a mind intervening? Or a car that could diagnosis its problems and have a system that could deliver the repair! Humankind is very creative and will probably be able to build machines like this in the future, but only because *we have a mind to conceptualize and design such machines* and because we have organic machines from which to learn! Stated another way, engineers regularly learn from the created world and get many of their ideas by reverse engineering the Creator's designs!

It is a fact that the complexity of the human body, for example, far exceeds the most advanced computers and machines man has made or will be able to make in the foreseeable future even with all the accumulated knowledge, technology, and design skills. And if humans can eventually duplicate those functions, it will only happen by using the metaphysical

---

[8] For a good explanation of the Lottery Fallacy, see http://rightreason.org/2010/the-lottery-fallacy-fallacy/

[9] See Hugh Ross's book, "Improbable Planet: How Earth Became Humanity's Home."

mind (operating system and application) the creator has given us; and through reverse engineering the incredibly complex organic machines that are the biological creatures on the earth.

The human body alone - not even considering the brain - is an engineering and design marvel that the smartest human engineers and designers cannot even approach regarding complexity and function. Think of all the inter-related and inter-dependent system the human body needs to function correctly.

- The skeleton to bear the load;
- The joints to allow for incredible flexibility of the movement of the components;
- The respiratory system which provides the energy of oxygen to the cells that require it;
- The digestive system to break down energy bearing materials to the right level for processing;
- The nervous system which transmits commands of the mind to operate our voluntary, and automatically sends self-sustaining commands to the involuntary muscles;
- The ability to see, and taste and smell and hear;
- The reproductive system;
- The dermatological system;
- The genetic code system that programs and self-directs the formation of the machine;
- The immune system that identifies and eliminates harmful agents.

Indeed, the human body makes even a space shuttle look primitive in comparison. And artificial barriers of organic versus inorganic does not in any way nullify the truth of that statement.

You need to ask yourself this simple question, dear reader. If it is unreasonable for your car or bicycle or phone or computer to exist without someone designing it, why is it reasonable for your body to exist without someone designing it?

If a more straightforward machine with inter-dependent subsystems like a car requires a designer, then why not acknowledge the self-evident truth that a more complicated device with greater functionality or more complex systems would need an even greater or smarter designer? This might be the first time you are considering the possibility that you have a designer and this ought to make you curious! (If you are a person that has experienced religion and you are saying, "yeah, I know God exists," please consider the possibility that the "god" religion has taught you about is not the Creator.)

Furthermore, it is unreasonable to believe that complex physical systems or machines comprised of interdependent sub-systems can exist without a designer. Again, it is absurd to think that a car or a computer would form itself from the raw materials if given enough time. You are free to read the many, many words of those scientific philosophers who would try and convince you otherwise. As you will see, their many words and the complexity associated with those many words; and the concepts those words form and advocate, have as their purpose trying to hide an elementary and self-evident truth. We will look at the practice of using complexity to hide things in a later chapter.

Comparing the most advanced human-designed machine – like the space shuttle – to the organic machine which is the human body – is to embarrass the designers of the space shuttle as being ignorant, rudimentary or puerile engineers. The human body with its genetic code/language that controls the characteristics of our bodies as well as our reproduction is fantastic. The human body with it interdependent systems and with functions like self-healing and the automatic immune system - is so far more advanced than the space shuttle *that it is ferociously irrational to claim that there is no designer behind the organic "machines" of the earth.*

It is true that claiming the Christian god is that designer does not logically follow as the non-theists rightly point out. The Designer's existence is evident, but the identity of that Designer must be established using good inductive and deductive reasoning, observation and perhaps the Designer communicating to humanity.

Therefore, human beings are inherently "religious" or "spiritual" because we find ourselves having the abilities listed above. We find ourselves using those abilities to look at flutterbys and sunsets or people we value and appreciating their beauty and marveling at the Creation. We can know we have wronged someone and we can feel the guilt. We are willing to die for someone out of our love for them. We know that even though we cannot sense (or physically account for) the spiritual abilities that we have, *that they are real and they do exist. We know that mere physical things –* atoms, molecules, acids, proteins, cells, tissue, organs, organ systems, i.e., building blocks - *cannot account for those abilities. Nor can atoms account for our experiences, or the design of the things created -* just like a computer's hardware cannot account for its software (nor can the hardware create itself!).

Non-theists will counter, "but in time we will understand that those abilities have a physical cause." That counter argument is weak at best. Time and physical investigation are going to enable us to understand that a computer's hardware did write/account for the software? Time and physical investigation are going to find the physical nature of numbers? Time and physical investigation are going to reveal the physical nature of reason and logic? Time and physical investigation are going to reveal the physical cause behind a person willingly giving their life away for another person? Time and physical investigation are going to prove that the concept of forgiveness is physical? The truth is time will not do that, for metaphysical or spiritual reality exists and is the best and only reasonable explanation for these things. Please do not choose the path of the irrational or maintain irrational "hopes" to avoid the simple truth that is right in front of you.

Another "defense" the non-theists will raise is "oh, those are old arguments that the author is making have been debunked for years..." or "Expert so-and-so has written a great book proving this fellow's arguments are wrong..." or something to that effect. They will then point you to some large, complicated book as their "defense" instead of providing a clear, brief explanation as to why the arguments I offer are not valid. They generally do this because they cannot reasonably counter the self-evident truth that complex machines (organic or inorganic) with inter-dependent subsystems require a designer.

Stated another way, the person arguing against the evident truths stated here cannot boil down the immense complexities that their favorite author offers in their book(s) because they do not understand them and for good reason! They cannot follow them because there are contradictions contained in all the convoluted arguments they make. It is no different than a fellow from one religious sect trying to "convert" another fellow into his sect by handing him a six hundred page book on theology from his esteemed professor at the seminary. (We will deal with using complexity in the "Hiding in Complexity" chapter.)

Again, those who point to "experts" so-called to refute the simple truths put forth here do this because facts cannot be reasonably denied and since they are unwilling to submit to the truth in this domain, they believe they need to come up with some defense. There is no reasonable refutation of the self-evident fact that complicated machines with inter-dependent subsystems – whether human-made inorganic or God-made organic – *require* a designer.

And as we shall see, mere physical things cannot in any reasonable way account for the most critical concept and aspect of life that we human beings experience and grapple with – true love.

One other quite silly response that people will provide to the "who created you" question is, "my mom and dad." I would respond to that person, "Did your parents" design and create you? I'd like to talk with them about their design planning and how the accomplished sentience, abstract reasoning, and a moral knowing—as well as the easier stuff like how they designed your brain to function. To say your parents "created you" is like saying the guy who drives the iron delivery truck to the auto plant created the plant's output, an automobile. The truth is that your parents just brought the raw materials together and then the Designer's "magic" happened to create you!'

So, having put forth a major premise of this book:

- That the billions of human beings that cover the earth are reasonably religious or spiritual;
- That humans reasonably have existential God beliefs to account for their existence;

Let us continue to build the framework and take a brief look at how humanity is doing and if religion is helping humankind be better as time moves forward. Or, stated another way, let us take a brief look at some of the facts and realities about human existence that meaningfully add to the broader framework that we are building and the worldview we are addressing so that we may make sound judgments as to whether Christianity is a successful failure.

Chapter Summary:
- We exist, and we have a cause for our existence – observation, reason, and logic leave no other option;
- Given the complexity of merely our physical presence, the only reasonable conclusion is that a designer exists—a designer capable of understanding and putting together all the complex systems of the human body. Complex bio-organic machines with interdependent subsystems don't just exist by random natural forces;
- We have metaphysical or spiritual aspects to our person or nature and to deny that is irrational and to demonstrate a physicalist bias;
- It is reasonable for people to have beliefs about God or to believe that a creator must exist.

2
THE STATE OF HUMANKIND

Opening Questions:
- Can we objectively assess how well human beings are doing?
- Why do we humans do so many bad things?
- What is Christianity's (or for that matter religions) role in the state of humankind, if any?
- If we ignore certain things we don't like to see or admit, does that mean they don't exist?

Christians like to say that Christianity has been an excellent and positive influence on humankind over the centuries. They point to the "successes" of Christianity to validate that belief. The Christians would generally define "success" as the number of members or adherents that participate; the amount of money and land and other material resources they possess and control; or the amount of money they spend on their charitable services. Other religions do the same. Evolutionary atheists and agnostics try to make a case that either the mysterious physical force of "evolution" is bettering humankind as the millennia tick by; or that their humanistic beliefs and actions are helping humanity; or both.

If anything, this book is dealing with root issues and problems and not painting a "pretty picture" over the pain, and suffering that in reality exists—this book endeavors to provide a solution to the root problems that plague humankind. Just like a physician cannot help a patient heal without properly diagnosing and understanding the problem, so we in this book cannot properly find a solution without looking closely at the "patient," who is us, humankind. *To deny realities is to be both deluded and furthermore not able to provide help.* To be able to determine if Christianity has been either a success or a failure and to be able to see what solution will work for the world's problems, we must first have an accurate view of the state of the world. Without an understanding of the state of the world, we would be unable to determine Christianity's impact on that world.

So, for those people who have bought into the positive thinking philosophy —no matter your ilk, religious person or non-religious person — let's leave the biased filter and instead take a real, unvarnished and unfiltered look at the "patient" to get a handle on the real state of things. (Later we will address why we as human beings have a strong bias against seeing clearly.)

The people of the United States are in the process of destroying themselves. The U.S., perhaps the most successful nation in history due to:

- It's being a stable nation-state (based on people creating and agreeing to laws to govern people's behavior);
- It's people being able to select their leaders (relatively politically free)
- Its people being able to pursue what they consider important in life (individual freedom and happiness);

…is in the process of destroying itself. The amount of conflict in the U.S. today is rapidly heading to the level of other conflict episodes in the nation's history like the civil war. The people no longer agree on a fundamental existential view of human life (absolutism versus relativism — we will look at those beliefs later in the book); nor do they agree on an ethical standard for determining good or bad human behavior (traditionally derived from some religious rule). Like their religious brethren who cannot agree on what the bible says, the political folks cannot even agree on what the U.S. Constitution states, a robust political standard if people could agree on what it says and means.

These choices of the American people have led them to the place where they no longer know how to tell if something is true or false, right or wrong. In fact, most Americans now take political freedom for granted and are not grateful for much of anything since greed and selfishness have grown exponentially in the hearts of the people. This book will not analyze the self-destruction of the American society, but it is noteworthy that politics, economics, business, religion or psychological philosophies are not what make a people healthy, functional and united. All of those domains are functioning well according to usual world standards in the U.S. - politics, economics, business, religion or psychological philosophies - and yet the people of the U.S. are starting to rip each other apart.

If you have eyes to see, you will know that conflict rages in every "corner" of the globe, from large national conflicts involving warring violence and tens of thousands killed and millions driven from their homes and becoming refugees, to tens of thousands of people committing suicide each year in the U.S. alone. Then there is the "commonplace" daily conflict like children hating or running away from parents or the silent animosity or "backstabbing" that characterizes so many workplaces as people compete for power or more money. These are but a very few examples of the root problem this book will address and provide a non-religious solution.

While many seek to deny the conflict, pain, and suffering that occurs each day by hiding from it and ignoring it in their perceived "place of safety," it does not change the facts. Just because a person lives in a relatively safe and free-from-crime housing development in the United States or Europe does not change the facts. Just because those same people can control what they choose to put in front of their face with their electronic devices; does not change the fact that billions of people are in conflict at some level, and billions are suffering or struggling in many different ways.

The facts also rebuke the idea that human beings are evolving into something better. The conflict problems don't go away as time moves forward or as the earth's population grows or as we get smarter with our technology of manipulating matter and energy. History proves that we are, in general, naturally predisposed to conflict and violence and the resultant pain, suffering, and destruction. There are ebbs and flows over history, for sure, but the basic fact of our human predisposition to enter into and remain in conflict remains undeniable.

In 2017, here is a small sampling of facts that illustrate well the state of humankind. Please think about what might be the root level causes for the following facts.

Problem 1: Few with most, many will little

"Nearly one-half of the world's population — more than 3 billion people — live on less than $2.50 a day. More than 1.3 billion live in extreme poverty — less than $1.25 a day. One billion children worldwide are living in poverty. According to UNICEF, about 22,000 children die each day due to poverty." [10]

Thousands of children are dying from preventable disease and starvation, while the number of billionaires has risen to over 1,800 and the number of millionaires has risen to about 16 million. What does that mean from a wealth/resource distribution standpoint?

- Half of the world's wealth belongs to the top 1% of the wealthiest people;

---

[10] Source: https://www.dosomething.org/us/facts/11-facts-about-global-poverty

- The top 10% of adults hold 85% of the world's wealth, while the bottom 90% hold the remaining 15% of the world's total wealth;
- The top 30% of adults hold 97% of the total wealth.

"According to the Organization for Economic Co-Operation and Development (OECD) in 2012 the top 0.6% of world population (consisting of adults with more than 1 million USD in assets) or the 42 million richest people in the world held 39.3% of world wealth. The next 4.4% (311 million people) held 32.3% of world wealth. The bottom 95% held 28.4% of world wealth." [11]

So, let's get the simple facts straight. Tens of thousands of children are outright dying each day, and millions more are suffering, neglected and abused, and billions of people are scraping by to survive each day. At the same time, a while a few hundred million people who could easily help them, don't, and instead ignore them, justify their lack of help and work to become wealthier. Clear enough? Even if you weed out the people who are self-destructive or unwilling to perform ethical work to "better their lives" in this world, the facts don't significantly change.

The simple truth is that there are more than enough resources on this planet for all human beings and with our improved technology; it would be a relatively simple matter to distribute those resources equitably.

Problem 2: Priority of Resource Usage - War Machines

The world's people/nations spend trillions of dollars on war machines, and they do this based on the primary corruptors of human nature – pride, fear and selfishness (we will look at this critical point in detail later). No murderous outer-space aliens are invading the planet to justify such behavior. Only pride, the pride that says, "we are better than you and more worthy than you and thus can take from you what we want." Fear says, "you are different than us so we don't trust you and you might try and hurt us so we must defend ourselves." Selfishness says, "we want something (perhaps what you have), and we don't care about the impact to you of taking what we want" (or we are going to take it no matter what it does to you). More self-pride which says, "try to stop us, and we will destroy you." and that, dear reader is the darkness of humanity. To deny it is irrational.

These motivations and associated behaviors account for the vast majority of conflict in human history. And it is these aspects of human

---

[11] The World Fact Book – Central Intelligence Agency. Distribution of Family Income – GINI Index. https://www.cia.gov/library/publications/the-world-factbook/fields/2172.html

OECD DATA. Income Inequality. https://data.oecd.org/inequality/income-inequality.htm

nature that justify spending a significant amount of the earth's resources on weapons. Can the reader think of any better use of the world's resources than making machines intended to kill human beings? What is it about humankind that they are so driven to build war machines and use them?

Problem 3: Mankind's Worst Enemy

No, our worst enemy is not a disease or natural disasters; instead, it is ourselves. The people who decide they are going to spend a large part or even the majority of our resources on war machines and weapons certainly want to use them and seem to look for opportunities to take and destroy. More people in human history have died at the hands of other human beings than any other means of physical death other than "natural" means of illness, disease or body function failure. Add to that "neglect" as a cause – meaning I could have saved a person but did not – and you paint an accurate picture of the human race...many hundreds of millions of people killed – or allowed to die when they did not have to - by other people.

Warring conflicts flare up all over the earth – the Middle East, Africa, Asia, and Eastern Europe to name a few in the last few years. Millions of refugees are fleeing the uncontrolled self-pride generated hatred of one people group and their beliefs against another and the resultant destruction. As a result, vast amounts of pain, suffering, and loss occur for what? A "new, better" political leader who will allow the power he/she will receive to corrupt them and start the violence cycle all over again? Another religious leader who will say, "Our God is the right God or greater..." and keep the people in darkness and start the cycle of fear and hatred all over again?

No doubt religion has contributed to a significant portion of the conflict in world history. Stated another way, people's God-claims and beliefs have been consistently used throughout history as justification to harm or destroy other people. How often has, "we have the One True God, and you must submit to him." been said, thought or acted upon? (A note for the atheist to not commit a logical fallacy by believing this acknowledgment proves that God is not real or that Joshua of Nazareth is to blame. Joshua of Nazareth taught AND lived out, "love your enemies" so no, he is not to blame for the violence in his "name'.) Other non-theists or agnostics try and blame all conflict on religion, and this too is wrong. Plain old greed and the desire for more or better material things including land has played a role. The willingness to take slaves to serve us and the desire to exercise power over others with non-God motivations (or using God claims as an excuse) equally have their place in history and the current state of affairs as the motivation for the conflict that exists.

Problem 4: People Killing Themselves or Suicide

People killing themselves has become the leading cause of injury-related death in the United States, overtaking auto accidents – a nation that people worldwide describe as one of the most desirable places to live. That means about 50,000 U.S. citizens are killing themselves each year or about 137 people each day. (https://afsp.org/about-suicide/suicide-statistics/)

The number of suicides has been steadily increasing over the years. The Reuters news agency published the following horrible and revealing facts on November 3rd, 2016.

"The suicide rate among U.S. *middle school students* doubled from 2007 to 2014, surpassing for the first time the incidence of youngsters *aged 10 to 14* who died in car crashes, a federal report released on Thursday said." So, not only adults are killing themselves by the tens of thousands, but now children are also killing themselves by the hundreds each year. What a horrific manifestation of the state of things in "the Christian nation" that is the U.S.

Add to the number of suicides those people who die from more-or-less purposeful drug usage and overdose, and you have about a hundred thousand people essentially killing themselves because they do not want to exist in this world anymore.

What evolutionary hypothesis fits with suicide caused by hopelessness? What political solution is going to fix those problems? How is money going to fix that? How are the latest psychological philosophies going to fix that? Is there some drug around the corner which will take away the hopelessness that drives much of the drug use problem? The answer is no since chemicals don't cause despair as hopelessness is a spiritual condition, not a physical one. And just as obvious is that while religion flourishes in the U.S., these problems wax, not wane, thus proving that religion is not an effective solution for these problems. Also, many Christians are part of the statistics of suicide and drug usage.

Problem 5: Drug Usage to Dull the Hopelessness

Using drugs to dull or numb the inner/spiritual hopelessness and pain people are experiencing in the U.S. alone, rises every year and at this point is in the tens of millions of people. Whether they are illegal narcotics or opioids dispensed by one's physician, the intent is the same, and the result is often the same. How many human beings worldwide are using drugs to dull their hopelessness? Billions?

The number of people in the U.S. that are addicted to some drug is about 20 million. The number of people in the U.S. who misuse alcohol is about 15 million. Get the picture?

Problem 6: Bigotry and Racism

Let's define the terms first. Bigotry is "a person who has strong, unreasonable ideas, esp. about race or religion, and who thinks anyone who does not have the same beliefs is wrong". [12] Racism is "the belief that some races are better than others, or the unfair treatment of someone because of his or her race." So, bigotry is a broader category of unjust discrimination whereas racism is bigotry towards people of different races or ethnicities.

This characteristic of the human race is one of the ugliest, worst and unfortunately widely held problems of people all over the earth. To judge people as somehow less human or less valuable based on their skin color or other racial or physical characteristics is plain evidence of the darkness in which human beings dwell. How much animosity and hatred exist due to bigotry and racism, and how much conflict does it generate on the earth each day? Undoubtedly, the hostility and conflict associated with bigoted views cause many millions of unloving thoughts and actions each day on the planet.

As soon as an individual starts seeing things through skin color, for example, they become racists, even if they do so to correct or speak about a perceived wrong or injustice to a particular group. Until people can get past all the labels and unimportant differences between people, the human race will continue to broil in potential and actual conflict, desiring to harm one another.

Please note that it is not bigoted to call out a particular group of people if they have beliefs or behavior that is harmful towards others or themselves.

Problem 7: Allowing others to be murdered and tortured when people can stop it

The people of the nation's allowing openly murderous individuals and their followers to roam the earth to rape pillage and murder freely. Groups like Boko Haram are paid mostly lip service while the "united nations" sits around doing nothing but arguing, bashing Israel and enjoying their New York lifestyle. With all the trillions of dollars spent on military junk, the only excuse the people of the world have for not preventing the murders perpetrated by groups like Boko Haram is the darkness of lovelessness and selfishness.

The world leader's position on Islamic "terror" is nothing short of atrocious. It is politically incorrect to critique a world religion, so the leaders of democratic nations blunder around with words to avoid the

---

[12] Cambridge Dictionary, www.dictionary.cambridge.org, April 2018

simple truth that the religion of Islam itself contains teachings from their primary prophet Muhammad, that includes sayings like "kill the infidels" (or non-Muslims). We shall address this in more detail later.

Problem 8: Human Slavery-'Trafficking'

"According to the International Labour Organization (ILO), forced labor alone (one component of human trafficking) generates an estimated $150 billion in profits per annum as of 2014. In 2012, the ILO estimated that 21 million victims are trapped in modern-day slavery. Of these, 14.2 million (68%) were exploited for labor, 4.5 million (22%) were sexually exploited, and 2.2 million (10%) were exploited in state-imposed forced labor." [13]

Human sex trafficking is enslaving and abusing millions of women and children for men's sexual pleasure each day, while the people of the earth who could do something about it turn away and pretend it is not a problem—or engage in it or facilitate it.

Problem 9: Only Helping Others with Basic or Critical Needs for Money

It is one thing to not provide a non-essential product or service to someone who cannot pay for it. It is another thing altogether, for example, to not provide a necessary medical procedure (for instance life-saving or pain reducing) because the person needing the help cannot pay for it or cannot afford it.

How would you describe only being willing to help each other with bodily illness or injury needs if we receive money for doing so? If you are injured or have a disease that you cannot treat yourself, how would you like it if the only way someone would help you is if you paid them money, but you didn't have the money? This dynamic essentially describes the "medical profession" in the U.S. The people operating the medical or healthcare industry are able and equipped with the means to help others who are injured or ill but will only do so if they get money. Here is a simple illustration to demonstrate this evil.

Let us say you are walking along a trail somewhere, and you fall and break your ankle and cannot walk. While you are laying there in pain and

---

[13] Special Action Programme to Combat Forced Labour (20 May 2014). "Profits and poverty: The economics of forced labour" (PDF -
http://www.ilo.org/wcmsp5/groups/public/---ed_norm/---
declaration/documents/publication/wcms_243027.pdf). International Labour Organization. p. 4. Retrieved 24 October 2016.

concerned about the coming cold night, a person with the ability to help you comes along, and you ask for help, and he says, "well, I'll help you if you give me 100 dollars'. You don't have the money, so he walks away and leaves you there or says, "oh, I will see if I can find someone who will help you for nothing.'

The simple truth is that the people who make up the medical or health systems of the U.S. operate on that same principle, all their objections notwithstanding. Of course, they hide behind receptionists and insurance companies; and in some places, they are forced by law to treat people. But that does not change the fact that they have the means to help the sick and injured, but will only do so if they receive a material benefit for doing so. This practice of just helping others for material gain is evil.

I do not propose that they not receive a wage for their work, for their work is valuable, but so is the electrician's work which provided electricity to the building, or the plumber who provided working toilets or the cafeteria staff who prepare food, or the cleaning service who cleaned the bathrooms, etc.

What I am saying is to deny competent medical help to a person based on money is morally wrong. It is also morally wrong to provide better medical care to those who can pay more.

Solutions include tax-based compensation for health care providers with appropriate incentives, peer, and patient reviews. A simple and practical solution would be to pass a law that says when a physician's rate exceeds, for example, $100 per hour; the physician must collect his fee in person from the patient. The law would be even better if it required the physician to say something like, "Please give me the $X you owe me for my $X per hour rate.'

One thing is sure - when you have many people who "cannot afford" good medical services and at the same time you have physicians occupying most of the top 10 highest paying jobs in the nation - love and compassion are gone, all the marketing slogans about "Care" notwithstanding.

Problem 10: Disrespecting and Devaluing Older or Elderly People

Most people in the United States regularly show contempt and hatred for those who raised them and provided for them for the first 15 to 20 years of their life – their parents. Parents are ignored, disrespected and dishonored by their children and finally, put away in a "nursing home" to die essentially alone – "cared for" by paid people who don't care. To not truly care for parents is evil even when the parents - **who have forgotten or never knew what love is** - say they want to be put "in a home." Only parents who believe they have nothing to contribute – no wisdom gained over their life, not even any love to give – would ask to be away from their children. Only parents who don't love their children would want to be away from their children. Only children who:

- Don't believe their parents are worthy of appreciation for all they did for them;
- Don't believe their parents are worthy of respect or honor;
- Want to live selfish lives;
- Don't love their parents;
- Would send their parents away to be "cared for" by people who are performing that work primarily for money.

Stated another way, only people who have believed or contributed to the lie that older people are worthless and younger people are valuable would participate in the evil of isolation from people they claim to love. Or, predicted by Joshua of Nazareth some 2,000 years ago, *"the love of most has grown cold."*

A significant number of suicides happen in these loveless healthcare facilities—is it any wonder why?

Problem 11: Fashionable Lying

Lying for selfish material gain is evil. The "sales" and "marketing" people of the earth have made lying into an art form. The standard in the U.S. is falling so low that people expect that a person selling something will lie to them, deceive them or withhold important information about something associated with "the sell."

It should concern people that the Real standard of honesty to which we will be held accountable is this - if I don't keep my word and don't apologize for breaking it, I have spoken falsely. If I make a practice of breaking my word and apologizing for it but don't change, I am a self-deceived liar. If I practice lying or speaking falsehoods for selfish gain, I am evil. If I withhold information to gain from someone selfishly, greed rules me.

Problem 12: The General State of Human Affairs

There are trillions of acts of unkindness that occur each day on the planet, all due to the three things that rule humans instead of love. From the coldness of not helping someone with some simple task, to ignoring people who would benefit from a kind word, to outright hurting each other in millions of ways each day. Yes, there are acts of kindness as well, but sadly, they are but a ripple under the tidal wave.

State of Things Conclusions

What is the conclusion that is arrived at by the above truths about the state of humankind? How about this saying of The Light?

And this is the judgment, that the people of the earth love the darkness rather than the light because their deeds are evil. (John 3:19)

From one important perspective, no other reasonable conclusion can be arrived at other than "guilty." Someone once said well, "Facts are stubborn things." Oh, you can whitewash all the above problems and ignore them and pretend they don't exist to live in a delusional state of selfishness, as we shall see in the next section...but that behavior does not make the facts go away. In like manner, focusing on the good things to the exclusion of acknowledging the bad things also does not make the bad things go away. For example, to say, "oh well, the tsunami will cause some fish to be available to eat on land," does not nullify the fact that the tsunami will come and kill many people and destroy much useful hard work.

It is just true that people are the same all over the earth for the past several thousand years. Nothing significant has changed except people's knowledge about physical things; how matter and energy work; and applying that knowledge to solve physical problems – thus the improvements in science and technology. Human beings and the issues caused by our nature has not changed one bit as the above fact examples illustrate. Religion has not solved those problems over the recent millennia and in fact, has caused much conflict.

That is not to say that some people have not been good people or that they have not made significant contributions to smaller groups of people. Some more recent examples come to mind like Gandhi and Martine Luther King Jr. and Nelson Mandela and others. They all made significant improvements within a nation, culture or a group of people on the earth. The problem is, when those leader's die, what happens? Do the things they stood for and the ethics or principles they believed or implemented remain and endure among their people or beyond? Sadly, history provides the answer to that question. Look at India, the U.S., and South Africa today. India has billionaires and remains deeply divided among religious and economic status. The U.S. is falling apart with identity politics, meaning racial, ethnic, gender and religious division are growing along with a deepening income/wealth divide. South Africa's racial advancements under Mandela are rapidly deteriorating.

The BIG picture is what is in view here, and given the facts above we are failing each other in a big way given the potential we have. *If you consider the possibility – all human beings working together for good, constructive purposes and projects and without conflict – the failure is magnified tremendously.* The simple fact is that people can work together without conflict, but instead choose not to.

This failure is worse because more than ever in history – through technology - we are capable of alleviating much of the non-human caused suffering that plagues billions of human beings. Food abundance and distribution means have never been greater. Drilling water wells and the methods to accomplish that drilling to provide safe drinking water all over the earth have never been better. Disease-fighting and other medical technology and cures have never been better, etc.

Furthermore, due to global communication removing the excuse of ignorance *and* due to the abundance of resources of some people groups/nations, we don't have a valid explanation for the above. All we have are the root problems, described in the next section, which causes what we see on the earth and causes us to be "guilty.'

If we (you and I) are not working to help improve things; if we (you and I) are not working to bring change in some way to problems we see, *then we are part of the problem instead of part of the solution.* What are Christians doing to solve these problems? Is it not true that Christians manifest the problems within their circles? And is it not true that Christians and Christianity claim to have the solutions to make the world a better place? And is it not true that organized Christianity has been around for millennia and yet the problems are not going away? Can you point to "Christian communities" where the "truths" of the Christians are consistently practiced and lived out? If you can, why are you not a part of them?

Here is a truth worth pondering: Few people are good, most are bad and the strong or powerful take advantage of, use or abuse the weak or powerless.

Don't believe that? Why? Perhaps you have the wrong standard to make that judgment? Or maybe there is something in the way of your being able to make that judgment properly? Or perhaps you don't want to see the facts? Or maybe you have a strong bias against the facts? In the next chapter, let us explore the premise that we have a strong and deep bias regarding how we view ourselves and others.

Chapter Summary:
- The world is a nasty place, and that reality can only be denied by ignoring the facts or by having a deficient standard to judge right from wrong;
- As we shall see, having some "positive belief" philosophy that one uses to ignore the facts presented in this chapter is both delusional and selfish;
- In as much as Christianity claims to "impact the world," it has not improved the general state of things, and in many cases, it has been the source of conflict and violence in God's name;

- Christians do not have widespread models of actual, real communities where their supposed beliefs and practices are lived out and manifested.

3
UNDERSTANDING HUMAN NATURE

Opening Questions:
- Is it essential to understand our nature?
- If we don't have a clear and proper understanding our nature, will it not be difficult to solve problems associated with that nature?
- What is our heart?
- What is our soul?
- What is our mind?
- What is our spirit?

So, as we can see, there is something wrong with us. The facts that we just reviewed are not necessarily facts. In other words, the people of the world do not have to be the way that we are, and the only thing to blame for human-caused wrong and suffering are we human beings.

It is essential to understand our nature so we can better understand ourselves and each other and thus be able to better see the framework and our part in it.

One of the most critical and fundamental questions we should ask ourselves as thinking beings is, "what exactly are we or, what does my nature consist of, or what makes me a human being"? As we have seen, many have believed the irrational concept that *we are merely atoms, molecules, acids, proteins, cells,* etc. - in other words, physical things are the entirety of who I am. That is as unreasonable as saying that the nature of a computer is merely its hardware—that no software is needed to account for the ability of the machine to do what they do. Instead of believing that which is unreasonable, why not observe well and make some good deductive realizations? The terms and concepts I am about to discuss are not mine alone.

The following concepts, while they have different terms/words to describe them, do not mean they are necessarily separate and distinct from one another from a metaphysical "substance" perspective. That means, for example, that while we have both a soul and a heart, those two unique, distinct and different *functioning* things could still be part of one whole metaphysical entity.

Our Spiritual or Metaphysical Nature

Our heart represents our will, the core of our being that controls the decisions we make regarding what we do with our both our life and the time we are given each day. Our heart determines what we value or consider important and thus it directs our will. Our heart motivates us to action.

Our soul represents both our emotional capabilities as well as our conscience.

Our emotions are what can color and bring depth and fullness to our experiences and our thoughts. We experience feelings based on things that happen in our lives or thoughts we have about our lives, others or our experiences. All people can experience emotions, but sadly, most people today are allowing their feelings to make life and relationship decisions instead of using their mind and reason. That is about as smart as needing to walk next to a cliff and deciding how best to walk next to that cliff based on how the cloud shapes in the sky make you "feel" instead of which direction the cliff is. Or, as another example, it is about as smart as a person who is dying of thirst in the desert deciding which direction the water spring might be based on which color or shape of sand makes him "feel the best" instead of deduced facts like plants live near water. You might think these examples are silly, but the truth is that more and more people each day - including probably you dear reader - are making decisions based on "I feel" instead of on "that is true." As people have turned away from the One who says, "I am the truth," and even *away from the fact that truth exists,* they are left with the *selfishness* of "I feel; therefore I decide this." An existence of being led by our emotions is a life of deep darkness and ruin.

Every human being has a soul.

Our conscience is that which intuitively tells us right behavior from wrong behavior or our ability to judge right from wrong on a non-intellectual basis. It is one key component of human nature that sets us apart from animals. Animals don't behave based on a moral compass of, "this action is wrong, and thus I will not do it," or, "this action is right and will help all animals in this area so I will do it." Instead, they are programmed with instincts that control their behavior. To deny that humans have a conscience is to believe that a child who lies has no idea that what they are doing is wrong—even the child who was never told that lying is wrong. Go, test what I say - find a child and ask them to tell a person that the blue car is a red car. Humans were given the innate ability - through our metaphysical conscience - to know right from wrong. I am not saying that people live by their conscience because in general and for many, they do not. Our will can easily overcome our conscience, especially when we perceive *we will gain or lose something valuable* to us based on some decision or circumstance. We can also dull our conscience by going against it so many times that it loses its sensitivity.

Our conscience is why no human being will stand before our *Life Judge* and successfully plead, "I am innocent" or "I plead ignorance."

Every human being has a conscience, but many dull or destroy their conscience through drugs (dull) or practicing wrong behavior (ruin).

Our mind represents our intellect - our ability to reason, use logic, process information and thus to identify truth from falsehood.

Our mind is distinct from our brain. To use a computer analogy, the brain is the physical hardware or "CPU, memory, data storage, and power source" while the mind is the metaphysical "software" or operating system and applications. Our mind is affected by our will and soul. In other words, our mind might successfully determine that something is true instead of false, but our will may take our conclusion and wash it away into non-action if we perceive we will lose something we want if we act upon the truth/conclusion.

If there is one thing that is needed today, it is for people to use reason well to arrive at truth. Tragically, most people do not because they have believed many false things about this realm called "the world." They think these false things because they are not willing to put truth above the comfort of their existence in this world. Stated another way, they love themselves and this world more than anything else - thus, they avoid using reason and logic to identify the truth and only use lesser truths to serve their desires in this world.

Every human being has a mind.

Our will interacts with our mind as our mind informs our will about the realm in which we exist and interact. Our will interacts with our soul as our soul provides "data" on what is right and wrong.

Our spirit enables us to know – be aware of – and commune with our Father and Creator.

Our spirit enables us to connect with our Creator. Through our spirit, we can connect or communicate with outside entities or beings, including our Creator—being to Being without words or language communication.

Every human being is born with a functional, living spirit.

Every child who has not passed out of innocence has a spirit that is alive through the Life given by the Creator. Innocence is the metaphysical or spiritual property which is the life of a child's spirit. For adults, faith in God (not a merely intellectual belief that he exists) is the life of our spirit.

Not all human beings have a living spirit, meaning their spirit can connect or communicate with (be aware of) their Creator due to choices they made - in fact, most adults do not have a spirit that is "alive.'

Without applications, a computer is essentially non-functional...it has an operating system and can function but it cannot produce meaningful or productive operations. So we are if our spirit is "dead" or not fully working or able to experience the fullness of its intended purpose.

What would a flower be without its color or odor? What is a kiss without love? What is a sunset without color? What is a smile without compassion? What is food without flavor or smell? What is a kind act without the right motivation? What would sex be without sensations or emotional aspects? What would a story be without a problem to overcome or conflict to solve?

So it is with our spirit when it "dies" and loses the connection to our Father—it becomes merely a colorless shadow rather than a vibrant, colorful living agent.

Our body is merely *the physical means we have been given to express who we are and what we value.* Yes, we are an integrated whole – spirit, body, heart, soul and mind – but just like a computer, our hardware (or body) is the lesser aspect of our existence.

Every human being who exists in the realm/dimension of our physical universe has a body.

Here is something to consider which makes a strong case that our body is *not* what defines who we are.

Medical science and art are improving to the point the following scenario is realistic. A forty-year-old woman Megan was caught in her house when it caught fire before she went to bed. She was so badly burned that her body was lost to burn injury and the medical people used an advanced artificial life support systems to keep her alive by essentially amputating her head from her body. Her face was also severely burned and disfigured so that you could not recognize her. When Megan gained consciousness, she was the same person who she was 30 hours ago when she went to bed before the fire started.

Her personality, as well as all her memories and experiences and commitments to and love for other people, were the same. All the people she had relationships with were the same. She was still Megan in every meaningful way except her body was radically changed, essentially lost, and her face was unrecognizable. The biggest challenge for Megan would be how she will react to losing the physical identity her body provided and the functions her body provided. In other words, after *the accident, she views* herself as a different person since she sees her body as the essential part of who she is. Her perspective about herself changed but in reality, who she is did not change at all unless she wills it. Due to her body change, she will have to face and deal with the choices of fear, self-pride and darkness OR faith, love, and light.

This proves that we human beings, while having a body, are *not* primarily physical beings. Our body does *not* make us who we are even if we choose to believe that delusion.

Next, we will take a look at the root problems that we have mentioned and alluded to several times up to this point. We will also see that we all fit into particular categories of types of people. Understanding the root problems will help us further build the framework we need to honestly "see" and make sound judgments about the successful failure.

Chapter Summary:
- Human beings have metaphysical or spiritual components to our nature;
- We have a will (our "heart"), which directs our decisions each day and in life;
- We have a soul, which is our emotional capacity as well as our conscience - that is our ability to know right behavior from wrong behavior;
- We have a mind, which provides us with our intellect and is the component that can use reason and logic to know that which is true from that which is false;
- We have a spirit, which can connect us to our Life Source, or Creator and Father;
- All children have a living spirit while most adults have killed their spirit due to refusing to accept what is true and justifying self-wrongness and thus not seeing their need for forgiveness and true Life;
- The contemporary term "personality" would be synonymous (the same as) with our heart and soul;
- Who we are is not primarily about our bodies unless we choose that warped perspective;

4
THE ROOT PROBLEMS AND FOUR DIFFERENT KINDS OF PEOPLE

Opening Questions:
- Does what kind of a person I am matter?
- Is it possible to be blind in a way that is not physical?
- Does self-pride play a role in my life and is its influence good or bad, constructive or destructive?
- Does fear play a role in my life and is its influence good or bad, constructive or destructive?
- Does selfishness play a role in my life and is its influence good or bad, constructive or destructive?

The world – that is the people of the earth who create, participate in or ignore all the problems – needs a lot of help as we saw in the previous "the State of Humankind" chapter. However, "humankind" is made up of individuals. Individuals are collectively causing the problems, and every human being fits into one of four categories regarding their contributions to the problems. There are the leaders, the participators, the ignorers and the fighters.

The leaders get the lion's share of the blame, the participators a good percentage and the ignorers also share some responsibility for all evil in the world. The fighters actively work non-violently using truth against the evil that the other three types of people create, support or refuse to fight. Therefore, we have to ask ourselves, "how is MY state of being?" which will determine which category of person I am. *I cannot decide for or control anyone else, but I can choose for and control myself.* I can and should influence others.

As we saw previously, there is a tremendous amount of unnecessary pain and suffering that occurs each day due solely to the actions – in inactions - of other people.

Let us pause for a moment to bring this down to the personal level since we have been talking at a high, impersonal level. Am I the best person I could be? Am I causing conflict or pain in other people's lives? Am I neglecting people in my life? Am I treating all the people in my life the right way, and how do I know what the right way is? Am I genuinely living by love? If not, what is the solution? Will politics or religion or economics solve those problems that I have? Will self-pride prevent me from admitting those problems?

So what are the root problems and how can we fix them first in ourselves and then in others? The following story will help you understand the difficulty in finding the solution.

There once was a man who was an engineer and whose work it was to investigate the engineering failure(s) that occurred that caused a massive loss of life. This fellow's job was to find out what structural engineering components failed. He liked his work except for the dead bodies he would encounter on his site investigations, which greatly disturbed him. So, being a creative engineer, he invented a helmet which had a feature that would filter out the un-pleasantries of the dead human bodies and body parts that were a regular part of his initial evaluations. With his invention, the man could now walk onto the site of the collapsed building, for example, and not see any evidence of human suffering or death.

Did you know a real helmet of this nature exists? And did you know that the vast majority of human beings have this helmet and use it all the time? *It is called the helmet of selfishness, and it has two primary power sources that make it work – self-pride and fear.* What this helmet does is mask the evidence of all the problems causing hardship, pain, anguish, and suffering. This helmet is most useful for the real situations that the wearer encounters every day, but it also works with the TV and internet.

What is the primary benefit that the wearer of the helmet appreciates about the helmet? The primary benefit is that the wearers *believe themselves to be free of responsibility to do anything about helping the people affected by the problems or of trying to fix the problems*! Of course, the helmet prevents a person from even knowing how to help others let alone wanting to.

Now would be a good time to pause and summarize what we have covered in this book up to this point.

So far we have established a few relevant facts. First, that it is reasonable for we human beings to be "spiritual" or "religious" since a designer clearly must exist to account for our bodies and lives on the earth, just like it is reasonable to conclude a designer exists to account for the existence of a computer. Furthermore, since we have metaphysical or spiritual aspects or components to our persons – our souls, minds, conscience, etc. – it is only reasonable to conclude that our "software" components had a designer/Programmer. Therefore, it is only reasonable that we be "spiritual" or "religious" because the physical realm cannot account for metaphysical realities like reasoning, forgiveness or love properly defined as selfless behavior motivated by compassion.

Second, we established that the human race has serious problems, and it does no one any good to deny those problems. The first step to solving any problem is first to admit it exists! For example, a surgeon denying a cancerous tissue exists will not help the patient overcome the problem.

Finally, we took a brief look at human nature so we could understand ourselves better.

So, as we saw, the following terms and associated concepts describe well what is happening amongst human beings on a daily basis all over the earth for the past several thousand years – war, conflict, violence, slavery, abuse, neglect, suffering, pain, greed, wrongful competition, greed, etc. Yes, there are ebbs and flows to these things, but they continue to exist without any significant advances in solving them. And yes, good people are doing good things on the earth, but they are few and far between and don't significantly impact the overall state of humankind.

As I have already alluded to, I suggest that if one looks closely enough, one will see that three things are the cause of most of our problems: *Self-pride, fear, and selfishness.*

Remember, the Christians will say, "oh, well, of course, there are problems in the world, but sin is the real problem." That is no different than the physician who is unable to treat the disease successfully because he is not willing to look closely enough to determine the specific cause but instead insists that "disease" is the problem. In this way, he convinces himself he can see and is good at his occupation, even while most of his patients die.

Before we address how Christianity is a "successful" failure, we need to address a fundamental aspect of human nature that will be at work in all people. We already addressed the "helmet of selfishness," but let us take a closer look at the helmet as well as its two primary power sources. If we cannot fully appreciate our fundamental problem, we are not likely to see our need for the solution.

There are three aspects to our nature, or predispositions to our nature, which keep us in a cage of our own making. Stated another way, these three aspects of our nature cause us to do much wrong…self-pride and fear and selfishness. Here are some examples to help the reader understand the concept of being "bound" or in a metaphorical cage.

Examples from the physical realm: Asking a physically blind person to look at a sunset and appreciate its beauty is irrational - they can't do that. Asking a disabled person who cannot walk to please walk to the store and get some milk is silly - they can't do that.

An example from the metaphysical intellectual realm: To ask a normal seven-year-old child to read and understand Einstein's advanced works on the theory of relatively, is irrational - they can't do that.

An example from the metaphysical, moral realm: Asking a person - who is bound up in bitterness towards another person who they believe has wronged them – to forgive the offender immediately, is irrational - they are in a state of their choosing which will not allow them to do that.

An example from the metaphysical, spiritual realm: Asking a person to live by the teachings of Joshua of Nazareth when they have not placed their faith in him is irrational – they can't do that. Oh, they can play a game in the intellectual realm and learn many things about "Jesus" in their mind, but they will not listen to him, nor believe him nor do what he says due to their lack of faith. Unlike the physical limitation examples above, in this case, the capacity can be chosen or rejected by our free will—we have a choice.

We, as human beings, have limitations. More importantly, we have aspects of our nature that cripple us or blind us or make us far less than what we were intended to be. The three elements of our usual human nature that bind us and blind us and seek to control us are self-pride, fear, and selfishness. These root problems have been mentioned and referred to previously, but now we will take a close look at them.

I challenge the reader to look at the conflict and human-caused wrongness in the world – including the conflict and wrongness that is occurring in your life with those you interact with or have relationships with – and find the cause of the conflict or wrongness. If you do this well, you will arrive - in the vast majority of the cases - at self-pride, and fear and selfishness as the causes of the wrongness or conflict or hurt.

If we cannot find a way to overcome those three things, we will be part of humanity's problem rather than part of the solution no matter how much our self-pride will spur us to object to the contrary. If self-pride or fear or selfishness bind us, then we are incapacitated and will be unable to find the freedom offered in this book. Said another way, if self-pride or fear or selfishness guide us, we are not good people as Joshua of Nazareth defines a good person. Ironically and sadly, self-pride will usually prevent us from admitting this simple truth!

What is self-pride? *Self-pride believes at the personal level, that I am more valuable, more important, more enlightened, more worthy, smarter or better than other people.* Self-pride causes a person to think that they have important things about life figured out better than most people, which results in an unwillingness to learn or consider new beliefs. Self-pride causes me to think that I deserve more good things than other people. Or that I am more worthy to get this thing – material thing, power, authority, etc. – than others.

Here are some examples of how people - who are making decisions or treating others based upon self-pride - think or express themselves.

- I am not going to listen to you because I believe I already have a better understanding of the topics you would like to discuss.
- You can't be part of this team/group because you are not worthy or don't have anything significantly valuable to contribute.
- I am just smarter than you – and have such-and-such a degree from college or university, or I scored this on this test, etc. - and thus you ought to believe what I say or do what I say.
- I've already looked into that, and I believe I have the answers, or the answers cannot be known, so I don't want to waste my time talking about that. (this could also be fear)
- Are you going to tell me you know more than that famous subject matter expert? Who are you? (Vicarious self-pride or fear.)
- We are just better than you and thus you ought to submit to us or do what we think is good and right.
- You ought to give us that (land, material things) because we deserve it for these reasons and you don't, and if you don't, we are justified in taking it from you forcefully.
- Why am I a leader-manager / executive / minister / senator / bishop / captain, etc. - because I deserve it and am more worthy than you.
- Why would I want to do that—that is beneath me.
- You want me to consider befriending that person? You must be kidding.
- You are going to hang out with or befriend that weirdo?
- You believe what about God? I have been through seminary, and thus I am better equipped to know what is true about God...
- The people elected me, and thus it proves I am more worthy than you to be a leader.
- I've got a bachelor's degree (or masters or doctorate) in that area so who are you to question my knowledge in that area?
- You didn't even attend college…what makes you think you can make a significant contribution to this discussion or work?
- Oh, I would never do or say that to someone…

- I am popular; you are not; thus you don't deserve the things I get due to my popularity.
- Don't you know that people with my skin color are better or just naturally more beautiful people?
- You have not been to college? Oh well, I guess you won't do much with your life.
- Our church is the largest, most successful church in the city, so we are receiving God's blessings more than others.
- My pastor graduated at the top of his class at Ivory Tower Seminary so you really ought to listen to him about God – I mean who are you to question him?
- Don't you know that I am from the United States, and we have the best nation on the planet?
- Oh, my child(ren) did this or that…they accomplished this or that…they are the president of this or that…they are a doctor or a lawyer… (women often express this vicarious self-pride, and the unstated thought often is, "because I am such a wonderful parent")
- Oh, I need to post that I went to the bathroom on Facebook because I am so important and all my "friends" need to know about all the important things I did today.
- Oh, that poor soul…he has so few material things.
- God has blessed us with all this money, and so we must be doing things right in his sight.
- That person (or those people) must be foolish to get themselves into that situation.
- I am too smart or clever to have got myself into that situation.
- I would never have let that happen to me.
- I would never have done that.
- I would never have gotten caught.
- What an idiot.
- What a fool.
- Those stupid people deserve what they got.

Of course, there are clever ways to soften or sugar coat the above utterances, but that cleverness or political correctness does not change the fact, no matter how "humbly" those things might be stated or thought.

What is fear?

It is a perception that something I value or want or need is at risk of being lost, damaged or destroyed.

Here are some examples of how people who are making decisions based on fear think or express themselves.

- I can't leave him – I know he mistreats me, but I am afraid of the unknown—at least I know where I stand here.'
- But if I give that away, I might not have enough…
- I can't walk away from that job…I might end up on the street…
- I am not going to make that decision because I am afraid I might lose this or that…
- If I say that true thing, then I am afraid people will not like me any more…
- I can't believe that because I am afraid I will be rejected from the comfortable social circles I am part of…
- I can't do (or say that, or believe that) because these people whose approval I value will no longer accept me…
- But if I don't treat that person this way, I am afraid I will not get what I want from them… (also selfishness)
- I'm not going to give up control of those people because I am afraid I will be worthless without it… (also self-pride)
- If I change in that way, I don't know what my life will be like, and I am afraid of change or what it might bring…
- I simply do not want to consider that because I fear what it might mean…
- I'm just not going to go there…
- I am not generous because I must save up for retirement or else I won't have adequate funds for the last years of my life.
- There is no way I am going to believe that, because if I believe that, that means all these people I love, or respect are wrong, and I can't face that possibility and what that would mean.
- I need the material security that my parents provide so I can't believe or do that even though it is right because they will punish or reject me…
- Jesus can't mean that…that would mean I need to….
- I am afraid to change because I don't know what that will mean for the way I want to live my life.
- All those people can't be wrong…I am afraid to consider that possibility and its implications.
- I'm afraid if I don't look like that, I will not be attractive to others.
- Jesus can't mean that…that would mean these people I esteem would be wrong, and that would mean…
- If I don't please that person, they will reject me and then what?

- If I don't get that job, I'll be out on the street.
- There is just no way I will consider that.
- I can't stop working primarily for money to work for Joshua; I might end up homeless or worse…

I would suggest that the most important fear that causes much human conflict and motivates much selfishness is fear of death. When people believe that they are going to die, fear usually grips them, and that fear unleashes their dark nature which causes them to do many wrong, evil and harmful things to others to preserve their life in this world. If you think about it, greed is often fear-of-death motivated. The thinking is, "I need this to pad my life so my risk of dying is diminished" or other such similar thinking.

So, the question becomes what if there was a cure for fear of death? *How many fear motivated wrong things that humans do to each other would go away?* What if people believed that there was a cure for death, could appropriate that cure, and thus be free of the fear of death as something influencing their life and life decisions? An essential aspect of this book is to reveal that Cure.

What is selfishness?

It believes that my wants are more important than others…or stated another way, I am not going to take actions that cause me to lose something I consider valuable…my decisions are going to be based on what I gain or get out of it.

Here are some examples of how people who are making decisions or treating others based on selfishness think or express themselves.

- I know you think that is a good idea, but what do I get out of it?
- If there is nothing in it for me/us, then it just doesn't make sense to pursue it…
- Why should I give that away, are you crazy?
- If I don't take care of myself, who will?
- I need my personal space, for that is only good and right and you ought to respect that.
- I only have one life to live, and I am going to live it to its fullest and that means having fun and spending money on myself.
- Hey, we deserve this…
- That seems like the right thing to do; look at what we lose if we don't do that…
- I have to look after number one…
- I just have to do what it takes in order to get what I want…I cannot be concerned about its impact on others…

- I deserve some personal time…that other person is going to have to take care of themselves…
- I know it seems selfish, but if you really look at it, it is for the greater good…
- I worked hard for that and so I have no obligation to share it with others…
- It's a dog-eat-dog world – you need to take care of yourself…
- Sometimes, we just have to take care of ourselves and trust God to take care of the other person…
- Don't call me selfish – I am just living out survival of the fittest…
- At the end of the day, if I don't take care of myself, no one else will…
- It all depends upon your perspective…maybe taking from others is what will be best for them in the end…
- If I try and help people, I may not have enough for me…
- People don't want help, so why try?
- Who am I to do anything?" Translation…I need an excuse not to take any risks that might negatively impact my relatively comfortable life…
- I can't make a difference…" Translation…I need an excuse not to take any risks that might negatively impact my relatively comfortable life…
- Let the experts handle that…" Translation…I need an excuse not to take any risks that might negatively impact my relatively comfortable life…
- It's not my fault that that is happening to people… Translation—I don't care about anyone else me myself.
- I just don't have time. Translation – I am too busy trying to earn money for myself or doing things that please me.
- Who defines what is wrong anyway. Translation – I don't care what happens to anyone but me.

These examples are merely a small sampling of statements and justifications thought and uttered billions – perhaps trillions - of times each day in various forms by the people of the earth. Maybe you have made comments like these or have thought them? *Perhaps you believe you are somehow exempt from accountability even though you operate each day with those three spiritual problems being the primary factors in your decisions, thus driving your behavior and creating your lifestyle?*

Some would argue that hatred is a root problem. Here are some synonyms of hate: extreme dislike, disgust, animosity, hostility or aversion.

Hatred is almost always caused by a combination of fear and/or self-pride and/or selfishness. Let's use an example to test this theory out. Racism is a frequent cause of hatred. What is racism? It is when one person wrongly makes stereotypical judgments and has some level of animosity about another based on their "race" which is often manifest by the color of their skin. What causes the animosity? Fear and self-pride cause it—fear says, "I don't trust 'those people' because they are different than me"; or, "I heard this about them"; self-pride says, "I am better than those people because of reasons X, Y and Z…"

So, when a personal interaction occurs between the two people - person A is the victim and person B is the racist - and the stereotype is perceived to be validated by some behavior by person A, the racist person B makes the judgment ('I knew those people were stupid" for example) and some self-pride based manifestation is communicated by person B to person A ("You are a @&#* just like the rest of your kind…" for example), at which point things often can escalate into hatred manifest by harmful behavior or violence. The root problem is that the "racist's" heart is already bad – ruled by self-pride - and it's looking to justify the hatred that racism brings.

Selfishness can also quickly turn to hatred for another person. If someone tries to take something from us that we believe is rightfully ours, we will soon move into a mode of hating that person. So, hatred is just a more extreme expression of fear or self-pride or selfishness. Or stated another way, hatred's foundation is offended self-pride or fear moving to a high emotional state and perception of animosity. When dislike turns to hate, it starts to dominate one's soul/emotions and thus makes a person more prone to uncontrollable wrong, immoral or harmful behavior. Self-pride and fear and selfishness are the root problems that can produce the often outwardly destructive cancer that is hatred.

The simple truth is, if the three root problems regularly influence your thoughts and decisions, then you are in one of the first three categories of human beings – you are leader, participator or ignorer of the evil in the world. Of course, it is possible to be in several groups depending upon the specific wrong (or evil). In other words, I could be a leader in one wrong thing, a participator in a different wrong thing, and an ignorer in yet another or several or many other wrong things. To put it simply, I am – each of us is - either part of the problem or part of the solution. *Being part of the problem or part of the answer is a direction thing, not a perfection thing.* In other words, my daily actions will be either fighting against the evil and wrongness in the world, or my daily activities will not. If I am passive in my words and behavior, I am part of the problem no matter what I claim to believe.

We are either overcoming the root problems and thus caring about what is true and right, or we are not. We are either actively working against that which is false and wrong, or we are not. It is a conscious life direction involving a daily evaluation and decision process.

Remember the problem is first individual and then collective. The solution is not collective; first, it is individual. If I cannot overcome fear and self-pride and selfishness, then I can never effectively fight against the collective manifestation of those things or the individual manifestations I encounter. Instead, I will be carried along in the river of humanity and at some frequency lead, participate or ignore the wrong or false things that contribute to the dark state of this world.

Most people are primarily ignorers. Many are participators. Some are leaders. Few are fighters.

What are you dear reader, really?

Are you living an exceptional life, an evidence of which is experiencing the animosity of those to whom you say some version of, "no, that is not true, or that is not right"? Or are you justifying your life of being part of the problem? Are you actively fighting against the evil each day and if so, how so? Be real with this self-examination because self-deceit and delusion is a sad and ultimately destructive way go through life. Also, don't forget about the concept of accountability, which we will look at a bit later. Perhaps there is one whom we cannot fool with all our self-justifications and excuses?

Perhaps the most important question we could ask about ourselves is how we can escape the "cage" of self-pride and fear and selfishness? Or, what do I have to do to change to a fighter? We will take a preliminary look at the answer to those questions in the next chapter.

Chapter Summary:

- Human beings enter into and are bound in a cage consisting of self-pride, fear, and selfishness when they turn into adults and make decisions for themselves;

- We filter reality through a lens of the cage of self-pride and fear and selfishness. In other words, we do not see ourselves or the reality around us as it is, but instead, we see them only through the prism of our cage.

- We are either part of the problem (leader, participator, or ignorer) or part of the solution (non-violent fighter). There are no other options.

5

AN ALLUSION TO THE SOLUTION

Opening Questions:
- How important is it to successful communication to have a common language with commonly understood terms?
- If people start moving away from standard definitions of terms/words, will that lead to unity and common understanding or disunity and confusion?
- Can things like religion, politics, psychology or philosophy solve my struggles with things like self-pride, fear or selfishness?
- Can religious beliefs or political doctrine or policies or psychological philosophies free us from our cage of self-pride and fear and selfishness and thus solve problems like greed or un-forgiveness?

Now that we have identified the root problems – and the categories of people we fit into - we have to ask the question, what will solve the root problems of fear, self-pride and the resultant selfishness? *Later we will look in detail at how Christians substitute a false religious problem for the real root problems.*

Now would be an excellent point to define a few critical terms so we can be on the same page when using them. Unfortunately, ten different people will read the word "religious," and each might well have a different definition. In fact, I have used the terms repeatedly already and no doubt ten different readers would have more than one meaning.

Defining terms/nouns correctly is becoming more and more critical as more and more people leave rational thought, turn away from moral absolutes, embrace relativism as their foundational existential view, and thus submit to no standard whatsoever except their personal opinions and emotions to understand what is true or false, right or wrong. We will look at relativism more closely in section three.

Relevant Definitions

Accountable:
"A situation in which someone is responsible for things that happen and can give a satisfactory reason for them." [14]
"An obligation or willingness to accept responsibility or to account for one's actions." [15]

Agnostic: Those people who believe a person cannot know whether God exists or not.

Atheist: Those people who believe God does not exist and who typically make a practice of actively promoting their belief or joining with others of the same belief. Atheists are typically a bit more proactive and outspoken and those characteristics are what set them apart from Non-Theists, who are more individual and quieter in their beliefs and behavior. In general, Atheist for many is synonymous with Non-Theist.

Bible, The: The sacred book used to understand God by the majority of Christians. There are two primary versions – the Roman Catholic which has seventy-three books, and the protestant, which has sixty-six books. The protestant bible has two parts – the first part is the Hebrew scripture which is called the Old Testament. The second part is called the New Testament, which contains the four gospel books documenting the life and teachings of Joshua of Nazareth plus mostly Paul's writings.

- Typically, the average Christian does not read the Bible but instead the Bible is read or studied by the Christian leaders, to whom the people look to understand the Bible's contents.

Biblian: Those people who look primarily to "the bible" (typically some flavor of "protestant') as their standard to select their beliefs about God. While they would include the words of Jesus of Nazareth as "in the Bible," they mostly ignore his teachings in favor of the other bible teachings. So, in reality, the Biblians have a sixty-two book protestant bible instead of a sixty-six book bible, since they mostly ignore and nullify the instructions of The Light of the world contained in the four gospel books with beliefs and teachings from the other sixty-two books and other sources.

Christ: One-third of the Tri-God of Christians *not* represented by the historical Joshua of Nazareth as he defines himself by his own words in the

---

[14] Cambridge Dictionary, www.dictionary.cambridge.org, April 2018

[15] Merriam-Webster Dictionary, www.merriam-webster.com, April 2018

four gospel books. Typically, the "Christ" of Christianity is poorly defined and can mean different things to different people, from a person to a religious ideology or philosophy to a mythical figure to merely the source of ethical or moral principles.

Christian: A Christian is a person who has God beliefs received primarily from their religious leaders, and other claimed experts, and those leader's and experts understandings of the bible or other "sacred writings." Christians are those who claim "Jesus Christ" as their God or figurehead yet who do not, in general, live by the historical person Joshua of Nazareth's core teachings as found in the four gospel books.

Christianity: The people, organizations, resources, beliefs, and practices of those people who claim some affiliation with the "Christ" preached by their religious leaders or "the church."

Disciple of Jesus of Nazareth: A person who has only the historical Person of Joshua of Nazareth as their Master and thus who looks only to him as the sole objective standard (his words alone as were captured in the four gospel books). Using Joshua's teachings as the foundation, disciples also value and use reason and logic to understand God – who God is, what God is like, what God wants and how to treat and live with other people.

Ethics: Essentially the same as, or synonymous with morals. The study of what is morally right and wrong, or a set of beliefs about what is morally right and wrong.

Existential: About or relating to one's existence.

Faith: A core level or deep trust or confidence in someone or something, typically that which cannot be verified with our senses.

Hope:

Nouns:

- "The feeling that something desired can be had or will happen" [16]
- "To cherish a desire with anticipation: to want something to happen or be true" [17]
- "A feeling of expectation and desire for a particular thing to happen"; "Grounds for believing that something good may happen" [18]
- "The feeling that what is wanted can be had or that events will turn out for the best" [19]

Verb:

- "To look forward to with desire and reasonable confidence" [18]

---

[16] Cambridge Dictionary, www.dictionary.cambridge.org, April 2018

[17] Merriam-Webster Dictionary, www.merriam-webster.com, April 2018

[18] Oxford Living Dictionary, www.en.oxforddictionaries.com, April 2018

[19] www.dictionary.com, April 2018

Human being need hope to function in a reasonable and positive manner. Hope can be placed in something real or in something that is not real.

Interpretation:
"An explanation or opinion of what something means." [22]
"The action of explaining the meaning of something." [22]

Joshua (or Jesus) of Nazareth: A historical person of humble means who lived about 2,000 years ago, and who performed miracles including defeating death, to validate his message. His teachings would radically transform human life on the earth for better *if* people listened to him and did what he taught.

Morals:
"Concerned with the principles of right and wrong behavior." [22]

Non-Theist: Those people who reject the existence of a God or god's but who don't make a practice of actively promoting their belief. This distinction with Atheist is not absolute, and Non-Theist for many is synonymous with Atheist.

Peace:
These two dictionaries define it from a societal, individually external perspective:

- "A period of freedom from war or violence, esp. when people live and work together without violent disagreements." [20]
- "The normal, non-warring condition of a nation, group of nations, or the world." [21]

These two dictionaries define it as individual, personal and inward:

- "Freedom from disquieting or oppressive thoughts or emotions." [22]
- "Freedom from disturbance; tranquility." [23]

Physicalists: Are those who deny all metaphysical or spiritual realities or stated another way, those who believe reality can be best explained by the model of matter and energy alone. There are relatively few physicalists in terms of the earth's population, but they also typically possess positions of power and influence in the world, a fact that is not coincidental. Physicalists generally are non-theists and usually look to science and technology to solve humankind's problems.

Politics: The beliefs and interactions of people who are involved in trying to govern or rule or organize other people.

---

[20] Cambridge Dictionary, www.dictionary.cambridge.org, April 2018

[21] www.dictionary.com, April 2018

[22] Merriam-Webster Dictionary, www.merriam-webster.com, April 2018

[23] Oxford Living Dictionary, www.en.oxforddictionaries.com, April 2018

Political Correctness:
A person adopting the popular view/belief to feel some level of acceptance or belonging with others who have the same view, even if:
   A) That acceptance and belonging is vicarious, virtual or has no basis in real relationships;
   B) This view cannot stand the test of reason and therefore is false.
Relativism:
"The doctrine that knowledge, truth, and morality exist in relation to culture, society, or historical context, and are not absolute." [25]
"The belief that truth and right and wrong can only be judged in relation to other things and that nothing can be true or right in all situations." [21]
There are different levels of relativism, and we will look at that and clarify that later in the book.
Religion: People's beliefs and practices regarding God things, spiritual things and the afterlife, which beliefs and practices have *no reasonable basis* in the teachings of Jesus of Nazareth.
Religious Person: A person who has sincerely held God or spiritual beliefs which beliefs have nothing to do with listening to the person of, nor following the teachings of, Joshua of Nazareth.

> A religious person typically has a moral standard derived from their religious beliefs, but all people have some moral standard, so having an ethical standard does not make a person religious. Instead, it is the non-ethical or non-relational practices and rituals that the religious person believes they need to practice to be acceptable to God or to have a positive afterlife experience – even if infrequent or without much conviction—that makes a person religious.

Responsible:
"Having the duty of taking care of something." [24]
"Able to answer for one's conduct and obligations." [25]
Here is a clarifying statement for distinguishing between accountability and responsibility:
"You were responsible for closing the gate, and your failure to do so cost the lives of three people, so now we are holding you accountable for that failure and here is the consequence."

We will define additional terms later as we move through the book.

---

[24] Cambridge Dictionary, www.dictionary.cambridge.org, April 2018
[25] Merriam-Webster Dictionary, www.merriam-webster.com, April 2018

So, back to the initial question of this chapter, what will solve the root problems and provide the solution that all human being need? *Let us continue by first taking a look at what will NOT solve the root problems for the individual.*

First up is religion. If religion would solve the problem of people operating by self-pride and fear and selfishness, then the world would be a much better place since there are billions of religious people and over two billion Christians! At least there would be significant societies or communities of people – communities in the millions – within each religion that are practicing the tenants of their religion and thus doing better than those who are not part of those communities. For Christianity, the fact is, there are not.

Any astute observer will conclude that religion is not solving people's root problems, and it provided much fuel to the problems of self-pride and fear, which leads to many conflicts. The source of the conflict is often beliefs like, "Our God is the real true God, and yours is false, and our God hates people who tell lies about him…'

Again, and at least significant problems should not exist within Christian circles if they are addressing the root problems – within the about a 2.5 billion people who take some Christian label. By any measure, this is not so, primarily because "Christian circles" or real communities do not exist and thus cannot be identified! We will look at why this is so later. The reality is that Christians are as unified as political liberals and conservatives! And that in spite of this saying of the real, historical Joshua of Nazareth:

> The glory which You have given Me I have given to them, that they may be one, just as We are one; I in them and You in Me, that they may be perfected in unity, so that the world may know that You sent Me, and loved them, even as You have loved Me. (John 17:22-23)

This predisposition to divide among the Biblians and Christians accounts for the tens of thousands of bible and Christian sects on the earth at this time.

The morals derived from Christian teachings, for example, have helped certain cultures or societies or nations do better than others. I don't deny that better ethics held by a group of people can make human relationships and endeavors among that group work much better. However, I would also contend that "doing better" by constraining evil or being a bit more generous is not enough as the previous facts about our world reveal. The Christian ethic has been propagated in this world for two millennia, and yet, we still have what we have. Furthermore, there are no significant Christian communities (especially concerning the approximately 2.5 billion Christians currently on the earth) where people can look at the Christian community and say, "Oh, wow, they have solved the problems within their community." We can do better than accepting how the world is and just ringing our hands and at the end of the day going with the selfish path and making sure the ones I care about and I are OK.

How about humanistic psychological philosophies? Well, those beliefs and practitioners have been around for at least as long as religion! The beliefs/philosophies have changed over time, and they come and go and ebb and flow, but the essential beliefs and practices have been here for thousands of years. Mainly, those beliefs are attempts to understand human nature (with newer western beliefs trying to do so without referring to God or spiritual elements) and to find cause and effect – experience and reaction - with significant relationships in one's life. Most contemporary psychological philosophies and beliefs try and understand humans without a creator or metaphysical elements to human nature (remember heart, soul, mind, spirit?); or at least not accounting for the why's of those spiritual or metaphysical aspects of human nature.

To those who put their faith in psychological beliefs, it is to their credit that not too much conflict arises over those beliefs primarily because God-claims are not typically involved. However, while psychological beliefs and practices do not in general generate conflict amongst people, neither do they solve the root problems. In fact, *the practice of insisting on getting paid to discuss these beliefs with someone who thinks these beliefs will help, removes the most critical aspect of human relationships and thus render's it essentially powerless.* If self-pride and fear and selfishness form a cage, then those who advocate psychological beliefs, in general, seek to operate within that cage and are thus powerless. There is only one thing that can get someone out of that cage, as we shall see later.

Some might say that politics or politicians will solve those problems. Politics and politicians have been around for thousands of years in different forms, and yet their solutions are not working well as history shows. Again, some political systems work better than others, but the ebb and flow of time proves that none can abide the cycle of eventual destruction due to human conflict, usually from within and due to the causes already identified. Specifically, people turning away from a unifying and good ethic for human living.

Politics and politicians are about people governing people and setting rules and laws for groups of people and directing money and resources. The root problems, on the other hand, are first individual in nature. Yes, they affect other people, and as a group of collective people operate under the sway of the root problems, things do not work well. Remember the above examples of some of the problems that are widespread in the world?

Politicians or the rules they make or the money or resources they can direct can never solve the root problems; they can only seek to constrain or minimize the damage of the manifestations of the root problems. Law cannot cause love or internal peace, just like money or material things cannot generate love or inner peace.

No, we need something else to solve our root problems of self-pride and fear and selfishness. We need something outside of ourselves or higher than ourselves to fix our problem. Or stated another way, we cannot get out of our self-made cage by ourselves. We do not innately have the key to the lock of the self-made cage of self-pride and fear and selfishness. We desperately need help to make it out of the cage. Religion, psychology or politics cannot unlock our cage either, for they are our creations! We made them while in our cages!

Another good illustration depicting our dilemma is a large, self-dug pit. We started thinking there was something valuable down in the earth – even though we heard a small voice from above telling us to look up – so we grabbed a shovel and started digging. Self-pride or fear or selfishness motivated each shovel full, and the pit got bigger and deeper. Finally, at some point when we did not find what we were digging for, we realized that we dug the hole so deep that we could not get out by ourselves. We need someone to reach down and pull us out.

As we explore finding the solution to people's problems, we will need a tool to do that. Finding solutions to vexing problems requires the most valuable tool that we human beings were given, and we shall examine those tools in the coming section. Furthermore, the successful failure that is Christianity – and more generally reality itself - cannot be well evaluated without using these tools well.

Chapter Summary:
- Understanding things by having clear definitions of those things is extremely important—it is the only way to know if something is true or false;
- Many terms/concepts have been redefined or are misunderstood, thereby clouding the picture of reality and hiding essential ideas and truths as well as obscuring or hiding the solutions to problems;
- It is self-evident and objectively true that religion, politics or other philosophies about human beings (psychological or humanistic) do not have the power to set us free from our cage of self-pride and fear and selfishness;
- We need something higher than ourselves to lift us above our flawed human condition—we need someone to unlock the cage or to lift us out of the pit.

SECTION 2:
REASON IDENTIFIES TRUTH AND LEADS TO THE SOLUTION

Theme:
- Reason, logic, and observation are required tools to understand reality and to discover and know what is true.
  - o If we don't use reason and logic well, we will not be able to identify the truth in any domain where observation is inadequate.
  - o Using reason and logic in the domain of God claims or religious claims is particularly important since many claims cannot be validated by our senses. Therefore, God claims and religious claims should pass the test of reason to be considered correct.

Section Introduction

We cannot solve problems – especially difficult ones – if we cannot first clearly identify and adequately understand them. The tools that we ought to use to identify and describe human relationship and behavior problems and then craft solutions are *observation, reason, and logic*. If there was ever a time in human history where reason and logic are desperately needed to sort through the mess that time is now. Unfortunately, most people, including Christians, in general, hang onto their traditions and regularly put reason aside to hold to their religious doctrine and the worldview it produces. In spite of their vehement denial, non-theists do as well—that is they also stick to their existential beliefs often in spite of reason and logic.

Let's spend a bit of time reviewing, exploring, and learning about reason and logic to be able to evaluate the primary premise of this book better, that Christianity is a successful failure.

6
REASON, LOGIC AND TRUTH

Opening Questions:
- How vital are reason and logic in determining what is true or false?
- What role do emotions or "feeling" play in the process of using reason or logic to determine what is true or false?
- How does faith fit with reason and logic?
- What is the difference between reason and logic?
- What role should reason and logic play in evaluating God claims?
- Does reason or logic create anything?
- Are reason and logic physical things?

"When reason is put aside and faith dies, our emotions will lead us into darkness."

Emotionalism rules the day. Anyone who reads the news and is somewhat engaged in the things happening in the U.S. culture at this time, and who uses reason well to evaluate those things, will conclude that reason is out of fashion and emotionalism is in. There are very few voices that use reason well to articulate themselves. Most have a feeling or opinion that they have not thought about thoroughly, and then they voice those opinions as fact. Most can no longer reason well because they have left any objective standard against which to apply reason. The evidence of this is that the average guest on the news that tries to defend some political position or policy will usually commit several logical fallacies when trying to articulate their position. Most will contradict themselves and will often not even address the problem or questions asked because their opinion is wrong and thus they stay away from reason.

Perhaps the most asked question in the U.S. culture at this time is "how do you feel about that?" instead of "what are your reasons for taking that position or holding that belief?"—*the distinction is CRITICAL.* The former is entirely subjective and emotions driven while the latter is more objective and reason driven—the former has one's personal view as absolute while the latter has common principles as the standard. The fact is that most people are regularly engaging in the former.

One of the significant adverse effects of emotionalism is the associated lack of discipline. Discipline requires clarity of knowing right versus wrong and good from bad, as well as having strength of will. Without having a clear, reasoned purpose for some task or responsibility, most people will fail at accomplishing that task or responsibility well. Perhaps the best example of this is staying physically fit. Most Americans say, "I don't feel like exercising" or "I don't feel like eating healthy food." This emotional approach to physical health has obvious negative consequences as the obesity rates, associated diseases, and harmful physical effects are running rampant in the U.S. population. Without discipline, people will not excel at anything, for discipline is required to excel. Substituting an emotionally driven life for a belief, purpose, and discipline-driven life will lead to mediocrity at best and ruin at worst.

Those that do use reason well often lock themselves into an ideological box which does not enable them to see past their box. Yes, there are boxes inside of our cages!

Politics and Reason in the U.S.

In the political realm of the U.S., it is painfully obvious how little reason plays a role. Those who identify as conservatives or part of the "right" have their doctrines and liberals or "the left" have their doctrines, and in large measure, each sees the other side as "the enemy." Both sides talk right past each other most of the time, seldom intending to significantly examine the merits of the "other side." In this way, they act just like religious leaders whose predisposition to divide accounts for the thousands of religious sects that cover the earth. This is not to say that each political ideology camp (conservative or liberal) is not right about individual issues. It is to say, however, that the current animosity over merely a label (left or right, liberal or conservative, democrat or republican) is incredibly destructive.

In general, conservatives do better with reason than liberals—their beliefs are more consistent and stand the test of reason better than some liberal views. Conservatives are more likely to talk about principles or policies in a reasoned fashion whereas liberals are much more likely to resort to identity-politics to defend a position. They do this because conservatives have some standard against which to reason—in general, they are not relativists (we will learn about relativism in some upcoming chapters. In short, a relativist says there are no absolute truths). Most people who take the label "conservative" have a moral framework from their religion which they regularly reason from regarding ethical issues. Thus, their arguments regarding ethical problems are more consistent or defensible against some more objective standard.

What is "identity politics"? Here is a good definition, "Identity politics, also called identitarian politics, refers to political positions based on the interests and perspectives of social groups with which people identify." In other words, people choose some demographic aspect of themselves or others – skin color, nationality, immigration status, citizenship status, gender, sexuality preferences, etc. – to associate with and then advocate for that group with political positions that benefit that group. So, what is most important to people who participate in identity politics is that *their* group gets benefits or relief, and they often believe it is good and right to demonize other groups that they perceive get their way or are "against them." This belief often results in other groups being viewed as "the enemy" since they cannot see the righteousness of *our* cause. This error is incredibly destructive and will be the end of any social or political unity in the United States.

Simply put, fighting for *objective principles* that they can defend as good or right have no place in identify politics—they have left the higher plane of principle, policy or law for tribal association or mere physical characteristic advocacy. In short, identitarians have taken a step down to a lower level of existence in their humanity due to relativism and human nature.

While many self-professed liberals often put reason aside and go with emotionalism or identity-politic positions, conservatives have positions and doctrine that also do not pass the test of reason, usually due to their commitment to other supporting beliefs. Another weakness of conservatism is that conservatives often fail to operate based on the concept of compassion—they put rules over mercy often for selfish purposes. This tendency is also due to their commitment to the ideology of capitalism or other self-serving or selfish beliefs or doctrines. So, while conservatives in general use reason better than liberals or can defend their views better, they do so assuming that their foundational ideologies – like capitalism - are correct or provide the best solution. Their assumptions and ideologies that they reason from may or may not be accurate or may not offer the best solutions to problems.

So, to sum up, and in general, conservatives do better with reason than liberals, but liberals have a few morally correct positions and views (according to Joshua of Nazareth) which are wrongly dismissed by conservatives. Unfortunately, most people who self-identify as liberal or progressive cannot defend well why they hold a particular belief, because most are existential relativists. We will learn what that is a bit later in the book.

Ironically, many conservatives generally believe themselves to be the "God" politicians, while many liberals do not. That is ironic and appropriate because of the truth that this book reveals. The conservatives "God" is the god of the bible particularly the god of the Hebrew Scriptures - the God of war and vengeance and wrath most of the time and the God of mercy a very little of the time—the God of rules and law over the God of compassion. While the true and living God and his representative, His Son, very much want peace and love, the very things many classical or previous generation liberals said liberalism "was all about." Unfortunately, some contemporary self-professed liberals want nothing to do with "peace and love" and instead are violent, aggressive, rude or uncivil, and sadly they are not usually rebuked by their genuinely peaceful brethren. In this way, they are no different than the violent racists which generally gravitate to what is traditionally considered conservative ideologies.

The simple truth is this book is putting forth the narrow way. In other words, *the political ideologies of both camps (liberal and conservative) mostly miss the person and teachings of Joshua of Nazareth.* The One who called himself "the truth," walks right between them with both sides yelling at him that he is wrong! (Can you recall another event where people were yelling at Joshua as he walked between them?) They will only refer to "jesus" when one of his teachings can be made to fit their position, and often that teaching is taken out of context or is twisted to fit their political dogma. In other words, they will ignore his most important teaching – love – to argue and have animosity towards one another. In short, the vast majority of Christians and Biblians who are involved in politics are not followers of the real, historical Joshua of Nazareth, but rather create a "christ" to justify their politics.

Religion and Reason

Let's turn the corner and talk about religion and reason. When many people think about religion, they assume that reason does not play a prominent role in people's religious beliefs, and in general, they are correct. In fact, it is prevalent to say things like, "reason cannot account for faith" or "you must have faith, and put reason aside and just believe" or "it's not about reason, it's about faith" and other such misleading or erroneous statements.

Christians and Biblians often put reason aside when it demonstrates that their God beliefs contradict. An example of this is the Christian belief (or premises) that God is both all-powerful and all loving. By almighty, they mean that He is both omnipotent and can and does act and intervene in this realm (our life on the surface of this planet) in our daily human affairs. Thus, the oft-heard phrase, "God is in control." However, as we will see in more detail later on, if God is both all-powerful and all-loving, then this world would not be racked with all the human-caused unjust pain and suffering that occurs each day. Surely that almighty God would intervene to prevent the unjust pain and suffering. That is the only reasonable and logical conclusion to those two premises. Non-theists know this and they rightfully rebuke the religious people for this error.

The simple truth is that faith, as we have defined, is a core or deep level trust or confidence in someone or something (in a God context, an additional element to faith exists in that we place our faith or confidence in someone we cannot see or directly validate with our senses). When a person puts their faith in something, that act is not an act of reason, but instead, it is an act of faith/trust/confidence.

However, reason DOES play an important role in faith, and it is this— a person can and *should* use reason to guide them in deciding *in whom or what to place their faith*. Again, reason – and its primary tool of logic – should play an essential role determining in who or what people choose to put their faith. For example, most people place their faith in themselves, money, material things, or a god of their own making. If you view your life and existence in a primarily selfish and materialistic way, then it is reasonable to place your faith in yourself and money and in the businesses that generate that money, and as you can see, most do. If you view your life and existence in a primarily selfish and materialistic way, then it is also reasonable to make up a god who "blesses" people with money and material things. (For the readers" information, Joshua of Nazareth *never* teaches that God does some special "blessing" for an individual, but instead showed that God provided the organic things naturally on the earth for all human beings sustenance.)

But from a pure existential view, placing our faith in ourselves is foolish, as we shall see, for we do not cause our existence and our efforts to preserve our physical lives are often feeble. Ourselves, money, businesses, careers or other such things have no power or ability to preserve our existence after our lives run their courses. Nor do they have the power to set us free or give us peace and contentment. Nor do they empower us to truly love.

This book is not going to teach reason and logic extensively; instead, it will provide an introduction and some basics. More importantly, this book will use reason and logic to present things that are reasonable and which pass the test of logic. In other words, this author endeavors to use reason and logic well to support my premises in this book. However, *unless the reader is willing also to use reason and logic well, it is unlikely that the reader will arrive at the same conclusions that I put forth.* If you believe I err in my use of reason or logic, please contact me with precise, reasoned statements, and if I err, I will correct it.

I have observed that we all very much tend to put reason and logic aside when they will not support where we want to go. In other words, if we sense reason and logic pointing us or leading us somewhere that makes us afraid, offends our self-pride or argues for a selfless life (which typically means we must change something we do not want to), we will usually abandon reason and logic. *We often only use reason and logic well when it supports what we already believe, or when it justifies us in some way.* This tendency is a terrible and blinding handicap. The three primary faults of our nature - fear, self-pride, and selfishness - work hard against reason and logic.

The reason Joshua said we need to love the Lord our God with all our heart, soul, mind and strength, is because he knew that reason would be a slave to our heart and soul. In other words, he put "mind" third after heart and soul, instead of first because if we do not want (will) to find truth (God), or we insist on allowing our emotions (particularly fear) to over-rule reason, then our mind cannot help us. In other words, our mind is key to finding God, but if we do not want to find God and we choose to allow fear to guide us, our mind cannot help us.

To love the Lord our God with our entire mind means *to be committed to using reason and logic well to find what is true in the spiritual or metaphysical domain.* Therefore, let's take a look at gaining a better understanding of reason and logic at least at an introductory level. We will start by defining a few important concepts.

Here are the dictionaries definitions of "reason":

Oxford Dictionary: [26]
"Noun: The power of the mind to think, understand, and form judgments logically."
"Verb: Think, understand, and form judgments logically; Find an answer to a problem by considering possible options; Persuade (someone) with rational argument."

Merriam-Webster Dictionary: [27]
"The power of comprehending, inferring, or thinking especially in orderly rational ways : intelligence (2):proper exercise of the mind (3):sanity.

---

[26] Oxford Living Dictionary, www.en.oxforddictionaries.com, April 2018
[27] Merriam-Webster Dictionary, www.merriam-webster.com, April 2018

"Noun: The power of the mind to think and understand in a logical way."

Cambridge Dictionary: [28]
"Noun: the ability to think and make judgments, esp. good judgments."
"Verb: to argue with and try to persuade someone."

Here are the dictionaries definitions of "logic":

Oxford Dictionary: [26]
"Noun: Reasoning conducted or assessed according to strict principles of validity."

Merriam-Webster Dictionary: [27]
"A science that deals with the principles and criteria of validity of inference and demonstration: the science of the formal principles of reasoning."

Cambridge Dictionary: [29]
"Noun: a formal, scientific method of examining or thinking about ideas; a formal scientific method of examining or thinking about ideas."
The Encyclopedia Britannica[30] does a much better job at filling in the understanding of the concept of "reason":

> "Reason, in philosophy, the faculty or process of drawing logical inferences. The term "reason" is also used in several other, narrower senses. Reason is in opposition to sensation, perception, feeling, desire, as the faculty (the existence of which is denied by empiricists) by which fundamental truths are intuitively apprehended. These fundamental truths are the causes or "reasons" of all derivative facts. According to the German philosopher Immanuel Kant, reason is the power of synthesizing into unity, by means of comprehensive principles, the concepts that are provided by the intellect. That reason which gives a priori principles Kant calls "pure reason," as distinguished from the "practical reason," which is especially concerned with the performance of actions. In formal logic, the drawing of inferences (frequently called "ratiocination," from Latin ratiocinari, "to use the reasoning

---

[28] Cambridge Dictionary, www.dictionary.cambridge.org, April 2018
[29] Cambridge Dictionary, www.dictionary.cambridge.org, April 2018
[30] Encyclopedia Britannica, www.britannica.com, May 2018

faculty") is classified from Aristotle on as deductive (from generals to particulars) and inductive (from particulars to generals).

Here is Encyclopedia Britannica's [30] definition of "logic":

> "Logic, the study of correct reasoning, especially as it involves the drawing of inferences.
> "An inference is a rule-governed step from one or more propositions, called premises, to a new proposition, usually called the conclusion. A rule of inference is said to be truth-preserving if the conclusion derived from the application of the rule is true whenever the premises are true. Inferences based on truth-preserving rules are called deductive, and the study of such inferences is known as deductive logic. An inference rule is said to be valid, or deductively valid, if it is necessarily truth-preserving. That is, in any conceivable case in which the premises are true, the conclusion yielded by the inference rule will also be true. Inferences based on valid inference rules are also said to be valid.
> "Logic in a narrow sense is equivalent to deductive logic. By definition, such reasoning cannot produce any information (in the form of a conclusion) that is not already contained in the premises. In a wider sense, which is close to ordinary usage, logic also includes the study of inferences that may produce conclusions that contain genuinely new information. Such inferences are called ampliative or inductive, and their formal study is known as inductive logic. They are illustrated by the inferences drawn by clever detectives, such as the fictional Sherlock Holmes.
> "Applied logic is the study of the practical art of right reasoning."

A good, short definition of logic would be *the art and science of reasoning.*

If you compare the definitions for reason and logic, you will see that they are not distinct, meaning they are tied to each other and dependent upon each other. "Reasoning" is broader than logic and can use methods that extend past logic's rules like observing things in the world. Proper reasoning depends on logic to some extent. For example, if I drive a car, I know brakes are necessary to slow or stop the vehicle. If a car crashes into a pole or tree, for example, it would be reasonable to consider if the brakes failed. One could reason through drawing pictures or diagrams to conclude something. If trying to figure out what caused a plane to crash, one could figure out the sequence of events before and after the accident and work backward through that sequence to try and find the correct answer as to why the plane crashed.

So, to summarize Encyclopedia Britannica and the Dictionary's content – as well as fill it out a bit - "reason" is human beings metaphysical ability, tool and process to order, sort, distinguish and clarify things – to find truth - in their realms of thought, observation, and experience. Logic is the precise metaphysical rules that our mind's use to process concepts, ideas or beliefs. *Logic is like our operating system, while reason is like exploratory applications that need our operating system's rules to function.* Our mind is the metaphysical element of our nature that can use reason and logic.

I also recommend reading Wiki's descriptions of "reason" and "logic," as the descriptions on Wiki are both solid and less complex than the encyclopedia definitions.

> (As an aside, confusion exists due to physicalist beliefs regarding distinguishing the brain from the mind. The two thing are as confused as "faith" and "religion"! The confusion is unwarranted because they are distinct. For example, let us say you had a team of the world's foremost brain surgeons and experts with all their technology opening up a person's skull to peer into that person's brain. Let us say that person was conscious and thinking about a strawberry. The fact is that team of surgeons and brain experts will never know what that person thinks because human thoughts are metaphysical and inaccessible to others. When a person is thinking about a strawberry, there is no physical manifestation in the brain of a strawberry—no little strawberry forms! Indeed the brain (hardware) produces physical signs of the mind (software) working that can be measured, like bioelectrical impulses or heat energy. However, heat (physical manifestation) or electrical impulses (physical manifestation) produced by the CPU (hardware/brain) does not amount to knowing what the software is processing. Nor is heat or electrical impulses the output of the computer's logic processing - it is merely an energy manifestation of the CPU/hardware (brain) as it runs the software (mind).

Formal and Informal Logic: [31]

The practice of the study of logic has two main components, formal logic, and informal logic. Formal logic is about pure reasoning in the abstract. The definition of "abstract," exists in thought or as an idea but

---

[31] Some of the information from this section was taken from the book, ***The Art of Argument: An Introduction to the Informal Fallacies*** **by Aaron Larsen and Joelle Hodge.**

not having physical or concrete existence." [32] So, formal logic does not deal with physical entities, but rather concepts (metaphysical things), much like pure mathematics.

Formal logic usually focuses on deductive reasoning, which means types of arguments in which the premises imply a necessary conclusion.

Here is an example of a deductive argument:

Premise 1:	Christians meet in a building they call a "church."
Premise 2:	Pentecostals are Christians.
Conclusion:	Therefore, Pentecostals meet in buildings they call a "church."

This type of argument is called a syllogism and has the characteristics that *the conclusion must be true* (Pentecostals meet in buildings they call a "church") *if the premises are true.* However, if one or both premises are false, then the conclusion will be false even though the form of the argument is valid.

For example:

Premise 1:	All Christians practice love.
Premise 2:	A Baptist is a Christian.
Conclusion:	Therefore, Baptists practice love.

This argument or syllogism is valid, meaning its *form or structure is correct.* If it were true that all Christians practice love and a Baptist is a Christian, then it must follow that Baptists practice love. However, in this syllogism, *premise one is false* even though the form of the argument is correct or valid. Since premise one is false, the conclusion is false. In conclusion, the argument is in a valid form, but one of the premises contains false information. If the premises were true, then the conclusion would also be true, just like in the first example above.

The form of premises that lead to a conclusion is vital in "form al" logic.

Please consider this argument:

Premise 1:	Forgiveness is real.
Premise 2:	Forgiveness is not physical.
Conclusion:	Non-physical things like forgiveness are real.

---

[32] Oxford Living Dictionary, www.en.oxforddictionaries.com, April 2018

Please think about that argument, for it is a crucial one, for it demonstrates that what most people call *the "scientific worldview" or at least the strict physicalist view is false.* More precisely, many people assume that science proves the physicalist worldview that the only things that are real and exist are physical, meaning things made up of matter or energy.

In contrast to formal logic, those who practice informal logic are not so concerned with form or structure; instead, they are concerned with arguments made using every day, ordinary language. Informal logic also tends to emphasize inductive reasoning instead of deductive reasoning.

The Latin word *"deducere,"* which is where the English term *"derived"* comes from, means "to lead down or away." Therefore, deductive reasoning starts with premises that "lead down" to a necessary conclusion. Deductive reasoning is "whole-to-part" reasoning. The arguments above regarding Christians, church, and love, are deductive arguments.

The Latin word *"inducere,"* which is where the English term *"induce"* comes from, means "to lead or bring in." Inductive reasoning is "part-to-whole" reasoning. Meaning, we begin with particular facts and try to prove a general conclusion. Inductive reasoning involves "bringing in specific facts to an argument in an attempt to prove a more general point.

Let's use a relevant example to explain these concepts.

I may "bring in" the fact that all Christians I have ever known "go to church," and I might say that that observation proves that *all* Christians "go to church."" In other words, inductive reasoning often works toward generalizations that are reasonably accurate but not necessary absolutely true. Inductive arguments are only *more or less probable, not absolutely certain.* So, in this case, it would be erroneous to state that all Christian's "go to church" since I do not have perfect and comprehensive knowledge to prove that.

In fact, almost all superlatives – like always or never, etc. – will falsify statements that include them, at least in everyday usage regarding human behavior. For example, the report "he is always late," will be a false statement, even if the man is late 98% of the time. Thus, when speaking about human behavior, it would be wise to eliminate all superlatives if we are concerned with accurate or truthful statements. (Generally speaking and frequently, when we use superlatives, the purpose of the usage of those superlatives will be to "hammer" another person to try and get them to see something we are trying to communicate. This can often lead to the perception that we are using "fighting words," which is not productive.)

Deductive arguments are either valid or invalid since they deal with pure metaphysical concepts like mathematics, while inductive arguments are said to be either strong or weak since they are based on physical entities or events that occur in the physical world. Deductive logic addresses things/concepts/beliefs/metaphysical things that are either "black" or "white" – 100% or 0% - while inductive arguments deal in shades of grey or probabilities less than 100% or 0% certainty.

Here is a summary of the two forms of logic to contrast and make clear the differences:

Formal Logic:
1. Uses deductive reasoning
2. Produces either valid or invalid conclusions
3. Provides certain answers if the premises are valid

Informal Logic:
1. Used inductive reasoning
2. Produces either strong or weak conclusions
3. Provides probability answers, not certain ones

What is interesting when dealing with God-claims is that formal logic plays a critical role because God-claims are mainly conceptual/metaphysical, *the strong suit of formal logic*! Thus, many of my arguments in this book are deductive. For example:

Premise 1:	God is All-Powerful (meaning he can do anything he wants in any realm—nothing or nobody can stop his will and work)
Premise 2:	God is All-Loving (meaning he cares deeply about the welfare of people and would not want them to come to – at a minimum – unjust harm or suffering)
Conclusion:	God prevents unjust harm or suffering in this world.

As one considers the conclusion, one will of necessity identify it as false, meaning the conclusion is not supported by the facts as observed in the world. Therefore, while the arguments form is correct, there is something incorrect in one or both of the premises since the conclusion is wrong. That argument is valid and is deductive. We take a closer look at the claim of God's "all-powerfulness" in a later chapter.

Next, we will identify the most common logical fallacies that are committed an untold number of times each day on this planet in human communication. And we should learn to appreciate how logical fallacies or false concepts play an essential role in the successful failure.

Chapter Summary:
- It is necessary to use reason and its tool logic well to find and know what is true and what is false, especially concerning claims or concepts that cannot be verified by observation;

- Emotionalism nullifies, disparages or ignores reason and logic and our emotions should not be the basis of our understanding things or our important life decisions;

- Faith is not opposed to, or contradicted by, reason and logic—rather one should use reason and logic well to understand what is best to place one's faith in;

- Formal logic applies deductive reasoning and results in true or false conclusions and should be the most important tool to test religious or spiritual claims—claims that cannot be verified by observation;

- Informal logic uses inductive reasoning which results in probability answers instead of certain true or false conclusions;

- Informal logic is the foundation of probability analysis and was used previously in the book to support the contention that it is not reasonable to think complex machines with inter-dependent sub-systems can exist without a designer;

- Reason and logic do not create anything new; rather, they are essential tools to sort out what already exists, both physical (reasoning from observation) and metaphysical (deductive reasoning).

7
COMMON LOGICAL FALLACIES

Opening Questions:

- What is a logical fallacy?
- What are some of the most common fallacies that people make?
- Are their categories of logical fallacies?
- I thought that a red herring was a fish?
- Can a person find non-observable truth without using reason and logic?
- Should you accept a person's argument when it is based on a fallacy?

A fallacy is an argument or idea that is false.

So, for example in the observation realm, if I said, "God miraculously physically heals people through prayer"; all one has to do is observe religious people who have a loved one who is injured or ill to see if they are miraculously healed. When they are not, then observation and reason conclude that "prayer does not result in the physical healing of people." That is an example of informal logic and inductive reasoning. A person could not say that "prayer never physically heals someone" because they cannot observe all the healing events on the earth in the past and present. However, they can say that if prayer normally physically heals people, then we would have tons of documented evidence of that and we don't. Therefore prayer does not usually physically heal people.

Another example would be if an atheist said, "God does not exist, and only children, fools, and other simpletons believe He does. Therefore, God is a delusion concocted by mental and emotional juveniles'. This fallacy is a version of the Appeal to Spite fallacy. That fallacy is an attempt to win favor for an argument by exploiting existing feelings of bitterness, spite, or schadenfreude in the opposing party (schadenfreude is the experience of pleasure, joy, or self-satisfaction that comes from learning of or witnessing the troubles, failures, or humiliation of another). It is an attempt to sway the audience emotionally by associating a hate-figure or despised or disrespected people with opposition to the speaker's argument. Simply put, what does a certain group of people's or certain types of people's beliefs about God prove about God's existence? Nothing.

I have already identified and described a few of the primary fallacies that are used by non-theists to justify their rejection of the existence of God. There are many logical fallacies that we as human beings can make. However, if we are doing a half-way decent job at trying to be better human beings, we must strive to avoid falsehood and error. If you have not been doing that, I urge you to start.

Four of the most common fallacies are *Tu Quoque, Sweeping or Hasty generalization, Anecdotal* and the *Straw Man or Red Herring.*

Tu Quoque is an invalid argument that assumes that a rival's recommendation should be discounted or dismissed because the rival does not always follow it him/herself. The Tu Quoque argument is otherwise known as the "reject due to hypocrisy argument." An example would be, "Christian's tell people to love each other, but they don't do that; therefore we should not love one another."

The Sweeping or Hasty Generalization is also known as the "don't throw the baby out with the bathwater" argument. It is a fallacy of induction argument that overextends a generalization to include facts or cases that are valid exceptions to it. An example of that fallacy would be, "Since Christians have delusional beliefs we should conclude that God does not exist."

The *Anecdotal* fallacy – a form of the *Hasty Generalization* fallacy - is using personal experience or an isolated example instead of a valid argument, especially to dismiss statistics or other objectively gathered facts. An example would be, "I know that the latest poll statistics say that the Christian divorce rate is almost as high as the general U.S. population, but I know Christian spouses who will never divorce each other."

Finally, there is the *Straw Man* argument. A straw man argument is a "red herring" type argument that attempts to disprove an opponent's position by presenting it unfairly or inaccurately. I will provide examples of these fallacies shortly.

A "red herring" argument is, according to Cambridge dictionary, "a fact, idea, or subject that takes people's attention away from the central point being considered." [33]

---

[33] Cambridge Dictionary, www.dictionary.cambridge.org, April 2018

Those are probably the big four fallacies regarding the number of people committing them on a daily basis. Therefore, I urge the reader to understand them well and not to make them—to examine your thoughts especially when you are in a defensive position when talking with someone.

Logic Categories Explained [34]

There are three major categories of fallacies - fallacies of relevance, of presumption, and of clarity. Each of those categories has subcategories.

"Fallacies of relevance have premises that do not "bear upon" the truth of the conclusions. In other words, they introduce an irrelevancy into the argument." [35]

There are three primary categories of fallacies of relevance, and they are *Ad Fontem* arguments, appeals to emotion, and red herring arguments.

Ad Fontem fallacies criticize the SOURCE of the argument rather than the issue itself. Those who offer *Ad Fontem* fallacious arguments are trying very hard to avoid a question they do not want to address. This behavior is pronounced in the political realm, where politicians, pundits, and media people spend much time personally attacking each other (*Ad Hominem* or "against the person" argument) instead of discussing the issue or policy. (By the way, you really should pause and think about the fact that so many U.S. politicians rely upon logical fallacies to try and support their policy positions.)

The *Tu Quoque* is a type of *Ad Fontem* argument since it focuses on the personal character of individuals to avoid carefully discussing what those individuals believe or the issue they advocate. Again, this fallacy is a STAPLE of politicians as well as the major news networks in the U.S. at this time.

The fallacies of *Appeal to Emotion* do just that; they appeal to emotions instead of facts and reasons. Most fallacies appeal to our emotions to get away from reason, but there are some particularly obvious ones. An example of the fallacy of appealing to fear is, "if you don't agree with me, I am going to do this to you or your family, etc."

The *Red Herring* fallacies are types of arguments that are irrelevant to the issue or situation. The *Straw Man* fallacy is a *Red Herring* fallacy. Another excellent example of the *Straw Man* fallacy is when people who support homosexual marriage call those who don't, "homophobes" or other such fear-based and distracting labels. All who charge their opponent with some "phobia" (fear), are attempting to characterize their opponent as

---

[34] Some of the information from this section is from the book, *The Art of Argument: An Introduction to the Informal Fallacies* by **Aaron Larsen and Joelle Hodge**.

[35] *The Art of Argument: An Introduction to the Informal Fallacies* by **Aaron Larsen and Joelle Hodge**.

irrational and thus not worth considering. The phobia fallacy is error and should be rejected and rebuked. Again, this fallacy is used probably millions of time each day in the U.S. as the LGBT folks use this fallacy regularly.

A very popular *Red Herring- Ad Hominem* fallacy that is used to bully someone emotionally is to call them "closed-minded." Or as usually happens, to be asked the question, "do you have an open mind?" People ask this question when a person believes that the person they are communicating with does not share their view on something. It is a trick to emotionally bully or shame the other person into believing their view on something. After all, who wants to have a "closed mind"?

If by "open mind" you mean will I consider believing contradictions, then no, for contradictions are false.

If by "open mind" you mean I will not reject things that are false, then no, for false things ought to be rejected.

If by "open mind" you mean I will believe spiritual or metaphysical claims that should have a manifestation in our physical realm but do not, then no, for empty claims with no evidence deserve skepticism.

If by "open mind" you mean I will share your belief that watermelon farmers on Pluto want us to worship watermelons, then no, for you have no reasonable evidence to prove your claim.

If, however, by "open mind" you mean I am open willing to consider new ideas while I remain open to the possibility that the ideas you are communicating to me could be true or false, reasonable or not; then yes, I have an open mind. *If a person cannot accept the possibility that an idea might be false, then their mind is not operating rightly and is not only not "open" but broken.*

A truly open minded person will critically examine all claims but will not accept them if there is no reason to believe they are correct. Furthermore, an open-minded person will not accept false views, ideas or concepts, for to accept them would be wrong and thus to be deceived.

Another of these type fallacies as a religious example would be something to the effect of, "oh, don't you know religious leader so-and-so graduated cum laude from Best Seminary, and thus you are a fool if you do not listen to him on this issue." That is a type of the *Appeal to Snobbery* fallacy. It does not matter what school someone went to or how well they did, what matters is that reason and logic are used well to find the truth of the issue being discussed or examined.

Another *Red Herring* fallacy is the appeal to ignorance. Religious people are often guilty of this error. This argument says a belief that cannot be disproved must, therefore, be likely. If a theist uses a form of the appeal to ignorance argument to "prove" God exists (because it cannot be disproved that He does not), they err. Theists should stick to the many valid arguments for the existence of God and stay away from fallacies.

The next high-level category of logical fallacies is called *fallacies of presumption*. These fallacies contain hidden assumptions that make the arguments unreasonable.

The most popular of these fallacies is the fallacy *of begging the question*, also known as *circular reasoning*. This argument assumes the very thing that one is trying to prove. Biblians are regularly guilty of using this fallacy. In defending a belief they got from the bible, they will say, "because the bible says so." For example, they will say, "the bible is the word of God." When asked what proof they offer to validate that claim, they will say, "the bible says so," or, "Paul says so" (a Bible author), or, "the scripture says so" ("the scripture" is synonymous with "the bible"). Those arguments are false or fallacious.

Another popular fallacy among religious people is the *Is-Ought* fallacy. This fallacy argues that because something is a certain way, it ought to be that way. The religious person, when asked why they have a particular tradition that does not make sense, might answer, "we have been doing it that way for 500 years"; or, "because God thinks it is good and right and thus it should be that way."

The next category of presumptive fallacies is the *fallacies of induction*. These fallacies use questionable assumptions about empirical data or inductive reasoning from that data.

The most popular fallacy of this group is the *Hasty Generalization*. Racism is an example of a belief whose foundation is this fallacy. It is the argument that because some (or even most) individuals with a particular physical or demographic characteristic I have experienced in my life are a certain way, then *all* people of that type are that way. When a racist encounters a decent person of the race they have animosity towards, they will filter that person out as an exception to their general racist beliefs.

The *Sweeping Generalization* is another popular fallacy among Christians. This fallacy takes a generalization that might be true and applies it to cases that are legitimate exceptions to it. An example would be, "Christians do not know well the teachings of the one they point to, so anyone who claims to 'follow Jesus' would likely also be ignorant of his teachings." It is true that the vast majority of Christians do not know the teachings of Joshua of Nazareth as found in the four gospel books. However, actual followers of Joshua do know both him and his teachings. Thus, to believe the genuine followers of Joshua of Nazareth are ignorant of his teachings (false) based on most Christians being unaware of his teachings (true) would be to make the error of sweeping or hasty generalization.

The *Anecdotal* fallacy is using personal experience or an isolated example instead of a valid argument, especially to dismiss statistics or other objectively gathered facts.

For example, let's say a young woman works for the President of the U.S. and she likes her job and wants to defend the President. She gets invited to an interview with a panel of people who are politically opposed to the President. One of the panelists brings up the crude, base, vulgar or arrogant comments the President has made. In response, the young woman who works for the President might say, "Oh, well, I can't speak to that, but I can share my personal experience with the President and tell you what a wonderful guy he has been to me." The panelist's point or argument is that the President does not have good enough character to hold that office. The fallacious response is to ignore the videos or audio tapes of the President acting in a crude, vulgar, crass or arrogant manner and instead substitute her "personal experience."

Here is another example. Let's say a woman who is pro-abortion is invited to speak to a panel of women who are anti-abortion. The anti-abortion women want to get the pro-abortion woman to admit to the fact that most abortions are performed as a form a "birth control" and not due to duress circumstances like abortion after a rape. The pro-abortion woman might respond, "well, I can only speak from my experience to say that when I was raped and became pregnant as a result, having an abortion allowed me to have my career." As you can see, her anecdote has no bearing on the fact that most abortions are performed for convenience and not due to difficult circumstances.

Experience is valuable regarding gaining an understanding of work or tasks or how things work or how people react. Therefore, older people have more experience in many things than younger people, and thus older people ought to be valued more highly regarding the expertise they bring to a task or in dealing with people. This is especially true regarding functions that are more complex or work that has many unstable variables needing to be taken into account to achieve a particular result.

However, experience has nothing to do with determining whether something is true or false, right or wrong. Therefore, a person having experience is not a valid factor in deciding whether something is true or false, right or wrong, unless, of course, one has much experience at practicing reason and logic.

The last high-level category of logical fallacies is *fallacies of clarity*. These arguments are false because they contain elements (words, phrases, syntax) that distort or cloud their meanings. There are three subcategories of this type of fallacy – *Equivocation, Accent and Distinction without a Difference*.

Perhaps the most popular of the *clarity* fallacies is the *Distinction without a Difference* fallacy. This fallacy is when people make a word distinction between two things that are not different from each other. For example, someone might say, "It's not that I don't like that person, it's just that they are a creep." This type of fallacy is the bread and butter of people who are led by their emotions and try and find "creative" ways to communicate negative things that their positive thinking philosophy says they ought not to say. In other words, people that have a predisposition to commit this fallacy often contradict themselves in spirit in the same sentence.

The previous fallacies are just a small sampling of the many fallacies that exist. I would highly recommend the book, *"The Art of the Argument: An Introduction to the Informal Fallacies"* by authors Aaron Larsen and Joelle Hodge. You can also find a good list of informal fallacies on Wiki at https://en.wikipedia.org/wiki/List_of_fallacies.

As I said at the beginning of this section, it is imperative that people think clearly, reason well, and know or learn how to use critical thinking skills. In fact, I would say it is the most vital life skill for human beings of all times but is extremely important for today's generation of U.S. citizens. Sadly, U.S. secondary schools do not typically require a class on critical thinking or reason and logic, and it is perhaps the worst omission the secondary schools make.

As we have seen, people destroy themselves by remaining in their cages and refusing to use reason well to find their way out of the cage. In the next chapter, we will move beyond learning about the tools one must use to know truth, to exploring what truth is. Understanding these things is an essential part of preparing to look at the successful failure.

Chapter Summary:
- Logical fallacies are incorrect reasoning methods that result in concepts or precepts or principles or beliefs that are false like saying that one plus one equals three in the mathematical domain, or like saying God is both all loving and all powerful in the God-claim domain;
- The four most common fallacies are *Tu Quoque, The Sweeping or Hasty Generalization, Anecdotal* and *Red Herring* or *Strawman* arguments. You would do well to get to know these fallacies well and avoid using them and be able to identify when someone else is committing them;
- If a person does not care to use reason and logic well in sorting out essential life questions, then they will never find the Truth about *their* life, or greater truth in general;
- It is imperative that people understand that any argument, position or belief that is based on fallacious reasoning is false and should be rejected.

8
FINDING TRUTH

Opening Questions:
- What is "truth"?
- How can a person know if something is true?
- How can a person know what is right or wrong regarding human behavior?
- Do religious people use reason and logic well to determine truth in the God domain?
- Do scientists use reason and logic well to find truth in the physical realm?
- Do scientists use reason and logic thoroughly to evaluate human nature?

We human beings use reason (the broader concept not constrained to metaphysical premises and conclusions) and the associated tool of logic (the narrower concept that is limited to the metaphysical realm of formal argument using premises and conclusions) to arrive at and know "truth." "Truth" or that which is "true" is that which is real, genuine, authentic and not fake or false. Here is Cambridge dictionary's definition of what is "true":

"Agreeing with fact; not false or wrong; based on what is real, or actual, not imaginary." [36]

---

[36] Cambridge Dictionary, www.dictionary.cambridge.org, April 2018

Here is Merriam-Webster dictionary's definition of "truth":

> "The body of real things, events, and facts; the property (as of a statement) of being in accord with fact or reality; fidelity to an original or a standard." [37]

Furthermore, to determine what is true one needs some original standard against which to judge it, as the definition of "truth" above states. An example in the material realm would be counterfeit currency. The standard to know whether a currency note or coin is fake/false is to compare it against the official standard, which would be a legally produced currency note—the real thing.

An example in the human event or behavioral realm (what could be described as the eye-witness testimony realm) would be a child telling their parent that they achieved a B+ on the math exam. To determine if that is true, the parent could ask to see the original exam or ask to see the teacher's official grade book.

This book uses observation, reason, and logic using the teachings of the historical Joshua of Nazareth as the standard of truth in the domain of God-things, spiritual things and human behavior.

The basis for using Joshua of Nazareth for truth in those domains is his statements as follows:

> But he *who practices the truth* comes to the Light, so that his deeds may be manifested as having been wrought in God. (John 3:21)

> *I am the way, and the truth and the life,* and no one comes to the Father except through me. (John 14:6)

> Therefore Pilate said to Him, "So You are a king?" Jesus answered, "You say correctly that I am a king. For this I have been born, and for this I have come into the world, to testify to the truth. *Everyone who is of the truth hears my voice.*" (John 18:37)

> If you continue in *my words/truths*, then you are my follower/disciple; *and then you will know the truth, and the truth will set you free*! (John 8:31-32)

> For I did not speak on my own initiative, but the Father Himself who sent me has given me a commandment as to what to say and what to speak. I know that His commandment is eternal life;

---

[37] Merriam-Webster Dictionary, www.merriam-webster.com, April 2018

therefore *the things I speak, I speak just as the Father has told Me.* (John 12:49-50)

Sanctify them in the truth; your word is truth. As You sent me into the world, I also have sent them into the world. For their sakes I sanctify myself, that they themselves also may be sanctified in truth. (John 17:17-19)

That is the primary reason why the errors of Christianity are so visible and easy to see—why we can make a reasoned case for the successful failure that is Christianity. If this author was still in a "biblical worldview", my only valid arguments could be to point to personal failures of Christian individuals (something Joshua warns us not to do) instead of corrections of principles, beliefs and cherished Christian dogma. That is part of what Joshua of Nazareth means when he says this:

If you continue in **my word** (*NOT Paul's or Moses or "the bible"*) then you are my follower; and then you will know the truth, and the truth will set you free! (John 8:31-32)

In this context, free from the darkness of ignorance and error about basic existential realities, about God, about human life.

What about in the realm of the metaphysical? Logic is an essential tool to determine truth in that realm since our senses cannot validate it. Mathematics is the purest form of reasoning with unambiguous and consistent rules. One plus one equals two, for example - that is called a formal proof. Logic is priceless when sorting out claims that cannot be physically verified, like in the realm of religious or spiritual claims. Unfortunately, more and more people don't care about what is true—how about you?

There is a great misconception that "love" (improperly defined) and logic are incompatible in a person. Or, stated another way that emotions and reason are contradictory in a person. (These misconceptions promote the wrong idea that love is primarily an emotion, and we will look at that falsehood later). This idea is championed in popular culture in many different ways, but perhaps most notably with the television and movie series Star Trek and the character Mr. Spock. The view that emotions and logic are incompatible is both wrong and damaging.

People who rely primarily on their emotions generally do not like reasoning minds and are apt to call someone who uses reason well, "dry," "strict," "dogmatic" or "humorless" other such negative labels. And the fact is that if the person is using reason well and the person is defending against the truth(s) that reason is revealing, then they are doing very poorly indeed.

Those who rely on reason instead of emotion for most decisions often do not like people who put their mind aside to rely primarily on emotions and might label them as "too sensitive," "wishy-washy" or other such labels. Either way, aspects of one's personality are not what are in view here, but instead, we need to know the best way or tools to use to sort out our existence, the claims we encounter and things that happen in our daily experiences.

The simple truth is that both reason and emotion play essential roles in our human experience. Feelings very much have their place in our experiences and perhaps some of the most impactful moments in our lives are colored the most beautifully by our emotions. For example, it might take our minds to plan and execute the best route to the top of a mountain. However, once we use our minds to map the way, and our bodies to get there, the beautiful view and sense of accomplishment at the top will create an emotion that will make that experience memorable. Thus, our Creator made us sentient beings, where our feelings color our thoughts and the experiences associated with them.

On the other hand, we were given by our Creator a mind to reason and a tool, logic, to know true from false. Virtually no human problems are solved through emotion, but instead, we need reason to identify them, and without identifying them, we cannot solve them. Emotions are not going to solve energy problems or waste problems or housing problems or food production problems or the worst problems that exist - human conflict problems. In fact, emotions often create, contribute to or exacerbate human conflict problems. Instead, our ability to reason out solutions to those things is what identifies those problems and provides the opportunity to use our wills to solve them.

One of the most significant errors that many people make these days is relying on emotions or feelings to attempt to judge or evaluate a situation or facts and then to make decisions based on those emotional feelings. *An emotionally led life will almost certainly lead to a life in the cage of fear, self-pride, and selfishness.* The best an emotionally driven life will lead to is some level of chaos and confusion. Emotions are personal/individual, which is to say they typically only affect the person experiencing them unless they act on those emotions. Since this is true and people are selfish, relying on our feelings to make decisions will typically result in selfish choices. In contrast, only living by principles (and beliefs) can lead to a consistently selfless life—living by principles like selflessness, unity, and love.

Many religious people have a severe problem with observation and reason, the tools of science. This aversion to observation and reason is very unfortunate since observation and reason are essential tools to assess and evaluate the things we humans experience on a daily basis on the surface of this planet and beyond. Those who like to call themselves "scientists" do a much better job at using observation and reason to evaluate the things they concern themselves with and to come to conclusions regarding the natural, physical world.

Unfortunately, many scientists don't do so well with solving human relationship problems since their trade or the domain of their interest does not have the tools to sort out human relationship problems and the metaphysical or spiritual realities behind them. In fact, many scientists are terrible at trying to solve human problems because they are blind to the fact that metaphysical or spiritual realities exist and this makes them poorly equipped to deal with that realm of human existence and relationship.

In the last chapter of this section, we will take a look at how cause and effect point very strongly to the existence of non-physical things. This will help those who tend to be physicalists open their mind and thus be more objective when evaluating the successful failure.

Chapter Summary:
- "Truth" is that which is real and not fake or pretend;
- To determine that which is true or real one needs some original standard against which to compare it;
- In the God or metaphysical or human nature or human relationship realm, the Standard to judge truth is the Creator's Messenger, Joshua of Nazareth;
- Religious people generally are poor users of reason and logic in finding or determining truth in the God domain;
- Empirical scientists typically use reason well to find or discover or validate that which is factual in the physical realm. Science is a valuable tool in solving many physically related human problems;
- Scientists generally do not do well in the non-physical domain or origin speculation due to their usually being committed to a naturalistic or physicalist worldviews and thus ignoring metaphysical realities like the human soul and human conscience.

9
FIRST CAUSES

Opening Questions:
- Does anything exist that does not have a cause?
- Do explosions organize matter?
- Do human beings – that is exceptionally complex, genetically coded organic machines with interdependent subsystems – exist?
- Do two people having sexual intercourse and fertilizing an egg amount to their designing a human being?
- Is the genetic code a language?

Before we move to the next section, let us take a look at one more significant aspect of inductive reasoning. Everything that exists has to have a sufficient cause to account for its existence. This statement applies to all things in the time, space, and matter universe. For example, a stone is caused by something; it did not "just appear." There was a geological formation process behind that stone as well as physical force that shaped and moved it to its present location. Anything physical that you can imagine had a cause…it did not just happen. Please think about that and confirm that it is true in your mind.

Furthermore, any relatively complex physical thing – like a human-made machine – has some cause sufficient to account for its existence. Gorillas or chimpanzees are not an adequate cause, for example, to account for the existence of a bicycle. The bicycle, although a relatively simple machine, nevertheless has dependent sub-systems that required a designer well beyond the capabilities of an ape to engineer the bicycle for its intended purpose.

As we have seen, physical things are not sufficient to account for non-physical realities like the human mind, soul or reason. A physical thing is not a sufficient cause for a metaphysical thing. As an analogy, a computer's hardware is not an adequate cause for its software. This author admits this is an imperfect analogy since software is physical in the sense it is made up of electronic bits. But electronic bits are the foundation for a language which uses the metaphysical laws of logic, which language was created by spiritual minds who reason.

Ironically, reason and logic themselves are metaphysical! While describing them and the principles by which they operate can be written down, they are in the mind of the human being before they are written down. Mathematics is the purest form of logic and the numbers used for mathematics don't exist physically, instead, they exist as concepts in human's minds which can find representation for those concepts in the physical world. For example, I am with someone, and we see three ducks swimming in a pond. The concept of "three" is represented by the number of ducks we see on the pond.

As another example of first and sufficient causes, atoms to organs and a bit of biochemical energy are not an adequate cause for abstract thought, moral intuition or sentience. There must be a cause sufficient to account for those things. Bricks, wood, metal, and plastic cannot account for the love story conveyed in the theatre. In the same way, atoms, molecules, acids, proteins, cells, tissues, organs and organ systems cannot account for the love or forgiveness that is real and exists among some people.

Love is real. It is perhaps the most meaningful aspect of human existence, and it has the power, so to speak, to solve the problems addressed in this book. Love – properly understood - is metaphysical. It has no physical aspect to it regarding its existence, for it is a concept held and known in the human mind and heart that causes behavior. This all-important concept called "love" is metaphysical and it *must* have a sufficient cause to account for its existence. Just like a computer application that can do a particular function must have had a programmer to account for that function.

The physicalists would have you believe that love is just an emotion based on chemical reactions. That is both the wrong understanding of the concept of love as well as one of the physicalists more irrational claims. Again, true love lays down one's life for another – selfless behavior empowered by compassion - and no evolutionary or chemical hypothesis is adequate to explain that reality.

For example, when a man is in a fighting situation and sees a friend who is about to be killed by a grenade, it is not emotion or chemicals that cause him to jump on the grenade and die for his friend. In fact, if anything, the feelings associated with the understanding of physical danger would tend to push the will towards self-preservation. Instead, he sees a friend who he cares about and decides to give his life for that of his friend. Love is first a value judgment—what do I value and how highly do I appreciate it. Once I identify that which is valuable, I then behave selflessly towards the person of that I value highly or love - unless, of course, I am in my cage of selfishness and thus value myself above all others.

We were not purposed to love things, instead only people. One could make a case for loving animals, but just if it is secondary to loving people.

You see, dear reader, reason points to a designer or a creator, the first and sufficient cause for metaphysical realities like our minds, our consciences, and love.

Non-theists will argue that God therefore needs a first cause for his /her existence and that is a valid argument - I admit it is a weakness in this line of reasoning. My response would be that perhaps metaphysical beings in other dimensions operate with different rules? In other words, the definition of metaphysical is beyond physical – not able to be detected by our five senses. Thus, it is reasonable to believe that additional or different rules apply in that realm. The same could be said for a dimension - or a being that exists in a dimension - that exists outside the matter, energy, time dimension in which we exist. A similar question on the physical plane would be, what causes the universe to end?

However, the question of "What caused God to exist," while interesting and valid, is not relevant to our existence, *for we do exist and their needs be a sufficient cause for our existence.* Since we exist and our bodies are complex organic machines with interdependent systems, a creator/designer is the required cause for that existence. Again, the fact that we exist is undeniable, so the question is what cause best explains our presence.

While non-theists and evolutionists try and put forth an alternative cause to our existence, that alternative is not reasonable for several reasons, one of which it is statistically impossible. Essentially, evolutionists argue, "In the beginning was hydrogen gas, and then something caused a huge explosion, and that explosion led to complex organic machines (hardware) with metaphysical components (software)." Not only do the second law of thermodynamics and the science of mathematical probability work against the physical aspects of that claim, but reason does as well. In fact, reason itself refutes the claim since it is metaphysical and reason says that it is unreasonable to claim that nothing creates something or that the hardware caused the software!

This author highly encourages the reader to in fact learn critical thinking skills for they are *essential* to both find truth and to help solve the problems this world is experiencing. In fact, not being able to reason well and putting logic aside will lead to falsehood, not truth, and yet this is where the majority of people are in the world today.

Let us take a look at this fact – that the majority of people in the world are no longer operating by sound reason in some critical areas – in the next section. If we do that well it will help in preparing us to understand the successful failure that is Christianity.

Chapter summary:
- Everything that exists has a cause to its existence;
- A gigantic explosion and natural forces cannot reasonably account for the presence of complex organic machines, nor can it account for our metaphysical components;
- We humans do exist; therefore we have a cause—we did not "just happen" through random natural forces any more than a complex inorganic machine like an automobile could happen through random physical forces;
- To claim that we exist due to our parent's sexual activity is a fallacious argument since our parents did not Design us but rather just brought the sperm and egg together which began the fantastic DNA code-led process of creating our physical bodies;
- Our first cause was a designer who understood and could create incredibly complex organic machines run by a genetic code that humans are only starting to understand.

SECTION 3:
FALSE BELIEFS, INADEQUATE VIEWS, AND MEANS TO DECEIVE

Theme:
- Identifying popular false beliefs that:
    o Demonstrate we need to care more about what is true;
    o Greatly hinder discovering more significant or ultimate truth;
    o Cause mind and soul traps that prevent people from learning;
    o Are fallacies that enslave and lead to the destruction of things that are good and right.

Section Introduction:

In this section, we will continue to develop the framework that will enable us to critically and successfully evaluate Christianity as a successful failure. Christians have certain foundational beliefs that are existential, and often those beliefs were not received from the Christians own stated standard for such things, the Bible. That means that they have adopted and go by majority opinion about most things in the world.

Before we look directly at Christian religion, we need to address some ways of thinking that will very much help establish our premise that Christianity is a successful failure. In other words, this section will provide the tools and insight necessary to adequately consider, evaluate and judge as wrong or fallacious, ideas and concepts that the majority of people have come to believe – including Christians. It will also help balance the view and assist in getting those readers of this book whose primary motivation is to prove their world-view right and Christianity's worldview as wrong.

We have seen (or I have put forth the proposition) that the root problems that cause almost all human conflict are self-pride and fear and selfishness. So, the question is what is the solution to those problems? Before I show how Christianity is not the solution, we must first remove the things in the way of seeing the answer. There are non-Christian or non-religious things that significantly hinder being able to see the solution clearly, or even knowing a solution is possible.

These things are primarily in the realm of thought, reason, and beliefs – the metaphysical realm – and they drive belief and behavior. We need the tools of reason and logic, and we need to use them well to identify these hindrances and obstacles that are in the way of seeing the solution. As another simple proof of metaphysical reality, this section proves that real barriers exist that are not physical or material. The beliefs we are about to examine are false and thus significantly hinder the search for truth for those who hold to them. We can know them to be false because they fail to pass the test of reason and logic as we shall see.

This entire book is essentially a criticism of Christian religion (and religion in general), so to be fair, some important rules must be laid out at the beginning to even the playing field.

I have found that some, perhaps many, non-theists and agnostics spend a good bit of time committing the logical fallacies of Tu Quoque, Sweeping or Hasty generalization and the Straw Man or Red Herring. The following will provide a review of the logical fallacies already introduced as well as relevant examples of those fallacies.

As we have seen, *Tu Quoque* is an invalid argument that assumes that a rival's recommendation, belief or behavior should be discounted or dismissed because the rival does not always follow it him/herself. This fallacy could otherwise be known as the hypocrisy argument. Unfortunately, Christians are very guilty – perhaps increasingly so – of hypocrisy. Their hypocrisy is unfortunate, yet even Christian's hypocrisy has a silver lining – without a knowable standard, no hypocrisy could be judged to exist! Please think about that.

Some teachings in Christianity (mainly Jesus of Nazareth's teachings) do set a high standard that not many Christians are willing to try to follow, even as they preach them to others. Of course, many Christians being hypocrites in no way proves that God does not exist, nor does it invalidate the teachings and claims of the historical person of Jesus of Nazareth.

Accusing others of hypocrisy without examining ourselves first is effortless. We all, as human beings, would do well to critically self-examine ourselves to see if we practice hypocrisy in some area(s) in our lives. The saying is true that to be human is to err. If the Christian is doing more good by helping others than the non-theist or agnostic, then the non-theist or agnostic would do well not to point out that person's hypocrisy unless they are willing to examine their own life equally critically and with similar diligence. Of course, if one has no objective standard to make that examination, then that self-examination will most likely be a futile exercise in self-justification. We shall look at that significant problem shortly.

The Sweeping or Hasty Generalization is also known as the "don't throw the baby out with the bathwater" argument. It is a fallacy of induction argument that overextends a generalization to include facts or cases that are valid exceptions to it. So, for example, a non-theist might argue, "since many Roman Catholic priests sexually abuse children, all Christian leaders have a predisposition to abuse children sexually". Trust me, my using that example is not to encourage people to trust Christian leaders, and I will spend a good bit of time explaining how they are primarily responsible for the thing which is a successful failure. However, because some Christian leaders sexually abuse children does not mean that all have a predisposition to, and claiming so is a logical fallacy. Just so the reader understands, some Christian religious sects (Roman Catholics for example) ask their staff/leaders to live in a way that they do not have the power to (celibate), and this causes many sexual related problems for these people and their victims.

The most important version of the logical fallacy of Hasty Generalization that is made by many is, "Since Christianity has so many false or wrong things associated with it (the bathwater), therefore Jesus of Nazareth (the baby) is false or wrong" (or an additional fallacy, that he is responsible for all that falseness and wrongness). It is surprising how many non-theists and agnostics stand on this fallacy to justify their rejection of God or the dismissal of the historical person of Jesus of Nazareth. It is also ironic how many non-theists and agnostics preach reason and logic as the answer to humanity's problems (and they are partially correct in this belief), yet some of their primary arguments against what they perceive as false beliefs, fail the test of logic!

Finally, there is the *Straw Man argument.* The Straw Man is a "red herring" type argument that attempts to disprove an opponent's position by presenting it in an unfair, inaccurate manner. A good example of this presented itself recently. Let's say a Christian/Biblian is appointed to an important federal government position. Let us say the position is Secretary of Education. Let us say the person has been judged by the political people that need to vet her as reasonably qualified. Lastly, let us say that the

Secretary made some religious comment not related to the task of leading, or setting policies for, the Education Department. A non-theist will commit the fallacy of the Straw Man by saying something to the effect of, "Oh, look, she is a Christian; therefore, the Education Department is going to be a mess." That is an unfair argument since the person's religious beliefs may not affect the policies he/she implements at the Education Department. The fallacy of that argument would be especially true if the person is not controlling *content* but rather methods or channels or platforms of education delivery.

So, for the atheist or agnostic or non-Christian or non-theist, it is essential for you to realize that to have logical fallacies as your primary "proofs" or objections to God's existence is a weak foundation indeed. I encourage you to not be like many religious people who hold to their dogma in spite of reason demonstrating their errors.

So, let's move on and examine some of the significant false beliefs or fallacies that many people currently hold in the western world. In doing this, we will expose wrong thinking that prevents a person from knowing truth, and thus we will remove obstacles to understanding why Christianity and religion in general, is a successful failure.

10
THE GREAT BLINDNESS: TRUTH RELATIVISM

Opening Questions:

- What happens when people cannot agree on what is true or false?
- What happens when people cannot agree on what is right or wrong?
- Are all things relative to the individual or a culture?
- Is torturing (the intentional infliction of unnecessary pain) a baby ever right at any time in any culture?
- If all things are relative, is the statement "all things are relative" absolutely true?

What if a group of people believed false things that impacted their ability to make correct decisions? How would the individuals of that group do at functioning in the world with other people? For example, let's say that a particular group of people believed that the results of mathematical equations would result in random answers (something false). Thus, if one of their children asked, "what is the sum of two plus two daddy," the parent would say, "well, we are not sure, maybe six, maybe three, or possibly four."

How well would their buying, selling or trading work?

How would their architects and engineers design things to build?

If a group of people denied the principles that mathematics operates on, then they would be hard-pressed to live up to their human potential, and would at best be primitive and at worst be in chaos.

As another example, what if a group of people could not agree on what was right behavior and what was wrong behavior? So, for example, one parent believes that it is OK when their son takes vegetables from their neighbor's garden without asking but others don't. Another parent thinks it is OK if their son bullies and forces his will upon others but others don't. An adult male thinks that twelve-year-old girls are "fair game" for his sexual activities, but most others don't, especially dads with daughters. If that group of people could not agree on what is right behavior and what is wrong behavior, how would that group do? Would there be harmony and peace, or would there be discord and conflict?

As far-fetched as the above examples might seem, the point is to demonstrate that there is a widely held belief by the people in the United States (and in other nations as well) that is serving as the foundation for - and enabling - people to in fact enter into the kind of destructive confusion in the examples above. That core level belief or worldview is called "relativism." Here are some dictionary definitions of relativism:

"The doctrine that knowledge, truth, and morality exist in relation to culture, society, or historical context, and are not absolute." [38]

"The belief that truth and right and wrong can only be judged in relation to other things and that nothing can be true or right in all situations." [39]

"Ethical relativism, the doctrine that there are no absolute truths in ethics and that what is morally right or wrong varies from person to person or from society to society." [40]

There are two primary factors to the source of blindness and confusion that is occurring in many people in the United States. *First, people denying that any universal standard (or ethic) regarding "proper" human behavior exists* - this could be known as "ethical," "moral" or "truth relativism." So, element one to the great blindness is the belief of "truth" or "ethical" relativism.

The second element is people being unable to use reason well to arrive at sound conclusions in any realm of knowledge, but particularly in the field of human beliefs and behavior. *People are turning away from reason being the primary means to sort out true from false claims in any domain of knowledge.* Relativism is the belief that facilitates this, and it leaves people with mere emotionalism - the idea that "human knowing" is primarily an emotional endeavor instead of an endeavor of reason especially regarding human relationships and behavior.

The Foundational Belief Driving the Blindness

Again, the relativism philosophy states there are no absolute truths (or standards) that exist to judge anything (of course "anything" would include human beliefs or behavior). This belief says that the individual's

---

[38] www.dictionary.com, April 2018

[39] Cambridge Dictionary, www.dictionary.cambridge.org, April 2018

[40] Encyclopedia Britannica, www.britannica.com, May 2018

perspective on any topic or event is that person's ultimate reality or complete truth by which no other person is bound.

It states that there are no absolute truths that people can hold to, "that all beliefs and behaviors are only real or meaningful or relevant to the person or persons who hold them and no one else (unless other people happen to hold to those same beliefs and behaviors). Stated yet another way, there is nothing outside of the *individual* human mind (which mind, by the way, certain scientists confuse with "brain" as we shall see!) by which human's behavior or beliefs can be governed or judged as right or wrong.

Furthermore, relativism is girded by physicalism which is the belief that there is no reality (metaphysical or otherwise) beyond the physical reality that can be measured by science. What is a physicalist? It is a person who believes that human nature, the world we live in and our human experiences are all best accounted for by mere physical matter. Physicalists should be distinguished from non-theists who assert that no God or gods exist, and from agnostics, who claim you cannot know if God or gods exist.

Not all non-theists (a- not, theist – God) are physicalists, although many are. Since most God claims involve spiritual or metaphysical claims, non-theists undoubtedly lean that way due to their desire to "prove" that God does not exist. However, you don't have to be a physicalist to be a non-theist.

Most agnostics (a-not, gnostic-know) are not physicalists since agnostics tend not to take a stand or a position. They tend to be content with "I don't know" and to move on to other things. Agnostics tend not to use reason well, for it would often defeat the claim of "I don't know." If I claim to know about things that impact human life, then I become accountable and responsible - if I claim "I do not know," I can go on my merry selfish way. Agnostics don't want to use their minds to come to a conclusion and thus be in the position of offending someone, nor be in a position of having to help other people. Simply put many perhaps most agnostics are cowards who believe in nothing and thus fight for nothing except their comfort, entertainment or pleasure.

Some people (physicalists) in the world have come to believe that we human beings are no more than the aggregation of atoms, molecules, acids, proteins, cells, tissues, organs, organ systems and a bit of biochemical energy. The truth is that physicalism is a selfish cop-out. Physicalists can either do a little work to find the truth that best explains human nature, the world we live in, and their human experience. Or they can take the lazy way out and say things like:

- "I don't care about anything but me and my comfort and pleasure";
- "I don't want to waste my time trying to make sense of things';
- "I don't want God to exist, so I don't have to consider being accountable for the way I live my life".

Physicalism is then adopted by that person to justify their existence. It brings the same "benefits" as non-theism or agnosticism in that one is now not accountable for how we live our lives, and thus we are now justified in our selfishness.

This book will not take a hard look at physicalism or atheism or agnosticism. Instead, this book focuses on those who claim to represent "Jesus" and thus is based upon the principle, "If you were blind, you would have no sin; but since you say, 'We see,' your sin remains." Or stated another way, if you were ignorant in the God realm, you would not be guilty, but since you claim to know in that realm, you are guilty. If you cannot guess, this principle applies primarily to Christians and other religious people since they claim they see concerning the God realm—what God is like and what God wants.

Relativism is a true belief for many lesser aspects of the human experience, like wealth accumulation, for example. Who defines what materially wealthy is? Each society or group of people will have different standards. The people in a village in Bangladesh will have a different standard than the people who live in a wealthy section of the city of Tokyo or New York, and thus a person's material wealth will be relative to others they encounter in their usual sphere of living. However, as global communication continues to grow and be accessible to more and more people, relativism will have fewer standards to scatter to, and people will become more and more accountable for their selfishness / loveless-ness.

While relativism is valid for many aspects of the human experience, it fails as the highest governing belief for an individual.

When you apply reason to moral or existential relativism, it is shown to be self-defeating. The statement from the consistent relativist is, "there are no universal or absolute moral or existential truths that can be known or applied to all humans." But when you ask the relativist who uttered that statement, "does your statement convey an absolute truth that applies to all people', they have only two reasonable answers - yes or no. If they answer "yes," then there is at least one universal truth, and thus their statement is false. If they answer "no," then they admit that relativism is false since there are universal or absolute truths that exist. Therefore, other absolute truths might also exist, so perhaps it would be wise to seek out from where absolute truth originates. Please reread this paragraph, slowly and carefully, for it proves (using logic) that moral or existential or truth relativism is a false belief, and thus if you hold it, you ought to abandon that which is false. Believing something wrong that is at a relatively high level – like a world or life view – is to be significantly delusional.

Existential or truth relativism leads to only one place – confusion, selfishness, conflict, and ruin. With no standard of right or wrong, people will be utterly bound by the core human nature problems of fear, self-pride, and selfishness. This bondage will lead to conflict as each person, or small group of people decides for themselves what is right or wrong human behavior. The leaving of an existential anchor or ethical standard has happened throughout history and is happening right now in the United States in the domains of human sexuality, marriage, and gender among other things. People are throwing out well established moral norms for a new view of human sexuality and even what it means to be male or female, and relativism is the world-view that enables this. They have left an absolute standard for human ethics and have adopted a "whatever floats your boat" worldview regarding human relationships. If human nature was good, this would not be a problem. But as we look at the world and the evidence, clearly human nature is not "good" if you define "good" as including not using or abusing or neglecting or harming one another.

Ironically, relativism regarding moral and existential beliefs is probably the most widely held belief among the "educated" people of the earth at this time. The opposing belief has traditionally been called "absolutism." This belief states that there are absolute truths that don't change due to a person's perception or human culture or time - and those truths exist not only in the physical realm (gravity, for example) but the spiritual or metaphysical realm as well.

Relativism is most popular amongst the educated elite in materially wealthy nations. Thus, the U.S. educational system and the teachers that staff it teach from the relativistic perspective. Teaching from a relativistic perspective is very unfortunate and is the leading cause of "blindness" and "madness" (believing and proclaiming things that are contradictory and false) in individuals in the U.S. at this junction in history.

Absolutism has far fewer problems with logic, represents reality better, and thus should be adopted by people who want to understand and sort out their lives and experiences using reason and logic.

"All things are relative." Is that statement absolutely true?

In the next few chapters, let us take a look at three fundamental relativistic and popular beliefs as they very much play a role in making Christianity a successful failure since many Christians adopt, hold and make these errors.

Chapter Summary:

- Existential relativism is a worldview, top-level perspective or operating system level belief that says, "the only things that are real and true are things that are real and true for me—there are no absolute truths that exist beyond the individual human mind and thus there is no binding reality regarding human ethics or relationship behavior principles";

- Lower level relativistic views are valid. For example, how wealthy a person is relative to all other people's wealth on the earth;
- Existential or truth relativism is a false view that is proved by their highest level statement, that "all things are relative; there is nothing that is absolutely true." When asked if that statement is true, if they answer "yes," then the statement is false. If they answer "no," then the statement is false. It is a self-defeating belief;
- Existential relativism leads to chaos, confusion and ultimately the ruin of groups that hold to that view. The current social environment and culture in the U.S. validates that claim as people switch from some form of absolutism and associated ethics to relativism;
- Absolute truth exists, and it is essential that people identify it and use it to guide their lives.

11
"DON'T BE JUDGMENTAL" AS I JUDGE YOU!

Opening Questions:
- Do you make judgments?
- Is it wrong to be a judgmental person?
- Should we hold fallacies as a guiding belief?
- Is all judgment wrong?
- Is it "unloving" to make a judgment about another person's beliefs or behavior?

The fallacy of existential or ethical relativism is making people unwilling or unable to discern truth and thus leading them to believe that judgment is wrong.

Many are quick to say, "oh, you'd better be careful about judging others" or "don't be judgmental." Like many things, that could be a true or false statement depending upon the context of the comment. One thing is for sure; most people are proclaiming, "don't judge" in a wrong way—in an extremely damaging way; a way caused by a more profound problem of denying right or wrong, good or bad exists; in a way driven by the false view of existential relativism.

The key point to understand about this topic is that *not all judgment is wrong, just various types of judgment*. In fact, some kinds of judgment are critically important, right and necessary. The types of judgments that are wrong according to Joshua include the following:
- Condemnatory judgment of groups of people based not on their ethical beliefs or practices but merely on amoral demographics. People are individuals and while they may be part of a group - "I'm a Russian" for example - it is fallacious to judge people based on an

amoral group label (race, gender, nationality) because it is individuals who are morally responsible for their actions.

- Another type of judgment that is wrong is to condemn individuals based on attributes that are merely physical and thus play no part in their behavior. Examples of things people cannot change include things like where they were born or the color of their skin or how "attractive" they are other physical aspects; or how "smart" they are, or what language they speak or don't speak, some disability or handicap, etc.
- Another wrong type of judgment is hypocritical judgment. Hypocritical judgment is to say to someone, "you should not do that" or "you should do this" when I am not abstaining from or not doing the very same or similar things. For example, if I say to another person, "you should not smoke cigarettes," while a few minutes later I smoke cigarettes. Or I say, "you ought to give money to poor people who want to work" when I am not doing so.
- Another wrong type of judgment is self-righteous judgment which is to have our judgment biased by self-pride. This would mean I think of myself as more valuable or more important than other people and thus my judgments are regularly critical of other individuals, looking for their faults and weaknesses and mistakes to put them down instead of constructively discussing beliefs, principles or concepts that affect us.

On the other hand, right judgment is commended by Joshua as we will see. *Correct judgment includes the judging of truth versus falsehood; of right and wrong human behavior; the sincere and sober judgment of our faults and weaknesses; as well as the gentle, and compassionate and thus non-condemnatory judgment and correction of other's wrong behavior.* People should be judged by *their character* which character manifests itself in words and action. Here are Joshua's statements commending right judgment:

> Do not judge according to appearance, but judge with righteous judgment. (John 7:24)

> You have rightly judged... (Luke 7:43)

> Yes, and why, even of yourselves, do you not judge what is right? (Luke 12:57)

> For God did not send the Son into the world to judge the world, but that the world might be saved through him. He who believes

in him is not condemned; he who does not believe has been condemned already because he has not believed in the name of the only spiritually birthed Son of God. (John 3:17-18)

As you can see above, Joshua of Nazareth *urges others to make right judgments and commends others for making right judgments.* Therefore, not all judgment is wrong.

He also says this:

> Do not judge so that you will not be judged. For in the way you judge, you will be judged; and by your standard of measure, it will be measured to you. Why do you look at the speck that is in your brother's eye, but do not notice the log that is in your own eye? Or how can you say to your brother, "Let me take the speck out of your eye," and behold, the log is in your own eye? You hypocrite, first take the log out of your own eye, and then you will see clearly to take the speck out of your brother's eye. (Matt. 7:1-5)

Are these sayings contradictory, or complementary? They are complementary.

If you look at the context of the sayings above where he is exhorting others to make right judgments or commending them for making right judgments, he is *addressing judging whether something is true or false, right or wrong –* he was not making judgments *about an individual's weaknesses or flaws.* Judging is especially critical with religious beliefs or beliefs about God. Joshua was regularly correcting people's wrong ideas about God and what God wants. This practice of his is what got him into so much trouble because people's pride was offended when he said in some form, "your belief about God is wrong" or "this thing you do for God He doesn't want" or other such corrections.

The latter saying above, where Joshua says, "Do not judge so that you will not be judged", is an excellent warning to us not to make the wrong type judgments. In that saying, he is specifically focusing on the self-righteous type of wrong view (which often lead to hypocritical judgments), where I am overlooking my faults and problems and instead focusing on another person's.

For example, if I see someone from another nation or who speaks another language or who is wearing clothes I don't like, and I say, "Oh, that person is inferior or wrong or bad or 'low class'" then I have made a wrong judgment. Unfortunately, I will be accountable to the same degree of strictness for things that do matter! Dear reader, you don't want that, because all you will do is condemn yourself—and if you can't see that, then you are bound by self-pride, and you are in a wrong place.

Inevitably you have either been accused yourself or have been the accuser, saying to someone something like, "you had better be careful, you are judging someone, and Jesus says we are not to judge." Typically, this response comes when you have said (or have heard someone say) something perceived as negative (in reality probably corrective) about some person's behavior or belief or event or organization.

The simple truth is we all make many judgments each day.

If you see a man beating up a young child, you will make a judgment that his behavior is wrong and needs to be stopped. If you hear a person say something you perceive as negative about your mother or children, then you will immediately judge that person's words! If you decide not to go into a specific neighborhood during the evening hours, then you are making a judgment. As you listen to some preacher say that God commands you this night to give your entire savings account to "his ministry," you will make a judgment. As you are reading my words in this book, you are judging them against your understanding of what is true. This type of judgment is a good thing, for Joshua commands it (John 4:24, 8:32), and it is part of the rational mind that God gave us to sort out that which is true from that which is false.

Those that are quick to say, "Don't judge" or "you are judgmental," are generally those people who don't hold to any objective truth or ethic, but instead believe that *their* beliefs are correct and others are wrong with no objective standard to rationally defend that. The whole stance or response of "Don't judge" or "you are judgmental" is a way to try and force others to their existential relativistic view that no objective or absolute truth exists. As followers of the One who says, "I am the truth," we reject that view and instead believe Joshua.

Telling people not to judge is irrational and wrong from two perspectives. First, as we have seen, all people make judgments, thus making the statement "you should not judge" without a qualifier, is at best poorly stated. More importantly, those who make the statement, "you should not judge" are being hypocritical because they have judged another's words or actions, and that is why they told them not to judge! As soon as you tell someone not to judge, you have judged their opinion or judgment as somehow wrong, and that is irrational - this practice can make for an irrational go around of accusations of "you better not judge."

The real issue that must be recognized before the emotions get too impassioned is what is the truth regarding the matter at hand. Instead of accusing one another of "judging," what should happen is the clearer thinking person should ask the question, "can we use reason to try and sort this issue out?" This approach is almost always the proper way out from accusations of "you are judgmental." Sadly, in many circumstances, those accusing another of "judging" are not interested in truth, but rather in protecting their own incorrect opinions or tightly held traditions of men.

Here is another example of a wrong understanding of "judgment." A contentious issue these days is "gay marriage." If a person says, "gay marriage is wrong," then they are highly likely to be subjected to people rebuking them saying, "you are a judgmental person" or "you should not condemn homosexuals" or "Jesus says to love, not hate."

All of those rebukes are fallacious.

Knowing right behavior from wrong behavior is critical for any people group who want to hold to some unifying moral ethic. Those who listen to the real Joshua of Nazareth know he teaches that marriage is defined as, and intended by, the Creator as between one man and one woman for life.

In the case of the "you are a judgmental person" rebuke, a proper response could be, "well, in context, thank you! It is critical that we judge right behavior from wrong behavior".

Regarding the "you should not condemn homosexuals" rebuke, a proper response could be, "I did not say that I condemn homosexual persons, I said I don't believe God's definition of marriage includes two same-gendered people."

Concerning the "Jesus says to love, not hate" rebuke, a proper response could be, "yes, he does teach that, and I did not say I hate homosexual people; I merely said that I don't believe God's definition of marriage includes two same-gendered people. Why do you accuse me of hatred when I don't hate homosexuals or any other kind of person?"

The real issue is that people in general, and by the millions, are leaving behind any concept of a higher being or deity giving absolute truth. According to this belief, since a God or higher being does not exist (or he/she/it cannot be known), then the only source of truth regarding right or wrong human behavior is we human beings. Only people make up our moral standards, and those standards will vary from one culture to the next and even from one person to the next. Therefore, it is wrong to try and say other people will be held accountable to some higher ethical standard; or stated another way, it is wrong to say people will be held to some moral standard of behavior. Ethical relativism is the "new belief" of the masses. And this belief generates many, "don't judge" or "you are too judgmental" responses to people who can identify true from false or right from wrong according to some standard.

Finally, any person who holds to the belief that God exists and provides rules or guidelines for human behavior will ironically be judged wrongly as "hateful" by relativists because relativists so desperately don't want to believe that there is a God who will hold people accountable for how they live their lives. You should wonder why this is so.

How do we untangle this mess about "judging"?

The solution is not difficult to understand, but it is difficult to live by. If you remember and live by these next five principles of Joshua regarding judgment, you will be doing well in this crucial matter of judging.

- First, *it is critical that we do judge what is true versus what is false in all areas of our lives with Joshua as our Standard and using good reason and logic.* This is a critical aspect of what it means to be a human being, and when people abandon this, the result will always be the same—chaos, confusion, ruin and the strong or powerful ruling over and using the weak or powerless.
- Second, we are to *judge people's behavior, words and beliefs against Joshua" words-teachings-truths,* for Joshua the Creator's messenger is the standard of truth (John 14:6; 17:17).

(Regarding this principle, it is imperative to distinguish between a person's beliefs and behavior versus their amoral behaviors or physical characteristics. We are to carefully judge all God beliefs and ethical beliefs against Joshua's teachings, and we are *not* to judge people's amoral behavior. Amoral behavior means customs, traditions, ceremonies or actions that have no moral or spiritual implication. For example, the way someone brushes their teeth, or how or what someone eats, or the manner of their speaking, etc. We are also not to judge someone's physical appearance, i.e., their body shape, skin color or facial features.)

- Third, when judging other's behaviors and words, we are to be *careful that we are not committing similar sins or errors* (Matt. 7:1-6). To be correcting someone for behavior that we have not gained control over is hypocritical and Joshua taught that hypocrisy significantly blinds us and prevents us from becoming better human beings.
- Forth, we are to be *slow to judge others and quick to listen and to forgive* (Matt. 7:1-6, 6:14-15). Be gracious; give people the benefit of the doubt; listen carefully and slowly weight the matter—treat others the way we want to be treated.
- Fifth and finally, we are *not to condemn anyone as hopelessly beyond the reach of God's love* (Luke 6:37). The follower of Joshua should never tell someone, "you're going to hell." Not even Joshua - the only one to ascend into heaven (John 3:13), and thus could justly give that judgment, and who certainly knew many people who were going to end up destroying themselves in hell - brought that condemnation to individuals. We can always change! There is always Hope!

In the next chapter, we will take a look at one of the most popular concepts in U.S. culture at this time – what it means to be a tolerant person - and try and make some right judgments!

Chapter Summary:

- All people make judgments – making judgments is not wrong and making judgments is very much a necessary part of being a functioning human being;
- If we do not judge what is true versus what is false, we will fall into deep darkness;
- If we do not judge what is ethically right versus wrong, we will be cowards who are utterly selfish;
- We should be careful in what judgments we make regarding other people – we should make judgments that avoid hypocrisy; in most normal social circumstances we should make judgments that are gracious and provide the benefit of the doubt;
- Our Standard for judging human behavior and beliefs ought to be Joshua of Nazareth;
- Correcting or rebuking false beliefs or views or correcting or rebuking wrong behavior is not wrong – even when people who are trapped by this fallacy call it "being judgmental" - but we should typically correct other individuals we know with sincerity, humility, and compassion.

12
I WILL BE TOLERANT OF BIRDS THAT I FLOCK WITH, BUT NOT OF YOU!

Opening Questions:
- Do you believe you are a tolerant person?
- What is a truly tolerant person?
- Do tolerant people hate, despise, have animosity towards or dislike other people who have different beliefs?
- If I claim to be a tolerant person, yet I judge and label a person as "intolerant," am I not being intolerant myself in that very action?
- How does a person who claims to be tolerant know what is right and wrong and thus worth holding or defending as a "tolerant belief"?
- Should I hold or rely on beliefs that are fallacious?

One of the most popular beliefs in today's western culture based on relativism is the belief called "tolerance." It sounds like a great belief to hold and to practice towards others. However, there are some important distinctions to be made about the idea. Sadly, those who preach tolerance the loudest are some of the most intolerant people. What this means is that these people hold a contradictory, self-serving belief that only makes them hypocritical and brings no light to others.

Following are three versions or possible definitions for a "tolerant person":

Version 1 - The Most Popular

> To be a tolerant person, you must accept all other people's beliefs
> or behaviors, and if you cannot accept something, you must not
> express disapproval towards the person(s) who hold the view or
> engage in the practice.

A belief that includes this principle - "you must accept all other
people's beliefs or behaviors" - is a self-defeating statement which means it
is impossible to practice. The person who says they hold to that belief and
encounters a person who "believes they should not accept all other people's
beliefs or behaviors," *will contradict their own belief by rejecting that person's belief
and judging it as wrong.*

So, for example, let's say person 1 is a person who says they hold to this
version of tolerance. Let's say person 2 comes along and says, "I believe
that homosexual marriage is wrong." Person 1 reacts to person 2's
statement and says, "oh, your belief is wrong, you are a bigot." Person 1 has
not accepted Person 2's belief and in so doing is in contradiction to their
own stated tolerance belief. Please reread this slowly to understand it.

In essence, this belief is promoted by those who desire to believe that
there is no universal moral standard by which people should live - just *their*
standard. In so doing, they practice hypocrisy regarding not applying their
tolerance belief to others who disagree.

Version 2 - Better Than Version 1 But Still Deficient

> To be a tolerant person, you must accept your culture's majority
> views/beliefs of acceptable human beliefs or behaviors, and if you
> cannot accept them, you must not express disapproval towards the
> person(s) who hold the view or engage in the practice.

This statement is better than the first self-contradicting and thus false
statement just examined, but it still contains two fatal flaws. First, who
decides what the "majority" views/beliefs are, and by what standard do you
judge them as right or wrong? For example, let's say most people in a
nation/society other than the United States believe that American people
are generally evil. Are the majority of people in that society "tolerant" of
American people? According to the above belief, yes they are if they do not
express disapproval of American people. However, the truth is that human
belief drives human behavior, thus exposing the second flaw. If a group of
people believes that American people are generally evil, then they will very

likely manifest behavior that aligns with that belief (Most Islamic Jihadists are a good example). It is unreasonable to believe that people who hold a belief like, "those people are evil" will not somehow manifest that belief with consistent behavior when opportunities arise.

Thus, the best this version of being a tolerant person can do is to leave people confused and unsure with no standard to reasonably sort things out.

Version 3 - The Truly Tolerant Person

> To be a tolerant person, you should not want to cause harm to others, nor desire they be harmed no matter how different they are from you or no matter how much you disagree with their non-ethical (not unethical, but non-ethical meaning not addressing how people ought to treat each other) beliefs. The genuinely tolerant person will be careful or sensitive in the way they seek to discuss an issue with the person with whom they disagree. (If they are engaged in a harmful behavior towards others, you should want them to stop and attempt to stop them. If they express an unethical belief, you should try and correct them.)

This statement is not self-contradictory and does not contain the significant flaws of the prior statements. Thus it should be adopted as the only valid definition of a "tolerant" person. It is not. Instead, people hold to some version of the first two definitions of "a tolerant person" above, and they do this due to relativism.

The qualifier's in the genuinely tolerant definition above of "ethical" and "non-behavior impacting" beliefs means we ought to desire to cause no harm to others nor desire harm come to them based on their ideas that would not produce wrongful behavior. However and for example, if someone shares a belief me that, "I think it is good to have sex with young children," I should want to stop them from acting upon that belief, even as I try not to harm them in that process.

At the most basic level, the popular concept of "tolerance" (version 1 above) is false. If a "tolerant" person judges another person as "intolerant," then their belief is self-defeating, meaning they contradict themselves. The moment a person proclaiming to be "tolerant" claims or castigates another as "intolerant," they have no reasonable basis to proclaim or believe that they are tolerant!

What many who proclaim "tolerance" the loudest are saying is that they believe and behave in a right and good manner and others must accept their beliefs and behavior. Those who disagree with their viewpoint are "intolerant bigots" or some other such intolerant label. As we have seen, this practice is illogical and thus false. This practice is also arrogant and virtually guaranteed to cause wrongful conflict. Despite these truths about this practice and way of thinking, it is one of the primary tools that is being used to shut down free speech or free expression of ideas in western cultures.

For example, some homosexuals seem to be eager to proclaim the "tolerance" belief - they want others to tolerate their beliefs and behavior regarding human sexuality. They say that it is intolerant for a person to say (or believe) that a homosexual belief or practice is wrong or harmful. They say that their ideas or behavior are good, right and acceptable and those that state or even believe otherwise are at a minimum intolerant.

It seems to this author that many outspoken homosexuals seem to be unable to refrain from more severe judgments against people who disagree with their beliefs or behavior, and use terms like "hateful," "bigots," "homophobic" and the like to label those who disagree with them. Do you see the problem? Even if a person is kind and caring and would never think of harming someone including a homosexual, they are judged as at least "intolerant" by people who hold to the belief - or practice it - and who want others to believe the same way. Even if a person is virtually perfect in gently and sincerely expressing their view that homosexual behavior is wrong and harmful, they are called "full of hatred" by many homosexuals.

What is the homosexual's standard to justify their beliefs and behavior? They have none other than where relativism leaves people - "because what I believe is right and true for me"; or "because this person or group of people believe it is acceptable." Unfortunately, it also makes the homosexuals who promote the "tolerance" belief, just as hypocritical as the religious people they appear to hate. As can be seen in the behavior and words of many outspoken homosexuals or those homosexuals who actively promote their lifestyle, they do not practice what they preach - they are among the most intolerant people (by any definition) towards others who don't agree with their beliefs and practices. The reader might want to question why that is. For a framework on human sexuality, see *Appendix 4, A Basic Framework for Human Sexuality.*

(Lest you think the author to be biased against homosexuals, I would also say that most religious people do not practice what they preach and also seem to have great difficulty avoiding hypocrisy. In fact, this author would say that we all as humans have difficulty avoiding hypocrisy to some degree. This author believes that a life well lived has two components: First, having the right beliefs to guide one's life, and second, consistently practicing or living out those beliefs. (Of course, this author will argue that the beliefs we ought to adopt as our standard are those given by the Creator's Messenger.)

Concerning avoiding hypocrisy, it is critical to make the distinction between a person's failures to live out what they say they believe in contrast to a person saying the standard they believe needs to be changed to accommodate their behavior. For example, I can say ('preach') that I believe that all high saturated fat food is unhealthy. My standard could be medical or scientific reports or data that demonstrate that indeed high saturated fat diet is bad for human health.

If, however, you catch me eating a high saturated fat food, my response will be telling. If I say, "Oh, well, the evidence that high-fat foods are bad for human health is suspect," then I am justifying my behavior and wrongly attacking the standard to do so. If, however, I said, "well, yes, high-fat food is bad, and I should never eat it, but I fail and occasionally eat it because I enjoy the flavor," my response is not attacking the standard, and thus my answer is more objective and humble.

Unfortunately, we as humans seem to lack clarity when it comes to seeing our faults, and we would rather get what we want (in this example, the flavor of high saturated fat foods), defend ourselves and attack the standard rather than being seen as wrong. What exactly accounts for that? Perhaps self-pride? How does that tendency fit into the physicalist's beliefs? In other words, what physical thing causes self-pride?

Here are some additional examples to illustrate the erroneous nature of the popular "tolerant" belief.

Example A:

An adult person believes that it is good to have sexual relations with 12-year-olds and lives in a nation where that behavior is not "illegal." The adult's belief is, "It is good and right for me to have sexual relations with 12-year-olds".

According to the popular tolerant belief, it would be intolerant to attempt to change or correct that adult's viewpoint.

Example B:

A person believes that teaching young children that people group X (Jews, Indians, Black People, etc.) is less valuable human beings than my flesh or "my people" is good and right.

That person's belief ought to be "tolerated," and to try to convince them otherwise would be intolerant.

Example C:

Adult person A believes that God exists and has given humanity a moral standard both by which to live, and by which they will be held accountable, including that the only acceptable expressions of human sexuality are between a husband and his wife (a man and woman committed to caring for each other for life).

Is this belief "tolerated" and "respected" by the many people who currently live in the US? Here is a very realistic scenario to test if Person A's is treated with tolerance.

Person B, a person who proclaims their "tolerance" belief regularly to others, yells at person A (as person A states his belief publicly calmly and appropriately) and accuses person A of "proclaiming hate speech."

Does the reader get the point? Will the reader use reason to conclude what is evidently and undeniably true? What is evident is that reason or truth does not play a part in Person B's reaction to Person A, and it is also apparent that Person B is contradicting his own stated "tolerance" belief and thus is acting hypocritically. As such, Person B's corrections of Person A should be ignored, and his hypocritical statements regarding the topic should be seriously questioned, in this case, his "tolerance" belief.

What happens in reality? Person B's words get published by the "objective press" while the same press paints Person B's words in a favorable light and context while subtly (increasingly not so subtly) supporting Person B's contention that Person A is in the wrong or even "full of hate."

When the laws are changed to support the homosexual view that believing or stating the belief that homosexual behavior is morally wrong is "hate speech" or "evil intolerance," what do you think is going to happen to those people who speak out their belief that homosexual behavior is wrong? Do you think they will be treated with tolerance?

When the LGBT "community" and those who support them and call people who oppose their agenda "hateful bigots" get the political power to enforce their view, how do you think those people are going to act towards we who disagree with them? Do you think calm and respectful reason is going to be the path? Do you think "tolerance" is going to characterize their actions towards us? Or do you think that the hatred expressed in their voices as they call us "hateful bigots" might escalate into persecution?

The widespread belief of "tolerance," while sounding good is built on the erroneous foundation of moral or existential relativism. This chapter has demonstrated the error of that widespread belief by showing people who hold to the incorrect definitions of "tolerant" contradict themselves and pronounce self-defeating statements. When people say things that are false - self-defeating or contradictory - those statements ought to be rejected, and reason should be used to find the truth of the matter. Or, at worst, people should civilly agree to disagree.

So, we saw what a truly tolerant person is in this chapter. What about the belief that I need to respect other people's views to be a good person? Let us examine that belief in the next chapter.

Chapter Summary:

- To be a tolerant person, you ought to desire to cause no harm to others, nor desire harm come to them no matter how different they are from you or no matter how much you disagree with their beliefs;

- The genuinely tolerant person will be careful or sensitive in the way they discuss something with the person they disagree with;

- Those who claim to be "tolerant" yet who call others "intolerant" or other negative labels because they don't like their beliefs are contradicting themselves, being hypocritical and thus their claims or judgments that caused them to be hypocritical or contradictory ought to be carefully examined, and usually one will find that reason does not support their judgments.

13
"WE MUST RESPECT OTHER PEOPLE'S BELIEFS" (AT LEAST THOSE WE AGREE WITH!)

Opening Questions:
- What does it mean to respect a person?
- Can I respect beliefs I consider wrong?
- Is it possible to distinguish between a person and their beliefs and respect the person even if I disagree with their views?
- Does redefining terms help clarify things or bring confusion and misunderstanding?

Let us take one last look at another of relativism popular beliefs. It is very much like the "tolerance" belief we just examined in the prior chapter, except it is built on another loaded term "respect."

Here is the "respect" popular belief:

> Each person has their own beliefs, and those beliefs must be respected and not sought to be changed by another person." Stated another way, "since there are no absolute truths, it is disrespectful to judge another person's beliefs as somehow deficient or wrong and thus needing changing or correction.

The above statement contains essentially three premises:

Premise 1. Each person has their own beliefs;

Premise 2. There are no absolute beliefs, meaning there is no unchanging universal standard to judge beliefs as true or false, right or wrong;

Conclusion. Since Premise 2 is true, it is disrespectful to judge another person's beliefs as somehow deficient or wrong and thus needing changing or correction.

Premise one is self-evidently true. (However, it is important to point out that two or more people can share the same beliefs and not have heard it from another person. It is also possible for two or more people to consider the beliefs that they share the most important beliefs to them.)

Premise two is not necessarily true. We will examine this in the following paragraphs.

The Conclusion is not necessarily true.

It is essential that the reader understand that the assumptive statement "since there are no absolute truths" needs to be true for the conclusion of the popular belief to be true - and without premise two being true, the conclusion is false. The "no absolutes" belief is often not spelled out, stated or clearly identified in the popular belief, but is assumed since it serves as the foundation of the popular belief.

Examining the Conclusion

The conclusion of the popular belief statement includes this statement - "it is disrespectful to judge another person's beliefs." So, not only is the conclusion not true if premise two is false, the conclusion itself includes a self-defeating statement even if premise two is true!

A self-defeating statement is one that contradicts itself. For example, "all red rocks are blue" (physical), or, "kind people enjoy hurting others" (moral) are self-defeating statements since within the statement the single subject or point in the statement is contradicted within the statement. In the previous two examples, the only subject or point is the color of all red rocks, and the contradiction to that single point is that red rocks are blue. In the next example, the only subject or point is what kind people enjoy, and the contradiction to that single point is that kind people enjoy hurting others.

As we have seen, the statement, "it is wrong to judge," is a self-defeating statement, for judgment is made with the statement!

As we have seen, the statement, "you are a hateful bigot" when stated by a person who says they are a tolerant person, is a self-defeating statement, for that person is being by their definition intolerant of the person they are condemning as "a hateful bigot."

The statement "it is wrong to judge" is merely a simplified version of, "it is disrespectful to judge another person's beliefs." If a person believes and expresses that "It is acceptable to judge another person's beliefs," then that person is *judged* as intolerant and disrespectful by the person who believes, "it is intolerant and disrespectful to judge another person's beliefs." Do you see the contradiction? When the person who says, "It is intolerant and disrespectful to judge another person's beliefs," judges another person's beliefs as wrong, then by their principle, they are "intolerant and disrespectful"!

The above examples of arguments are proved false by using logic. One of the laws of logic says that if two things/concepts/ideas/beliefs contradict one another when addressing the same subject, and both claim to be true, then at least one is false. These statements demonstrate that principle; "all red rocks are blue" or "it is wrong to judge." In the latter, the subject, "judgment," is said to be wrong or is judged to be wrong. Thus, the statement is false as it contradicts itself.

Let us look at the central issue again from a slightly different perspective to help the reader grasp this critical point.

Consider the statement, "It is wrong to say something is wrong."

This statement uses a synonym for "judge," namely a type of judgment, "wrong-ness," to make clear the false nature of the statement. The statement claims that it is wrong to say something is wrong - a clear contradiction. It is the same type of statement as "It is bad to say (or judge) something is bad." Judgment is the discernment and subsequent declaration of something as right or wrong, good or bad, true or false. The nature of the term "wrong" is undeniably an essential aspect of human judgment and an integral part of human's ability to reason. A person cannot utter a coherent, non-definitional statement containing the word "wrong" (and its associated concept) without making a judgment.

Therefore, the statement, "It is wrong to judge" is a false statement as the statement contradicts itself; for the person uttering, "it is wrong to judge" is himself proclaiming judgment and thus is doing what he says is wrong.

Defining "Respect"

This widespread belief relies heavily on the concept of "respect," for the popular belief says all people must "respect" other people's beliefs. Thus, it is important that the term "respect" be defined and adequately understood.

The people who believe this popular belief define the term "respect" as meaning, "a person should not say anything negative about another person's beliefs nor state that they believe it is false." The concept of "respecting someone's rights" might seem akin to this, but is significantly different for the following reason. A "right" is a legal concept and to respect someone's right to "free speech" for example, means to agree they are allowed to express themselves - it does not address the content of the speech, but rather a person's "freedom" to speak at all no matter what they say.

The widespread belief we are looking at has everything to do with the content or nature of a person's ideas for we are told we must "respect" other's beliefs. In other words, the popular belief is not defending some innate human "right," but rather is attempting to *shut a certain kind of people's expression down, namely, those people who reject relativism and believe there are absolute ethical, moral and existential truths.*

Here are some definitions of "respect" (in the context it is used in the widespread belief) from widely accepted dictionary sources in the United States.

"A feeling of deep admiration for someone or something elicited by their abilities, qualities, or achievements." [41]

"Esteem for or a sense of the worth or excellence of a person, a personal quality or ability, or something considered as a manifestation of a personal quality or ability: Example: "I have great respect for her judgment."" [42]

"Admiration for someone or something that you believe has good ideas or qualities." [43]

All these definitions assume there is a basis for one person respecting another. In other words, these definitions imply that *the first person sees something worthy of respect in the other person.*

For example, if you have never met someone and during your first encounter with the person, the person is doing something you believe is wrong, you are unlikely to "respect" that person. You would not likely say you respect a person if the first time you met them, all they are doing is sitting on a chair. If you did want to make that statement in those circumstances, then this author would suggest what you are saying is, "All humans deserve respect," which statement has a very different meaning than a personal respecting of a person due to their characteristics or behavior.

The attitude of "respect" or state of "respecting" is based on the judgment of the person doing the respecting. Thus, *to "respect" someone means that the basis of that "respect" is valued and thus sought to be emulated, adopted or mimicked by the person doing the respecting;* this would hold true for behavior, traits or beliefs. Thus, if I "respect" someone for their character trait of honesty, then I would like to be honest myself. Or, if I "respect" someone

---

[41] Oxford Living Dictionary, www.en.oxforddictionaries.com, April 2018

[42] www.dictionary.com, April 2018

[43] Cambridge Dictionary, www.dictionary.cambridge.org, April 2018

for exercising each day and thus staying physically fit, I would like to have the discipline to be physically fit. Finally, if I "respect" someone's belief that people with darker skin are valuable humans just like people with lighter skin, then I too will share or adopt that belief.

In the popular statement above, "respect" is re-defined to mean "having no concern for truth or rightness"; or, "not seeking to change another person's beliefs." (A person's beliefs should be "respected," e.g., not sought to be changed.) As we have just seen by the most commonly held definitions of respect, this popular belief re-defines (or uses a minority or uncommon definition) the term "respect" to mean *"it is wrong to judge another person's beliefs as wrong."* This author believes the purpose of the re-definition is to bully the reader into adopting this popular belief since most people want to exhibit respect - or be respectful (an act of humility) - as correctly defined above.

Furthermore, the proper understanding of the concept of "respect" is in contrast to a philosophy which states that "a person is free to believe whatever they like, for whatever they believe is right or true to them." This philosophy is what this widespread belief is advocating, and this philosophy seeks to remove all judgment of good and evil, right and wrong, true and false from the human experience, and thus it is both unreasonable and undeniably false. In other words, reason is removed as a guide to rational thought or behavior to hold to this belief.

It seems to have good intentions - to remove improper judgment of other people not guided by humility or compassion - but unfortunately, it has a false basis. What the belief does is remove all ethical or moral judgment from the human experience as well as force people to reject specific undisputable facts about human nature or even historical events. As we shall see, a person using reason and concerned about right and wrong ought to reject such a belief as VERY harmful to human existence and relationships.

Testing This Popular Belief

Let us first test the popular statement's basic premise using some example statements. Here is a restatement of this widespread belief that we are going to test:

> Each person has their views, and those beliefs must be respected and not sought to be changed by another person. Stated another way, since there are no absolute truths, it is *disrespectful* to judge another person's beliefs as somehow deficient or wrong and thus needing changing or correction.

So, the question is, should the stated beliefs below be "respected"?

Examples:

"I believe that all people with a dark skin color less evolved as people with lighter skin, and thus they are less human and ought to be relegated to some servant status only, for this belief is true and right to me."

"I believe that people who have different religious beliefs than I do are inferior to me, for this belief is true for me."

"I believe that it is good for adult men to sexualize young girls, for this belief (and desired subsequent behavior) is true for me."

"I believe that Christians are all untrustworthy aggressive people who ought to be defeated and subjugated to non-Christian people, for this belief (and desired consequence) is true for me."

"I believe that non-Muslims are all untrustworthy evil people who ought to be defeated and subjugated to Muslim people, for this belief (and desired consequence) is true for me."

"I believe that people who say they believe God exists ought to have their foolish God beliefs removed from their minds to be enlightened by those who have a proper understanding of reality, for this belief is true for me."

"I believe that it is good and right to protect myself (which protection includes harming them) from other people who frighten me due to their differences from me, for this belief is true for me."

"I believe that it is good and right to distrust people who are different from me, and to allow that distrust to become fear and hatred, for this belief is true for me."

"I believe that those who have less material things should forcibly take material resources from those who have more and who will not willingly share, for this belief and behavior is true for me."

"I believe that "non-normal people" (handicapped, retarded, disabled, etc.) are a drain on society and thus ought to be eliminated, for this belief is true to me and ought to be true for everyone."

Given the statements above, how does the "each person has their own beliefs and those beliefs must be respected and not sought to be changed by another person" philosophy hold up to your reasoning? The philosophy sounds good at first glance, but it does not lead to human freedom and true respecting of one another. Rather, it can be (and is) used to justify evil (the unjust harming of people) and opens the door wide for the strong or aggressive to take advantage of those who are weak or vulnerable.

Some would seek to qualify the philosophy of "a person is free to believe in whatever way they like, for whatever they believe is right or true to them" with the premise "as long as what a person believes does not cause harm to others." This harm clause does not fix the fundamental flaw with the belief which flaw is that it begs the question regarding what standard of human behavior to use in the first place. The harm clause cannot overcome the same problem - what standard is used to determine "harm to others'? In other words, who or what is the standard a person turns to in order to know what causes harm to others? Furthermore, is the absence of harming one another an ethic that will produce love for one another? As we shall see, the answer to the latter question is no.

Let us look at some examples to illustrate the fatal flaw in the "harm clause" proposition.

Is it harmful to people to serve or sell food or consumptive items that are known to be harmful to people?

'I believe that it is good that I can profit off of selling food (or tobacco) that is proved to contain harmful elements to other people, for this belief is true for me.'

Is it harmful to a woman who "willingly" performs sexual acts in front of a camera to make money "harmful" to anyone? What standard do you use to make that judgment?

"I believe that it is good for women to believe and be trained that they should be used for sexual pleasure by men, and to earn income for such a belief and associated activities, for this belief is true for me."

Is it harmful to children to be allowed or led by their parents to play-act or enjoy violence?

"I believe that it is fine for parents to allow their children to play video games that involve explicit, unjustified, personal and gratuitous violence, and which games promote and glorify violent behavior, for this belief is true for me."

Or, "I believe that it is good for children to learn to enjoy perpetrating violence by partaking in virtual violence and thus training their minds as such, for this belief is true for me."

Is it harmful to people to believe and thus practice that using a powerful narcotic is an excellent way to "relax" or to worship God?

"I believe that it is good for me to use LSD (or whatever the latest drug is) to connect with my god, for this belief is true for me, and I am not harming anyone."

Is it harmful to one group of people to raid a neighboring group, and to take their women and children for slaves for their group?

"'I believe that un-contacted tribes in the Amazon basin have a right to be free of all outside influence due to evolutionary principles and relativism; which leads me to believe that all their behavior is right for them (which tribes do in fact forcibly take

women and children as slaves from neighboring tribes), for this
belief is right for me."

Is it harmful to one person to see another person being harmed, and
yet do nothing about it?

"I believe that I should have done nothing today when I saw
the old man in the trench coat reveal himself to the little girl in the
park because this belief is right for me."; or,

"I am free to believe that I did not have to do anything to help
the person lying on the street bleeding today - I don't owe them
anything, and they might sue me if I do something wrong - because
this belief is right for me and I am not harming anyone."

Is it harmful to one person to see another person being verbally
abused, and yet do nothing about it?

"I believe that I am not responsible for helping that young girl
I saw crying today due to being yelled at and called all kinds of
terrible things by her dad – she needs to deal with that herself, its
none of my business – for this belief is right for me and I am not
harming anyone".

Is suicide harmful to others?

"I believe as a hopeless young person that I can kill myself, and
I know that I am not harming others when I do so, for this belief is
good and right for me."

The above examples demonstrate the erroneous nature of the "as long
as it causes no harm to others" clause. If each person determines what is
"true and right" for them, and their definition of "harm to others" if
different than another person's (which is a reasonable assumption), then
some people will be viewed by others as harming other people. What then?
What happens when others see one person as hurting another person or
allowing harm to come to another person? Which side will the referee take?
What is the referee's standard to make such judgments for that matter?!

What is the right action to take? Without any standard of right and
wrong beliefs and behavior, who is to say what is right and wrong? Indeed,
if you follow this philosophy consistently, it has and will lead to destructive
human conflict within any given human group (or among groups). This
philosophy will lead to the physically stronger dominating and using the
weaker persons as their slaves - in other words, human history.

Let us take another look at this widespread belief in light of the
relativism doctrine.

"Each person has their own beliefs, and those beliefs must be
respected and not sought to be changed by another person. Stated
another way, since there are no absolute truths, it is disrespectful to

judge another person's beliefs as somehow deficient or wrong and thus needing changing or correction."

As you can see, this widespread belief is merely a slightly different wording for expressing relativism. This widespread belief goes a step further than just stating relativism, however, and seeks to defend relativism by providing "ought not's."

As we have seen, this is a self-defeating exercise since relativists state there are no "ought's" (no universal moral standard by which to judge right and wrong for human beliefs or behavior), so how can there be "ought not's"?

This widespread belief piggy-backs quite closely with relativism since it promotes the following idea: That a person should not be pressured to hold a different moral or existential belief or adopt behavior that they did not hold before the person desiring to use reason to examine their belief approached them. Trying to convince someone that a view is better than what they currently hold would be wrong since there are no universal truths that apply to all human beings. This author has used reasoned arguments to demonstrate that this belief is false - it is self-defeating or self-contradictory. Thus, this widespread belief ought to be rejected and a better understanding adopted.

Let's wrap up our examination of relativism and the popular beliefs it is built on in the next chapter. In so doing, we will help the reader be able to see more clearly, and thus be in a better position to judge whether Christianity is indeed a successful failure.

Chapter Summary:
- To "respect" someone means to esteem or honor *their person or their character*, not one or more of their beliefs;
- The term "respect" has been redefined to mean "agree with someone's belief or view or perspective or position." The term's meaning has been shifted away from a view of one's person or character or behavior, to a view of a person's beliefs;
- This redefinition is harmful and is contributing greatly to the strife that exists in the U.S. culture at this time;
- We should not "respect" a person's wrong view of something, but we should respect a person if they have good character even if they hold a wrong view or a belief we disagree with unless that view or understanding is immoral or unethical according to Joshua.

14
TRUTH OR ETHICAL RELATIVISM IS FALSE AND DESTRUCTIVE

Opening Questions:
- If everything is relative, is the premise "everything is relative" absolutely true?
- If you judge me as a bad person, are you judgmental?
- If you don't like my view on homosexuality, for example, and thus have hatred towards me and judge me as a bad person, are you tolerant of me and my view?
- Do you respect my belief those women who put their young children into daycare instead of caring for them themselves because they want more money or love money or material things more than their children?

Relativism as a guiding belief applied to human morality, ethics or existentialism (and by extension its derived popular beliefs) says that there are no absolute truths that apply to collective humanity. When a person who holds that view declares a foul by stating a person "ought not" believe or behave in a certain manner, they are stating a contradiction according to the laws of logic. A consistent relativist contradicts themselves when they say to another person, "you should not believe that" or, "you ought not to do that." If asked "why not?" a relativist who answers with anything other than, "because I say so" (and thus identify themselves as The Standard) will contradict themselves.

Some will counter, "I am not saying I am the standard, but this expert person I like with all those credentials should be The Standard." This is a bit better than each person being their standard, but it just shifts the problem back a bit. In other words, for each belief and person who claims to be some authority or expert, there is another with equal credentials with the opposing view. Think the "social issues" beliefs of the two political parties and their leaders in the U.S. Or think the divided world religions. The unnecessary division and contention over inferior standards are precisely why human beings need a standard higher than ourselves to guide us.

Unfortunately, those who have either chosen or ebbed into a relativistic mindset are bound to utter contradictory and hypocritical statements. *As we have seen above in three of the primary guiding relativistic beliefs, all those who hold to the popular views of judgmentalism, tolerance, and respect, are much like robots with a bad piece of code and thus stuck in an erroneous loop…they cannot help but contradict themselves and act hypocritically.*

In the religious realm, relativists will frequently offer the "you are too dogmatic" defense, which means they are offended when their relativistic hypocrisy is exposed. To the Christian religious relativists who have made up their own "jesus" to fit their beliefs, I offer this:

> I am the way, and the truth, and the life; and no one comes to the Father but through me. (John 14:6)

…and I recommend you take your offense at absolutism (what you often call "dogmatism") up with the One who said that. We will take a closer look at religious relativism later.

From a slightly different perspective, any statement of the nature of judgment such as "that is wrong" by a person who claims to hold or believe the popular beliefs (or its parent, truth or existential relativism) is a self-defeating statement. Since this is true, people who make self-defeating statements and who practice hypocrisy ought to abandon the belief that puts them in that position in favor of the idea which will not. Put plainly, absolute truth does exist and to reject that truth is to deny reality, short circuit your operating system and thus make you irrational to some degree.

Conclusions Regarding Relativism:

So, we have looked at existential relativism and ethical relativism and have found it lacking and not able to stand the test of reason and logic. We have looked at three of the most common erroneous beliefs that many people believe – that all judgments about other people are wrong; that it is wrong and intolerant to criticize any people group or individual's behavior choices, and that to respect someone means to accept (or not correct) anything/everything they believe.

Existential and ethical relativism is the core worldview that is driving people to practice hypocrisy, and to use force and violence to get *their* way. When a person leaves or never had an absolutist worldview – absolutist meaning certain behaviors are right and wrong in all cultures and all times, and that there is some standard higher than human beings – they will typically hold a relativistic worldview. The only thing holding back relativists from chaos and ruin is the human conscience, which conscience the Designer and Source of Good and Right human ethics gave us.

This very truth is playing itself out right now in the U.S.A. Those who self-identify as the "left" or "progressives" or "liberals" are generally those who are existential or ethical relativists, and some of those people who, when they don't get their way, are resorting to force and violence and trying to shut down free speech. They are trapped in blindness and hypocrisy because they cannot see that they break their own stated beliefs of non-judge-mentalism, tolerance, and respect when force and violence are used against those with whom they disagree. They are unable to see that they are little tyrants or "fascists," the very thing they often accuse others of being. Their worldview typically leads to only one place – anarchy.

Definition: Anarchy

- "Absence or denial of any authority or established order" [44]
- "A state of disorder due to absence or non-recognition of authority or other controlling systems." [45]

Existential and Ethical relativism will be the belief or worldview that will justify those people who are destroying the United States. One of the logical conclusions of ethical relativists is that anarchy is better than "evil authority" since they believe all authority is wrong or evil because "who is another person to tell me what is right or wrong or suggest what I should do"? Since there is no higher right or wrong for the relativist except for what they believe, it is an insult to them when another person says, "no, you are wrong, there is absolute right and wrong, and we can know it and practice it." This insult is created by self-pride and leads nowhere good.

Remember, a characteristic of existential or ethical relativism is the belief that there is NO right or wrong *except* for what an individual perceives. So, if there are no transcendent moral truths for all people, then no one has a right to "force" anyone to live by any rules or ethics. Instead, those people who come across each other and happen to hold the same beliefs will flock together to get THEIR WAY, certain that they are doing the right thing since the other's they have flocked with will validate that their individual belief is good and right. Their individual belief that they share with another individual did not come from any higher place or

---

[44] Merriam-Webster Dictionary, www.merriam-webster.com, May 2018

[45] Oxford Living Dictionary, www.en.oxforddictionaries.com, May 2018

absolute reality – it is just chance that those individual's arrived at the same belief. *This belief is the irrational denial of the both the Source of the human conscience as well as The Light given to humankind.* Destructive tribalism is just around the corner.

There is absolutely a spiritual component to this problem, and that component is the turning away from either an ethical standard or one's conscience as a moral compass, to perpetuate what one believes is necessary to get their way. This rejection of traditional ethical standards or one's conscience includes using violence to get what you feel is good and right. Indeed, the principle of "the ends justify the means" is a significant belief used by existential relativists. So, for example, and in the political realm, since Mr. Trump its viewed as evil due either his poor character or the beliefs he holds that impact public policy, the existential relativists will believe that using violence is a legitimate means to end the rule of Trump. The end – no longer having a ruler who is offensive to them – will be justified by the use of violence as the means to achieve that end.

The principle of "for the greater good" is also used by existential or ethical relativists to get their way. It is essentially a slightly different version of "the ends justify the means." So, again, to use the political realm as an example, those who disagree with Mr. Trump's views will believe that violence is a legitimate means to achieve the greater good, which is the U.S.A. without a ruler whose "right and wrong views" are offensive to the relativists. Please note this is in no way an endorsement of Mr. Trump, his character, or his immoral beliefs or behavior. Rather, it is merely pointing out the difference between an ethical absolutist (Mr. Trump and "conservatives') and ethical relativists who typically self-identify with "the left" or "liberal" or "progressive" labels.

In sum, existential or ethical relativism will always lead to conflict, anarchy, destruction, and the absolute rule of the human cage of self-pride, fear, and selfishness. And when anarchy happens, then it is only a matter of time before a single ruler – the strongest or most powerful person – will end up ruling.

There are other dominant false and deceitful beliefs and practices out in the culture besides relativism, which lead many people astray. One of those ways to get people to think wrongly is to redefine language. We will examine that practice in the next chapter. In so doing, we will remove another obstacle to people seeing whether Christianity is a successful failure or not.

Chapter Summary:
- Truth or ethical relativism is an erroneous worldview;

- We were designed to acknowledge and think using absolute things/concepts in the domain of human behavior and in the reality in which we exist on this earth;
- Human beings are NOT a trustworthy source of ethics—we need Someone Greater than ourselves;
- Ethical or Truth Relativism will always lead to anarchy, suffering, and destruction due to the deeply flawed human nature we possess.

15
REDEFINING LANGUAGE

Opening Questions:
- How well can people communicate if they have different understandings of the same words?
- If two or more people disagree with the meaning of words in their language, is it likely they will reach unity on matters to which those words pertain?
- If essential and valuable terms are redefined to something different, less essential, less valuable, or even false, then isn't something important lost?

So, we have made the proposition that reason and logic are being put aside and emotionalism is taking their place. Furthermore, we have taken a brief look at relativism and a few of the more popular beliefs based on relativism. Those beliefs have been shown to be erroneous using reason and logic as our tools to evaluate what is true versus what is false. There is a strong correlation between emotionalism (putting reason aside) and the rise and popularity of a relativistic worldview. Not believing that objective truth can be known will push people towards emotionalism. With standards gone and using reason on the wane, what sense is there in trying to make sense? That which will rule is, "I feel that is right" or "I feel that is wrong," and that marks the beginning of the end of unity for any group of people.

Additionally, we just saw how the term "respect" has been redefined or its previous commonly understood meaning has been shifted to mean something different, and that different meaning has serious negative consequences. That fact is a good lead into this chapter.

Another way to befuddle reason or to try and destroy truth is by redefining language. Language is critical in communicating and understanding concepts or each other. The importance of sharing a language is most evident when two people who don't speak the same language try and communicate. Usually, body language, facial gesturing, and pointing are used to communicate. Anyone who has tried to describe something more complicated to a person who does not speak the same language knows how difficult it is to communicate in a deep, precise, detailed manner.

What if a group of people believed that each person must decide what a particular noun means (that the meanings of the nouns in that culture's dictionary are incorrect)? In other words, they agreed on a basic vocabulary regarding the word's existence, spelling, and pronunciation, but left the definition of the words up to the individual. How well could that group communicate? If a group of people turned away from a common standard for knowing the meaning of nouns, then would not confusion and chaos result? Imagine this grocery store scene, "Excuse me, sir, could you please tell me where the apples are?" the worker answers, "well, what do you mean by 'sir' and 'apples'?"

Language is not inflexibly permanent. In other words, language can change over time, and new words are added, and old terms let go. However, even though language is more pliable than stone, it still needs to be consistent for it to work as a means of clear communication. Nouns and verbs need to be stable in their meaning and not change based on an individual's whim or a culture's fad.

When terms are re-defined, then language loses its ability to communicate concepts clearly. A recent sub-cultural example of this was the use of the word "bad" to mean "good." That is about as confusing as it gets!

Many terms have multiple definitions, but the primary meaning is usually stable and consistent over time in any given language and culture/society. If you look at dictionaries for the English language published in the last one-hundred years, you can validate this truth.

A valid question is who is the Keeper of the Standard for what terms mean? Typically, this has been a collaborative endeavor by the people who publish dictionaries. No single person is appointed as "The Keeper of English Nouns" for example! However, and concerning English, some terms have older origins than others. When a new word is created, it is called "coining" a term. Many new words have been created over the past half a century particularly in areas of growing knowledge like technology and science. However, terms that describe basic human existence and relationships have not changed significantly over time. This is so *because human life and the ways people relate to one another have not changed over time.*

So, let's look at a few more important terms and their associated concepts—to define them properly versus how the popular culture defines them.

False Cultural Definitions of "Love":
- An emotional bonding or infatuation with a person whom you want in some way, usually to have for yourself often to fill insecurity needs, e.g. "I want you to be my girlfriend/boyfriend…"
- Romantic feelings towards another person; e.g. "I love you and want you to be my spouse/partner…"
- To like or have a strong affinity for something; e.g. "I love ice cream."
- Sexual expressions: e.g. "Let's make love."

The Proper Definition of Love:
- To value someone at least as much as one's self, and to behave selflessly towards them based on having compassion for them and thus help them in every good and right way possible and to want to share life with them as friends.

False Cultural Definition of Faith:
- A religion or a person's religion
- A pie-in-the-sky, highly unlikely hope

Proper Definition of Faith:
- A simple, core level existential trust or confidence in something or someone;
  - In the case of God-beliefs, the above definition has the additional component of trust or confidence in someone or something *you cannot see or validate with your senses.*

False Cultural Definition of the Church:
- The religious building that people go to for their religious "services."
- The programs, services, and staff of the religious organization.
- The people who participate in and support the religious organizations which take some Christian label – or who profess or identify with one of the many "christs" and sects of Christianity or the God of their parents.

Proper Definition of the Church:
- The collective followers of Jesus of Nazareth especially as *they live together and share his Life together in daily life in one location*; the called out ones who don't value or pursue many of the things the people of the society or nation they are in says are valuable or important.

False Cultural Definition of Community:
- People in close proximity; people living in the same housing development; people who live within a smaller geopolitical entity like a town or village.
- People who self-identify the same way even while they might not know each other or encounter one another or communicate with one another, e.g., the LGBT community.

Proper Definition of Community:
- Derived from the root term, "Commune";
- People living communally, meaning sharing their resources and participating in each other's daily lives to support one another, help one another, and join in the work required to support those in the community;
- People holding shared, significant common beliefs (often political or religious views) that come together and are unified in sharing life together.

False Cultural Definition of Peace:
- Lack of outward conflict, e.g. "the middle east peace process."

Proper Definition of Peace:
- Internal lack of conflict or stress manifesting calm with no animosity or ill intentions towards other people.

False Cultural Definition of Marriage:
- The legal joining together of any two adults to gain material benefits or "rights" or privileges typically from a government as well as a legally-based acceptance or approval of that relationship from the society or their natural relatives.

Proper Definition of Marriage:
- The joining of a man and woman together as complementary life partners and a concept that provides a commitment to the having and raising of children and the best model to accomplish that vital responsibility.

False Cultural definition of Gender:

- A fluid, vague, non-specific, unstable, confused view of male-ness and female-ness no longer associated with the actual physiological anatomy of the person—determined by personal emotions instead of physiological aspects and character traits, and subject to change.

Proper Definition of Gender:

- Male-ness associated with males (those with male anatomy) and having masculine character traits, and female-ness associated with females (those with female anatomy) and having feminine character traits.

The above definitions are just a small sampling of the redefining of vital, significant and meaningful terms. As you can see, essential terms have already been redefined, and the critical, proper definitions and concepts of those terms have been mostly lost or destroyed, often by relativists who drive political correctness and desire to force others to their irrational worldview.

Another "great" way to hide wrong motives or to destroy simple truth is to use complex concepts or processes to do so. The next chapter will examine that practice in the culture at large and then again in the religious sub-cultures in a later chapter.

Chapter Summary:

- Having a common language is critical and necessary for people to communicate ideas, concepts, and needs successfully. Having a standard and stable definition of nouns is crucial for having a stable and consistent common language which is critical for good communication and to have any hope for unity on critical human relationship matters;
- Words or terms are being redefined due to relativism and people moving away from a shared understanding of reality or a universal shared ethic;
- Through redefining terms, essential ideas are being destroyed or lost, and worst of all, the most important concept of all - love - has been more or less destroyed as we shall see.

TIM SPIESS

16
HIDING IN COMPLEXITY

Opening Questions:
- Do you like it when things are so complicated it is difficult to understand?
- Can complexity be used to hide things?
- If you cannot understand something in an area you believe you have a need, will you not be dependent on others to get your need met?
- Why are so many human service domains complex – domains like legal or financial?
- Do most things regarding human relationships or services need to be complicated?

In addition to redefining language terms, another way truth is hidden away, concealed, obscured, corrupted or destroyed, is through complexity. Let's use an illustration to help the reader understand.

Once there was a young boy, six years old. His dad would regularly play building blocks with his son. They would build all kinds of interesting block structures, and when done, they would usually knock the buildings down. The boy knew from experience that he and his dad built the block buildings. Now the boy's dad often had to go away on business, and he would fly on planes to travel. One day, the dad said to his young six year old son, "Son, did you know that when we are flying at Mach 1.5 up at 10,668 meters; and when we fly above the arctic circle where the Aroura Borealis often

130

occur; that if you leave a pile of blocks on the plane's floor during the night; that when you wake up the pile of blocks will have formed itself into a structure hexagonal structure?" The boy is likely to say, "Really dad, wow, that is so cool."

What the dad did was to interject factors – or complexities - into his story that the boy could not understand or did not experience. This same dynamic is what the world uses to push their selfish falsehoods and lies.

When a person starts speaking to another person about things they do not or cannot understand or have not experienced that speaker can then lead that person where they want him/her to go.

Human life, meaning people interacting or communicating with one another, is only complicated because people try to make it that way to hide things and get things. Complexity is often used by people with greater intellectual ability to gain control or power over those with less mental capacity. Or, people on about the same intellectual level can make a matter complicated to deceive or take advantage of others.

An individual can also use complexity to avoid responsibility. If I want to hide something about myself – perhaps laziness or selfishness - I can claim that something is too complicated for me to understand so I can be less responsible or not perform a task I don't want to.

Simplicity reveals things or makes things easy to understand.

Complexity hides things or makes things difficult to understand.

Most people can speak in simple, clear terms.

Indeed, if a person has the intellect and articulation skills to make something they claim to understand complex, then they certainly can make something they claim to understand simple and clear.

This complexity dynamic is no more evident than in discussions between atheists and people who believe God exists or theists. It is as simple as acknowledging that an automobile or space shuttle – examples of relatively complicated inorganic machines created by people – require a designer or designers to account for their existence. The simple truth is that the human body - as an example of a complex organic machine – makes the space shuttle look like a poorly designed child's toy. Nothing more needs to be said, and yet the non-theists will write many large books that they claim represent "real science" to try and disprove that simple, self-evident truth…that complex physical machines defined as including inter-dependent subsystems - whether inorganic or organic - require a thoughtful designer to account for their existence.

So, whether a person is looking for knowledge in the area of origins of life or more mundane matters like health or taxes or finding good work or a myriad of other areas of human life, simplicity is almost always the selfless route and complexity is often used for selfish purposes. Sadly, the very goal of many people is to make things complicated to hide the selfish motivations behind their elaborate designs.

Of course, some things are natively or naturally complicated. Some kinds of science (some of the ways and aspects of the physical nature of our fantastic biology, for example), as well as advanced mathematics (rocket science for example), are examples of realms of knowledge that can have complex concepts. *However, this chapter and its context are all about human relationships and a basic understanding of our existence and purpose, NOT science or mathematics or physical things!*

Good communicators take more complex concepts and simplify them so that more people can understand the idea. Their desire for the listeners to grasp the idea is a significant part of what makes them "good" communicators. Bad communicators don't care about making things simple; rather they care about getting what they want out of their communication or making themselves look "smart."

Many people like using complex communications to control people or get something from people. Using complicated communication accomplishes two purposes. First, it makes them look "smarter" than the people who cannot understand them. Second, it makes the people dependent upon them to understand the concept *for* them. People who hire lawyers or psychologists or doctors or investment experts or tax experts do so for help because they either cannot or do not want to try and understand the complex concepts that those domains contain. Thus, they trust the "expert" who claims to understand the domain for which they claim to be experts.

- Laws do *not* have to be complicated.
- Human nature is *not* complicated.
- Tax codes do *not* have to be so involved.
- Physicians could communicate essential concepts to customers (they like to call us "patients", but we are just customers to most physicians) without using advanced medical terminology *if* they wanted to. Investing in some business does *not* need to be a complicated endeavor.

So the question is why are they? Why are the laws/rules so complex? Why do lawyers or psychologists or medical people speak a language only they understand? Why won't medical people communicate well? Why do the tax laws have to be so complicated? Finally, why does theology have to be so complicated?

The answer is simple – *because those who want power over others, or who want something from others, benefit from complexity so they can get people to rely on them and thus exercise control over them and take things from them (usually money).* The goal is to be able to say some form of this statement, *"Oh, dear person, this is so complex, so you need to rely on me and pay me to handle it for you.*" (And don't forget the lie, "because I care about you.")

This selfish manipulation is one of the primary ways of the world.

- Taking, not giving.
- Hiding, not openness.
- Complexity, not simplicity.
- Selfishness, not selflessness.

Don't forget about the new and popular term "transparency" and the ridiculous hypocrisy practiced by many who use the term. Many people in business and government like to claim they want "transparency," supposedly meaning they want openness and honesty. For most leaders, the term is merely used to manipulate people and fool them into believing the leadership wants transparency. However, business as usual means that power and control are often held onto through secretive, purposely vague and sophisticated communications.

It is a primary manifestation of the darkness of people…a darkness rooted in taking advantage of others—of self-pride thinking that only I know what is good and right for people—and of the lovelessness that selfishness motivates.

Knowledge is a form of "light." It is the opposite of ignorance, which is a form of darkness. One primary goal of every human beings life ought to be to grow in knowledge and thus decrease in ignorance. Sadly, the world works very hard fighting this process and using complexity is one of their means of fighting.

There are three primary ways that people use complexity to take from others. First, is advanced or specialized vocabulary. Second, is using many more words than are necessary to bring a point across. Third is the speed of delivery of communication.

Lawyers, psychologists, medical people, scientists, financial people and religious people are just some of the domains of knowledge and types of people who use advanced vocabulary to snow or deceive other people. This is not to say that some advanced vocabulary is not valid and useful. However, when communicating with someone unfamiliar with that vocabulary, it is only decent and thoughtful to use more straightforward or common language to convey the concepts the advanced vocabulary represent…—very rarely is that impossible to do.

Using many words to obfuscate or hide or cloud a concept is another way that people use complexity to conceal something. This is especially true in the legal, psychological, political and religious fields. If I want to disguise a contradiction; an ugly truth I don't want to admit, or I don't want someone else to see; or an unpopular or irrational idea or policy I want people to accept; all I need is complex vocabulary or a few hundred or thousand words to do so.

Religious leaders and a variety of religious leader called "apologists," specialize in using complexity to avoid certain falsehoods upon which Christianity is built. In fact, they have the unenviable job of defending Christianity's falsehoods. I just ran across a great example of using many words to attempt to hide a contradiction – and the implications of that on one's "theology" – he is unwilling to accept. A popular apologist Ravi Zacharias has an article in which he attempts to defend the falsehood that God is both all-powerful and perfectly loving.

If you want a great example of a person using complexity to try and avoid a truth they do not wish to accede, then Mr. Zacharias' article is a prime example. Mr. Zacharias uses about 8,500 words to attempt to avoid the simple truth of a syllogism or argument of 33 words! The article is/was posted on the web at http://rzim.org/just-thinking/why-suffering-the-question/, and it is entitled, "Why Suffering." Mr. Zacharias puts forth many dozens of irrelevant arguments, as well as committing several logical fallacies, all because he refuses to let go of religious dogma that he cherishes and has committed himself to defending. Why does a smart man like Mr. Zacharias do this? Well, if Mr. Zacharias varies from Christianity's cherished beliefs – if he refutes "orthodox" dogma - will he have a "successful ministry" and the influence and money that go along with that?

Psychologists are just substitutes for good and wise friends. Just like prostitutes sell sex, psychologists sell friendship or "caring." Another accurate way to view psychologists and psychiatrists is as replacements for religious leaders. They are the secular priest class who are only too happy to have broken free from the religious, "please provide a donation" model, to the "you must pay fee per hour" model! Since most psychologists reject important aspects of human nature as given by the Creator, they are only too happy to make up their complicated views of human nature and to have customers come and pay them for their opinions. They have huge books that grow every year which they fill with new disorders, syndromes and other sundry and largely imagined mental maladies. They are the ultimate "put a label on people" people. Instead of saying a thought or behavior is wrong, sinful or harmful and should cease, they instead give it a name and provide a "therapy solution" involving many paid visits or drugs. They are only too happy to keep building the complexity because that has a direct impact on their ability to earn money.

Lawyers make the laws and rules complex, so people are dependent upon them to understand something or to get something done in the legal domain. This author has tried to go "Pro se" in a legal matter, and I could not even make it to the playing field. In other words, not only is legal language complex, and not only are the law's complex, but the process to contest a matter in a court of law is complicated. Lawyers are genuinely the worst when it comes to taking from others and using complexity to hide their motives. For this reason, Joshua of Nazareth singled out only two "vocations" or "professions" for rebuke - lawyers and religious leaders.

The Light of the world had this to say about lawyers:

> But He said, "Woe to you lawyers as well! For you weigh men down with burdens hard to bear, while you yourselves will not even touch the burdens with one of your fingers." and, "Woe to you lawyers! For you have taken away the key of knowledge; you yourselves did not enter, and you hindered those who were entering. (Luke 11:46, 52)

As you can see from his sayings from about 2,000 years ago, *nothing* has changed. Lawyers, in general, are not willing to help their clients in a truly selfless way—they are *not* going to risk their "career" (code for the ability to make money) or even a bit of their own money to take a stand for their client. And lawyers – all of them participate in this in some degree – take the away the key of knowledge, which is *simplicity* or the simple truth. As such, they do not enter the Kingdom of God, and they seek to prevent others from entering, just like their religious leader brethren.

> Truly I say to you, unless you are converted and become like children, you will not enter the kingdom of heaven. Truly I say to you, whoever does not receive the kingdom of God like a child will not enter it. (Matt. 18:3; Mark 10:15)

Dear reader, children operate in the mode of clear and pure and innocent, unless they have adults who are training them against those good things.

The same is true of other "professions" or domains, but to a lesser extent than legal. As we have seen, the psychological counseling profession is built on complex concepts of human nature which only the self-serving psychologists can understand. People who are lost and thus are hurting themselves or others go to these people for help, and what they generally get is nothing valuable, only the opinions of the new priests who usually go in circles as much as is possible to bill more.

The medical profession is made highly complicated, and physicians use complex language or concepts often to help justify a procedure that will gain them a good bit of money. It is easy to use complicated medical vocabulary or concepts when talking to a patient to push them towards a procedure they may not need. And how about the billing process! Talk about complex! All that complexity makes it easy to hide one's greed-based actions. Complexity also makes it easier to cheat since it is much harder to catch.

The financial and insurance industries are quite complex. It is human nature to want to be a person who understands something better than the other person for then I have power over them...they are dependent upon me to get something they consider valuable. Once people are dependent upon me, I can now either exert control over them or take money or other resources from them. How much money is in the law, medical, financial and insurance industries? *It is not a random associative fact that the businesses or human service industries with the most money are some of the most complex in nature.* In manufacturing and engineering, for example, one cannot hide results or failure in complexity, for they are self-evident when the physical process does not work or the bridge fails, for example.

Government policies are often complicated. Think tax laws or health care laws. Typically government regulations, rules or policies are created or written by lawyers or assisted by people in the industries that are subject to the laws, like legal or medical, etc. Sadly, most legislators at the U.S. federal level are lawyers at this point, thus accounting for the failure of government. It is no surprise that the laws and rules and policies are so complex since the people who wrote them or guided their creation are "experts" in those domains and thus gain from complexity. For example, how many people make money for assisting with tax filings? And who makes money from that endeavor? Often, the same people who wrote or helped shape the complex laws or rules or policies that people now need help navigating.

So, to boil down the service business (lawyers, psychologists, physicians and other medical specialists, financial and investment advisors, etc.) general mode of operation, it is this—*'you believe you need some information from me that I understand and you don't, so you will need to pay me or give me something to get it'.*

We cannot forget scientists, especially "scientists" who do not use empirical methods to defend their "facts," particularly "facts" that happened long ago that cannot be validated by empirical means or that go against current natural law or physics.

There is no doubt that as a scientist delves into their specialty and they learn and apply more and more detail to their work and understanding, that they develop new words or more advanced vocabularies to express the facts/things they encounter. However, a good communicator will have no problem not getting bogged down in details and thus explaining a process or aspect of the science they are working on in a generally consumable manner. And yet, some scientists and most scientists-so-called (those dealing with origin speculations in particular) regularly communicate in a sophisticated way, thus making it easy to hide inconsistencies, contradictions, non-plausible hypothesis or false or questionable or untestable assumptions.

Concealing contradictions or false things is also true of the spiritual realm. Religious leaders are very much like their lawyer brethren in that they want their theologies to be elaborate so that people will be dependent upon them to understand God, a paramount concern for many people. How many large theological books exist and have been written - undoubtedly many thousands, and probably tens of thousands? So, when a person asks the simple question, "How can I know God?', the religious person responds with some variation of, "well, I have a degree from Great Seminary and have studied the bible extensively and have read many hundreds of books about God, so I am best qualified to tell you about God."

So, the first line of complexity is the source documents. The bible is a large and complicated book. Have you ever seen or read the Roman Catholic catechism? It is large and complicated. The same is generally true of most of religion's primary "sacred" documents. Add to the major or base documents, new "revelations" like Joseph Smith's work the book of Mormon, or things like The Urania Book and you pile the complexity higher and higher. Those piles of books have one purpose, and that is to hide some essential and simple truths and thus be used by religious leaders to get something from you, namely power over you or money from you.

Religious leaders have taken complexity a step further, for they have an advantage that people in other domains don't have. Many God claims cannot be verified, which means that you can make something not only complicated but contradictory and ask that people believe it because our senses cannot validate it! (Of course, this only works when people are not able or willing to use reason, logic or observation well or they are unwilling to value reason as the means to understand God-stuff.)

It should be interesting to the reader that the religious leaders of the thousands of Christian and Bible-based sects have just such a belief as their top belief. With all of their division, they agree on this belief! They say that the people must believe this inherently contradictory concept to avoid going to hell! They place this belief at the top of their doctrinal membership statements and have given it a catchy name, the Trinity.

The trinity has been a fundamental belief of the Christian system for many hundreds of years. The doctrine states that God is one God yet three Persons.

The trinity concept is very simple regarding its nature. It is religious leaders - who want to control or influence people and who want an "easy living" – creating something complicated and using religious fear and irrational claims to make people dependent upon them and willing to support them.

Here is how it works. People are afraid of God due to religious leaders preaching God's wrath and vengeance and justice, etc. to people over the millennia, as well as people, feeling guilty over their sins due to the conscience God gave us. So, people search for answers about God - what He is like and what He wants - and so they go to people who claim to be experts on God. These "experts" say that God is a just God and does send people to hell. The people then turn to the religious leaders and ask, "Well, what does God want from me to avoid hell?" And the religious leaders say some form of, "you need to listen to us to understand God, and what He wants and you need to support our organization (really pay me)."

So, the first question many people ask is, "what is God like"? And the religious leaders, liking people looking to them to understand God say, "Well, the first thing you must know is that he is a trinity being." The religious leaders know at some level, that if the people figure out who God is and what He is like, they will no longer be needed. So, they invented and promote this belief of "the trinity," *and* they say you *must* believe in this "trinity" to avoid hell. They tell the people that the trinity god is three persons but one god. Or, stated more simply, that three equals one. So, they have communicated a contradiction to the people and told the people that they must "believe" this contradiction or else they will go to hell. And they tell the people that while they don't fully understand the trinity, they do have a better understanding of it/him than "the laymen," so you better listen to them.

Trap accomplished.

So, Christian leaders accomplish a significant step in making people dependent upon them by having what they claim is an essential belief, a complex (actually contradictory) belief about God. Having people dependent upon the religious leader is a massive step in hiding the Light.

(For more on the trinity doctrine, see *Appendix 5, The Trinity Trap*.)

In addition to the trinity, here are some of the more complicated theological concepts that religious leaders like to rely on to make things complicated to hide the Light and have the people dependent upon them.
Atonement:
"The action of making amends for a wrong or injury." [46]
Vicarious:
"Experienced in the imagination through the feelings or actions of another person." [46]
Propitiation:
"The action of propitiating or appeasing a god, spirit, or person." [46]
These three concepts – two taken from the Hebrew scripture, Atonement, and Propitiation; and one borrowed by Christian theologians,

---

[46] Oxford Living Dictionary, www.en.oxforddictionaries.com, April 2018

Vicarious; together make the heart and soul of the Christian salvation concept. Here is an accurate statement of that concept:

"Vicarious atonement is the idea that Jesus Christ took the place of humankind, suffering the penalty for sin. Atonement is a term meaning "reconciliation" or "amends." Vicarious means "done in place of or instead of someone else." So, in literal terms, the Christian concept of "vicarious atonement" is that Jesus was substituted for humanity and punished for our faults to pay for the sins we had committed and reconcile us to God. Vicarious atonement is also referred to as "substitutionary atonement" or "penal substitution." [47]

In a nutshell, a wrathful, vengeful god will not forgive people who sincerely ask him but instead demanded that an innocent person – his beloved and obedient Son – be tortured and killed to "pay" for the wrong-doings of guilty people so that God can forgive people. Please note that *none* of those concepts are taught by Joshua of Nazareth, as we shall see later.

In summary, when you hear someone say, "Oh, that is complicated" regarding a people problem (that is relationships among people; how our behavior ought to be; how people ought to act; what people value or moral truths) or some God issue, a little red flag ought to go up in your mind. That red flag should point you to think, "This person is confused or likely hiding something they don't want to admit or face, or they are trying to get something from me." Then, apply reason well to the problem they say is "complicated" and if you do, you will be rewarded with the truth! You may not like what the truth reveals, but it is much better to live in reality than in a delusion.

Another way people stay away from that which is correct is to adopt philosophies which gloss over what is real and promote their favorite delusion. This practice can be appropriately described as adopting or holding "positive thinking" philosophies. Versions of those philosophies are trendy in both religious and "secular" cultures, and we will take a look at those in the next chapter.

Chapter Summary:
- Creating or using complicated concepts is a common practice in the world—people hide their ignorance or selfishness in complexity;
- The usual reason for a person using complex ideas associated with human "service" offerings is because they want to conceal something from people or because they want people to depend on them to get something from another person or persons;

---

[47] Taken from www.gotquestions.org

139

- Realms or domains that people make complex to get people to rely on them include legal, financial/insurance, religious, psychological, government laws or policies and medical. Good empirical science can be complicated by nature, but origin speculation is also purposely made complex to deceive people;
- The vast majority of human communication – especially regarding human relationships - does not need to be complicated and with a little effort, the concepts that are claimed to be "complex" are simple if one is not trying to hide something.

17
POSITIVE THINKING, NEGATIVE OUTCOMES

Opening Questions:

- Do positive thinking philosophies represent reality well?
- What is the purpose of positive thinking philosophies?
- Does believing something make it true?
- Is it possible that positive thinking philosophies are detrimental to most people?

The philosophy of positive thinking has no doubt been around in some version for a long time. Author Norman Vincent Peale wrote a very popular book entitled, "The Power of Positive Thinking" that was published in 1952, thus he could be credited with promoting the latest version of the philosophy in the U.S. In more recent times, religious leader Robert Schuller made positive thinking popular and widely accepted among U.S. citizens particularly religious ones.

Here is what this author believes is a good quote summing up the belief:

"Positive thinking is a mental and emotional attitude that focuses on the bright side of life and expects positive results. A positive person anticipates happiness, health, and success, and believes he or she can overcome any obstacle and difficulty." [48]

At face value, this belief is very appealing to many people. It promotes "happiness, health, and success" and it appeals to the "I can do anything" crowd. Stated another way, the belief can easily be used to inflates one's ego or boosts one's self-esteem.

---

[48] Taken from www.successconsciousness.com/index_000009.htm

Two questions are relevant to ask about the philosophy. First, can it be found in the teachings of Joshua of Nazareth? Second, does it make people better human beings?

The answer to the first question is no, Joshua does not teach it. Perhaps the easiest way to demonstrate what he teaches would be to contrast it with the positive thinking summary above. Here are the two statements together for easy reading:

"Positive thinking is a mental and emotional attitude that focuses on the bright side of life and expects positive results. A positive person anticipates happiness, health, and success, and believes he or she can overcome any obstacle and difficulty."

"Faith is a core level trust in God that focuses on our Father's love for us and our responsibility to seek and promote truth and rightness. A person of faith has Hope for their future with their Father; believes that love can overcome all of humanities worst problems, and works to help others."

As you can see, the two summaries are incompatible. The positive thinking philosophy is inherently selfish…it is all about *me* and how I can achieve happiness, health, and success for myself. The way of faith in Joshua, on the other hand, is other's focused and has us seek to give away, not take since it is love based.

With that contrast, we have also answered the second question. Any life-philosophy which encourages selfishness will not produce better human beings from God's perspective or a standpoint that a selfless life is a better life than a selfish life.

The reader might ask, what about the glass-half-full versus half-empty truth doesn't that support the positive thinking philosophy? No, it does not. All it proves is that different people can look at the same physical thing and use different words to describe it. For a selfless person in a particular situation – say taking care of a sick person who needs to hydrate - they could look at the glass half empty and say, "Oh, its half empty, good, I'm glad Rebecca drank half the water." I would suggest the glass half empty phenomenon is primarily situational and the same person could judge that differently depending on their situation or "where" they are in their life.

I do not deny that certain people have a general outlook of either optimistic/positive or pessimistic/negative. I also think that people with the former will likely have less stress and stress does put a load on our biological systems sometimes creating or exacerbating health problems. However, neither of those facts support that the positive thinking philosophy is true or that it is ultimately beneficial to people. As we have seen, the positive thinking philosophy is, at its core, selfish. And as we have seen, selfishness is a primary root problem of human beings. There are far better ways to reduce stress than living in a selfish, comfortable bubble.

The selfish focus of the positive thinking philosophy is very damaging in that it is in fact used to justify ignoring bad things in the world. For example, imagine the doggedly positive thinking person walking amidst the aftermath of a bombing scene, with severely injured people crying out in pain and suffering and needing help. Now, according to their philosophy, they will be trying real hard to find the "bright side of life" in that situation, and so their natural reaction must be something like, "I'm glad it wasn't me"; or "oh, don't be so upset, you only lost one leg, not both legs"; or, "the pain could be worse". Of course, upon walking upon the scene, they could also turn around and walk away to save themselves the difficulty of maintaining a selfishly positive view in that scenario. What they certainly will not think about is "why did this happen," because the answer will NOT fit into their white-washed delusion of "reality."

Ultimately, the positive thinking philosophies are used by people as part of their selfish helmet, as we learned earlier. They will use that belief to filter out things that will not contribute to their attaining "happiness, health and success." If you are a selfless person with compassion for others ("blessed are you who weep for others"), then you will see the injustice, pain, and suffering in the world and you will seek to help people—you will work to bring what you believe is the solution to help others. If you are trapped in a selfish view due to a positive thinking belief, then you will look to primarily help yourself attain the happiness, health, and success you believe you deserve.

A final illustration for this topic: Two people were walking in the desert, dying from thirst. They happen upon a partial glass of water. The positive thinking person sees the glass and says, "wow, a half-full glass of water" and runs to drink it to attain happiness, health, and success. The person with faith and love says, "wow, I'm glad you are now likely to survive...enjoy the water." They both die while trying to escape the desert. The positive thinker goes to the destiny he/she choose with his/her selfish life-guiding philosophy of positive thinking. The person with faith goes to the future he/she decided with his/her selfless/love life-guiding faith. To believe that both destinies are the same is to deny the metaphysical conscience that is trying to inform you otherwise.

So, what dominant false beliefs, inadequate views, and means to deceive are left? How about religion! Let us take a very brief and straightforward (whew!) look at religions other than Christianity in the next and last chapter of this section. In so doing, we will have completed the process of identifying wrong concepts and wrong ways of thinking that block a person from using reason well to properly evaluate the successful failure that is Christianity.

Chapter Summary:

- Positive thinking philosophies or beliefs often ignore what is real and true;
- Positive thinking philosophies and beliefs are inherently selfish and encourage the person believing them to be primarily concerned about themselves;
- Different perspectives on the same thing – like a glass of water filled halfway – can exist, but the different perspectives don't change reality, they only allow for different potential reactions to reality;
- A person will never be more positive or improve upon the truth that they have a Father who loves them dearly; and that loving others – behaving selflessly motivated by compassion for others - is the best way to have a fulfilling life;
- A positive belief or attitude will not produce eternal life, and every person can have a much-improved existence after death if they are willing to give up the selfish life.

18
OTHER WORLD RELIGIONS

Opening Questions:

- Can all God beliefs - if they have contradictory elements – be true?
- Can one religion contain more true beliefs than another?
- If religion has false beliefs or harmful practices, should it be "respected'?
- Does religion genuinely meet the real spiritual needs of individual human beings?
- If God/the Creator exists and he/she did send a Messenger to humankind to communicate, how could we identify that Messenger?
- If God did send a Messenger and a group of people hides that Messenger and his message, should they not be more accountable?

Karl Marx supposedly said, "Religion in the opiate of the masses." He actually said this, "Religion is the sigh of the oppressed creature, the heart of a heartless world, and the soul of soulless conditions. It is the opium of the people". The saying has been taken to mean that religion is like a drug that dulls people to the realities of the harsh world and keeps then inactive in trying to solve problems. If that is what he meant, then he is correct. Religion is the hope of people expressed in non-helpful or non-productive ways...often in ways that contradict some of the very religious/ethical principles the religious people proclaim. It can be the comfort of people, but comfort which often is selfish or comfort which is not based in reality. Christianity is not exempt from this correct observation of Marx, but this chapter will take a very brief and narrow view of other religions. (My using and clarifying a famous and often quoted saying of Marx in no way provides some blanket endorsement of his beliefs.)

Many people have come to believe and will say that if observable facts or occurrences cannot prove something, then it is not real, or at least it is not relevant to human existence. As we have seen, two observable facts strongly point to – in fact, demand – that a creator exists. First, is the physical complexity of the living organic beings that populate this planet. It is irrational to believe that natural forces created highly complex, DNA coded, replicating biological machines with inter-dependent sub-systems…as a legitimate analogy, it is unreasonable to encounter a computer or a robot and believe that natural forces built its hardware.

Second, human beings have a metaphysical "operating system," if you will—the ability to reason is not physical; the desire and ability to forgive and to want forgiveness is not material; the ability to know right moral behavior from wrong is not physical; etc. Thus, our hardware has software.

So, a fair question is why I should believe "the creation narrative" and worldview of this Joshua of Nazareth instead of many other people or "religious" or existential claims or possibilities? The reason is threefold. Before I answer that directly, please understand these qualifying statements in response the question. Joshua of Nazareth does not give any extensive, detailed "creation narrative." Rather, he says that God created "male and female" human beings. So, there is quite a bit of room for speculation regarding how exactly God created human beings, and by inference, the rest of the life on this planet.

Now I will answer the question directly.

First, because he defeated death to prove that what he said was true about himself and God – he is the only person in history to conquer death in an authentic, genuine way or context/narrative. Read the accounts, and you will see. If you dismiss the accounts due to the miracles, that dismissal demonstrates that you are biased against a metaphysical reality even though the evidence of such is right in front of you as has been previously extensively revealed.

Second, because Joshua of Nazareth is the only person in history whose views on the world best represent the reality that we human beings experience each day. Human beings have both light and dark in them, but the dark in general rules and thus most of the causes of pain, suffering, hardship, and conflict are created by human beings. People also can do well, but their nature, in general, overrules their knowing what is right and consistently practicing it. Remember the second chapter in the book on the state of humankind which proves this point?

Third, because he provides the solution to human kind's most significant needs and worst problems – leadership/guidance, truth, hope, and love. The only person qualified to lead human beings is the One who taught and practiced, "Love your enemies."

146

This chapter will very briefly look at other major world religions with the goal of arriving at a reasonable conclusion that the other world religions do not provide the solutions to humankind's most vexing problems. Frankly, if one would apply reason well to world religion's claims, they would collapse fairly quickly or at least they would be found to have significant contradictions, inconsistencies or to waste time, energy and resources.

As stated earlier, the world religions are very much alike. While the monotheistic religions have different names for their gods, the people have pretty much the same view of God and live pretty much the same lives with the small exception of the nature of the religious rituals they partake in, which rituals do not significantly affect their life view or daily life behavior. In other words and in general, Christians, Jews, Muslims, Buddhists, Hindu's, etc. all live pretty much similar lives—they live and work for money and material security, and they are only willing to share their material things and daily lives with blood and legal relatives or family. Their religion is just a minor aspect of their social life – it does not drive their basic everyday behavior; it does not overcome their desire to stay in the cage of fear, self-pride, and selfishness; it does not lead them to live lives of true love.

Let's take a small step back and review some important facts before we directly address other world religions. We observed that while spiritual things cannot be validated physically by observation - concepts, principles or beliefs can be verified as true or false using reason and logic. For example, consider this mathematical statement, "the sum of one plus one does not equal three." We need no physical things to validate that statement, but our mind, using reason, tells us that is a true statement.

Here is an example from the realm of God claims – "our God says love other people and we can harm them as well." The statement contains a contradiction and thus is false, e.g., loving other people and harming those people are contradictory or mutually exclusive – you cannot both love another person and at the same time intentionally hurt them. What are a few of the leading possibilities that could reasonably explain such a statement?

1. God does not exist, and a poorly reasoning person made the statement up;

2. God contradicts himself and cannot reason well;

3. God did communicate something, but the communication was unintentionally messed up;

4. God did communicate something, but the communication was intentionally messed up;

5. God said love one another and man added the harm clause;

6. God said harm one another and man added the love clause.

If people who hold to God beliefs applied reason more diligently to their God beliefs, there would be a whole lot fewer God-claims as well as less confusion and division.

Sadly, they do not, and there is a reason for that the Light identifies.

The normal mode for religious people is, "this is what I believe, and you are not going to change my mind" – a statement driven by self-pride and fear. *Religious people, in general, manifest the attributes of stubbornness, closed-mindedness and a healthy dislike of reason!* Ironically, most non-theists and some agnostics – while rejecting they possess a "religious view" – still have a worldview, and they hold to that worldview just as stubbornly as the religious people they mock or condemn. Of course, they will claim that their worldview is "scientific and provable (meaning physical) facts," even while they use the metaphysical elements and means of human beings called the mind and reason to argue so!

It is reasonable to conclude that if the Designer wanted to communicate to us, and for whatever reason, he or she could not do that directly:

- Due to some constraint like the Designer existing in a dimension that prevented direct communication that could be received or understood by the physical means we have, or;
- Some condition existed that was temporary or occasional that allowed the Designer to interact with our realm intermittently or temporarily;
- Due to some metaphysical constraint, like human's inability to receive the Designer's communications due to some problem with our nature, i.e., he/she gave us a two-way radio, but we broke it.

...then he or she would use the best indirect means possible to ensure his or her message was understood correctly. Generally speaking, face to face conversation with the other person is the best way to communicate something. If the Designer for whatever reason could not do that him or herself then sending or enabling a representative or messenger who could deliver his or her message would be best.

So that leaves us with trying to figure out whom, if anyone is that representative.

There have been, and are, millions of people who claimed, or currently claim, to speak for the Designer or God and many millions of God claims. Using observation and reason, we can eliminate many of those gods and the religion associated with them. For example, we can reject gods that cannot design and create the human race. We can eliminate gods who state contradictions, for they - at best and if they exist - would not be worthy of the designation "God."

Furthermore, we should reject any god claims that cannot pass the test of reason. For example, perhaps the paramount belief of many Christian sects is the trinity doctrine, which states that one god is three persons, or said more simply, that 1 equals 3. All the theological equivocation with the associated complex vocabulary used to hide the contradiction notwithstanding, one does not equal three. Thus the trinity belief ought to be rejected as false (we will look more closely at the trinity belief later).

Some of the earth's religions with many adherents include Islam, Christianity, Hinduism, Buddhism, and Judaism. There are hundreds of more beliefs and practices that people hold that could be considered religion, but the five mentioned above probably account for about 75% of the humans on the earth, so we will address those five.

In addition to the five major religions themselves, there are many hundreds of divisions in each of those five religions, so rational people should reject any pretense of unity. However, the central question is who is correct with their essential claims? Muslims says Mohammed is God's messenger. Buddhists look to Siddhartha Gautama. Jews look to Moses and their prophets as God's messengers. Christians say "Christ" but this author has found that the Christian's "Christ" does not represent the historical Joshua of Nazareth, and many Christians spend most of their time quoting everyone but him for their God beliefs, especially Paul and Moses.

In addition to those people who lived in the past, many living people say they are God's messengers. So again, who is correct? How can we validate claims? Is Christianity the only one which is a failure? Do they all speak for God? What about the many contradictions between each of those supposed messengers and their messages? As we have seen and agreed, if something that can be evaluated by reason cannot pass the test of reason, then we will not consider it, for we should not be interested in believing things that are false.

So, getting back to someone representing God and our ability to know what the Designer is like, where do we go from here? God could be anything from a non-caring, apathetic distant being that sees his human creation as an afterthought, to a being passionate about his created beings. (Of course, there is the assumption there that the Creator would create beings that had attributes similar to himself/herself or with characteristics he/she cares about.) So, what is the Designer like? Remember we need a way to validate that the messenger is sent from, and accurately represents, the Designer. Anyone can claim anything, so how could we validate those claims?

A primary way to accomplish that validation would be if the Messenger had special powers that other people did not have. If the Designer's Messenger could do things that no one else could do, then that would be good evidence that that person's claims – if they also claimed to represent the Designer – were valid.

Other proofs the messenger could prove could include that he or she could see into the future, or if the messenger fulfilled prophesies that were communicated long ago - things they could not manipulate nor fulfill by their own will. Thus, they would have proof that they were not bound by time and therefore would be a likely candidate for someone who knows the Designer if the Designer exists outside of time or can see through time.

Perhaps the least objective and yet the most effective validation is if our conscience or our mind validate the messenger's message. That is to say that we know the things they teach or taught are true and right, for who can argue with true and right? Validating their sayings with our conscience becomes especially important with any God claims the supposed messengers made or make.

So, where does this leave us?

Let's add another layer of possibility to this puzzle of finding the Designer's spokesperson. What if the Designer's messenger said things that were so unpopular that people who heard them would naturally draw away and not want to consider or receive the message? For example, have you ever tried to communicate something to an arrogant teenager that went against what they wanted? How does that go? Do they "hear" you?

What if the Designer provided a singular messenger and a clear message that could not be reasonably misunderstood unless the people who heard it were afraid of the message and the message's implications on their lives? In other words, what if the Designer sent a messenger or messengers, but people, in general, don't want to hear the message? If that were so, then the human race would have a non-physical deafness so-to-speak that would work hard against identifying the messenger and the message. However, we are currently in the endeavor to identify a Messenger, not whether or not the intended recipients of the message were worthy or able to receive it.

As we have said, we need a way to validate if a person who claimed to represent the Designer did or does. I would suggest the following criteria for confirming messengers. Of the primary messengers who say they were representatives from the Creator of the human race, which one's message provides the best solution to humanity's problems, and which messenger validated their message with an event(s) that were a sure sign or "signature" from the Creator—an event(s) or feat(s) that would rise above normal human experience? Here is what I suggest are the basic validations that any messenger needs to pass to be considered as "The Messenger" from the Creator.

First, *they need to have claimed to speak directly for the Creator.* If the Creator wants to communicate with his created beings through a messenger, then that messenger would claim that they speak for the Creator. If the Messenger knew the Creator and knew they were sent by the Creator to provide his/her message, then they would convey and proclaim that essential truth as part of their message.

Criteria two or second, the messenger *needs to have provided and lived out the solution to humanity's most significant problems.* As we have identified, humankind's primary problem is fear, self-pride and selfishness causing us to take from, harm, unjustly rule over, harm, abuse, and neglect others. In other words, *we do not live by love.*

Third, they *needed to validate their person and message by an act(s) or event(s) that marks them as extraordinary and unique deliverers of the Designer's message.*

I would encourage the reader to consider these criteria and try and find fault with them. If you cannot, then you should be excited that by these three criteria, the Creator's messenger or messengers will be revealed.

Let me say that a brief chapter cannot possibly contain an in-depth analysis of this topic of the claims of messengers from the Designer, so you, reader, if you are not persuaded with the simple truths herein, will need to do some research to validate the claims made in this chapter.

Messenger Search

In this chapter, we will only consider those alleged messengers from whom most of the people on the planet are looking (approximately 75%) to know God and his or her will—so let's do that now.

First, let's consider Islam's messenger, Muhammad since Islam is making some significant waves at this time across the globe. Does he pass the three criteria? Muhammad indeed claimed to speak for God, so he passes the first criteria.

What was his solution for humankind? It was to spread Islam – the teachings of Muhammad who claimed to speak for God - to all humans to get them to submit to Allah and his rules using whatever means necessary, including force or violence. Here are a few quotes of Muhammad from the Quran in that regard.

Qur'an 9:29-Fight against Christians and Jews until they pay the tribute readily, being brought low."

Qur'an 4:91- If the unbelievers do not offer you peace, kill them wherever you find them. Against such you are given clear warrant.

Qur'an 9:7-9-Don't make treaties with non-Muslims. They are all evildoers and should not be trusted.

Qur'an 9:12-14-Fight the disbelievers! Allah is on your side; he will give you victory.

Qur'an 9:5 - Kill the nonbelievers wherever you find them.

Qur'an 2:191-2-Kill disbelievers wherever you find them. If they attack you, then kill them. Such is the reward of disbelievers.

Qur'an (5:51) - "O you who believe! do not take the Jews and the Christians for friends; they are friends of each other; and whoever amongst you takes them for a friend, then surely he is one of them; surely Allah does not guide the unjust people."

Qur'an (2:65-66) Christians and Jews must believe what Allah has revealed to Muhammad or Allah will disfigure their faces or turn them into apes, as he did the Sabbath-breakers.

Well, as you can see, the solution Muhammad laid out for humanity seems a bit flawed! Using force and violence to accomplish one's goals – even if the end is said to be good – is wrong. Now, of course, the Muslim theologians will cry foul and cite other sayings of Mohammed that contradict the ones above – sayings about peace and love. However, that proves that the god Mohammad is supposedly speaking for contradicts itself, and thus is not worthy of believing.

Other teachings in the Quran, of course, provide for human leaders that the other followers of Allah must submit to, thus setting up a religious system controlled by men. Indeed claiming an angry God wants people to submit to him and that his followers are right to use force, threat and violence to achieve that end – hardly solves humankind's problems! In fact, that kind of belief is the cause of much of the hatred and violence in the world.

Just because many who take the religious label Muslim ignore, deny, cite contradictory sayings or seek ways to avoid the plain meaning of these verses in their holy book and uttered by their "prophet of God" in no way nullifies the fact that they do exist in the primary Muslim holy book, the Quran.

Nor does quoting sayings from the Quran which contradict with the ones cited above negate the fact that Allah supposedly said the above-quoted sayings through Mohammed. All the contradictions do is to demonstrate that "Allah" makes mistakes and is not clear on what he wants, thus disqualifying him as a worthy god.

Nor does the fact that many Muslims renounce violence and are not aggressive or violent people negate the fact that it is reasonable that other Muslims take those sayings of Muhammad in the Quran at face value and act upon them, thus the jihadists and those who empathize with, and support them.

Finally, what means or event did Muhammad use to validate he was a special messenger from the Designer? None, for he lived a normal life and died in a normal way. Thus, the supposed messenger Muhammad fails two of the three tests.

For more on Islam, see *Appendix 6, Islam.*

OK, what about the Buddha, or Siddhartha Gautama? Did he claim to speak for the Creator? No, he did not; therefore, he is eliminated by the first criteria! Siddhartha had a good focus to his teachings – essentially the overcoming and alleviation of suffering - and he certainly did not teach that force or violence was justified to achieve those, or any, earthly ends, to his credit. His solution for humanity was far less flawed than Muhammad's, but it was still too narrow and did not explicitly address the root problems nor provide the answer. Since Siddhartha did not claim to speak for the Designer, he needn't have validated his person or message, and in fact, he lived a relatively normal life.

OK, what about Hinduism? Did it have a founder or a chief messenger? No, it does not. Instead, it is a set of existential or religious philosophies only. While some of Hinduism's beliefs and philosophies seem good and right and would help alleviate some of the problems in the world, those beliefs and views cannot be validated as having come from the Designer, nor do they address the root problems or supply the solution. There are also many conflicting claims and views in Hinduism, so it fails to present a unified worldview.

OK, what about Judaism? If you had to pick the chief messenger from Judaism's standpoint, it would have to be Moses. How does Moses do with our three criteria? He indeed claimed to have spoken for God, so he passes the first criteria.

What does Moses say is the Designer's solutions for humanity's problems? Many Christians and some Jews would argue the Ten Commandments. However, the Ten Commandments so-called do not address the root problems of fear, pride, and selfishness – they merely attempt to constrain some bad behavior. Furthermore, Moses teachings do not provide the critical element of the solution. Moses' Ten Commandments do try to restrain bad behavior, and that is good, but they do *not* lead to peace and love among people who are not "Jewish." Please consider the following in that regard.

Moses says, "You shall not take vengeance, nor bear any grudge *against the sons of your people*, but you shall love your neighbor as yourself; I am the LORD." (Leviticus 19:18) Note how the neighbor is qualified as having to be one of "the sons of your people." Here is what Moses says God says regarding people who are not "the sons of your people":

> Then the LORD spoke to Moses, saying, "Take full vengeance for the sons of Israel on the Midianites; afterward you will be gathered to your people. Moses spoke to the people, saying, "Arm men from among you for the war, that they may go against Midian to execute the Lord's vengeance on Midian. "A thousand from each tribe of all the tribes of Israel you shall send to the war." So there were furnished from the thousands of Israel, a thousand from each tribe, twelve thousand armed for war.

Moses sent them, a thousand from each tribe, to the war, and Phinehas the son of Eleazar the priest, to the war with them, and the holy vessels and the trumpets for the alarm in his hand. So they made war against Midian, just as the LORD had commanded Moses, and they killed every male. They killed the kings of Midian along with the rest of their slain: Evi and Rekem and Zur and Hur and Reba, the five kings of Midian; they also killed Balaam the son of Beor with the sword. The sons of Israel captured the women of Midian and their little ones; and all their cattle and all their flocks and all their goods they plundered. Then they burned all their cities where they lived and all their camps with fire. They took all the spoil and all the prey, both of man and of beast.

They brought the captives and the prey and the spoil to Moses, and to Eleazar the priest and to the congregation of the sons of Israel, to the camp at the plains of Moab, which are by the Jordan opposite Jericho. Moses and Eleazar the priest and all the leaders of the congregation went out to meet them outside the camp. Moses was angry with the officers of the army, the captains of thousands and the captains of hundreds, who had come from service in the war. And Moses said to them, "Have you spared all the women? "Behold, these caused the sons of Israel, through the counsel of Balaam, to trespass against the LORD in the matter of Peor, so the plague was among the congregation of the LORD. *"Now therefore, kill every male among the little ones, and kill every woman who has known man intimately. "But all the girls who have not known man intimately, spare for yourselves.* (Numbers 31:1-18)

So, as you can see, some part of Moses was a merciless religious guy who used his fear and God as his justification to kill many people. Vengeance never leads to peace; it only works hard to perpetuate more violence and conflict.

Jesus of Nazareth later provided an improved version of the Ten Commandments, thus demonstrating the original commandments were imperfect and incomplete and therefore not from a perfect being (see Matt. 5). On these bases, Moses does not pass the second criteria.

What about the third criteria? Moses indeed did allegedly perform – or call upon God to work - miracles to validate his message to the Egyptian leadership. *But notice who the validating signs were directed at - the Egyptian people at large and not constrained to the leadership responsible for the injustices to the Hebrew people.* The alleged miracles performed by the god of Moses were of the nature of destruction and killing...of violence and force. In this way, they vary very little from the Muslim's God's way.

Destructive acts against the Egyptian leadership – not acts against the common Egyptian people – could be justified from the viewpoint of the oppressed seeking relief from the unjust oppressor. However, the violence of the Hebrew god was against the innocent children of the ordinary citizens of Egypt instead of against the guilty Egyptian leadership. That is unjust and morally wrong.

Furthermore, is violence the only way or the best way to achieve relief from oppression? No, it is not. See the stories Gandhi or Martin Luther King Jr. to validate that truth. Or better yet, see the story of the Savior of humankind!

If we assume that the Designer is above some of our more base desires – like harming others to get our way – then we should reject the possibility that the Designer would use or advocate or approve of violence to achieve various ends, even just ones. So, while Moses did allegedly perform things that would seem to validate that a super being was behind his words and actions, the unjust and immoral acts of destructive violence against innocent people themselves disqualify Moses and the god he represented.

As we will see in more detail, Christianity fails the test because Christians don't listen to Joshua of Nazareth, they look to Paul or Moses or their favorite religious leaders.

All religions are not equal. Some provide better ethics than others thus accounting for the different general behaviors of Muslims versus Jews, for example. Stated another way, some religions have fewer ethical contradictions and fewer immoral teachings than others, and thus present a better moral framework or principles for humankind than others.

Many others throughout history claimed to speak for God, but none of them met all three criteria except one. And no one except one provided The Ethical Principle that could solve most human conflict problems, and that principle is "love even your enemies."

I think we have built an adequate framework to evaluate whether and why Christianity is a successful failure, with one exception, which we will take care of in the next chapter. In the next section, we will examine the primary beliefs and practices of Christians to evaluate whether or not it is successful according to the teachings of the historical person of Joshua of Nazareth.

Chapter Summary:
- The four largest religions are Christianity, Islam, Secular/Non-Theist, and Hinduism – their adherents account for about 86% of the people on the planet, or about 6 billion human beings;
- Religions and their God claims can be evaluated using reason and logic by finding contradictions within their religious claims/belief

or by identifying non-factual claims of those religions against facts established by everyday observation and experience;

- All religions are the same concerning trying unsuccessfully to meet the real spiritual needs of people;
- If you sort through the claims of the main person, originator or founder of religions on these three bases:
    - o They claimed to speak for and represent the Creator;
    - o They lived out and provided the solution(s) to humanity's most significant problems/needs;
    - o They performed extraordinary or miraculous works as evidence to back up their claims that they represent the Creator;
    ...all fail except for one;
- Religions other than Christianity have as many or more problems, errors, falsehoods, destructive ethical principles or contradictory claims as Christianity;
- Christians are more accountable for their erroneous religious beliefs and practices since they use the Creator's Messenger for their selfish purposes instead of listening to him and doing what he asks, as we shall see.

SECTION 4:
CHRISTIANITY: A SUCCESSFUL FAILURE

Theme:
- Christianity is a "successful" failure
  - Christians do not listen well or at all to the one they call their God;
  - Christianity and by extension Christians, do more harm than good since they bring so much wrong judgment, division, contention, and conflict;
  - In general, Christians live no differently than people of other religions or atheists, agnostics or non-theists;
  - Organized Christian religion increases hypocrisy in people;
  - It would be better to be ignorant than to claim knowledge and that knowledge be wrong;

Section Introduction:

Christians are not entirely wrong about all God things. All religions contain both truth and falsehood, but all religions do not provide the solutions to human kinds most intractable problems. Other world religions like Islam, Judaism, Hinduism, Buddhism, Taoism, etc., all have both true teachings about human nature and/or God, as well as errors and falsehoods (remember we can rightly make that judgment based on observation, reason, and logic!), but examining those other religions is not the topic of this book. What my focusing on Christianity means is that Christians are more accountable for their error because they have easy access to the One who is the actual Solution from the Creator and who says, "I am the truth" and is the One True Standard. In fact, they claim to worship him and call him their God even while they mostly ignore him or explain away his most important teachings!

Please consider this illustration. There once was a man who was looking for driving directions to a specific destination. He asked several people and got several different answers. The first person gave him instructions that were way off and did not take him to his destination. The second person gave him directions that guided him towards his destination but still left him many kilometers away. The third person gave him instructions that could lead to the destination, but she didn't know the specifics about the way, so several parts of the routes could quickly lead to dead-end roads or perilous road situations that would lead most drivers to drive off a cliff! The last person gave him instructions to what **he** believed was the right destination instead of the destination for which the man asked!

This illustrates the story of Christianity and the Christian's who proclaim and defend it.

Sincere people looking for the answers to life's most essential questions encounter Christians of the various sects/divisions who give them the wrong directions. Please consider the following sayings regarding people saying they understand but indeed don't:

> From everyone who has been given much, much will be required; and to whom they entrusted much, of him they will ask all the more. (Luke 12:48)

> If you were blind, you would have no sin/fault/guilt; but since you say, "We see," your sin/fault/guilt remains. (John 9:41)

As one who has spent about the last forty years experiencing or thinking about the Christian religion, I can tell you what the statement most Christians would make, "Christ is the figurehead of our religion" does NOT mean. *It does not mean that the leaders of Christian religion and their followers have the historical Jesus/Joshua of Nazareth — that is the subject of the four gospel books - as their Master.* The term "Master" means a person looked to for complete, comprehensive and best-available knowledge in the domain of which they claim mastery. Therefore, to reason well, if a Christian had the historical person of Joshua/Jesus of Nazareth as their Master, then they would hold and practice their Master's teachings. What are the domains of mastery that Joshua claims? *Joshua's claimed domains of Mastery the Creator of the human race (called "God"), and the nature, drives, and needs of human beings.* I ask the reader to slow down, re-read that last sentence and ponder it.

The remarkable fact is that Christians do not have the historical person of Joshua of Nazareth as their Master. Oh, they will collectively call some jesus figure "Lord, Lord" billions of times each day, but as Joshua said some two-thousand years earlier to the religious people of his day as he quoted one of their favorite prophets…

> "This people honors me with their lips, but their heart is far away from me.
> "But in vain do they worship me, teaching as doctrines (venerated content of the "statements of faith") the precepts of men."
> Neglecting the commandment of God, you hold to the tradition of men. (Mark 7:6-8)

Dear reader, nothing has changed in 2,000 years *except* the religious leaders now use "Christ" as their bait or figurehead to push their "precepts of men"—*their* beliefs about God, *not* what the historical person of Joshua of Nazareth actually taught. Sound incredible? Sound unbelievable? Sound absurdly fantastic? Read on!

Various Flavors of Christians

There are several varieties of Christians. The variety of type of Christian is set by the degree to which they have faith and are familiar with the teachings of Joshua of Nazareth.

There are those that are Christian in label only who might be able to repeat a few teachings of Joshua. These folks have no expressions of their loosely claimed religion, and if you were able to watch their lives over a week, there would be nothing that would "give them away" as Christians. These might go to their religious organization a few times a year if at all. How they live their lives and what they care about is indistinguishable from non-Christians, and if given a test on the teachings of Joshua of Nazareth, they would fail.

Then there are the "church going" Christians who are actively participating in their religious organization. They might be able to repeat several dozen sayings of Joshua, but not the ones that go against their church religion. There are different degrees of participation in the religion of these Christians, but at a minimum, they religiously "go to church" and look to their organization as a significant, if not important, aspect of their life in this world. Other than their "church going," these Christians also have virtually no manifestations of their religion during "normal daily life." Again, how they live their lives and what they care about is indistinguishable from non-Christians, and if given a test on the teachings of Joshua of Nazareth, they would fail.

Then there are the Christian leaders and other more zealous "non-clergy" who not only are active in their sect or religious organization but who diligently study the Bible and their denominations/organizations other literature. These are not too different than the former type of Christian in that they might be able to repeat several dozen sayings of Joshua, but unfortunately, they diligently stay away from the sayings of Joshua that would harm their religious practices. Worse, they typically work pretty hard to explain away the teachings of Joshua that get in the way of their God beliefs.

Then are those who build, promote and defend their religion, their sect/denomination and their organizations they call "the church." The primary manifestations of these Christians are that they are typically more harshly judgmental regarding things they ought not to be. They usually fit their "building, promoting and defending" work of their religion into a box called "ministry." What "ministry" means is that they are a formal organization recognized by the world and operating on generally the same principles of "success" and how to achieve "success" as the businesses and other organizations around them. However, like their less zealous brethren, and after their "ministry" work is accomplished (40 hour week), their "normal lives" are virtually indistinguishable from those they call "unbelievers." Again, how they live their lives and what they care about is indistinguishable from non-Christians, and if given a test on the teachings of Joshua of Nazareth, they too would fail.

Finally, there is the tiny number of Christians who understand and seek to practice some of the fundamental teachings of Jesus of Nazareth and thus who live differently than the people around them. The echoes of the Light have penetrated them to some degree. They practice some of the teachings of Jesus of Nazareth. They are kind and forgiving towards others and generally spend a good bit of time working to help other people. They are typically not materialistic, and thus they don't live for money and are generous. These are those who are active in organizations that feed the needy or build shelters for those with none, etc. In other words, the faith that they have in the Light of the world is real and thus active—these are those who have some understanding of what love is and try to practice what they know.

Their primary problem is confusion about the standard and thus their not understanding the root problems or the solution. This confusion usually means they will be part of a religious organization, thinking that is the only way to "serve God." Their worst problem is not having a clear understanding of how love should be lived out amongst the disciples.

In spite of these weaknesses, they do better than the previous three categories of people. These, unfortunately, are a *vast* minority among those that call themselves Christians—as a percent, probably in the low single digits. These have pretty good hearts, but due to their error about the Standard, how they live their lives and what they care about is mostly indistinguishable from non-Christians, and if given a test on the teachings of Joshua of Nazareth, maybe a few would pass. In as much as they love other's well, they are doing well!

Perhaps inaccurate generalizations, but maybe not—I will let the reader judge especially if you take a Christian label. Beware of the all too common self-deception of "not *me* or *my* church."

The Non-Religious Conundrum

Much of the non-religious crowd can see the falsehoods of the religious crowd and are only too eager to mock and condemn the religious people for their duplicity, hypocrisy and the false things they believe and promote, like "God is all-powerful and also a God of pure love."

The non-religious people can be hypocritical as well in as much as they say to the religious people, "you ought to be doing good" if they are not. And what standard do non-religious people have even to know what is "good"? As we saw, relativism leaves them without a standard, and thus hypocrisy is prevalent, and unity will be virtually impossible.

Sadly, there are also a significant number of non-religious people who spend a good bit of time in a state of bitterness mocking the religious people and thus are in a worse state than many of the Christian people they mock. It is better to be a kind person trying to do some good on a consistent basis – even if you are doing so for wrong or pretend reasons - than a person who sees the errors of religious people yet is living a selfish life. In other words, it is better to be in the cage and reaching your arms out of the cage to try and do some good, than to be content in the cage and throw things at people in the cages around you. Of course, the best is to be out of the cage and thus free!

So, in general, the religious crowd acts more hypocritically then the non-religious folks, but much of the non-religious people have mostly bitterness against the religious masses to stand on, instead of answers to real needs and essential questions. Again and in general, the religious crowd does more good works than the non-religious crowd; however, the religious crowd also causes much unnecessary conflict whereas the non-religious folks not so much.

So, that is the high-level view, and thus we have completed the framework and in fact, have built a good bit of detail as well. We are now ready to look carefully at Christianity to see how and why it is a successful failure. We will start by looking at Christianity and addressing one of the most compelling beliefs that has given its leaders much power and control over the people for many centuries. Unless a person can overcome fear, they are unlikely to consider Christianity as a successful failure.

This section will use the standard of the teachings of the historical Jesus of Nazareth as found in the four gospel books to bring to light the successful failure that is Christianity.

In the next chapter, we will define and seek to understand some critical terms and concepts that the reader must grasp to be able to comprehend how and why Christianity is a successful failure.

19
DIFFERENCES BETWEEN BELIEF, RELIGION, FAITH AND GOD

Opening Questions:

- What are the differences between the critical concepts of "belief," "religion," "faith" and "God"?
- Do I have an equally valid or plausible explanation for humanity's presence or my existence?
- What is the best definition of "Religion"?
- What if most people misunderstand the vital concept of "faith"?
- Are beliefs *about* God, and God, the same thing?
- Are beliefs and faith the same thing?

I have been talking about the need for a framework or context to properly evaluate whether Christianity is a success or failure. I believe we have accomplished that with one exception. Let's take care of that exception now in this chapter.

Let us perform a brief review of the book thus far. We have learned that it is reasonable for people to be religious since there is a creator and we as human beings have bodies that are extremely complex and aspects to our nature that are more than just molecules. We as human beings have metaphysical or spiritual components to our nature.

Furthermore, we have seen that humanity is not doing well. There are ebbs and flows to the conflict, neglect, and suffering, but as the centuries tick by, the pattern and cycle are the same. Individuals make up the collective humanity, and the vast majority will not come out of their cage of self-pride and fear and selfishness and thus will not do what is right on a consistent basis. Therefore, you have what you have as we took a brief sampling of in Chapter 2, "The State of Humankind."

Religion has not changed the human condition in significant, meaningful ways and has in fact been the cause of much conflict – from outright violent wars to everyday animosity. Just look at the Jews in Israel and the Muslims in "Palestine" for a current day example of the animosity and hatred that religion causes (in that example, most of the hatred is coming from the "Palestinians" due in large part to their religion which is used to justify the hatred).

We have learned that the underlying problem with we human beings is that we exist in a cage of self-pride and fear and selfishness and this is the fundamental cause of all the human conflict and lack-of-cooperation that plagues the human race. From another perspective, that the individual problem forms the collective problems of conflict with people.

We have learned that all solutions, including the most difficult and important ones regarding human nature, can only be solved by using the tools of reason and logic…that reason will always lead to the solutions we need, and logic can identify when we err on that journey. Of course, we need something more than reason and logic, we need a Source to know right from wrong before we can make progress, and our conscience works well enough to point us in the right direction as we seek answers.

We used reason and logic to look at a few important concepts that many people hold in their minds, which thoughts are wrong and get in the way of finding the solution. We saw that existential relativism is a self-defeating belief that should be rejected by those who want to order their reality by that which is true. We saw how many people who hold to relativism are unable to make sound judgments, contradict themselves, and act hypocritically due to the erroneous usage of "judge-mentalism," "tolerance" and "respect." We looked at several of the things people use to hide from truth, like complexity, redefining language, "feel good or positive" philosophies, and of course religion.

Having reviewed all those things has enabled us to get to a place to successfully evaluate Christianity and the Christians that make it up and who claim that Christianity is the solution to the world's problems—to humanity's problems. We have set the playing field, so to speak, and provided a framework and context to judge whether Christianity is a successful failure.

One last thing we must do before we look at Christianity is to clarify some essential concepts. Without understanding these concepts correctly, we will not be able to evaluate Christianity successfully, or at least we will not be able to arrive at sound, reasoned conclusions.

Important Misunderstood Distinctions

Let us take a close look at some essential concepts and reveal some crucial distinctions among those concepts. Let us start by contrasting the definitions of the critical concepts identified by the terms "belief" and "faith" and "religion."

Belief: A thought, concept or idea held or understood in a person's mind.

Belief is not faith for it does not reside at the core existential level of a person nor do most beliefs require trust of something or someone. Beliefs may or may not drive or influence a person's behavior. Beliefs are metaphysical things.

The term "believe" can refer either to a mere intellectual concept or it can be used synonymously with a faith concept. If a person has a firm conviction associated with a belief, then they will typically behave consistently with that belief (and its representation in reality) which they value. For example, people are willing to die for various causes, and thus the beliefs associated with those causes are strongly held or perceived as very valuable. For example, some environmentalists have strong beliefs. However, if someone is willing to die for a view – say to protest the way a government is treating people they care about – that does NOT mean they placed their faith in the people they care about or in the belief that the government is wrong.

All people have beliefs about the fundamental questions of life, the purpose of their existence, and what is truly valuable, even agnostics and non-theists and even if they are not willing or able to articulate them.

Faith: Placing one's deep or core level trust, or having confidence in, someone or something to meet some real or perceived need, especially in people/things which cannot be validated by our senses.

Faith reaches from the heart to the mind, and thus one can articulate into what they have put their faith. Faith is different than belief for it resides at the core level (the "heart" or will) and will always guide behavior…who or what we have our faith in will have behavior consequences.

Many people have some level of faith in something, usually in themselves, money or material things, their religion or a god of their own making, but NOT the Creator or his Messenger who is only revealed by His Messenger.

Religion: People's beliefs and practices regarding God things, spiritual things and the afterlife, which beliefs and practices have NO REASONABLE BASIS in the teachings of Jesus of Nazareth.

Religion's primary behavior consequences are ritual and moral "don't do" rules. Without faith, the "don't do" rules are generally not objectively applied or observed but instead are usually followed when one perceives they will benefit from doing so or to avoid punishment.

The world is filled with many religions as well as billions of religious people.

A person can believe that God exists and have other associated God beliefs but that person could not have placed their faith in that God. *In fact, most people reasonably will not put their faith in someone or something they do not know, are not familiar with or of which they are afraid or uncertain.* That is why Joshua taught that everlasting Life itself is facilitated by "knowing God through himself" (John 17:3). If you get to know Joshua by reading his words and deeds, you will likely place your faith in him and the Creator he represents because you will understand his core nature of love, Light, and Life.

A religious person can have many God beliefs that they could be tested on to see if they know them, and take a test and pass that test about their God, but that does not mean they have placed their faith in that God. It also certainly does not mean they have put their faith in the actual Creator of life on the earth who is only well revealed and represented by Joshua of Nazareth.

A person can –and most do - have faith "in an unknown god," or a god that is part or all of their own making often created in their likeness and with the same nature. That is why the schizophrenic Bible god is so popular – wrath and love, vengeance and forgiveness!

The world's mass media are confused regarding the distinction between "faith" and "religion," and they work hard to make the terms synonymous. In other words, the world's media on television will as a matter of practice use the terms "faith" and "religion" as meaning the same thing.

The King and His Rules

We have used the concept of faith many times in this book up to this point, and we have defined it several times. However, it is imperative that the reader has a clear understanding of the two terms which are typically used synonymously.

Here is an illustration to help clarify the difference between faith and religion.

There once was a King whose name was Sebastian. He was an outstanding man and was an exceptional leader. He genuinely cared about his subjects throughout his kingdom, and he treated all the servants in his castle really well. As a result, the people in the castle enjoyed working for the King and appreciated all the beneficial things he gave them.

King Sebastian had a handicap that did not allow him to travel easily, so it was difficult for him to go out of the castle and travel around his kingdom. One of the critical tasks he spent his time on was figuring out rules for people in the kingdom. The King wanted his laws to be both fair and just, and he wanted them to both facilitate the freedom of the people in his kingdom as well as prevent conflict. Once every six months, he would publish his latest set of rules for some domain in his kingdom like housing or buying and selling or transportation or resource distribution or conflict resolution. He would have these rules posted on the village squares where all the people could see them and read them.

King Sebastian had both an excellent character and was an outstanding thinker as well, so his rules were excellent and would accomplish what they intended for the people—freedom and peace.

There were four basic kinds of people regarding how they would react to the King's rule postings.

The first kind of person would not even bother to read the rules but would ignore them, and if they ran into a situation where they needed to know the rules, they would deal with that at the time.

The second kind of person would react negatively, along the lines of, "oh, that King thinks he knows better than us. I'm not going to listen to his stupid rules! I want to do what I think is best for me'.

The third kind of person would say something along the lines of, "oh, wow, what a great rule! I can see how that will help us order our lives in this area. That King is very wise; I can't wait for his rules regarding commerce.'

The last kind of person would read the King's rules—really read them and think about them. After a few readings of the King's laws and thinking about them, they would say something along the lines of, "I need to meet with this King, get to know him and serve him, for he is an exceptional human being." These people would leave the village they might have lived in for years and set out to find the King and to be with him and serve him in his castle.

And so it is with religion versus faith.

The first two people represent those who don't believe God exists or that what God wants cannot be known – non-theists and agnostics. They also represent people who are offended to submit to anyone's authority, believing they are most "free" by living the way THEY want regardless of how their choices might affect other people – anarchists and existential and ethical relativists.

The third person represents the religious people of the earth. Religious people are willing to submit to moral rules and say they believe God exists, but they are NOT willing to change their basic life pattern. In other words, they like assuming that they will survive death and that God will receive them into a happy place, but they are not willing to do anything to hasten or facilitate their being with the God they claim to submit to because there is little or no faith in, or love for, that God!

Religious people like to study "god stuff," and they like to partake in rituals they enjoy and to gain social contacts through their religion. But they are unwilling to leave their "life in the village" to find, know and serve the King. While they have many god beliefs, and will even kill over them, they lack faith in the One True King and the Father he represents. As stated, they will obey many of the rules, but not the ones that cost them something they value in this life. Most importantly, they don't understand WHY the King gives the rules nor do they want to know why.

The last person is the person who enters into faith in the King. They choose to trust the King to take care of them, and they are no longer bound by fear and a controlling power in their life. They leave their life in the village and journey to the King. They try diligently to get to know the King and what he is like and what he wants so they can express their love for him and serve him well. They experience the King's love and forgiveness and understand that it is love that motivates the King and he gives the rules because he cares about us and wants what is best for us!

Continuing Some Extremely Important Distinctions

So, we can now see the distinction between faith in God and beliefs about God. Those who place their faith in God change, grow, and live differently than the people around them. Those who merely have God beliefs are not affected by those beliefs if they don't also have faith…they typically do not significantly change themselves or their lifestyles concerning their God beliefs…they will blend into the general culture or society.

God and Religion

Let us continue making essential clarifications and distinctions. Let us focus on the difference between God and religion. Are they the same? No, they are not. God would be a metaphysical being or entity, while religion is the stuff people do or believe in the name of god or to appease or be accepted by their god.

Do you see the difference?

It is like the difference between a famous person (god) and the things that person's fans do to get the famous person's attention or affections (religion). Or like the difference between the real person (god) and that person being described in a non-fiction book about him but written by people who did not know him well (religion).

So religion is the stuff people do – rituals performed or partaken in - or the things they believe about God to be accepted by their god or gods or to try and get to a good after-life; which rituals or beliefs have no basis in the teachings of Joshua of Nazareth. So, can religion bring peace to a person's soul? It might bring a relieving distraction or a temporary comfort or change of focus or even good habits, but will religion consistently bring peace and purpose to a person? No, it will not.

Religion is not a being; therefore religion is not God. Thus, while religious leaders may claim to speak for God, they are not God nor do they have any good way to prove they are accurately representing God with their teachings. Is there a way to get the answers we need directly from God?

Faith and Religion

The world commonly makes faith and religion synonymous, meaning they use the terms interchangeably because they believe they mean the same thing. They are wrong as we have seen. Faith is merely a core level trust or confidence in something or someone, while religion is the beliefs and practices of people regarding God things, spiritual things or metaphysical things apart from the teachings of Joshua of Nazareth.

It should be evident that religion would not have the answers from God in the same way the famous person's fans would not know for sure what kind of person the renowned person is since they do not know him/her personally. If you are looking for answers from the famous person, you need to ask the famous person, not the "stars" fans. The "stars" fans would not know all the things the famous person has done let alone their character or way of life. Only the renowned person themselves (or someone who honestly knew them well, meaning lived with them for a while) could provide, with full assurance, questions about what they are like, what they want, why they make individual decisions, or about what they value in life or about their existence.

As another analogy, the readers of a book can only know the author if the author tells them about herself in an honest manner. If all the people have are the author's storybooks, then they will have a difficult time personally knowing the author. If, however, the author's good personal friends wrote a biography about the author, then a person could get to know specific vital facts about the author, her character, her motivations and her life.

Therefore religion – the second-hand stuff people claim about God – cannot provide any certain answers about God.

Religious people often do not represent well even the god they claim as their god. Religion is the distorted creation of people claiming they know the Creator. Religion can reveal the Creator just as well as Madison Avenue's marketing claims can reveal the products it describes.

There are often good aspects to religion – it's promoting good moral behavior – but sadly, the bad outweighs the good—distorting the Creator is an evil that far exceeds the ethical aspects. And most importantly, religion prevents people from DOING what the Creator wants.

So what if faith is necessary to "hear" God? How do you know what God in whom to place your faith? What if you put your trust in the wrong god?

Can you have faith in the wrong thing or person? Just ask all the abused children if their faith in the abusing parents was rightly placed. Just ask the boys - who looked to religious leaders to represent God, and who were sexually abused by those men - if they had their faith in the right place.

Religion is *not* the answer, and faith does play an essential role in being able to receive the answers we need. Sadly, most people are putting their faith in the wrong thing, and often that includes a god of their own making.

It is good to believe God exists. It is better to have faith in God, even if you have facts wrong about Him. It is best to have faith in the Creator/Father that Joshua of Nazareth alone reveals.

In the next chapter, we will look at the primary thing that religious leaders have used through the centuries to control people.

Chapter Summary:
- Important distinctions exist between the terms/concepts of "belief", "religion", "faith" and "God";
- All people hold beliefs about their existence and the why's of their existence even if they are unable or unwilling to articulate them. Beliefs about their existence are not faith, and they are not necessarily religious;
- "Religion" is people's beliefs and practices regarding God things, spiritual things and the afterlife. From Joshua of Nazareth's perspective, the definition of religion includes this important qualifier – which beliefs and practices have *no reasonable basis* in his teachings;
- "Faith" is placing one's deep or core level trust or confidence in someone or something to meet some real or perceived need, especially in someone or something that cannot be validated by our senses;

- "God" is a being or entity, not beliefs about him/her. The actual, real Creator is not the invention of religious people. Instead, He is the Agent or Cause behind human existence—the Creator, Designer, and Father of human beings.

20
THE THREAT OF HELL AND OTHER FEAR TACTICS

Opening Questions:
- How important a role does fear play in religious people?
- Does fear encourage learning and considering different viewpoints?
- Is fear used by people to get what they want from others?
- Is hell real?
- If we are acting in love towards another person, would that include calling that person a nasty thing or labeling them with some negative label?
- If we are secure in our heavenly Father, will we act in fear towards others?

Perhaps one of the most potent things used to control people is fear. Unfortunately, we humans are very susceptible to fear guiding our beliefs and behavior. In truth, we as human beings don't need to be governed by fear. However, we do need another motivation for us to do what is right if we don't have fear guiding us, and that other and higher motivation is love. Remember, the core of God's love is valuing others and selfless behavior motivated by compassion. If that love motivated all people, this world would be a radically different and an infinitely better place.

Unfortunately, this is not so, so in place of the purest love, most have fear motivating them to avoid doing wrong things. In other words, fear would drive me to do whatever it takes to prevent loss or damage to my person or life—to defend my life in this world or defend what I want in this world. Selfishness motivates me to preserve or advance my well-being in this world no matter how it might affect others. Fear is a powerful trap due to our selfish nature, motivating us to protect our self-interests at all costs. Unfortunately, we do not naturally love so our default motivation is fear and selfishness.

Political leaders use fear for their political ends when they say things like, "that nation wants to harm us so we ought to strike them." or, "those extremists are among us and must be rooted out." Business leaders use fear when they say things like, "this bad thing is probably going to happen, so you need to buy our products or services to be ready.'; or, "if you don't have this product or service, people won't like or accept you'; or, "if we don't make our profit margins, we are all going to be out of jobs.'

Religious leaders use fear when they say things like, "if you don't believe this, God will be mad at you or send you to hell'; or, "if you don't do this or if you do that, God will condemn you to hell." *The threat of hell is a potent fear motivator, perhaps the greatest ever created and used by people against others.* "Hell," as defined by the religious leaders, is a place and state of eternal torment, where a person's soul will be tormented forever. Many people will reasonably do whatever they think is necessary to avoid everlasting torture! Thus, most religions, including Bible/Christian religion, have been very effective, over the centuries, at controlling many people by fear.

Here is the ultimate fear trap explained in a bit more detail.

Belief 1: Part of God's character is that he is an angry, vengeful, wrathful, bloodthirsty being, who is eager to want to punish and destroy those people who fail to meet his perfect moral standard – the sinners and transgressors—see the Hebrew scripture and Paul to validate this. In fact, this god had his perfectly honoring, obedient and loving son killed in a horrible way so that he could forgive the guilty sons and daughters.

Belief 1 is entirely false.

Belief 2: Due to that part of God's character of anger, vengeance, and wrath, he created a place to torture eternally those people who don't meet his moral standards.

Belief 2 is false in that God did not create hell as a place to send human souls, nor is it a place for eternal torture.

Belief 3: Therefore, those who don't meet God's moral standards (as given and explained by the religious leaders) – will be sent to eternal torment by God.

Belief 3 is false. God sends no one to hell; instead, we can send ourselves to either Life or justice and destruction. While God did set up the system, He does not decide what an individual chooses.

Along come the religious leaders with their self-serving religious system to allegedly try and help people avoid hell and instead enter into heaven. What is perhaps the most popular "protestant" solution to the hell problem? It is something like, "just believe these things about God and participate in our religious organizations (in reality, give money to us), and by grace, you will be heaven bound." The Catholics and "Orthodox" are mostly the same, and they say believe God exists and believe this stuff about God that we tell you and do these required rituals.

As an actual example of religious leaders using fear for money, much of the billions of dollars of wealth that the leaders of the Roman Catholic religious system control, came from the fear concepts of purgatory and hell that they propagated and used for many centuries to take money from people.

In essence, religious leaders say that if you don't believe and do what "God wants," you are going to hell – a place where you will be tormented forever. In reality, if you don't believe and do *what the religious leaders want (not God)*, then they tell you, you are going to hell. Tragically, the religious leaders do not represent Joshua's Father, our Father, and the Creator as we shall see in more detail later on.

As you have seen if you have read and understood his teachings well, Joshua says that he is to be people's life/spiritual leader, not anyone else. And Joshua wants people to love one another each day, and not play foolish, selfish, empty games based on men's religion. God does not exist in the little box called "religion" that people put Him in. Instead, He is the great Spirit which created our soul and spirit, and He wants human beings to love each other all the time in all contexts of daily life—he wants us to do what is right, chiefly love one another.

The reality is that we set our after-physical-death-destiny by what we choose to do with the life we are given. *God condemns no one, nor does He send people to hell – a real place of justice and destruction - not of eternal torment.*

Joshua speaks for the Creator, God and he says:

> I did not come to destroy men's lives, but to save them. (Luke 9:56)

> For God so loved the people of the earth, that He gave His only begotten Son, that whoever puts their faith in him shall not destroy themselves, but rather have eternal life. For God did not send the Son into the world to judge the world, but that the world might be saved through Him. (John 3:16ff)

Please note, Joshua did not say:

'For God was so pissed off at the people of the earth that he sent his son so that he could condemn the people of the earth to an eternal torment in hell.'" And yet, if you listen to many religious leaders long enough, that is essentially what they teach at least some of the time.

Furthermore, most religious leaders teach that **what** *you believe* is what determines if God sends you to heaven or hell. There are two falsehoods and one truth in that statement. One falsehood is that what one believes is solely responsible for one's after-physical-death destiny. The other lie is that God determines a person's fate. The truth is that a person's beliefs do play a role in determining one's future, but only a part, not the sole determining factor as we shall see below.

Joshua teaches that our choices around faith, beliefs, and behavior are what will determine where we end up after our body dies. We determine our after-physical-death destiny by our decisions regarding these three things.

1. **Whether we choose to place our faith in our Creator Father**, an act of our heart or will illuminated by our soul.

If we don't believe God exists, we cannot place our faith in Him. We can also believe God exists and not place our faith in Him. Many people believe God exists, but they have never put their faith in Him. *Faith is the sure way to enter into Life, and faith is merely a deep, whole person, core level trust in someone or something.* It is best to place one's faith in the Creator Father revealed by the only person in history to defeat death to prove that all he said about God was true. In other words, we can place our faith in the right thing (the Father revealed by Joshua) or the wrong thing(s) like ourselves; money; a god of our own making or the making of religious leaders; etc. Faith is what causes us to be appropriately motivated to execute the third point below. If we place our faith in a god that we are confused about or wrong about - a god of our own or other's making or a corruption of the real Creator - that will lead to wrong understanding and likely wrong behavior and that will hinder us or prevent us from attaining the Life that the True God offers.

2. **What we choose to believe ABOUT God (not whether he exists or not)**, an intellectual act of the mind which can affect behavior.

A person only has two choices regarding the things they believe about God. One is to believe Joshua of Nazareth, and thus believe right things about the Creator. Two is to believe one or more of the many other voices – both dead from books, living people, or self – who claim to know God, what God is like and what God wants. Those who choose the former – those who listen only to Joshua of Nazareth to understand God – will have the best opportunity to come to know the Living Creator God. Please listen to the Light regarding the importance of truly knowing the true and living God:

> And this is eternal life, that you might know God and the one whom He sent. (John 17:3)

Furthermore, to know God is to love Him and to love Him results in doing what He wants. Those who choose to listen to people other than Joshua of Nazareth (or in addition to Joshua of Nazareth), will at best be confused about God, and at worst, will be badly wrong about God. The people who make up the world's religions make this critical mistake – Muslim, Jew, Hindi, Christian, Buddhist, etc. To have wrong beliefs about God, His Person and His desire for human beings, will hinder us or prevent us from attaining the Life He offers.

3. **Whether we choose to DO what God says we ought to do, the primary of which is to love other people**. We need to change into better human beings—real, measurable progress enabled by faith and effort and guided by the Truth who is Joshua of Nazareth.

Finally, we should do what the true and living God says. Why? The Creator made human beings and knew his intent for those created beings. He had a purpose for creating us, and His Messenger provided that purpose. His Son, the Messenger, Joshua of Nazareth, says that a primary way to manifest our love for our Father is to do what He says. Is that not true of parental human relationships? In other words, if our child values us, won't they want to please us by doing what we ask? And what God wants us to do is not difficult to understand at all.

The real and living God's top priority is that *human beings love and care for one another (and by definition, "love" means we don't ask for anything in return for that caring and help) and that they don't harm each other and destroy themselves.* Yes, it is that simple.

But no, "love" is not primarily an emotion, nor is it refraining from harming or hating others, nor is it selfish—rather, love brings people together to care for one another in the life we have been given; and NO, "together" does not mean you in YOUR house on YOUR property, etc. Instead, love means we will be together in a measure proportional to our love for the other person as we shall see in a later chapter.

Furthermore, our choice in making God's appointed Leader, our Leader, will lead us into unity, harmony, peace with other followers and cause a desire to help others through the things that we do. If we don't do that, then we fail at the primary purpose of the life we were given, and again, this will prevent us from attaining the Life He offers.

In summary, it does matter what we believe about God and our existence. But what matters equally as much is whether we place our faith in the correct God and how we choose to live our lives each day based on The Light's teachings. In other words and for example, there are hundreds of millions of people who say something to the effect of, "Oh yes, I am a Christian, and I believe in the Lord Jesus Christ," but then the next moment they will justify killing their enemies. Or, they make little or no effort to get to know this "Jesus" by reading HIS words in the four gospel books. Or they will seldom or never speak his important truths to others. Or they will not significantly share any of their material things with non-natural-family members. Or they will deceive others to gain money. Or they will very seldom treat others the way they want to be treated. Or many other things which contradict the Light's teachings! *So, their stated beliefs will not help them—will not bring them into everlasting Life,* but will likely only serve to bring greater condemnation upon themselves. The more we know, the more accountable we will be for acting upon what we know.

> If you did not claim to see, you would not be guilty, but since you claim to see (and yet reject my truths), your guilt remains. (John 9:41)

Many will respond to these truths by saying, "well, you are right back to fear as the primary motivation for listening to God, because you are saying that if we don't listen to God, then we condemn ourselves to destruction." That is a false or incorrect statement. God does not produce fear in people nor does He use it to motivate or manipulate free-will human beings. Rather, people are trapped **in fear** and this in spite of the Creator's love and His reaching out to us in love. Self-condemnation is a consequence of *our* choices to enter into, and then remain in, the state of self-pride and fear and selfishness, and *no one* has to choose to stay in that state of being. Joshua came and offers anyone who will listen to HIM the key to open our self-made jail cell and thus be truly free. Again, we condemn ourselves to destruction; God does not. *God merely set up a just system of accountability as well as a Way out of a wasted, selfish life.*

Humans are not neutral beings, meaning we are predisposed to a state of self-pride and fear and selfishness due to our nature. Our choice is simple to understand but challenging to make. Remain bound or guided by our nature of self-pride and fear and selfishness, or reach out past ourselves to the One who can set us free…the One who can lift us out of our self-made pit.

When things are wrong in my life, the correct question is not, "how come God…", but rather, "why don't I want to practice love as God defines that and asks of me." Or, "why will I not admit the truth on this matter and move forward?" Or, "why do I refuse to do what is right?" Or, "why do I continue to be driven by fear?"

Why is it wrong for the Creator to have set it up that free-will beings would need to choose love to be rewarded with the Greater Life? Why would that be unjust?

God gave us our soul and gave us a free will to choose what do with the life he gave us on this earth. Do you fault Him for giving you life? Would you prefer never to have existed? What about, "it is better to have loved and lost than never to have loved at all'? Do you believe that is a true saying? What it is saying is that love is perhaps the most important aspect of human existence and to not experience or practice love is to miss out on the most important aspect of human existence—to miss the purpose of our creation. And that "missing" was not God's fault, but ours.

Is that not also true about existence? In other words, it is better to have existed and had a chance and opportunity to better one's self and preserve one's existence (through faith and love) than to have never existed at all. We don't have to choose to condemn and destroy ourselves by a life lived in bondage to self-pride, fear and selfishness and all the wrong behavior those things bring—there is a Way out of that darkness.

Furthermore, many people, when they hear the truths of Joshua that this book conveys, react with fear by saying some version of, "Oh, but my husband was a Christian, so are you saying they went to hell?" or "But my wife or child was a Christian, so are you saying they went to hell?" This author has no power to send anyone anywhere! We each must choose our eternal destiny. And if anything, this book should give you hope that your loved one will stand before a Judge of love instead of a Judge of wrath and hell.

Religious Fear and Pride

How many people have been, are, and will be harmed due to the manifestations or behaviors associated with religious fear and pride? Well, we can answer the "have been" as it has been many millions of people, and that is not counting the Nazi persecution of the Jews.

Here is an example of the religious fear and pride dynamic played out.

Person 1 says something about God that contradicts challenges or calls into question person 2's beliefs about God. Person 2 says to themselves some form of the statement, "Oh if I am wrong about God, I might be rejected by God and perhaps sent to hell." That statement is a fear-based statement.

Person 2's next thought is something to the effect of, "Well, I have all these intelligent people I respect who gave me my belief about God (or "I studied the scripture myself') and they can't all be wrong, so I am correct, and that other person is wrong." That is a statement of self-pride.

Person 2 then says to person 1, some form of the statement, "Sorry, but you are wrong about God for this reason..." If person 1 does not "admit" they were wrong, but instead uses reason well to try and show person 2 they are wrong, then the mixture of fear and self-pride will often turn into hatred. Hatred is an intense dislike of another person who one perceives wronged them, or strong dislike by seeing a person as worthless and worthy of punishment, harm or death.

This simple dynamic - while not comprehensive and while coming in slightly different forms - has played itself out probably trillions of times over the millennia. Sometimes it just leads to merely a friendly disagreement between two people. Sometimes, it leads to war with countless thousands killing each other in the name of God. One thing is sure, though; fear and pride are at the heart of it. Not necessarily fear of the other person, but rather fear of God due to ignorance—fear of what God might do to me if I am wrong about who He is or what He wants of me.

A disciple of Joshua will experience this dynamic regularly if they are faithful in speaking the Light's truths to people they encounter. Here is how it usually plays out. The disciple is talking to a religious person and hears the religious person say something that is contrary to what the Light of the world teaches. The disciple will quote the teaching or saying of Joshua that demonstrates the error in the religious person's belief about God. The religious person will typically be offended to some degree and will want to argue with the disciple.

The disciple might make some clarifications as to why the belief is wrong as the discussion progresses. If the religious person will not listen to the Light's teaching but instead will try and defend their error, the tone for the religious person will often demonstrate the fear that is driving their effort to hold onto a wrong belief. At some point - usually when the disciple uses reason well several times to try and show the person their error - the religious person will move from fear to self-pride and start making personal attacks on the disciple. Since the disciple is using reason well to demonstrate the other person's false beliefs, the person with wrong beliefs has nothing left to respond with except personal attacks, and so they attack the messenger instead of humble themselves and receive truth and change their understanding.

What personal, fear-based attacks are most common? Some of the most popular attacks from Biblians and Christians are calling the disciple a "heretic" or "a cult leader" or "part of a cult." The Biblian or Christian who has failed in their argument(s) has two choices - be humble and accept the truth the disciple is trying to convey (and thus face change), or let fear and self-pride drive them to attack the messenger. Sadly, the latter is the most common response.

So, what exactly is a "heretic" or a "heresy"? Merriam-Webster says "heresy" is "adherence to a religious opinion contrary to church dogma"; "an opinion, doctrine, or practice contrary to the truth or to generally accepted beliefs or standards." [49] Thus a "heretic" is a person who holds that opinion or doctrine or belief.

So, the question is who determines the correct "church dogma" or "generally accepted beliefs or standards"? The Roman Catholic people and the Protestant people cannot even agree on what books to include in their "sacred scripture" or Bible and called the "other side" heretics - and killed them - for centuries! In fact, the Biblian/Christian religious system is made up of thousands of divisions, which divisions are caused by one sects/denomination's religious opinions or dogma differing from the others, thus the division! The Biblians and Christians seem to thrive on excommunicating one another - by some estimates, there are tens of thousands of divisions - and often in their forming a new sect, the reason they give was that their previous sect was starting to "adopt heresy" or that "God has given this guy/gal some new important revelation'. Ironically, the new teaching that causes the division is often offered by some charismatic individual who says some version of "God says listen to me" - see "cult" below!

How about the "cult" accusation and attack? Merriam-Webster defines "cult" as "a small religious group that is not part of a larger and more accepted religion, and that has beliefs regarded by many people as extreme or dangerous"; or, "great devotion to a person, idea, object, movement, or work." [49]

In the U.S. culture at this time, a cult is generally thought to be a religious or social group with socially deviant or novel beliefs and practices. However, whether any particular group's beliefs and practices are sufficiently atypical or unique is often unclear, thus making a precise definition problematic. In the English speaking nations, the word often carries derogatory connotations, but in other European countries, it is used as English-speakers use the word "religion," sometimes confusing English-speakers reading material translated from other languages. The word "cult" has always been controversial because it is (in a pejorative sense) considered a subjective term, used as an ad hominem attack against groups with differing doctrines or practices, which lacks a clear or consistent definition.

As you can see, labeling someone a "cultist" is problematic. The first problem is the lack of an authoritative standard to judge whether any particular group's beliefs and practices are sufficiently deviant or novel - precisely who makes that judgment! The second problem is the term is often used as an ad hominem attack (personal attack) against a person or

---

[49] Merriam-Webster Dictionary, www.merriam-webster.com, April 2018

other group who does not tow the party line of the religious person (or their sect or division or denomination) who is leveling the accusation.

I find the accusation of "cult" by Biblians and Christians against disciples of Joshua like myself as particularly ironic and irrational. Here are two reasons that support that the accusation is based on fear or self-pride.

1. We, disciples, have "Jesus Christ" (specifically, the words of the historical Jesus or Joshua of Nazareth as recorded in the four gospel books) as our ONLY Standard for knowing God just as he says we ought! Odd that that would be such a problem or offense for those who claim "Jesus Christ" as their God!

2. Those who define "cult" as more of this - "great devotion to a person" - seem to be quite blind to the fact that many religious people venerate and follow their leaders, thus fulfilling the definition of "cult"! Think any prominent religious leader like Joel Osteen, etc.

Ironically, we as disciples of Joshua seek to follow by faith ONLY the real Joshua of Nazareth revealed by his own words in the four gospel books! In other words, we disciples try very hard to reject the adoration of other people towards us since our Master says "do not call another person a spiritual leader or teacher"—rather, we point people towards the Light instead of ourselves. In contrast, the religious world (just like the other world realms, like entertainment, for example) is filled with men and women who have many followers who are devoted to them to some degree. Those religious leaders encourage this adoration since they like the power over of all those people looking to them, and thus are considered "successful" as a result. In short, many Christian leaders and sects fit the world's definition of "cult" and "cult leaders"!

In truth, any God-belief that varies from a religious person's beliefs - and whatever sect they are a part of - if spoken with conviction and shown plainly to contradict what the religious person considers essential religious beliefs - will likely be judged as "heresy" or "cultic" or worthy of rejection.

In truth, throwing "heretic" or "cult leader" at someone is done so by a person who is losing or has lost the "truth" battle and is operating by fear or self-pride and thus attacking the messenger. It is merely another logical fallacy tactic as we have seen.

In times past and in certain places, that could get a person burned at the stake. In many nations still today, you might well be killed for expressing a God-belief that goes against the ruling or majority groups "accepted orthodoxy'. Today in the US, and for the moment anyway, they will throw you out of their religious organizations or "unfriend" you or stop "following" your page on Facebook!

In conclusion, religious fear and pride cause a tremendous amount of conflict in the world - it always has and it ever will. Human's "operating system," as given by their Creator, includes a conscience which knows at some level that having a proper understanding of one's existence and what to do with that existence/life is very important. Thus God-beliefs are a very sensitive issue for many billions of people—and fear of the Unknown God causes that sensitivity. Whether Christian or Muslim or Jew, etc. - they all have the same schizophrenic scary, vengeful, wrathful god who sends many to hell - *one of the great lies that the religious people of the world believe and propagate to stay away from the Creator and His Light.*

The good news is that you don't have to be afraid of your Creator—you don't have to be ruled or controlled or heavily influenced by fear. Nor do you have to put yourself in a cage of ignorance created by your self-pride. All you need to do is to care about what is true and right no matter where that leads you, and if you do, you will find the Life He so much wants you to have!

I placed this chapter here because we are about to enter into the fear realm of many religious people. In other words, the chapters that follow will show how the success failure's beliefs and practices do not match up with the One who called himself, The Son of Man, The Light of the world, and the way, truth and life. You have a choice if you are a religious person. You can push past fear and evaluate what is presented, or you can allow fear to "protect you" from truth.

Chapter Summary:
- Fear of hell has been a significant factor in preventing people from considering different views of God or our existence;
- Threatening people with hell has been a benchmark of religious leaders control over people for many centuries;
- While there is a spiritual place of destruction that Joshua refers to as "hell" (fashioned after the real place of Gehenna); and that place is everlasting; the beings who send themselves there do not last forever there. Instead, they receive justice and are destroyed;
- God does not send people to hell; instead, people send themselves there to receive justice for refusing to live by love, truth, and rightness;
- Being labeled a "heretic" or "cultic" or other such fear labels is a hallmark of a religious person losing an argument and using an ad hominem fallacy to try and shut their opponent up;
- Fear is an effective motivator to prevent people from doing certain things due to fear of the consequence or justice or punishment;
- Joshua did not teach that fear ought to be our motivation for what we do with our life or how we behave, but instead, *love should be our motivation.* He did teach that fear as a secondary motivator – if we

refuse to be motivated by love – is better than harming other people.

21
PRIMARY FALSEHOODS OF CHRISTIANITY

Opening Questions:

- What is the difference between a falsehood and a lie?
- Is there a valid way to determine if Christian's beliefs are true or false?
- What Do Christians have right about God?
- Why would most Christians fail a test containing questions about the historical Joshua of Nazareth's teachings?

The chapter title contains the term "falsehoods," so now would be as good a time as any to explain the difference between "falsehoods" and lies. As you might be aware, religious people regularly react to someone who brings a belief that contradicts one of their religious beliefs, by accusing the person bringing the contradiction as "lying" or "speaking lies." As we learned, generally religious people are very defensive about their religious belief because they are afraid to have their religious beliefs tested against reason and logic—they are worried those beliefs will be exposed as wrong or false. Thus, they tend to bring the worst accusation (lying) than the lesser, more accurate allegation (saying something is false).

In short, the act of lying or something being a lie contains intent. That is to say, when I purposely communicate a falsehood, then I am lying, or I lied. Most things which are not accurate which are communicated by human beings are falsehoods, not lies. Falsehoods are typically communicated due to ignorance. For example, if someone says to another person, "Islam is a religion of peace," they are more than likely doing that out of ignorance. That is to say, they do not know that Mohammed's violence-justifying-sayings are real and contained in Islam's sacred writings.

So either they are just ignorant of the facts about Mohammad's writings, or they have believed the falsehood many speak and communicate that Islam is a religion of peace. (A true statement would be that Islam is a religion of peace for the majority of Muslims due to their ignorance of, or their explaining away of, Mohammad's violence justifying sayings.)

Again, lying is purposeful…the person lying is purposely trying to deceive the listener. Perhaps the best example of the distinction between lying and communicating a falsehood is counterfeit currency. The person creating the counterfeit currency is perpetrating a lie as they hand the false currency note to a person and say, "here is a twenty dollar bill." The person who takes the counterfeit currency note and does not know it is a false note and then passes the note on to another saying, "here is a twenty dollar bill" is communicating a falsehood, not a lie.

So it is with Christians and Christianity.

The lies in the spiritual realm are not typically generated by human beings, but rather by a powerful spiritual being that Joshua identifies as the prince of this world. However, the Christian leaders ought to know that many of the things they teach are false because they have easy access to Joshua's teachings and can use reason and logic. However, and tragically, since those Christian leaders believe the foundational lies which hide the actual Standard, they speak many falsehoods when it comes to their Christian beliefs as we shall see.

I don't believe that many Christian leaders know they are speaking falsehoods. The vast majority is indefensibly ignorant of Joshua's teachings, yes, but they are not knowingly telling people untruths …they believe the falsehoods are correct, which is what it means to be deceived.

Let us turn a corner. As we saw in the chapter on "Hiding in Complexity," I have found that if people are not willing to accept that $1 + 1 = 2$, then they are certainly not going to be willing to accept $((100 - 50)/50) * (3 - 1) = 2$. In other words, a lengthy discussion and revealing of the error will not convince a person who is in a mode to defend their religious beliefs. If one has a genuinely open mind and thus will allow reason to inform them and logic to correct them, then simplicity is not only all that is needed but is best. However, I know some people want (or believe they need) more, so I will address a few of the more tightly held "sacred" beliefs as appendices. Also, we have covered some of these errors previously, but I have found that redundancy can be an aid to consideration or acceptance, so please bear with me.

The thing that calls itself "the church" is comprised of organizations of various sizes – from large like Roman Catholicism or Eastern Orthodox, to Protestantism to Pentecostal to Anabaptist to small groups of people. The people who make up those organizations are all organized around the idea that who God is and what He wants can be found and understood through the Bible (minus Joshua's primary teachings) and that organization's leadership. (Most world religions work the same way.)

Some will say that Christianity is about "Christ", but Christianity's "Christ" is still at least partially derived through the Bible and those who say they are experts on the Bible, or who claim to "have the Holy Spirit's anointing" or are graduates of Best Seminary or some other such subjective claim.

The simple truth is that the source would be the best place to go to understand the source!

This the Christians do not do.

As we have seen, instead they substitute a huge book and their esteemed and chosen leaders, so they don't have to look directly at the Light. Or stated another way, they like the house with the really "cool" flashing Vegas type lights instead of the house with the clear, pure, bright light.

So, what are some of the fundamental beliefs and practices of Christianity?

1. That the Bible is the word of God to humankind.

This fundamental belief of who or what is to be humankind's standard for knowing God is false as we shall see in the next three chapters.

The truth is that Joshua of Nazareth is the Word of God to humanity, NOT the Bible. Even the Bible says that! See John 1:1, Luke 1:2, Rev. 19:13.

(See *Appendix 7, Protestant Biblicism Debunked.*)

2. That the concept of love is just something to be talked, preached, sung about and "felt," but not to be lived out.

This is a false belief and practice. As we shall see, since "love" is defined in the culture as primarily a feeling – and the Christians are very much part of the culture of the nation they live in - how can a feeling be lived out anyway?

Truth: God's love is not an emotion or a feeling, nor does it have anything to do with the male to female attraction. But believing the wrong thing about the all-important concept of "love" is a "great way" to avoid having to love people. *Love as the Creator defines it, will bring people together to live together and share His Life together – a communal life of faith and love—it is that simple.* Followers of the Light will be together, helping one another in daily life, being the Family/true community that we are told to be. We will take a closer look at this crucial topic later in the Solution section.

As an aside, can you imagine if your spouse went around signing and talking about how much you love them? "Oh, Bob loves me so much" or "Sally loves me so much." Furthermore, can you imagine if your spouse was doing that because they thought they were something extraordinary that deserved your love? The Christians need to think about that.

3. **That God cannot be known or known well or we rightly cannot understand why He does things**. (The scripture quoted to justify this is often, "For my thoughts are not your thoughts, nor are your ways my ways," declares the Lord. For as the heavens are higher than the earth, so are my ways higher than your ways, and my thoughts than your thoughts." Isaiah 55.)

This is a false belief.

Truth: As we have seen, Christian's enjoy putting reason aside as soon as someone points out some contradictory belief they hold about God; and a common defense is —that we cannot know God or his ways.

While it is true that we cannot know some aspects of God – like His infinite aspects or the extent of His glory, for example – *we certainly can understand his thoughts since Joshua came and gave them to us!* The very purpose of God's Messenger was to **reveal** God – His character and His will for how human beings ought to live.

The Light says:

> And this is eternal life, that *they may know you Father/God*, and me whom you have sent. (John 17:3)

> I praise You, Father, Lord of heaven and earth, that You have hidden these things from the wise and intelligent and have revealed them to infants. (Matt. 11:25)

> Unless you change and become *like little children*, you will not enter the kingdom of heaven. (Matt. 18:3)

God can be known, and it is very beneficial to get to know God! In fact, knowing God well provides eternal Life (John 17:3), so please start loving God with all your mind and get to know Him through His beloved Son/Messenger. The process is not some "super intellectual" exercise; instead, it is an exercise in faith and humility and perhaps finding out what true love is all about.

4. **That God is BOTH a Being of Wrath and Vengeance as well as a God of love.**

This is a false belief.

Truth: The Creator is our Father, and He is not a Being of wrath and anger and bloodthirsty vengeance as the writers of the *Hebrew scripture* - and *Paul, the author of most of the "new testament" and believer in the Hebrew scripture -*

imagined Him to be. Rather, He is a Being of love and compassion, *just as Joshua of Nazareth revealed.* Joshua never says that his Father is a Being of wrath or anger or vengeance—but "the Bible" certainly does! In contrast to "the Bible" god, here are some sayings of the Light to help us understand the character of his Father:

> If you have seen me, you have seen the Father. (*Joshua's revealing of the Father.*) (John 14:9)

To the woman caught in adultery:

> Neither do I condemn you. Go and sin no more. (John 8:11)

On the cross, speaking to the men who just nailed him up there to kill him:

> Father, forgive them for they do not know what they are doing. (Luke 23:34)

To humankind:

> Love your enemies. Matt. 5:44

Presenting a god who is wrathful and vengeful some of the time and loving and merciful some other of the time is almost worse than a purely wrathful being! Imagine the child of a dad who on three days of the week is angry, wrathful, impossibly strict, merciless and eager to harshly punish; and then on four days of the week is loving, kind, patient, etc. Will not the child fear that dad perhaps even more than a purely wrathful dad since the child will not know what is coming the next moment—when, after a moment of compassion shown by the dad causes the child to run to the day only to have the dad strike the child down in anger due to some other infraction. There is one concept that will be primary in the relationship between that dad and his child—fear. Thus the schizophrenic god of the Christians – wrath and vengeance half the time, love, patience, gentleness the other half of the time - effectively and understandably keeps people away from the Real Creator/Father through fear—a fear and uncertainty the religious leaders exploit to their own benefit.

5. That God had Christ sacrificed/killed to pay the penalty for people's sin so that God can forgive people.
This is a false belief.
Truth: No, God did not have his beloved, and obedient Son punished and killed for the wrongdoings of the other disobedient and guilty sons and

daughters (human beings). That would be morally wrong and horribly unjust – to punish the innocent for the guilty - and *God does not do what is wrong*. Remember, God is a God of love and a God who values what is real and right, and a loving father does NOT punish an innocent son for the wrongdoings of guilty ones!

"Why was Joshua Actually Killed?"

The Christian narrative is that "Christ died to pay for the sins of the world." That is a "nice" theological platitude that supports their gospel, but it is false, and Joshua never teaches that as we shall see. Please note two important things about that answer to the question of "Why was Joshua killed?". First, it does not answer the question; instead, it states their opinion about the reason for his death, and *not* why people killed him. Second, it states a religious concept – propitiatory and atoning sacrifice – that Joshua *nowhere teaches* as we shall see.

He was murdered because he spoke offensive and unpopular truths about their religion and people hated him for that and killed him for that. The plain, simple and truthful answer as to why the religious/political rulers of his day murdered Joshua of Nazareth was because he offended their self-pride by essentially saying, "your God beliefs and your associated religion and politics are wrong" and thus they feared him and the truth he spoke. However, he did use their evil to accomplish an amazing and beautiful good – *he paid a ransom through that experience…a ransom that enables a human being to be set free*!

(You can read a more extended defense of this fact at the end of the book, *Appendix 8, Forgiveness and Blood Sacrifice*.)

6. **That God sends people to hell** (a place of eternal torture) if they don't believe what "the Bible" or their Christian leaders say is right about God or God stuff.

This is a false belief.

Truth: The Creator sends no one to "hell'; rather, we send ourselves to justice and destruction (not eternal torture) if we refuse to live a life characterized by love for other human beings. What we believe is important, but what we do or how we behave and choose to live our lives is equally important. If we preach love but don't live it, we are not doing well and are hypocrites. If we love others but don't preach love, we are doing better for our actions speak louder than our words. If we love others and turn people to the Leader and spread The Light's teachings especially about love, then we have done the best.

A loving Father does not harm or destroy his children, *but* his children can walk away from him and harm or destroy themselves.

For those who don't like the reality of being held accountable for our actions, please consider this question. Should Hitler and Mother Teresa have the same after-death experience? If you have a conscience (a spiritual part of your soul) left and are listening to it then everything in that conscience should scream, "no that would be horribly unjust!" And yet this is the "reality" the atheists, physicalists and many religious people would like you to embrace.

Or, as another example, say you have two neighbors on either side of your home. One neighbor is very kind and very helpful and becomes a good friend. The other neighbor is very unkind and creepy and ends up sexually abusing your children and then murdering them and does not get caught. If both of those people were to die accidentally, would it be fair and just for them to experience the same after-death experience?

The Light of the world teaches that we have a heart, soul, mind and spirit and those things make us who we are and those things will endure after our physical body fails.

7. That people need to "go to church" – a religious building that Christians" build to meet in and sing songs they call worship and in which to perform other rituals and "ministries out of.'

This is a false belief and practice.

Truth: God does not want people building temples to him and calling them "churches" and using them for meetings which provide a substitute for actually loving one another, for the Light says that his followers, who are called out of the evil world, are "the church." And no, God does not want people listening to people who misrepresent His Son, who don't teach His Son's truths and who don't live as His Son taught we ought to live, i.e., religious leaders. And no, singing songs about God-stuff or love is not necessarily worship if we are not living what we sing about, for "God is seeking those who worship in spirit and in truth" not who sing songs which lyrics include false beliefs or who don't DO the right things about which they sing.

(See the forthcoming chapter, *What is So Bad about Going to Church?*, as well as Appendices 9 and 10 for more on this issue.)

8. That Christ is God and God is the Holy Spirit, and the three are all the same being.

This is a false belief.

Truth: Joshua/Jesus of Nazareth is who he plainly says he is, "The Son of God" (John 3:18, 5:25, 10:36-37, 11:4; Luke 22:70). Of course, he does not mean a physical offspring, but instead, he is the closest and dearest representative of the Creator, and he carries the Creator's authority.

Joshua of Nazareth never says, "I am God," but rather talks about his "Father in heaven" over 40 times in the four gospels. Therefore, if he – as was recorded in the gospels - was regularly talking about and to "my Father who is in heaven," he could not be the same person as the Father he is talking to, could he -at least if you want to use reason to know truth. If you are a religious person, don't make the mistake of ebbing into the irrational defense of, "but God's ways are higher than our ways…'

The few sayings where he talks about his perfect unity with the Father do NOT contradict nor nullify his plain confessions on who he is, the "Son of God."

> But of that day and hour no one knows, not even the angels in heaven, nor the Son, but only the Father. (Mark 13:32)

(See *Appendix 5, The Trinity Trap*.)

9. That people do not sin to go to heaven with sin generally being defined as doing bad things that their religious leaders identify - sometimes using the Bible, sometimes not.

This is a false belief.

Truth: One of the primary problems with Christians is that in general, they don't work to solve the root problems of people. They don't work to solve the problems because they have not identified those problems. Instead, they have created a generic religious problem they call "sin" and have created a false solution for that problem, as we shall see. By denying the real or more profound or fundamental problems with our nature, Christians will not work to solve them. This denial or ignorance leaves Christians in general *not* being part of the solution, but rather part of the problem.

If we confess our wrongdoings and have remorse over it and ask for forgiveness, God forgives us. Of course, if we are genuinely remorseful, we will not do it again, or we will fight and struggle to stop. Jesus does teach what makes us "unclean" before God - see Mark 7 for example - he does talk about sin and teaches we should not sin. *However, we condemn ourselves by our lack of faith and love which keeps us trapped in our self-pride and fear and selfishness, and thus living a mostly loveless life – which is the great sin* - even while we abstain from some sins (or practice religion or morality). Some things that religious leaders say are sinful are not (for example, drinking alcohol), even while they ignore the greater sins.

I am not saying sin is okay. Nor am I saying that sin does not have a negative impact on people. What I am saying is *abstaining from "sin" is not what eternal Life is about*! Or, stated another way, if sin is rotten apples on the apple tree, then removing those rotten apples does not provide life to the tree! The tree's life comes from the living water and Sonlight (faith), *not* from its fruit—the fruit is merely what the tree produces. "You will know a tree by its fruit." You cannot change a tree by its fruit. Faith and love – the tree's life - are what leads to eternal life. And yes, if we are living by faith and love, our fruit will be good—meaning there will not be a lot of rotten apples (sin).

10. That people participate in a ritual of eating bread and drinking wine to commemorate Christ's death to please God and stay in good stead with Him.

This is a false belief.

Truth: The Living Being that is the Designer and Creator of the human race does not care about rituals that take the place for that which he does care. He cares that His Son be honored, and if the Living Bread is not honored, then all the empty rituals in his name are meaningless and an offense - we are swallowing a camel and choking on a gnat – *meaning we are doing what is far less important because we refuse to do what is really important.*

A god that grants favor through ritual participation is not worthy of human's love or praise, but of course, you need to know the Father to know that!

11. That people get dunked in water or have water poured on them to go to heaven or due to the ritual are accepted by God.

This is a false belief and practice.

Truth: To think that the Creator would only accept people who participated in a little ritual involving water is to have a seriously wrong understanding of the character and heart of God. To think He would send people to eternal torture based on not participating in a water ritual is to reveal complete ignorance—to expose the utter darkness of the human heart, and the utter foolishness of religion in God's name—in other words, to reveal **not knowing god**. See point F above, i.e., "And this is eternal life, that they might know God..."

So to sum up, you mainly have three convenient rituals – "going to church," baptism and "the Lord's supper" – substituted for what God wants—love practiced, rightness practiced, and truth cared about and sought. Not doing what God wants is the heart of the successful failure. Let me say that again. God wants people loving each other, not forming and joining religious social clubs, playing religious games, performing religious rituals, and adhering to a moral code that merely constrains bad behavior. The former, the Christians will not do, the latter, they do.

12. That "the holy spirit" is our guide and teacher and leader and that he will empower us to do what God wants.

Part true, part false.

Truth: The role of the Holy Spirit, according to Joshua of Nazareth, is apparent and straightforward.

- First, he is to be the disciples' enabling-teacher, enabling us to receive *Joshua's teachings* *as preserved in the four gospel books*. In other words, it takes more than mere intellect to absorb "love your enemies."

- Second, he also works to bring people to repentance by working with our conscience to convict the people of the world of sin (how we fall short of doing what is right), and righteousness (knowing and living by what is right and wrong) and judgment (how we are guilty). See John 16.

- Third, he is the disciple's comforter, the one who both made our spirit alive when we were born from above, and who continues to help us (our spirit) connect to our loving heavenly Father.

The Holy Spirit can empower us to do the right thing when we are weak in our flesh, but just like our Father, he does not force us or manipulate us in any way.

There is much "holy spirit" religion out in the world today, and most of it is merely emotional and delusional religion which is nothing more than cheap entertainment or silly spectacles or those seeking emotional adrenaline rushes. How many foolish things and behavior are attributed to "the holy spirits" workings'? These sects like to think they are "alive and not dead" due to their emotionalism but in fact, they are further from the one who calls himself "the Truth" due to their reliance on emotionalism instead of on the truths of the One who calls himself "the truth."

As I have stated previously, our emotions are a gift to color our life experiences, but we were given a mind to reason and a heart/will to choose how to live our lives. In as much as we follow our feelings or emotions we are solidly in the cage and indeed lost and in darkness. In other words, we should not allow our emotions to inform our thoughts and decisions. To follow *any* aspect of ourselves or self-generated beliefs is **not** to follow Joshua of Nazareth. It is especially sad to justify one's emotional approach to life by saying "the holy spirit" is the one doing that.

I will elaborate more on the Holy Spirit in the upcoming chapter entitled, *The Holy Spirit or a Silly spirit?*

In the following chapters, we will take a closer look at some main errors or falsehoods introduced in this chapter and upon which the successful failure is built. We will also look at the methods and means the religious leaders use to encourage people to be dependent upon them instead of dependent upon our heavenly Father and the Leader He sent.

Chapter Summary:

- Almost all of the fundamental beliefs of Christians and their religion Christianity are false either as compared to the teachings of Joshua of Nazareth; or as compared to science or the reality we experience each day on the planet.

- About the only things Christians have right about God-things are the following:
    o God exists;
    o His Son is Joshua of Nazareth (although they contradict themselves on this point when they say he is also God the Father and God the Holy Spirit);
    o God is concerned about how people behave—how human beings treat each other;
    o There will be an accounting for how each of us live our lives;

- When a disciple/student/pupil/follower of Joshua of Nazareth gives a Christian a test/quiz about the teachings of Joshua of Nazareth, the vast majority will fail the test/quiz thus proving they are not listening well to the real, historical Joshua of Nazareth as he revealed himself by his own words and actions in the four gospel books (Just such a quiz can be taken here - http://thepeacefulrevolution.info/quiz.html).

22
IF YOU CAN'T DESTROY IT, HIDE IT

Opening Questions:
- What would be some good ways to hide critical written truths?
- If a truth exists and cannot be destroyed outright, what would be an effective way to attack it or make it of no effect?
- Was it a good idea to place the four gospel books containing the life and teachings of Joshua of Nazareth in "the Bible"?
- Why do so many Christians use a belief of Paul to define their whole or primary standard of understanding God instead of having the Person and sayings of Joshua as their Standard?

A parable is a story with a hidden meaning which meaning addresses something important.

These parables are about something precious which has been lost.

Please, have ears to hear and consider these parables.

Imagine you were kidnapped and put in a horrible place, and other than the kidnapper, there was only one person on the planet who knew where you were. Fortunately, this person cared about you, and although they were halfway around the earth, they knew someone near you who could rescue you. So, they wrote a message to the prospective rescuer, telling him exactly where you were and how you could be saved. They then mailed the message to the potential rescuer. The message arrived safely at the remote post office; however, the post office employee only delivered mail to the rescuer occasionally. So, he took the letter and placed it in a large envelope with many other notes to the rescuer, and on the outside of that envelope was written, "The Envelope of Important Messages." By the time the rescue letter was delivered to the rescuer, it was just one note among many hundreds in the large envelope labeled, "The Envelope of Important Messages." Therefore, your note drowned in a sea of other people's notes, and thus you had little hope of being free from your bondage any time soon.

Here is another illustration to help you understand what has been lost.

Imagine you are stranded on a remote island with only one piece of paper, pen, and bottle. So you write a note to tell those who find the bottle where you are, and your situation and you throw the bottle into the ocean. The bottle finds a current which carries the bottle towards land, but there are thousands of other bottles in that current as well. It seems there were many people who, while not desperately needing to be rescued like yourself, never-the-less greatly enjoyed putting messages in bottles and throwing them in the ocean. Unfortunately for you, all those other bottles found their way to the same current which carried your bottle, and thus your bottle arrives at the beach with thousands of other like bottles containing "urgent" (but pretend or false) messages. Therefore, you have little hope of your message being found anytime soon, and little hope as well of getting free from the captivity of the island.

Perhaps the most accurate illustration of that which has been lost would be as follows.

Let us say you wandered into a vast and Dangerous City - dangerous due to the many people who would look to use you for their selfish purposes - and got yourself lost in a maze of streets, and you desperately need directions out of the city. Let us say that a person who knows the way out of the dangerous city - because they made it out - has clearly and concisely written the directions down in two sentences on a page of paper. That person makes those clear directions available to any who request them and many groups and organizations of people take the instructions and use them for their purposes. In your case, the person from whom you ask the directions is a member of one of those organizations, and that organization feels they need to add to the instructions, even though they don't know for sure the way out of the city because they have never been out of the city. So they write, on a copy of the correct directions, their beliefs on how to get out of the city. And so, when handed the one-page document, the two sentences containing the way to freedom are surrounded by many sentences which contain errors and which at best confuse you and at worst, hide the truth in the two sentences of the way out of the dangerous city. Thus, you don't find your way out of the perilous city because, in your sincere efforts to read the directions, you get more and more lost due to the confusion caused by the errors and inconsistencies contained in that page.

To continue that illustration, let us say that many people regularly get lost in the vast and dangerous city, and so there is a regular need for clear directions out of the city. However, the central authority of the city benefits economically from having more people in their city, even if some are lost and don't want to be there. The paper with the two sentences of clear directions becomes well known amongst the city dwellers, as well as the one page that contains both the two sentences of clear directions surrounded by the erroneous opinions of others. The city authority and those who run the organizations give to those people lost in their city, the confused and error-ridden one full page of "directions" instead of the two clear sentences out. The authorities do this because they discovered that when they give the people the document with errors more people stay in their city, and they all have much to gain from that. They justify it by saying clever but misleading things like, "well, the directions document does contain the truth" and "the directions document contains the way out as we say." Thus, they tell a very clever half-truth and thus deceive themselves and those to whom they hand the "directions."

So the city authority and the organizations formally make a diligent practice of telling the people that the one-page document is "the truth" that people need to get free from their lost-ness in the city. They also tell those people who find out about the page with the two clear sentences of correct directions that that document is "inadequate," "incomplete" and "too simple" and people should not rely solely on that document or its instructions. Now, if a person looking to escape the city respects that authority-person more than wanting to know the truth (correct directions), then what will happen to their ability to find their way out of the city? Will it not be compromised at best, or destroyed at worst? If disagreeing with the authority will have uncomfortable consequences, or even cost the person something they want, won't they be in even a worse situation to find the truth buried in that one page?

One final step to complete the illustration:

In the same way, what if there is a book which contains sixty-six chapters, and only four of the sixty-six chapters include what you need to be set free. And what if an authority that many people respect including yourself, and who claims to know the book better than you, tells you that all sixty-six chapters contain the truth that you need to be set free. And what if they tell you that the four chapters which provide what you need to be set free are "inadequate, insufficient and incomplete"?

If you respect the authority more than wanting to know the truth, then what will happen to your ability to find the actual truth in the four chapters? Will it not be compromised at best, or destroyed at worst?

And what if the cost of rejecting the authority's beliefs about the book will mean being rejected by family and your cherished social or religious circles of friends? Perhaps you will pretend the dangerous city is not so bad after all? Or maybe you like the dangerous city, and thus you are not looking to be set free since you have deceived yourself and think that you already are?

Which brings us directly to that which is most valuable which has been lost?

What if there was a Man who said:

I am the Way, the Truth and the Life, and no one gets to the Father except through me. (John 14)

And;

If you continue in my Word/teachings/truths, then you are truly disciples of mine; and you will know the truth, and the truth will set you free. (John 8)

And he performed many miracles including defeating death to prove what he said was true;

But other's come along after he leaves and, like countless others to come, they say that they have the truth that people need to be accepted by God—to be set free from the things that *bind* us;

And they place these people's words in a big book along with the one sure and final Word of God, and say, "this whole book is the truth, not just the person who says, "I am the truth";

And the religious authorities who like exercising authority over others and who enjoy the lifestyle they gain from the people paying them for their position say, "you need more than the red letters, you need the whole counsel of 'God's Word,' and **you need us** to understand it";

And as years, decades and centuries pass, the book is handed down from generation to generation, each generation before it, listening not to the Light, but to another voice, saying that the whole book contains the truth that people need. And if a person can't understand the book due to the errors or contradictions or complexity, the people's religious leaders say, "well, **you need us** or Christian leader so-and-so or Bible scholar so-and-so to understand the book";

And the religious leaders, whose authority the people respect, **point people to themselves** and the book as well as many other voices, both dead and living, in addition to the one who says, "I am the truth." The religious leaders say, "the book and all these other voices which quote the book are "the truth" you need to know God, not just the one who says, "I am the Truth"—not just the one who says, "If the Son sets you free, you will be free indeed".

If this happened, then isn't the truth of the statements above by the one who says, "I am the truth", **lost** as the people look to the book, and other's words and other voices, and those other words and voice's nullify, cancel or make of no effect the one who says:

I am the Way, the Truth and the Life, and *All who are of the truth listen to MY voice.*

Those eternally valuable truths:

I am the Way, the Truth and the Life, and no one gets to the Father except through me.

And;

If you continue in My word, then you are truly disciples of Mine; and you will know the truth, and the truth will set you free.

Have been drowned out — nullified — buried — **lost.**

Remember the Dangerous City above and the two sets of directions to get free from the city? Sound familiar?

And so, that which is extremely valuable, and which is lost, is revealed.

The Father sent One beloved, error-free Messenger – *one voice* - who can bring freedom from your hopelessness, but his voice has been drowned out, hidden, nullified, and obscured.

The Beloved One says plainly:

All things have been handed over to me by my Father, and no one knows the Son except the Father; nor does anyone know the Father except the Son, and anyone to whom the Son wills to reveal Him. (Matthew 11:27)

This is eternal life, that they may know You, the only true God, and Messiah Joshua whom You have sent. (John 17:3)

No one knows the Father except the Son and a person's eternal destiny is determined by understanding the Father by looking **only** to the One who knows Him, and yet people do not listen to the Son, but instead, listen to all the other voices that say they represent the Son — especially Bible author voices.

It is a painful truth to receive, but in fact, the teachings of the One who calls himself the Light of the world have been covered, buried and for all practical purposes, lost. His Voice has been drowned out by thousands of other voices. In fact, at an essential level, his Voice has been replaced by a book, "the Bible" or "the Scripture" or "God's Word," by a clever slight-of-hand Paul provides which says that *the book is* his voice!

His statements, "All who are of the truth listen to **my** voice"; and "nor does anyone know the Father except the Son"; have been changed and corrupted to:

"All who are of the truth listen to the Bible" with all its over 700,000 words and its many contradictory precepts, accounts, and teachings; and "Nor does anyone know the Father except the other people who wrote the Bible", thus pointing people away from the *only one who knows the father first hand, perfectly.*

The one the Light refers to as the prince of the world is the author of the great lie, just as he is the father of all lies about God and human existence. *The great lie is that The Light of the world is NOT all one needs to overcome darkness and death.* The prince of the world has had many agents to spread the great lie. However, there was one agent who people choose to make up most of what they would call the new testament, the one called the apostle Paul, who would be particularly useful in propagating the great lie. We will look at that in a bit more detail later.

Perhaps the reader has believed the falsehood that the Bible has no contradictions? Here is just one of many:

> Do I not hate those who hate You, O LORD? And do I not loathe those who rise up against You? I hate them with the utmost hatred; they have become my enemies. (Psalms 139:21-22); (The Biblians/Paulians say that this was written under the inspiration of the holy spirit, whatever that means.)

And;

> A time to love and a time to hate; A time for war and a time for peace. (Ecclesiastes 3:8)

And;

> Then Samuel said to Saul, "The Lord sent me to anoint you as king over His people, over Israel; now, therefore, listen to the words of the Lord. Thus says the Lord of hosts, "I will punish Amalek for what he did to Israel, how he set himself against him on the way while he was coming up from Egypt. 3 Now *go and strike Amalek* (your enemies) *and utterly destroy all that he has, and do not spare him; but*

put to death both man and woman, child and infant, ox and sheep, camel and donkey." (1 Sam. 15:1-3)

Versus

You have heard that it was said, "you shall love your neighbor and hate your enemy." "But I say to you, love your enemies and pray for those who persecute you, so that you may be sons of your Father who is in heaven; for He causes His sun to rise on the evil and the good, and sends rain on the righteous and the unrighteous. (Matthew 5:43-45)

One can pretend there is no contradiction, but that only proves that one is not listening to the one who says, "I am the Truth" and instead wants to emulate a lawyer! Unfortunately, they are deceived by Paul's teaching of all scripture being inspired by God, and they will defend apparent contradictions to protect their key belief that allows them to bury and thus ignore the Light in "the Book."

With all the dozens of Bible versions and hundreds of books about "Christ", it should be curious to the reader that there are very few which use only the Light's Words to tell us who he is. Why is it that so very few are concerned about focusing wholeheartedly on HIS person and teachings *only*? Perhaps, just perhaps, it is for these reasons:

This is the judgment that the Light has come into the world, and men loved the darkness rather than the Light, for their deeds were evil. (John 3:19)

But because I speak the truth, you do not believe me. (John 8:45)

Many who claim to speak for God but don't will arise and will mislead many. (Matt. 24:11)

For false leaders and those who claim to speak for God but don't will arise and will show great signs and wonders, so as to mislead, if possible, even the elect. (Matthew 24:24)

Maybe the truth is that the one Voice that brings freedom offends the vast majority because they love their life in this world more than they love their heavenly Father? Perhaps Biblians are especially loath to turn to the Light because they very much like believing they are "saved" and heaven bound while they continue not to forsake anything this world offers and thus continue to love their life in the world?

In summary, the fundamental problem is that people are not listening to Joshua of Nazareth. Instead, the people have substituted a *large book* that can be used to justify any behavior including those that nullify or contradict *the Person* who said, "I am the Life" and "love your enemies." They have chosen the wrong standard to know God and what God wants and being that they regularly read / encounter/ have readily available to them the teachings of The Light, they are most accountable.

In the next chapter, we will take a closer look at how the Bible is the central prop in the successful failure that is Christianity.

Chapter Summary:

- If a truth about something or someone important cannot be destroyed due to a small number of people successfully propagating it to a point where it cannot be contained (i.e., it broke out), then a "good way" to try and get rid of that truth is to hide it and attack it through various means;

- Christians have buried/hidden the truths of The Light of the world in a giant religious book they call "the holy Bible," which book many people worship or substitute for the Person and teachings of Joshua of Nazareth;

- Christians are so confused about the difference between "the Bible" (meaning the opinions of the authors of the sixty-six books of the "protestant Bible") and the accounts and sayings of Joshua of Nazareth that they generally cannot distinguish between the two. This critical error exists because people choose to believe Paul's teaching that "the scripture is inspired of God";

- The Word of God to humanity is Joshua of Nazareth, NOT "the Bible" or "the scripture." Paul is wrong, and Joshua is right.

23
THE PROP OF THE DARKNESS

Opening Questions:
- Did Joshua make future predictions in the gospels?
- Did Joshua predict that a book would be written that contained his Father's words and that people ought to look to that book and those authors to understand God?
- Is "the Bible" Joshua of Nazareth or God?
- Do the Bible authors accurately represent the Creator? How would we know?
- Does the Bible contain contradictions?
- If a contradiction is found in the Bible, how likely are people who believe that the book represents God, to accede the contradiction?

As we have discussed in prior chapters, the fundamental error or purposeful mistake is to substitute a large book people call "the Bible', for the Person and teachings of Joshua of Nazareth. The error has two aspects. The first is human nature that very much wants to participate in that error. The Light said this:

> And this is the condemnation, that the people of the world love the darkness rather than the light... (John 3:19)

This love of the darkness is THE spiritual cause that puts us in cages and causes us to be governed by self-pride and fear and selfishness. Here are the other key discipleship teachings of the Light that harmonize with the teaching/truth above:

He who has found his life will lose it, and he who has lost his life for
My sake will find it. (Matt. 10:39)
For whoever wishes to save his life will lose it; but whoever loses his
life for My sake will find it. (Matt. 16:25)

For whoever wishes to save his life will lose it, but whoever loses his
life for My sake and the gospel's will save it. (Mark 8:35)

For whoever wishes to save his life will lose it, but whoever loses his
life for My sake, he is the one who will save it. (Luke 9:24)

Whoever seeks to keep his life will lose it, and whoever loses his life
will preserve it. (Luke 17:33)

He who loves his life loses it, and he who hates his life in this world
will keep it to life eternal. (John 12:25)

I quoted all of this saying from the Light to make the point on how
fundamental a teaching it is of the Light. It occurs in all four gospel books
as you can see, multiple times.

If we "love the darkness," we will endeavor to "save, keep, love" our
life in this world—a life primarily of selfishness and ignoring all the wrong
and evil in the world—we will refuse to love as the Light defines that. We
know at some level that if we speak about the wrongness we encounter
each day – wrongness in relationships and how people run or operate
businesses or governments or "ministries," etc. – we will be rejected and
perhaps worse. So, what do we do? In general, we keep our mouths shut,
which is how we keep our lives in this world. We do not speak the higher
truths of the Light – that people are in darkness and need the Light as their
Leader - and we even have trouble expressing the lower truths of people
doing wrong things. This cowardice is particularly evident with
homosexuality and transgenderism in the U.S. at this time.

The other thing we do is to try and have our cake and eat it too, and
this is called "religion"! For Christians, they have selected as their
distraction and nullification of the Light – their prop, if you will - the large
book they called "the Bible." By calling or believing the book is the "word
of God" to mankind, they in one stroke both nullify the Light *and* can
justify almost any behavior in the "name of God." The Bible is replete with
examples of an angry god bringing his wrath and vengeance upon many
millions of people. Since God does this, then surely we human being are
justified in acting like him and in "doing his will" in this regard!

The crusades were a more recent good example of this. All that killing
in the "name" of the One who said, "Love your enemies"!

For a person using their mind even just reasonably well and who seriously studies the Bible, that person can only conclude that there are hundreds of contradictions and hundreds of evil deeds that are justified in the name of God in that book. This fact rightly frustrates non-theists as they bring these contradictions and falsehoods to Christians only to have Christians deny the plain contradictions and falsehoods or worse defend and justify them. In fact, the Christians make a practice of writing large books with the express purpose of defending the contradictions and falsehoods!

Here is a short list of obvious, non-moral contradictions from the Bible:

Hebrew Scripture Errors

- Gen. 25:1 versus 1 Chron. 1:32, wife versus concubine
- 2 Kings 24:8 versus 2 Chron. 36:9, 18 years old versus 8 years old
- 1 Kings 7:26 versus 2 Chron. 4:5, 2,000 versus 3,000 baths
- Ezra 2:5 versus Nehemiah 7:10, 775 versus 652 sons (It must be asked why the translators translate the same exact Hebrew word transliterated "bane" as two different English words?)
- 1 Kings 9:27-28 versus 2 Chron. 8:18, 420 versus 450 talents of gold
- II Samuel 24 :1 versus I Chronicles 21:1, God versus Satan
- Isaiah 34:7, King James version, "unicorn" an animal of Latin-Greek mythology
- Isaiah 13:21, 34:14, King James version, "satyr" a half-human, half-goat creature of Latin-Greek mythology

New Testament Errors

- Matthew 27:9-10 cites Jeremiah, yet the prophesy is clearly contained in Zechariah 11:12-13
- Matt. 1:16 versus Luke 3:23, Jacob versus Heli
- Matt. 8:5 versus Luke 7:3,6, Centurion himself versus "elders of the Jews" or "friends"
- Matt. 8:28 versus Mark 5:2, 15, "two demon-possessed men" versus one man.
- Mark 14:69 versus Luke 22:59, The same servant girl the second time, or "another saw him; Man, I do not know what you are saying" when previously he said to the servant girl, "Woman, I do not know him."

- Acts 12:4, King James version uses the word, "Easter," while almost every other major translation uses the word "Passover." So, which translation is correct?

- Eph. 2:8-9 versus James 2:24, Oh, the tap dancing and sleight-of-hand used to try and reconcile the plain contradiction between, "saved through faith alone—not of works" versus "justified by works, and not by faith only."

- Eph. 4:11 versus John 10:16, The same Greek word "poimen" is translated "Shepherd" in John 10:16 and "pastor(s)" in Eph. 4:11. What rational explanation exists for that except the translators wanted to avoid the plain contradiction.

Then there are the moral or ethical wrong-doings or justifications by a supposedly "holy, perfect, righteous, just, loving God." Here is a short list of just a few of the many of those immoral teachings in the name of God.

- The Exodus story has God killing many thousands of innocent male babies, boys, and young men – the eldest male child of the Egyptian families living in Egypt – instead of killing the guilty Pharaoh and those directly enforcing his unjust and oppressive ways;

- God "inspiring" (according to Paul) the pornographic rebuke of Ezekiel in his book, chapter 23. Certainly the language in Ezek. 23:20, for example, is hardly necessary to bring a rebuke, and is difficult to imagine a holy God "inspiring";

- The Old Testament teaches, "The law of the LORD is perfect, restoring the soul" (Psalm 17:9). Most Bible leaders take that to mean Moses teachings in the Torah. In stark contrast and rebuke, the Light says in reference to Moses teachings, "You have heard that it was said, "YOU SHALL NOT COMMIT ADULTERY" (a teaching of Moses in Exodus 20:14 or Deut. 5:18); but I say to you that everyone who looks at a woman with lust for her has already committed adultery with her in his heart." (Matthew 5:27-28) According to Joshua, the law of Moses was quite imperfect, incomplete and unfulfilled. If this is so (and Joshua says it is) then how could Moses" writing be inerrant or perfectly portraying the Father's mind?

- King David: "I hate them with the utmost hatred; They have become my enemies." (Psalms 139:22)
  o The Light: "You have heard that it was said, "YOU SHALL LOVE YOUR NEIGHBOR and hate your enemy." "But

I say to you, love your enemies and pray for those who persecute you..." (Matthew 5:43-44)

- o Comments: Does the Holy Spirit inspire these words of David as Paul teaches? Not according to the Light. All arguments to justify David's words because he was in the Old Covenant commit the error of begging the question. Has God the Father changed so much between the covenants that in one case His Spirit "inspired" David to express and justify hatred, while in the other, His Son teaches just the opposite? Do perfect beings change?

- "The prophet" Samuel: "Then Samuel said to Saul, "The Lord sent me to anoint you as king over His people, over Israel; now therefore, listen to the words of the Lord. 2 Thus says the Lord of hosts, "I will punish Amalek for what he did to Israel, how he set himself against him on the way while he was coming up from Egypt. 3 Now go and strike Amalek and utterly destroy all that he has, and do not spare him; but put to death both man and woman, child and infant, ox and sheep, camel and donkey."" (1 Sam. 15:1-3)
    - o The Light: "You have heard that it was said, "YOU SHALL LOVE YOUR NEIGHBOR and hate your enemy." "But I say to you, love your enemies and pray for those who persecute you." (Matthew 5:43-44)
    - o Comments: So Jesus" Father supposedly speaking through Samuel orders Saul - based on the motivation of vengeance - to go kill thousands of "women, children, and infants." To try and reconcile the Light of the world's command to "love your enemies" with murderous vengeance is to be deluded—it is the perfect example of how religion blinds people to simple truths. And the simple fact is that the god of the Hebrew scripture is one made by men while the God revealed by the Light is the Creator of the Human Race!

- King Solomon: "A time to love and a time to hate; A time for war and a time for peace." (Ecclesiastes 3:8)
    - o The Light: "You have heard that it was said, "YOU SHALL LOVE YOUR NEIGHBOR and hate your enemy." "But I say to you, love your enemies and pray for those who persecute you." (Matthew 5:43-44)
    - o Comments: Does the Holy Spirit inspire these words of Solomon as Paul taught? Not according to the Light.

Joshua teaches that God the Father rewards mercy and loving your enemies, and thus God's Spirit at no time taught that there is a time for "hate" and for "war" for those who are listening to Him. Of course, one is free to explain the truth away with philosophies (which philosophies Joshua did not teach) about how God's commands do or do not apply to nations.

- Judges 9:22-24: "Now Abimelech ruled over Israel three years. Then God sent an evil spirit between Abimelech and the men of Shechem; and the men of Shechem dealt treacherously with Abimelech, so that the violence done to the seventy sons of Jerubbaal might come, and their blood might be laid on Abimelech their brother, who killed them, and on the men of Shechem, who strengthened his hands to kill his brothers."
- 1 Sam. 16:14: "Now the Spirit of the Lord departed from Saul, and an evil spirit from the Lord terrorized him."
  - The Light: "You have heard that it was said, "YOU SHALL LOVE YOUR NEIGHBOR and hate your enemy." "But I say to you, love your enemies and pray for those who persecute you." (Matthew 5:43-44)
  - Comments: These passages in the Hebrew scripture have God sending "an evil spirit" between two people groups, the result of which was treachery, violence and murder, and another evil spirit to terrorize Saul! To show the foolishness of trying to somehow reconcile these passages with the character of God revealed by Joshua of Nazareth, let's re-write a famous saying according to the Hebrew scripture, "For God so loved the world that he sent evil spirits to terrorize them"?!

- Job 42:8: God supposedly speaking: "For I will accept him so that I may not do with you according to your folly, because you have not spoken of Me what is right, as My servant Job has."
  - Comments: If these words in the scripture are correct (and according to Paul's doctrine they must be), then whatever was recorded in the preceding chapters of the book of Job that was said by Job's friends about God is wrong - "you have not spoken of me what is right." How could the Holy Spirit allow scripture to be wrong about God, for whatever was recorded of the friend's words about God in those scriptures is wrong?

I could provide many hundreds of similar contradictions and wrong-doings justified by the god of the Bible—the god of the authors who wrote most of the books included in the Bible.

Sadly, I have found that when we want to believe something that we consider important, or that we think we have adequately vetted, then we will believe it even if the only tool or means we have to know true from false – reason and logic – clearly shows it is false. And so it is with the Bible and the Christians and Biblians who cling to the book ignoring its darkness, or, perhaps, secretly glad about the darkness and thus justifying their behaviors? "Hey, if God did it or blessed it, then I can do it too."

So, to sum up the section thus far, we have seen that the great falsehood upon which most of the Christian religious/business system is the belief that the Bible is God's word to humankind. Or stated another way the great lie of the prince of the world is that Joshua of Nazareth and his truth is not adequate for freedom and eternal life.

In the next chapter, I have some questions to ask and comments to consider for those who defend the primary error of the successful failure.

Chapter Summary:
- The Bible being considered "the word of God" is perhaps the greatest falsehood of this time and perhaps the last many hundreds of years;
- In the last few centuries, the Bible has become a substitute for the Person of Joshua of Nazareth and his life and teachings;
- The Bible is full of contradictions IF you are a person willing to use reason and logic well;
- The Bible - while having many good stories about people of faith; and much good human wisdom; and recording many fairly accurate historical events regarding human history in that part of the earth – is not the "word of God" to humanity. Instead, Joshua of Nazareth is;
- To place the life accounts of Joshua of Nazareth into a large book, which book has many contradictory concepts to Joshua's teachings, is a very effective way to hide The Light and destroy his Message.

For a clear contrast between the Biblian view and the view of a follower of the Light, see *Appendix 7, Protestant Biblicism Debunked.*

24
SOME QUESTIONS FOR BIBLIANS AND CHRISTIANS

Opening Questions:

- Should a sincere person who is seeking to understand Joshua of Nazareth use Joshua's own words and deeds to understand him, or other's people's opinions to follow him?
- Who understood Joshua best – Paul and the other New Testament writers or Joshua himself?
- Who understood Joshua best – Moses and the other Hebrew scripture authors or Joshua himself?
- Who understood the Creator better – those who had never been with the Creator, or the One who was with the Creator and sent from the Creator?

If God exists and He wants humans to know Him so He can help us and so we can know what He wants for us, would it not be of primary importance to understand how to accomplish that?

Most Christians (and all Biblians) claim that a person needs "the Bible" as the source of knowledge to know God. They are only partially correct, and their understanding of the Bible is wholly incorrect. They are partly right because the Light we need to know God *has been placed/ hidden in the Bible in four small books* towards the back of the book. They are wholly incorrect in thinking that the authors of the other sixty-two books of the protestant Bible had true insight and understanding of God. The simple truth is that all authors of the Bible's books did *not* have a full or proper understanding of our Creator Father—we can know that because the Light tells us so!

It is also a simple truth that there was One Man who did have a full and correct understanding of God, and he is the **subject** of the four "gospel" books of Matthew, Mark, Luke, and John. He was not the author of the books, but rather the authors were with him and saw him and knew him - or knew those who were with him and knew him - and wrote down what he said and did in those four books.

Many Biblians and Christians are very offended when a disciple of the Light says that we only listen to the Light to understand our Father. They are angry because our belief contradicts their belief about a crucial issue - how we can know God and what God wants.

The fundamental error of Biblians (and most Christians are Biblians) is to believe that the sixty-six *authors* of the "protestant Bible" and their writings, views, statements, and opinions about God revealed God as well as the Person and words of Joshua/Jesus of Nazareth. They believe this because Biblians believe Paul's *scripture beliefs* and thus they look to the scripture to understand God instead of to Jesus/Joshua of Nazareth.

In contrast and contradiction to Paul, Jesus/Joshua says look to *him and him alone* to know and understand God. The quotes below will verify this claim. In other words, the Biblians/Christians use *Paul's teaching* to nullify the plain teachings of the Light of the world (Ironically, Paul's saying in 2 Tim. 3 - "All scripture is inspired by God..."- does not address what would later be called "the new testament" but is constrained to the Hebrew scripture).

Please note that Joshua/Jesus could indeed have told his original disciples that a book would be compiled one day that would reveal and represent God. The fact is he both did *not* say that, and he said many things contrary to that as we shall see below.

It is brilliant to hide the four eyewitness recordings of Joshua's life and teachings (the four books that contain Joshua's words/teachings/truths) in a large book, which book contains many statements that contradict Joshua's statements. To then say *that book* is "God's Word" to humanity completes the clever deception. It is difficult for people to distinguish between "the book/Bible" at this point, and the **subject** of the four gospels books, which books were placed in the larger book, the Bible. However, as I try and remind people regularly, Joshua/Jesus is not "the Bible" and his Words Alone - not all the other authors of the Bible books and their opinions about God - are the Words that lead to Life!

Biblians and Christians looking to defend their Bible belief against the Person and words of Joshua of Nazareth often ask, "But where do you read Jesus" words from?" Of course they want me to say, "the Bible". The simple truth is that I have access to the words and deeds of the historical Person of Joshua of Nazareth from the four gospel books of Matthew, Mark, Luke and John, which four books were placed in the compiled book people call "the Bible'. To make the distinction clear to a Biblian I make the following argument:

1. I inform the Biblian that I recently published a book that just contains the four gospel books (http://www.amazon.com/Light-World-Teachings-Jesus-Nazareth/dp/0692300481);

2. I ask the Biblian, "If I hand my book to someone, are they able to get to know Jesus of Nazareth by reading my book?" The answer of course is "Yes".

> (Of course, some Biblians will argue that a person needs the rest of the Bible to "know Jesus" but that is a fallacious argument from two perspectives. First, that the original source is always best when trying to understand an issue related to the original source. Second, Joshua of Nazareth himself says that people ought to look only to him to understand him and the Father he said he represents.)

3. My final question is, "Is my book 'the Bible'?" The answer of course is "No" thus proving that "the Bible" is not necessary to hear from and get to know the One who says, "I am the way, the truth and the life".

Therefore, one does not need "the Bible" to get to know the historical person of Jesus or Joshua of Nazareth!

So, for you Biblians and most Christians, I ask that instead of condemning me, you use reason well to answer the following questions in a simple, straightforward manner.

Joshua says, "*If you continue in MY word* (teachings, truths), *then you are my disciple; and then you shall know the truth, and the truth will set you free.*" John 8:31-32

1. Whose words? Paul's? Moses'? Contemporary Preachers? Bible college professors? Popular author or theologians? "The scriptures'? "The Bible'?

2. By definition, to be a disciple/student/pupil of Joshua of Nazareth means he is our Master, and thus he alone defines what is true and real regarding God, spiritual things and human nature. He says IF we continue in HIS words (no one else's) *only* then are we his disciple/student/pupil which makes perfect sense; and by remaining in only *his* words, a person will be set free. Thus, if we listen to others teachings and continue in other's teachings, why would we think we will be set free?

3. All the truth someone needs to be set free is found in the Person and words of Joshua of Nazareth, so why would you be looking to others if you want to be set free? Stated another way, who or what else can set you free? "The Bible" with all the God-justified fear/hatred and

violence? How exactly can a book containing hundreds of core-level contradictions about God set a person free?

4. His word includes, "*love your enemies*," a clear principle for ordering our lives. So, when a Biblian says, "oh, but the Bible says...", and they turn to some other voice (passages like 1 Sam. 15:1-3) to try and convince a disciple that Jesus" Father (or if you are a Trinitarian, that Jesus himself) really does "kill his enemies"; we ask the Biblian to please be set free from rejecting the Light and ignoring or nullifying the Light's teaching of "*love your enemies*".

Joshua says, "*I am the way, the truth, and the life and no one comes to the Father except through me.*" John 14:6
1. Who or what is the way? Paul's? Moses'? Contemporary Preachers? Bible college professors? Popular author or theologians? "The scriptures"? "The Bible"?

2. Who or what is the truth? Paul's? Moses'? Contemporary Preachers? Bible college professors? Popular author or theologians? "The scriptures"? "The Bible"?

3. Who or what is the life? Paul's? Moses'? Contemporary Preachers? Bible college professors? Popular author or theologians? "The scriptures"? "The Bible"?

4. So, if Joshua plainly says that HE (faith in him as he reveals himself by his own words in the four gospels) is the sure way Home, all the Truth that matters, and Life everlasting, then why look to other sources for God understanding?

5. So, when you stand before the King and he asks, "Why did you listen to all those other voices, many of which nullified or contradicted my voice?"" What are you going to say? "Oh, Lord, they did not nullify or contradict your voice." So, you are going to rebuke the King about his wrong understanding on this matter? Or, "Well, Lord, where is Paul, he will explain it all to you." Poor "Lord Jesus" needs Paul to explain God-understandings to him...

Joshua says, "*Everyone who is of the truth hears MY voice.*" John 18:37
1. Hears whose voice? Paul's? Moses'? Contemporary Preachers? Bible college professors? Popular author or theologians? "The scriptures"? "The Bible"?

2. If I am not "of the truth" (or don't care about what is true) regarding God-things, perhaps I will want to listen to other voices? And if I don't hear his voice, then am I "of the truth"? And if I listen to other voices, then am I not at risk for being deceived, for he does say, "Many will come in my name and deceive many"?

3. If a disciple repeats a word/teaching/truth of the Light and the person who hears it reacts negatively to it and rejects it because it contradicts one of their religious beliefs, is that person "of the truth"?

Joshua says, "*I am the Light of the world; he who follows* **me** *will not walk in the darkness but will have the Light of life.*" John 8:12

1. Follows who? Paul? Moses? Contemporary Preachers? Bible college professors? Popular author or theologians? "The scriptures"? "The Bible"?

2. Who is the Light of the world? Paul? Moses? Contemporary Preachers? Bible college professors? Popular author or theologians? "The scriptures"? "The Bible"?

3. If I follow Paul (for he does say "imitate me" - 1 Cor. 4:16; Phil. 3:17) for example - or anyone else - then will I not walk in the darkness?

4. Does Joshua teach that we should follow others instead of, or in addition to, him? No, he does not.

5. If in "following Joshua" we make him our Master, how many masters can a man have in one domain? Joshua says, "No one can serve two masters..." (Matt. 6:24) and the context is God-understanding or the God domain.

6. If I am following the Light as he reveals himself by his own words, am I not doing well? And if I am doing well in that regard, why would you want to condemn me?

7. Would "following him" include believing that the Father that Jesus reveals kills people, including thousands of "women, children, and babies" (1 Sam. 15:1-3) when Jesus teaches "*love your enemies*" and "*God so loved the people of the earth...*"? Does not Jesus speak for the Father? Does not believing that Jesus' Father murders people prove that I "walk in the darkness"?

Joshua says, "*He who rejects me and does not receive my sayings, has one who judges him; the word I spoke is what will judge him at the last day.*" John 12:48

1. The word who spoke? Paul? Moses? Contemporary Preacher? Bible college professor? Popular author or theologian? "The Bible"?

2. Does not receive whose sayings? Paul's? Moses? Contemporary Preacher? Popular "pastor"? "The Bible's"?

3. Will Paul or Moses or anyone else's words judge us on the last day? If not, *why listen to them regarding what it takes to pass judgment?* Are they going to improve upon the sinless One's teachings? Are their sayings superior to Joshua's sayings?

4. Joshua says, "*love your enemies*" and Joshua says that he is speaking the Father's words, and logic proves that perfect beings do not change. When you believe the author of 1 Samuel who says Jesus" Father said— "Thus says the Lord of hosts, "I will punish Amalek for what he did to Israel, how he set himself against him on the way while he was coming up from Egypt. 3 Now go and strike Amalek and utterly destroy all that he has, and do not spare him; but put to death both man and woman, child and infant, ox and sheep, camel and donkey.'" 1 Sam. 15:1-3 — are you not *rejecting Joshua's plain saying of "love your enemies"*? Or are you going to do the "theological dance" and play the lawyer and deceive yourself into believing there is no contradiction?

Joshua says, "*Heaven and earth will pass away, but **my** words will not pass away.*" Matt. 24:35

1. Whose words? Paul's? Moses'? Contemporary Preachers? Bible college professors? Popular author or theologians? "The scriptures"? "The Bible"?

2. So if "my words" mean the words of Joshua of Nazareth, which it surely does, then why would you think that other's words will not pass away?

3. Who else in the Bible makes that claim? And even if they made it, who else defeated death to prove what they said and did was true?

4. If I listen to, memorize, take to heart, etc. words of people other than Joshua of Nazareth, then am I not hanging onto that which

will pass away? How will that which will pass away help those who do not pass away?

Joshua says, "*Blessed are the meek and humble*". Matt. 5:3, 5
Paul says:

> Since many boast according to the flesh, I will boast also...But in whatever respect anyone else is bold—I speak in foolishness—I am just as bold myself. Are they Hebrews? So am I. Are they Israelites? So am I. Are they descendants of Abraham? So am I. Are they servants of Christ?—I speak as if insane—I more so; in far more labors, in far more imprisonments, beaten times without number, often in danger of death. (2 Cor. 11)

So, it doesn't make sense that an admission to speaking (or writing) foolishly takes away the wrongness of speaking (or writing) foolishly.

1. Can I boast and at the same time be meek and humble?

2. Would God "inspire" words of boasting, conceit, arrogance or other such words/teachings?

3. Would God inspire speaking or writing "foolishness"?

The Father says, "*This is my beloved Son in whom I am well pleased - listen to him.*" Matt. 17:5

1. So, will the heavenly Father will be upset or displeased with a person because they do this—they only listen to Joshua? Are you aware of the Father ever speaking audibly from His dimension at any other time in history to tell us to listen to anyone else?

2. Can you explain to me why our Father would be upset or displeased with a person because they have made His Son their sole/soul standard for knowing Him? Why would God be bothered by having made Joshua one's Master, and Master by definition means we don't look to anyone else to teach us about God? *Please try and keep the sayings of the Light above in mind when answering this.*

3. Also, can you explain why if a person listens only to "the Way, Truth and Life" they would be displeasing to our Father?

4. Can you provide me a quote by Joshua to the effect of, "Listen to others to know and understand my Father"?

5. If our Father would not be upset or displeased with a person who listens only to Joshua to understand Him, why are disciples like myself condemned by Biblians and Christians as "heretics," "cultists" and the like?

6. Would heeding this saying, "Many will come in my name and deceive many" be consistent with listening only to Joshua who elsewhere says, "I am the Way, truth, and life"; or would it be consistent with listening to MANY voices who claim to represent Joshua, like Paul and the millions of religious leaders and people who are like Paul?

7. For those who still cling to the Bible and "the scripture" other than Joshua's words, please provide me with one quote from Joshua where he says something to the effect of, "listen to the Hebrew prophets to understand and know my Father." Even if you do find it (which you will not), how it can be reconciled with "This is eternal life, that they may know you, the only true God, and me (Joshua of Nazareth) whom You have sent."?

So, we have established that looking to "the Bible" instead of to the Person and teachings of The Light of the world is grievous error and seeks to perpetuate the great lie that people need more than Joshua of Nazareth to enter into and remain in eternal life.

In the next chapter, we will take a look at the thing Christian's call "the gospel."

Chapter Summary:
*   Reason and logic - using Joshua's sayings as the standard of truth for understanding God - conclude that Joshua stated that **he** (and now by extension, his recorded words, and deeds) was the best way to know and understand the Creator;
*   Joshua plainly said that we should look only to him to know and understand God and that other people/sources should not be relied upon to understand God;
*   Joshua taught that we gain eternal life by knowing him (not the Bible) and the Father **he** revealed by his own words and deeds as recorded in the four gospel books;
*   Biblians/Christians rely on several fallacies to attempt to defend their belief that the Bible is the word of God to humankind;

- Biblians/Christians reject reason and logic regarding God claims and instead go with their traditions, which traditions largely nullify the teachings of Joshua of Nazareth.

See *Appendix 2: The Bible Conversation* for more information on this topic.

25
WHICH GOSPEL?

Opening Questions:
- What does "gospel" mean?
- To whom should we go to understand "the gospel" of Joshua of Nazareth - Joshua or other people like Paul or Billy Graham?
- If something is false, how good can it be?
- If something is popular or widely accepted, does that prove or mean that it is true?
- What is the real "gospel" as given by the real, historical Person of Joshua of Nazareth and his words and teachings in the four "gospel" books?

OK, we have clearly and thoroughly addressed the central error of Christians/Biblians. Let us move on and take a closer look at what the Christian's call "the gospel" or the central message of the Christian religion. We will take a look at what is believed by most to be the primary or core message of Christianity given by perhaps the most popular and successful modern proclaimer of that message in recent times, Billy Graham.

The following material is taken directly from the late Mr. Graham's website here – billygraham.org:

"How to Know Jesus

In four brief steps, you can come to an understanding of how to find eternal life. During Billy Graham's landmark 1954 London Crusade, his team developed a simple system to bring people to faith known as "Steps to Peace with God." Since that time, and in various printed and electronic forms, this succinct and clear presentation of how to have a personal relationship with Jesus Christ and experience peace with God has been translated into dozens of languages and shared with millions of people.

"Steps to Peace with God" is the natural overflow of the Gospel message Billy Graham has given around the world. It clearly conveys God's love, forgiveness, and plan for each person's life."

So, to sum up, Billy Graham's team is going to provide people with steps to peace with God as well as the "plan for each person's life." He goes on to list what he believes are the four steps that will get people into heaven or peace with God. The source quoted as the authority to validate that the steps are real and right is "the Bible." Out of the 15 quotes from the implied standard of the Bible, only two or 13% are from Joshua of Nazareth! So, while the Christians claim to represent Joshua of Nazareth, they do not look to him for the core of their beliefs or their gospel or good news. They do this because Joshua does *not teach* their "gospel" as we shall see.

And what do they provide as "the plan for each person's life"? It appears to be "join a religious organization, otherwise known as a church." That is a very deficient, shallow and narrow plan for anyone's life since church-going accounts for about 1% of people's waking hours per week and generally does not affect the way one lives for the other 99% of their life!

Let's take a look at Christianity" core message as given by Billy Graham's organization.

Step 1 of the popular version of the Christian gospel is entitled, "**God's purpose: peace and life**."

Please note that while Joshua of Nazareth does want his followers to experience peace, he does not state anywhere that that is the Designer's primary purpose for people. Here is an illustration to help you understand.

Their once was a family trapped under a house after a tornado except for one child, a son. The dad says to his son, "go, and find help to get us out of here."

So the boy goes looking for help. Of course, the dad would like his son to be safe and not to be afraid while he searches for help, but his safety in traveling and managing his fear is not the primary purpose. Instead, it was to find help to rescue his family.

In like manner, God's primary purpose is not for people to have a good life on the earth. Therefore, this claim from Mr. Graham is only partly true and is falsely represented in its context. God does want us to have inner peace *with Him as the source*. Joshua represents a "good life" on this earth, and it is **not** a comfortable life as Christianity portrays it. In fact, there was no better life lived than Joshua of Nazareth, and for that the people killed him!

Step 2 of the Christian gospel is entitled, *"The Problem: Our Separation."* Paul and the Hebrew scriptures are used as the basis for this belief instead of Joshua of Nazareth. The fundamental teaching is because we sin; God is angry with us as a result and will not give us heaven unless a sacrifice is paid to Him so that He might forgive us. *This is false.*

As we have seen, we as human beings are naturally captured by our self-pride, fear or selfishness (part of our nature which produces most sins) which prevents us from turning to any person who could help us. This is the real cause of separation from our Creator. While adult humans have self-pride, fear and selfishness ruling their person and are thus in a state of captivity; and while human adults remain "captive" if they do not turn to the Freedom Giver in faith; the fact is that God is not angry with people. Christianity's god of wrath and vengeance who demands that His innocent Son is brutally killed as a sacrifice to appease his rage is a drastically wrong characterization of our heavenly Father, and it keeps people *away* from Him.

Step 3 of the Christian gospel is entitled, **"God's Bridge: The Cross."** Step three contains no quotes from Joshua of Nazareth to justify or back up the content behind the step. This step says that "Jesus Christ" was the sacrifice God needed to forgive people. It states that God required that His innocent Son be sacrificed on the cross to pay for the sins of the guilty children so that God could forgive people and give free tickets to heaven to all who believe that religious doctrine. Please note how they make the instrument of his death central to their gospel – the cross – instead of the person himself. *This belief is grossly wrong.* God did **not** punish his Son by having him killed in order to forgive the wrongdoings of the guilty sons and daughters. Instead, God forgives everyone who comes to Him with a sincere and contrite heart and asks for forgiveness.

Step 4 of the Christian gospel is entitled, **"Our Response: Receive Christ."** Again, no direct quotes from Joshua of Nazareth to support the content associated with the step. This step is a clever "sleight of hand" that contains truth, yet only enough truth to psychologically entice and manipulate people. *Whatever "Receive Christ" means, what we can be entirely sure that it does not say is to make the real, historical Person of Joshua of Nazareth the Leader and Master of your life and thus live according to his teachings as recorded in the four gospel books.* Instead, it is merely some empty words – an incantation of sorts – that lead people to believe that by saying the words and participating in religious organizations, they get to go to heaven. They even provide the words of the incantation – what they call a prayer - for people to read off the website.

Billy Graham and the many who seek to emulate him or be Christian evangelists have one thing in common. They do not use the teachings of the historical Joshua of Nazareth as the basis of their "gospel" or if they do quote Joshua, his words and teachings will:

1. Be a minority of their "gospel" (in this case, only 13 percent), not supporting their key principles, or;
2. Be taken out of context, or;
3. Are twisted to conform to Christianity's gospel.

So, to sum up the Christian gospel, it is believe the stuff about God and how to know what God wants that the Christian leaders say is, and if you do that, you will go to heaven. In general, the only actual behavior requirements stated by the Christian leaders in their "gospel" is to attend and support (give money to) their religious organizations (what they call "the church"), partake in their rituals, and to abstain from doing grossly wrong things.

Of course, some will take issue with using Mr. Graham's version of "the gospel," and this is typical since Christianity is made up of rival sects, thousands of them. Never-the-less, Mr. Graham's version of "the gospel" is representative of what most Christians believe. All one has to do is do a bit of research on the internet of various Christian organization's statements of belief to validate this claim.

The False "Gospel" of Christianity

Let us restate in a clear, detailed fashion Christianity's "gospel."

God sent His Son to die on the cross to pay for our sins so if we believe the stuff **about** the jesus and god our religious leaders tell us; we will go to heaven when we die.

- That God, being a being of wrath, anger, and vengeance some of the time, decided to have his beloved son - which innocent son loved him and honored him and obeyed him - tortured and killed:
    - o As a blood sacrifice to sate or appease his wrath and anger against people for people's wrongdoings;
    - o And for punishment and atonement for the wrongdoings of other people who did not love or honor or obey this god.
- The Bible god will not forgive people unless he gets paid to do so (thus, by definition, he never forgives people, for true forgiveness does not require payment!), and the payment he selected was the torturing and killing of his "beloved" and *innocent* son who honored him and obeyed him;

- Now, this schizophrenic god has good moments too. On those good days, he loves us and wants us to put our faith in him; though on his bad days, he has his *innocent*, perfect, honoring and obedient son tortured and killed in a fit of anger about the wrong-doings of **guilty** sons and daughters (as well as having many thousands of women, children and babies killed - See 1 Sam. 15:1-3);

- Nothing significant has to change in you or your life pattern—you can stay exactly how you are and continue to live and work for money or the other things you love in this world, and you don't have to love anyone truly. We only ask that if you have any major outward sins, you must hide them, so they don't disturb other members of the organization or reveal the falseness and lovelessness and powerlessness of our religion;

- If you will believe the things about the Bible god the religious leaders tell us - and you do the things the religious leaders tell us (but are usually unwilling to do themselves); and you "go to church" and support the religious leaders with your money - you will go to heaven when you die.

The True Good News of the Light of the World

Let us now contrast the above false gospel of Christianity with the real and truly good news the Creator's Messenger gave.

The Good News in a Nutshell

See our condition of captivity; have remorse over our wrongdoings which are evidence of our imprisonment; and in order to escape, place our faith in Joshua (or Jesus) of Nazareth as he reveals himself and our Father through *his own words* in the four gospel books and *thus be set free from our cage of self-pride and fear and selfishness*. Make Joshua the Leader of *my life (not of your "religious time" or your "church life")* and stop living for the things this world values particularly money and material things. With this new found freedom and purpose, *change ourselves and go and make a change in people's lives where we can by introducing them to the Freedom Giver and our Father and by living out love with them and speaking that which is true and doing that which is right according to Joshua.*

Following Joshua is the primary life endeavor and passion ("To love the Lord your God with all your heart, soul, mind and strength" and to "serve God"), NOT a part-time religious hobby which the *counterfeit of Christianity* offers. If we do this, we will be set free, and we will enter into eternal Life in this life - and if we stay faithful - we will enter into the fullness of Eternal Life after our body dies.

The Gospel of Joshua of Nazareth

Joshua quoted from the beloved Hebrew prophet Isaiah about his mission because Isaiah provided a saying that hit the core of his mission, and he knew the Jewish listeners would pay more attention since they venerated their prophet:

> The Spirit of the Lord is upon me,
> Because He anointed me to preach the gospel to the poor.
> He has sent me to proclaim **release to the captives**,
> And recovery of sight to the blind,
> **To set free those who are oppressed**,
> To proclaim the favorable year of the Lord. (Luke 4:18-19)

Joshua later said it this way:

> If you continue in My word, then you are indeed disciples of Mine; and you will know the truth, and the truth will make you free. (John 8)

And:

> For even the Son of Man did not come to be served, but to serve, and to give His life a ransom for many. (Mark 10)

Please note the crucial part of his good news is that he will ***set us free***. Also please note that this real, pure gospel of the Freedom Giver has *nothing* to do with blood sacrifice!

As I have been saying throughout the book, we human beings place ourselves in a cage during our adolescent years. We transition from innocence to guiltiness. Our conscience becomes fully formed and thus informs us that what we are doing is wrong and we have to willingly – at some level – ignore or push away the "voice" of our conscience. That is the equivalent of walking into our cage of darkness, locking the door and throwing away the key. Our self-pride and fear and selfishness (root level sins) form our cage and keep it closed. Our cage – and our unwillingness to look for a way out – will ultimately destroy us. We cannot escape that cage without help—we cannot be set free from that condition without a Freedom Giver greater than ourselves.

The Freedom Giver's good news is that we don't have to stay in our cage and thus forfeit our existence; we don't have to destroy ourselves and forfeit our true Life; we don't have to lose the ones we love. We can have a compelling, meaningful and beautiful purpose to our lives here on the earth.

God, the Designer and Creator of human beings, exists. This God can be known, and his will for us can be understood. The best way to know this God and what He wants is by looking to His Son, as his life, words, and deeds are recorded in the four "gospel" books placed at the beginning of what people call the New Testament. To truly know God is how one attains to eternal life (John 17:3) – a, better, enduring Life that is entered into after one's body dies. The good news is the Son of Man did the following for us:

- *He paid a ransom for us to set us free from our self-made cage of self-pride, fear, and selfishness* and he invites us to take advantage of that ransom and offer of freedom, through faith in him, and the Father HE reveals (Matt. 20:28, Mark 10:45; Matt. 18:4, Luke 14:11; Matt. 10:26, Luke 5:10; John 15:13);
- He taught us right versus wrong and how to treat other people (Matt. 5 for example);
- He showed us what *real love is and how to live it out* (John 8:1-11, etc.);
- He will give us *a new life and a new Family that really loves us* IF we and others are willing to listen to him and do what he says (Matt. 12:48, Mark 10:29);
- He has and will continue to *show us the Way Home to our Father* by helping us change and leading us into the fullness of eternal Life (John 5:24, 14:6).

The Light teaches that our Father will forgive us for all our wrongs if we see our guilt - the worst transgression we have committed being ignoring him and His Messenger or playing a religious game as a substitute. If we see our guild and ask Him with a sincere and remorseful heart to forgive us, He does (He does **not** need/want/require some weird blood sacrifice to forgive us! :)). If we will turn to our Father in faith during our time of remorse - and to His appointed Leader of humanity, Joshua of Nazareth - then we will be born from above, enter into Life, and start the most fantastic journey any human being can undertake. This journey is arduous, but anyone can make it **if** they have but a little faith and love. While the journey is daunting, it is the best, most meaningful and fulfilling journey human beings are called to enter into by our Creator.

That is the sure Hope of the good news of Joshua of Nazareth.

Let us continue to contrast Joshua's gospel to the Christian "gospel" from a different perspective to provide additional insight into this vital matter.

The Christian gospel will have x marks, followed by Joshua's gospel with check marks:

⊗ Believe what the Christian leaders say – both dead and living especially Paul - about God and their understanding of the Bible – a schizophrenic god who acts in love part of the time and wrath and vengeance the other part of the time and who sends people to eternal torment in hell, versus:

✓ Believe what Joshua says and place your faith in him and the Father HE reveals by his own words ONLY in the four gospel books – a Father who truly loves you and demonstrated that love by sending His Son to save us *from ourselves*—a God who is *not* a God of wrath and vengeance who does *not* send people to eternal torment in hell;

⊗ Believe stuff about "Christ" to go to heaven with virtually no consequences on why or how you live your life, including remaining popular with most people, versus:

✓ Place your faith in the Light and make him the Leader of your life with radical consequences on WHY you live your life and significant implications on *how* you live your life, including being rejected by most people;

⊗ Go to a religious organization the people call "the church"; support the religious organization and its work; partake in the rituals at "the church";
  o The religious organization's work is primarily to build a building for the people to meet in to hear their leaders talk about God, and have programs that the people enjoy, and to build more organizations and buildings for the same sect. This work is *secondary* or *tertiary* for 95+ percent of the people (who merely give money to accomplish it) while all the people's *primary* work is making money for themselves in regular "secular careers" and "secular jobs" in order to be comfortable in this world just like the rest of the people of the planet.

✓ Live out the new command with other disciples, genuinely loving and caring for each other thus sharing his Life together and doing HIS work together;
  o God's work is to bring the Leader and his truth and love and spiritual healing and therefore Life to other human beings and to help them do the same for others. This Life and work is the *primary* work for close to 100% of the people/flock/Family.

⊗ Do not do bad things, e.g., don't hurt yourself or other people when "unjustified.'

✓ Living out the new command of loving one another is primary and is lived out by helping one another and others in daily life.

⊗ Do these things (religious rituals, belief remembrance and abstention from gross sins of commission), and you will enter into heaven.

✓ Actually love other people and care about what is true and right and thus be a model and a change agent in this world, and you shall Live; and *that* Life will not end with the death of your body; and all the love you tried to express to others in your life will remain and grow in the next.

This contrast should also be used to understand the essential concept of faith versus beliefs **and** the concept of placing one's faith in the correct thing.

What is the result of these two gospels?

For those who choose Christianity's gospel, its result is the successful failure that covers the earth at this time, as well as individual's likely self-condemnation for those who participate in it.

That which calls itself "the church" is nothing more than a religious social club built on Paul's or the Hebrew scripture author's or their religious leader's teachings. It is a group of people that feed themselves and is judged as successful by its members and the world of which they are part. It is successful if the organization gives them what they want-nice music, good moral or emotionally touching messages, good children programs, assurance of heaven, etc. And it is judged successful based on the amount of money it controls and through what money can buy, and the number of people it controls or influences.

For those who choose Joshua's good news, the result is a meaningful life; a life truly well lived; an exceptional life; *and* a painful experience with the same pattern of treatment/reception that Joshua received while here on the earth. This troublesome Life, however, will provide the fullness of Eternal Life when our body dies.

In the next chapter, we will look at the empty ritual that Christians substitute for actually following Joshua.

Chapter Summary:

• The "gospel" of the Christians is not the good news that Joshua of Nazareth taught;

- The Christian gospel is a clever mix of truth with falsehoods which might result in a person sincerely coming to faith in God, but which faith will be in the god created by the Christians. If the individual who entered into faith clings to Joshua and starts to learn from **him**, he/she will be rejected by the religious people. Once that rejection starts, only one of two outcomes typically result – either their faith will die, and they will become a member of "the church"; or their faith will grow, and they will leave the religious system and speak against it, just like Joshua did some 2,000 years ago;

- The Christian gospel's good news is about as good as free hamburgers at McDonald's – a very popular offer of something free which is not substantive; does not address the real problems; will not lead to a truly healthy, well-lived life; and will not lead to eternal Life;

- The Christian gospel, in a nutshell, is, "believe this stuff about God and you will go to heaven";

- The True Gospel of The Light is: "Let me set you free. Have faith in me. Turn from a wasted and selfish life and do my work, the most important of which is speaking truth and practicing love. If you do this, you will both enter into Life Everlasting, and change the lives for the betterment of the people around you.

See *Appendix 8, Forgiveness and Blood Sacrifice.*

26
WHAT IS SO BAD ABOUT 'GOING TO CHURCH'?

Opening Questions:
- How much did Joshua teach about the concept "church"?
- Doesn't the Person who started/invented something have the best understanding of how it is defined?
- If religious leaders define "the church" differently than Joshua of Nazareth, who knows better about what it actually is?
- Other than religious vocabulary, how different is "the church" versus other organizations like the Elks or Moose Lodge or the Masonic Lodge or the Knights of Columbus or other religious organizations like Mosques or Synagogues or other such organizations?
- If I participate in and support something that is a substitute or counterfeit for something that is important, am I doing well?

Christians are all about "going to church." That is THE main ritual that they believe pleases God or is required to be in good stead with God. And of course, they have their scripture (not Joshua's teachings) and tradition to back that belief up.

When one pictures in their mind a bunch of Christians in their building singing songs about God, hopefully, one doesn't see "people doing evil things," for in general, they are not. In their "church going," they are only doing what they know and are taught, and they are not hurting anyone in the process except themselves. Meeting in a building to hear nice speeches with some moral truth and to sing songs about God and other things is not wrong in and of itself. Instead, the problem, error, and fault occur when gathering in a building and singing songs *are done in the name of "jesus" and substituted for what the real, historical Jesus of Nazareth wants.*

Christian religion would be fine if it did not use the historical person of Jesus of Nazareth to justify their religion. When Christians point to the historical person of Jesus of Nazareth to explain their religion – as they use him as the figurehead of their religion - *they then become accountable to him and his teachings.* Christians would be far better off if they left the Light of the world out of their church religion.

To further illustrate the reason why it is destructive for those who "go to church," here is a little story to consider.

Once there was a governor of Texas, a humble man who genuinely cared about people. He was aware of a significant problem that was occurring in his State. Disabled people were increasingly neglected, abused and mistreated. Many thousands of disabled people were increasingly viewed as worthless, and as merely resource drains on society (consistent with the evolutionary worldview which promotes survival of the fittest). The governor had a disabled child himself, so he was quite sensitive to the handicapped people's plight. So, he decided to create small communities or centers for disabled people around the state. He initially built three - one near Dallas, one near Houston and one near Austin. The intent was to find the disabled people who were being neglected, abused and mistreated and invite them to come and live in these communities. In these communities they could help one another, get what they needed and have the governors state workers help care for them when they could not care for themselves.

The governor asked the state health and medical workers to make this disabled program their top priority. The state health and medical workers were initially enthusiastic about this program the governor was implementing. However, they soon learned that it was more work than expected. They had first to identify the disabled people, find them, approach them or their legal guardians and ask for permission that they leave their current situation and move to one of these communities. Many times they would encounter resistance from the disabled people's legal guardians even when that legal guardian was not involved with the person and had abused them. It did not take long for the state health and medical workers to talk among themselves and come to the conclusion, "we did not sign up for this." They much preferred their prior work that was much easier and restricted from 9 am to 5 pm.

So, the state health and medical workers decided that instead of helping these disabled people, they would build a monument to the governor and sing songs about the governor about once a week at the monument. They figured that would please and satisfy the governor and prevent him from being angry with their refusing to implement his program for the disabled people.

And so it is with the Christian religion.

The governor represents God. The disabled people represent people without hope, not experiencing love and not having a useful purpose to their life. The state health and medical workers represent Christians who are misguided. The illustration is an imperfect analogy, but it does convey the truth that needs revealing. Christians – like all other religious people – make up their religion to serve primarily themselves and what THEY want. They don't want the challenging work of living out true love and living selflessly and thus sharing their lives with other people. They much prefer building their monuments to their god and singing songs about him and living a life of love for this world instead of love for Him and each other.

Here is another brief illustration to drive the point home. Let's say a dad says to his son, "son, I need you to get water from the stream because our well is dry and your sister has had a bad fever all night and needs to hydrate." But instead of going to the stream and getting the water which is needed, the boy instead decides to sit down and draw a nice picture of angels to give to his little sister. So it is with the Christian religion. That which is important and badly needed (in this story water - in reality, love, compassion, rightness, justice), is ignored while that which is trivial or not needed is practiced (in this story the drawing of angels, in reality "going to church" etc.).

In short, our heavenly Father does *not* want us "going to church", rather, He wants us to be the called out ones (which is what the original language word behind the English transliterated word "church" means) showing the world what love really is and looks like lived out among his people—his called out ones.

(For more on this subject, see *Appendix 9, Church Conversations.*)

But I'd Rather "Go to Church"…

A substitute is something that changed out for an original item. Merriam-Webster defines the term, "Substitute" as, "a person or thing that takes the place of someone or something else." [50] An example would be a substitute teacher at a high school. If the proper or original or authorized teacher cannot teach a given class, a substitute teacher will take their place. Unfortunately, there is also a wide-spread practice of substituting inferior items for the original. Think about the widely used marketing saying of, "accept no substitutes."

For example, before you can tell if a currency note is counterfeit, you must first know the legitimate or real or standard note very well.

The purpose of this book is to free the Messengers message from a system, and that system's agents who have destroyed that message.

To accomplish that, we must contrast truth with falsehood and right with wrong. Before a person can successfully identify a counterfeit, she must first have a standard to which to compare it. One of the things the Messenger teaches is that we human beings have a profound bias against Light, Life, and love. We prefer darkness, destruction, and coldness of heart. Or stated another way, we are only willing to truly love a small number of people who are related to us by blood or law.

As previously stated, the Standard for this book is the words/teachings/truths of Joshua of Nazareth as recorded in the four gospel books.

Here is the definition of "substitute" again - "a person or thing that takes the place of someone or something else."

Here is the definition of "counterfeit" - "made in imitation of something else with intent to deceive."

The substitute deceives most religious leaders. Some religious leaders proffer a counterfeit.

The Creator sent a Messenger to tell us what he wants for his created beings - we human beings. As we have learned, we humans have a significant problem with pride, fear, and selfishness. We also have a deep dislike of being held accountable for our behavior or words. We desperately want to do whatever we want and generally what we want does not involve losing things we think are valuable. This characteristic makes us strongly independent beings who don't like what is true or right if we perceive we don't get something out of it. We want to decide such things for ourselves, and in our self-pride, we take great offense at even the suggestion that we need help in either knowing what is true or doing what is right. We are all just so sure that we have everything figured out or that we have the best world or existential view possible. Or at least we are confident we are not wrong about significant or critical things about human life.

So, when the Messenger comes and says, *"hey, you are wrong about really important things like, there IS a Creator, what your Creator is like and how he wants you to live"*; what faithless people hear is, "your religion is wrong", or "the

---

[50] Merriam-Webster Dictionary, www.merriam-webster.com, April 2018

understanding you have concerning your existence is wrong". Given our self-pride and fear, what is the natural reaction?

It is to reject the Messenger as wrong or reject the Messenger's messengers as wrong.

Remember the saying, "don't kill the messenger for the news or information he brings." If you know the facts about Joshua of Nazareth, you know that is exactly what happened to him. People killed him out of the offense he caused by telling the truth about people's wrong concepts and understandings of God and how God wants human beings to be and to live.

Do you, dear reader, really believe that human's nature has changed over time? Do you think that people are better and freer from self-pride, fear, and selfishness than people of past times? If the Messenger and his message still offend people, what would be a smart way to handle that; in other words, how could "we" both ignore the Messenger and at the same time use him to gain power or money? How about merely using the Messenger's name while at the same time changing his person and his message? That way, people can have their cake (pay lip service to the Creator the Messenger spoke of just in case He does exist) and eat it too. Meaning, not listen to the Messenger, not do what he says, but rather create a religion in his name and continue to live bound by self-pride and fear and selfishness and thus for the empty things of this world. The Messenger is not like other leaders who you can see and touch, so it is *much* easier to merely pay him lip service ("oh lord jesus...") and in reality ignore him and never seriously intend to listen to him or do what he says.

Bible or Christian religion *substitutes beliefs about god* taken from a giant book (the Bible) with its many contradictory statements about God, *for faith in god and his appointed messenger* Joshua of Nazareth. In other words, Christians make a big deal about beliefs that avoid what is important to God and instead deal with stuff that has little to no bearing on how human beings are to live our lives. (Please read that again, slowly, carefully and think about it!)

Or, another version of the substitute is to misdirect what people put their faith in, like the Bible or religious leaders or some ritual or anything else except *the person* OF Joshua of Nazareth. Instead of getting to know the Messenger, listening to him and DOING what he says, the people:

- "Go to church" and songs they call "worship";
- Read and admire the Bible (at least the parts that don't contain the Messenger's teachings they don't want to hear or consider like it is difficult to follow him);
- Place crosses on their walls and around their necks, etc.

In other words, they do their Bible or Christian religious stuff in "jesus" name, all the while not *doing* what the Light says. It is such a smart and effective substitute that it is hard to imagine that it is not also a counterfeit—a counterfeit not created by the men who profit and benefit from it, but rather from a being with the power to propagate falsehoods that serve to deceive both the people and their appointed leaders.

Dear reader, please understand that you will not find the Light in what people call "the church"—that you will not find the Light in Bible or Christian religion. Furthermore, accept the fact that the Light is against religion—he is especially against religion in his name. What he is for is love as HE defines that - caring about each other, caring about what is true and right, standing up against that which is false or wrong, sharing our lives like people who actually, genuinely care about one another (See the upcoming chapter on love). Instead, we choose to be prideful, fearful, selfish, autonomous people who don't see the need to share his Life together.

The simple truth is that that which calls itself some form of "the church," is nothing more than a religious organization run by, and attended by, people who reject Joshua of Nazareth and in his place substitute another "jesus" or "Christ" and their shallow ritual religion. The Light of the world says, "Many will come in my name and will mislead many." *This deception has come to pass ever since he left and it is the Christian leaders who have come in his name.*

The leadership of Bible/Christian religion has taken the place of Joshua of Nazareth, and instead of living the Life he offers, they instead offer the death and darkness that comes with empty, shallow, loveless religion in his name. Of course, they market their death, darkness, and poison with very attractive "packaging" and spins, and the people eagerly participate in the substitute because they love their lives in this world. It is a mutually serving system - the leaders/rulers get their vocation with their money and their power or influence over people, and the people get the blessing of the religious leaders who say they are good with God and heading to heaven.

The current Biblian/Christian religious system is both foreign and alien to Joshua, as well as against him. The model of "ministry" or "church" has one or a few people "at the top" (minister, pastor, reverend, priest, and other paid staff) and the majority of the people doing virtually nothing except listening to speeches, singing songs and giving the leadership money. That model is anathema to Joshua's new command and the Families he came to build. Truly, that which calls itself "the church" is not significantly different than any of the other world religion's sects or social clubs or "societies" like the Rotary Club or the Elks Lodge or the Masons or the Moose Lodge or the Knights of Columbus, etc. The only significant difference between those organizations and "the church" is the God vocabulary used. The actual primary difference is that those people who call themselves Christians are much more accountable than the people in non-Christian organizations.

The simple truth is that we talk about whatever we love supremely. If we have in fact been saved from ourselves and out of the darkness of a life with little or no love or faith, then we will be compelled, out of love, to talk about our Father and our savior/master. All disciples tell other people about the Light, and all disciples seek to build and be part of the Family and thus the Kingdom of God—the kingdom of love, truth, and rightness. If we are not actively working to bring his Kingdom to pass, then we are not submitting to God's Leader (His Son), and we are not serving him, all our justifications and excuses notwithstanding.

The Light and Truth has said, "This is the condemnation, that people loved the darkness rather than the Light because their deeds are evil." It is evil to reject God's Leader Joshua and instead substitute other men and women in his place, which men and women do not listen to or follow Joshua, but instead encourage people - encourage **you** if you are participating in Bible-church religion – to stay in the darkness that is ignorance, falsehoods, and lovelessness.

I know this is hard to understand for many readers since you have been taught and believed that there is no significant difference between "jesus christ" and Christian or Bible religion you experience in that name—in truth "jesus christ" is merely the figurehead of your religion - the bait to draw you in. However, if you can see the difference between the historical person of Joshua (Jesus) of Nazareth and HIS words and teachings and deeds as found only in the four "gospel" books - and religion in his name - you have taken one simple but critical step in the right direction.

So many who ask good questions about God stuff can never get past throwing the baby (that which is valuable, Joshua of Nazareth) out with the bathwater (that which is worthless, Christian and Bible religion). Or, they cannot distinguish the baby from the bathwater, having believed for years that they are the same thing.

In sum, religious organizations – that which calls itself "the church" - cannot fix basic problems because they are essentially a business or social club, **not** a living, organic group of friends who actually care about one another (truly love one another) and thus work to solve their own, and then others, problems in as much as it is possible. Religious organizations – what people call "the church" - are largely dead and useless. Being merely social clubs that don't want to "rock the boat" – whose members very much want to conform to the ways of this world - they are powerless to bring change. They cannot bring significant life change within their organization's membership let alone bringing change to those outside of it.

In the next chapter, we will look at a significant problem – how to fix "sin" and the Christian's remedy for that problem.

(For more on "church," see *Appendix 10, Christian Church Doctrine Debunked*.)

Chapter Summary:

- Joshua of Nazareth only used the term "church" twice in all his teachings, and his definition of "the church" is very different from the current common understanding of the term;

- "The church" as Joshua of Nazareth defines it, are his people who allow themselves to be chosen out of the world by Joshua and into the Kingdom of God; who submit to King Joshua as their only spiritual Leader and Teacher; and who live together as actual brothers and sisters;

- "The church" is *not* a building or an organization or clergy/religious leaders or programs or ministries or rituals;

- The organizations that call themselves "the church" are nothing more than religious, social clubs which have as much power to bring a person into Life as a McDonalds can bring a person into dietary health;

- Those who participate in a religious organization are actively contributing to hiding The Light of the world and thus are working against him since they support and promote the substitute/counterfeit.

27
HOW DO WE FIX SIN?

Opening Questions:

- What is the difference between "sin" and wrong-doing?
- Is it okay to be vague, confused or inaccurate when trying to communicate a problem?
- Should we not focus on what is more important than what is less important?
- If our God beliefs do not motivate us to change us to better human beings nor to living a better life, what good are they?

Previously in the book, we said, "Later we will look in detail at how Christians substitute a false religious problem for the real root problems." Now is an excellent time to address that.

If you recall, the root problems that cause most of humanity's problems are fear, self-pride, and selfishness. Christians, on the other hand, say that "sin" is the root problem that needs to be fixed. Christians define "sin" as essentially things I do wrong-a missing of the mark. They talk about a valid concept they call sins of commission (things I do that are wrong) and sins of omission (things I don't do that I should). Their lists of "sins" are almost entirely focused on sins of commission instead of sins of omission. Yet lack of love is an omission problem, and it is the biggest problem of all, as we shall see. Examples of sins of commission include getting drunk, swearing or cussing, cheating, lying, stealing, smoking cigarettes, fornicating, disobeying laws or rules of governments, etc. The Christian's list of sins would be long, but it would generally omit the three root problems of fear, self-pride, and selfishness.

Some Christians would say that self-pride and selfishness are sins, but they would say they are just different sins not any more important than any other sin. They would not typically classify fear as sin.

In essence, what the Christians do is to focus on the symptoms instead of the root causes, and call the collective symptoms The Problem. Or to put it another way, they focus on that which is less important while ignoring the stuff that is most important. Joshua said it this way:

> Woe to you, Bible experts and religious leaders, hypocrites! For you give ten percent of your income (*to your religious organization*), and have neglected the weightier provisions of the law: justice and mercy and faithfulness; but these are the things you should have done without neglecting the others. You blind guides, who strain out a gnat (*keep religious rules*) and swallow a camel (*don't live by justice, mercy or faithfulness*)! (Matt. 23:23-24)

A great and current parallel example of the Christian error of vague or misleading labels of a problem would be calling Muslim Jihadists "terrorists." By calling people "terrorists" who are actually motivated by specific religious beliefs found in Islam's holy book is to at best obfuscate the facts and at worst, to hide them altogether. The symptom – a horrible one at that – is the violence that causes "terror" in the victims or potential victims. The cause is some Muslims following some of the teachings of Mohammad, Islam's prophet and spokesman for God, as found in the Quran. (See *Appendix 6, Islam*).

So, the Christians focus on their dandruff while they are dying of brain cancer.

They step on the broken glass and put Band-Aids on their feet, and step on the glass again the next day, thinking the Band-Aid is the solution.

They are most upset and focused on Johnny's poor grades at school while Jonny is bullying others.

They keep putting fires out in their community's houses while ignoring the electrical appliance that is causing the fires.

They focus on Betty's college entrance scores while Betty is having sex that will likely lead to HIV and her death and possibly others.

In short, they are worried about and focus on "disease" (the vague unclearly defined concept of "sin"), yet they never look closely enough to properly diagnose and treat the cause behind "disease" (self-pride and fear and selfishness). They do this because it is *much easier* to focus on symptoms (sin) than to consider the cause (loving my life in this world and thus having no faith and little love because I am in my made cage of self-pride and fear and selfishness). *It is far easier to abstain from minor or perceived moral wrongs than it is to engage in a life of self-change and using truth to foster, encourage and implement change in our lives and the lives of others.*

Furthermore, they say the way to fix the sin problem is to "accept the substitutionary (propitiatory, vicarious, etc.) death of Christ for the forgiveness of your sins." *This belief is perhaps the most damaging aspect in the concept-belief realm of the substitute that is Christianity.*

Christians are wrongly taught and hold that "by believing that Christ died on the cross to pay for your sins you are forgiven, and heaven bound." This belief is sadly and horribly wrong as we have seen. Joshua teaches no such thing – in contradiction, he says let him set us free, so we can care about what is true and right, proclaim and fight non-violently for those things, and above all love one another.

Furthermore, a reasonable belief of being accountable for one's behavior including lack of helping others (or said another way, lack of love) is replaced with Paul's "gospel of grace" and their doctrines of eternal security derived from non-Joshua sources. Many Christians are only too glad to push away any notions of accountability and responsibility with their favorite Paul doctrine of salvation by grace.

So, there is a three-fold falsehood that is the knock-out punch in substituting the false religious problem for the real problems identified earlier.

First, don't look solely to Joshua of Nazareth to understand who God is, what God is like and what God wants. Instead, they look to "the Bible," their religious leaders and their favorite Christian authors or "scholars." This mistake is the fatal error, and this error makes it easy to adopt all the other errors, including the next two.

Second, of gaining forgiveness from God for one's "sins" and thus acceptance from Him by "believing" (merely mental only) that Christ's death was a substitutionary sacrifice for you and your deserved death or punishment demanded by God's justice; thereby absolving you from your "sin."

> As has been discussed, not seeing ourselves as guilty human beings and *not* believing what is true nor practicing what is right - especially love - is how we condemn ourselves (being a prisoner in our cage of self-pride and fear and selfishness). Being genuinely remorseful for our realization of the state of our soul, and looking with faith to the True Light of the world to save us from ourselves is what brings us out of our cage and into everlasting Life.

Third, that after having received the forgiveness for one's sins, one continues to be "saved" (headed to heaven) by God's grace (and "going to church") and thus God will not hold you accountable or responsible for how you live your life or at least there are little or no consequences for one's decisions and behavior in life. This falsehood successfully turns people away from Joshua of Nazareth and to Paul or others and their erroneous religious doctrines.

After having entered into Life, what keeps us on the difficult way and abiding in eternal Life is we make sincere and real efforts to do what Joshua says motivated by our love for him and his Father.

Please note this saying of Joshua which validates that Paul's "gospel of grace" is wrong.

> Do not marvel at this; for an hour is coming, in which all who are in the tombs will hear His voice, and will come forth; those who **did the good deeds** to a resurrection of life, those who **committed the evil deeds** to a resurrection of judgment. (John 5:28-29)

Many religious people cement the third error by their doctrine of "eternal security," meaning once a person is "saved," they are always "saved" and cannot lose their salvation. In essence, they say to themselves, "Isn't that great! Just believe this stuff about our christ and his blood sacrifice to pay for our sins, and we are heaven bound-now we can get on with loving our life in this world to its fullest-me, me, me and money too!"

The thing that its leaders and members call "the church" is now justified in their "sin forgiveness" aspect of their religion by those three errors that they make and hold. People are not taught to think about how fear and self-pride and selfishness affect their daily lives. And if they are not motivated to identify, recognize and work on those three root problems of our nature, will they ever be part of the solution? Of course, not-they will remain in darkness and be part of the problem. They will put Band-Aids on arteries squirting out blood. They will flail at their sins and ignore their self-condemnation.

Christians are very complacent in their delusion, "they just know" that they had their sin forgiven when they "entered into a relationship with christ" - religious lingo for having some emotional experience or of affirming or adopting the intellectual doctrine of their "church."

In the prior chapters in the section, we have taken a close look at the significant falsehoods that Christianity is built upon, namely the Bible instead of Joshua, a false gospel, the central ritual that substitutes for what Joshua asks for, and an inadequate and negligent understanding of our real problems. In the next few chapters, we will look not at specific errors and wrong practices that Christians hold and substitute for what God wants, but rather a few of the primary methods and beliefs the Christian leaders use to nullify, hide or make of no effect the teachings of Joshua of Nazareth.

Chapter Summary:

- Christians teach that "sin" is the primary problem for human beings, but they do not define sin clearly and which sins are important will vary according to the religious leader;
- The true root problems for us are a nature ruled by fear, self-pride, and selfishness;
- Christians teach that we can have our "sin" problem fixed by "believing Christ died for your sins." What that generally means is if I merely make an intellectual or emotional profession in Christianity's Christ, my sin problem will be gone. That is a delusional belief which leads to much hypocrisy;
- Joshua teaches that repentance for the wrongs I committed in my state of non-faith and entering into faith in HIM and the Father HE reveals are what brings me forgiveness and into eternal Life. Joshua teaches that living according to his Way of love and caring about what is true and right is what keeps a person in the state of eternal Life.

See *Appendix 8, Forgiveness and Blood Sacrifice.*

In the appendix, "Forgiveness and Blood Sacrifice," the following facts will be established:

- Joshua never said that his death would be a sacrifice for sins;
- Joshua never taught that his Father required a sacrifice for sins;
- Joshua did speak about the meaning of his death, and he spoke of it as paying a ransom, not being a sacrifice for sin;
- Joshua provides no basis to support the primitive Hebrew belief of requiring blood to be spilled to receive forgiveness;
  (Some will point to Luke 22:20 to try and argue that Jesus did teach his death was a sacrifice. Here are arguments against that.
    - The passage does not use the term "sacrifice".
    - Some manuscripts do not have the phrase, "given for you" or "poured out for you".
    - It was ancient Hebrew practice to seal a covenant with blood.)
- Only a terrible and unjust dad would punish his innocent child for the wrongdoings of a guilty child;
- Forgiveness is granted to those who are sincerely remorseful for their wrongdoing(s) and thus desire to change.

28
RELIGIOUS LEADERS USE COMPLEXITY

Opening Questions:
- If religious leaders make things complicated so that people believe they must go to those religious leaders to understand important God truths, then don't the religious leaders gain much power by doing so?
- Could complexity be a significant factor in the dividedness of Christianity?
- What does it mean when Joshua's teachings are pure while Christian leader's instructions are often complicated?

As we saw in the previous chapter, *Hiding in Complexity*, people who want people to be dependent upon them to take things from them will often use complexity to accomplish that. If using complexity to hide things is more difficult when used regarding things that can be verified (like physical things), how much easier will it be regarding God things many of which are not verifiable? Religious leaders excel at using complexity to get the people to be dependent upon them. Please note Joshua's teaching on this issue of complexity:

> Truly I say to you, unless you are converted and become like children, you will not enter the kingdom of heaven. (Matt. 18:3)

So, Joshua does not use complicated language to convey his teachings, and he plainly says that if we want to enter the kingdom of heaven, we must become like children - and children do not communicate using complex concepts.

An excellent way to tell the difference between two things is to compare them. So let us compare a primary error of Christianity with the truth of The Light of the world by contrasting the stated beliefs of a representative religious organization with the teachings of Joshua.

As we have seen, many people hide in complexity, and this is a great example of religious people doing just that. The following is a list of the topical areas of the Doctrinal Statement from Dallas Theological Seminary which I consider generally representative of much of "protestant" Bible-anity. (Many religious organizations call statements like this a "Statement of Faith" which wrongly defines "faith" as synonymous with "religion" as we have seen.)

1. The Bible is God's Word or "All scripture is given by inspiration of God"
2. The Godhead or the Trinity
3. Angels, Fallen and Unfallen
4. Man, Created and Fallen
5. Dispensations
6. The First Advent
7. Salvation Only Through Christ
8. The Extent of Salvation
9. Sanctification
10. Eternal Security
11. Assurance
12. The Holy Spirit
13. The Church, A Unity of Believers
14. The Sacrament or Ordinances
15. The Christian Walk
16. The Christian's Service
17. The Great Commission
18. The Blessed Hope
19. The Tribulation
20. The Second Coming of Christ
21. The Eternal State

Here is a reference to that page - http://www.dts.edu/about/doctrinalstatement/. Each of those twenty one *Articles of Doctrine* has several paragraphs explaining them and that amounts to about 4,200 words!

In contrast, here is a disciple's suggested statement of core existential beliefs.

1. Joshua of Nazareth is the unique Son of God (Luke 22:69-70; John 3:16,18; 5:25; 10:36; 11:4), the Messenger and Leader sent by God the Creator to humankind to save us from ourselves / our sins (John 3:16). You can best know Joshua of Nazareth and his Good

News (or gospel) through his own words and teachings as
preserved in the four gospel books. The Bible is not the word of
God to humankind; instead the Person and teachings of Joshua of
Nazareth in the four "gospel books" is the word of God to
humankind. To look to "the Bible" or "the scripture" apart from
Joshua's teachings is a tremendous error and thus we should look
only to Joshua.

2. To begin following Joshua, we must:

    • Repent of our sins (see ourselves as guilty, be remorseful and
      receive our Father's forgiveness for our wrongs, and stop
      practicing what is wrong)(Matt. 4:17);
    • Be born from above by placing our faith in Joshua and thus
      transition from spiritual death to eternal Life (John 3:3-7);
    • Turn away from or forsake all we have believed is valuable in this
      world, especially money, material things, and people who don't
      want us to follow Joshua (Luke 14:33; John 12:25; Matt. 10:34-
      39; 12:46-50);
    • Stop working for money as our primary pursuit in life, and start
      working for Joshua and his kingdom as our primary passion in
      Life (Matt. 6:24; 4:19; 9:9).

3. While there are many sins we can commit, there are three aspects
    of our nature that we must be aware of and seek to be no longer
    controlled by - self-pride, fear, and selfishness. Self-pride prevents
    us from learning and having a critical character virtue that we
    desperately need to learn and be better people - humility (Luke
    18:9-14). Fear not only prevents us from learning but also
    dramatically hinders us from using reason well in our seeking what
    is true and decision making (Matt. 10:26, 31; Luke 5:10; 8:25).
    Selfishness works hard against love, and both self-pride and fear
    contribute to that as well (John 15:13; Matt. 6:19-21; Mark 8:35).

4. Joshua refers to this critical term - truth - over a dozen times in the
    four gospels. For example, he says, "I am the truth" and "all who
    are of the truth hear my voice" and "the truth will set you free."
    Furthermore, he says we are to "love the Lord our God with all our
    mind." Loving God with all our mind can only be reasonably
    understood to mean to use reason and logic well to find, know and
    understand God. Therefore, it is **critical** that we as disciples do
    our best to use reason and logic well and to be willing to "go"

where ever those important tools lead us—even if reason or logic lead us to reject some of our most tightly held religious beliefs or practices that we picked up over the years. If someone uses reason or logic well to show us that we believe something erroneous, we ought not to be offended and instead seriously consider if what the person is saying does in fact pass the test of reason as well as line up with all of Joshua's teachings (if he addresses it) in that area/topic/domain.

5. In Joshua's teachings, he does provide us with how we should treat each other as human beings. In fact, he gives the universal "ethic" in this saying, "Treat others the way you want to be treated" (Matt. 7:12). If we would keep this in heart/mind and act upon it, we would avoid *many* mistakes and wrongs done to other people.

6. To love Joshua means we will want to obey him (John 14:15). To know what to obey, we must first know HIM and HIS teachings and no one else's (John 8:12, 31-32; 12:48; 13:13; 14:6 Matt. 23:8-12; 24:35). His teachings are readily available to us in the four gospel books in any Bible.

7. In order to obey Joshua's new command of "love one another as I have loved you", we must join with other disciples and help them in real, daily life as we all serve God together as manifestations of His Family (Love means to value someone highly and to treat them with compassion and with selfless behavior). Our neighbors often choose not to love us back. What is the disciple's excuse? (Mark 10:28-30) (See also Acts 2:44-45 as an example of the teachings of Joshua about love lived out);

8. Serving God means we follow Joshua our Leader and Master/Teacher together, and we do the Greater Work of proclaiming Joshua's gospel in all manner of ways, making disciples and forming little flocks and cities on hills (groups/Families of people) (Matt. 5:14; 28:18-20; Mark 8:35; Luke 12:32); and we do the lesser work of helping each other with what is needed to live on this earth (providing food, shelter, and clothing)(Matt. 20:8; Luke 3:14). By this Life, we will demonstrate his living Way so that the world may know that we are his followers due to our love for one another and the unity we manifest (John 13:34-35; 17:20-21).

9. Eternal life is a state of being or existence which a person enters into through faith in our Father as revealed by Joshua. A person

remains in eternal life through faithfulness to God as given by Joshua of Nazareth by his own words in the four gospel books. (John 3:3-4, 5:24, 8:12, 12:48, 16:6, 17:3, Luke 7:50, Matt. 11:27

There are about nine-hundred words in the above disciple's statement of beliefs - that is about *eighty percent less than the Christian statement of God-stuff doctrine.* Some of those nine-hundred plus words are only there for corrective or clarification reasons due to widely held falsehoods as represented in the Dallas Theological statement. I also repeat certain things for the sake of helping the reader understand. Finally, please note how the disciple's statement is Joshua centered and addresses both essential spiritual as well as practical things.

Frankly, the disciples" statement of existential or spiritual beliefs could be as simple as this:

> To save yourself from yourself, place your faith in and listen to, the historical Joshua of Nazareth as he reveals himself and God by his life and own words in the four gospel books, and do what he says.

About thirty words. Beautifully simple, something a child can understand!

The more child-like our approach and attitude is towards the Light, the fewer words are required. As he says, "Truly I tell you, unless you change and become like little children, you will never enter the kingdom of heaven." (Matt. 18:3)

Notice the difference in content between the two statements of beliefs. The Christian statement is heavy on "angles on the head of a pin" stuff, stays away from Joshua, and is light on practical instruction. Aside from the MANY words, perhaps most revealing is that the Christians statement's category titles *are missing the most important teaching of Joshua, "love."* The absence of love is no coincidence. Joshua gave many teachings, instructions, directives, etc., but he only issued one "new command," and it is this:

> A new command I give you: Love one another. As I have loved you, so you must love one another. By this everyone will know that you are my disciples if you love one another. (John 13:34-35)

The Christians ignore the one teaching that he explicitly labeled a "command" and yet it is the only way people will know that a person is a disciple/follower of the real, historical Joshua of Nazareth. *Telling—ironic, and self-condemning—religious social clubs substituted for love in practical, daily life.* The Christians should confess, "we like Bible knowledge, apart from The

Light's teachings, and we will do just about any ritual or keep any tradition instead of complying with the new command."

Furthermore, the two statements bear out the distinction between what standard is looked to for each person-type to know God. The "protestant" Christians look to the Bible with its many hundreds of voices and opinions about God and its many contradictions. Of course, the "protestants" also look to their leaders and their writings as well, although many will say they use on "the Bible." The non-protestant sects look to their leaders and their writings and the Bible, making many more thousands of voices claiming to represent God.

The disciples of Joshua look to only One Person and One voice, the One whom we call our Master. That One person made this remarkable statement of unity and representation:

"If you have seen me, you have seen the Father/Creator/God"; and "All things have been handed over to Me by My Father, and no one knows the Son except the Father; nor does anyone know the Father except the Son, and anyone to whom the Son wills to reveal Him." (John 14; Matt. 11)

Remember the previous chapter on complexity? This comparison of beliefs is a great example of how the One who says "I am the truth" is hidden through Christian complexity. I am not saying that they purposely make something complex that ought to be simple. I am saying that they cannot help themselves because they refuse to listen to the One Voice that matters and at a deep level they want to stay away from him. I am saying that their unwillingness to make The Light their Master causes them to have the wrong standard to know God – the Bible or other's teachings – and to thus be confused and wrong about God, and their pride or fear will not allow them to admit that—hence the many words.

Even if your religious organization has a "statement of faith" that is not nearly as long as Dallas Theological Seminary's, I can pretty much guarantee you it's focus is *not* on Joshua of Nazareth and *his* teachings.

As a general rule, the more words it takes to address a single principle of human interaction, relationship or God belief, the more likely it is the author is lost and is trying to hide that lost-ness among the many words. Ask the Christian leader to boil down their "statement of faith" into about thirty words, and you will see what I am talking about here. Since Joshua is not their Leader, their thoughts are scattered.

In the next chapter, we will revisit relativism or at least a minor strain of it that applies to religious leader's ways.

Chapter Summary:
- Christian leaders hide The Light of the world in their complex believes and their false "gospel" narrative;

- If you ask one hundred people who are lost in a forest how to get out of the forest to a particular town, you are likely to get many dozens of answers—so it is with Christian leaders and thus the thousands of divisions of Christianity;
- The contrast between the simple teachings and truths of The Light of the world versus the complex doctrines of the Christian leaders is remarkable;
- "Unless you change and become like a little child, you will in no way enter the Kingdom of God."

29
RELIGIOUS RELATIVISM OR 'JESUS DIDN'T REALLY MEAN THAT...'

Opening Questions:

- Is it possible that the authors of the four gospel books accurately recorded the words, deeds, and life of Joshua of Nazareth?
- Is it possible that human beings have not changed very much over the past several millennia, meaning our nature and our problems regarding human relationships have not changed?
- If someone said two thousand years ago, "lying for selfish purposes is wrong," why would that ethical principle be invalid today?
- If relatively simple human relationship concepts are translated accurately from one language to another, why would anything about those concepts change over time?
- Is it possible that a perfect ethic for humans was communicated a long time ago and written down and that same ethic is entirely relevant for human beings today and in the future?

This content could be placed in the preceding chapter on Complexity since it is effective due to the elaborate arguments of those who practice it. Religious relativism is the primary tool that the religious leaders use to nullify the truths of the Light of the world. Like its sister, pure ethical relativism, religious relativism seeks to destroy the possibility that ideas, concepts, truths communicated in times past can be binding or relevant today. *Its purpose is to demolish the fact that almost all of Joshua of Nazareth's sayings regarding human relationships or what is valuable in human life apply in all times and all cultures.*

This form of religious relativism is communicated probably millions of times in various ways each time the religious leaders get on their stages and read the words of Joshua of Nazareth in the four gospels. Its primary purpose is to use complexity to convey that only the religious leaders through their religious education can understand "what Jesus was really saying." Essentially, they say, "you cannot understand that teaching or principle properly unless you have our education and can thus understand the culture in which it was said or in which it happened."

Like most clever deceptions, this philosophy has merit but only when applied to non-relational or non-ethical concepts that Joshua taught. For example, if a text says, "And twelve stone jars were used at the wedding feast"; that statement about twelve stone jars might well benefit from some understanding of the wedding ceremonies at that time. However, I would argue that getting a fuller understanding of the purpose of the twelve jars is a silly waste of time!

However, when Joshua of Nazareth gave principles that apply to human relationships or what is truly valuable in human life, those principles are not subject to cultural relativism, since human beings have not changed, nor has God changed His mind! So, for example, please consider this saying:

> Do not think that I came to bring peace on the earth; I did not come to bring peace, but a sword. For I came to set a man against his father, and a daughter against her mother, and a daughter-in-law against her mother-in-law; and a man's enemies will be the members of his household. "He who loves father or mother more than me is not worthy of me; and he who loves son or daughter more than me is not worthy of me. (Matt. 10:34-37)

The religious leaders – not willing to comply with this teaching themselves and knowing that they would be very unpopular for conveying the simple truth of this saying - resort to cultural relativism to nullify the Light's teaching. They will say something like, "oh, you have to understand the culture in Judea at that time to understand why that saying does not apply to us today…"

The other way the religious leaders nullify sayings of the Light is to use good old complexity, typically in some form of this statement: "You need to understand the original language of Hebrew, Greek or Aramaic to truly understand what Jesus is really saying here."

So, for example, in the above case, they might pick a few words like "sword", "set", "against", "enemies" or "household" and then "dive into the true meaning of the Greek, Aramaic or Hebrew" in order to nullify the plain meaning of the saying. When finished, they have redefined essential terms to fit what they want to believe. *They hide in the letter to avoid the spirit, just like their lawyer brethren.*

It is rather amazing how the average religious leader – who has merely an introductory knowledge of those languages if even that - *all of a sudden becomes a Hebrew, Greek or Aramaic language expert surpassing the TEAMS of experienced language scholars who translated into English the Bible version they are reading!* However, this use of complexity is extremely effective, so they use it regularly. The average person sitting in the pew is only too glad that Jesus didn't really mean, "love your enemies"; or "love your enemies means those enemies"; or "loving each other means we actually share our lives together"; or "you cannot serve God and money"; so no questions are asked. Everyone is happy, and the people have their religious leader telling them they are OK with God and that they can remain in their selfish death-style. And the religious leader has his money-paying vocation or "career" and people admiring him/her.

As I acceded, having some understanding of a past culture might be helpful in understanding issues that are not relevant to us today like how ancient governments worked or why wedding ceremonies were held a certain way. However, Joshua provides teachings that deal with human relationships or what is valuable – for example the essential principle that Joshua gave of "love your enemy" or "honor your father and mother" – then *cultural understanding or original language clarification is not needed to understand what he taught. Human relationship and value principles are timeless as given by Joshua of Nazareth. God was not confused about what is valuable in human life or how people ought to behave towards one another—God has not changed nor have we human beings.* People are the same in every time and every culture. God, through Joshua, has given approved and disapproved human behavior and those principles do not change with time or culture.

The phrase most used by religious relativists to avoid the plain sayings of The Light is, "Oh, well, it is a matter of interpretation". What they really mean by that is when they hear or read Joshua saying something they don't like they will conclude he really doesn't mean what he says. The fact that most people who use that saying to nullify, cancel out or ignore a truth or teaching of Joshua have never read Joshua's words in the four gospel books makes no difference to them. They are just sure that what they believe on a particular matter is correct so if Joshua's recording saying contradicts what they want to believe, it must me a "matter of interpretation". And of course the plain meaning of Joshua's saying in context is not the correct interpretation.

For example, most folks are just sure that people ought to be able to express their sexuality in any way they want. They are just sure that 'jesus' believes the same thing, or that he would back up their beliefs regarding expressing sexuality. Please consider this saying of Joshua:

That which proceeds out of the man, that is what defiles the man. For from within, out of the heart of men, proceed the evil thoughts, fornications, thefts, murders, adulteries, deeds of coveting and wickedness, as well as deceit, sensuality, envy, slander, pride and foolishness. All these evil things proceed from within and defile the man. (Mark 7:20-23)

The term "fornication" means sexual immorality, or more specifically, two people having sex who are not married. The term "adulteries" means a spouse being unfaithful sexually. The term "sensuality" means to promote one's self in ways sexual. So, the real, historical Joshua of Nazareth plainly teaches that we human beings have a problem with controlling our sexual urges and he gives clear teachings on what is acceptable and what is not. And yet, how many people will say, "oh, well that is a matter of interpretation" when hearing of Joshua's constraints on human sexuality?

In fact, in many critical areas of Joshua's teachings, people who don't want to listen to him nor do what he says, yet who still claim some Christian label-people who want to have their cake and eat it too-will brush off his teachings with "it's a matter of interpretation".

- You cannot serve God and money.
- A wealthy person cannot enter the Kingdom of God.
- Love means to actually care for one another as actual brothers and sisters.
- The good news is we can be free from our bondage, not that God killed His Son as a sacrifice.
- Love your enemies.

For those who don't care about what is true or right, all things "God" are "a matter of interpretation". At the root level, what they are saying is, "Jesus cannot really mean that we have to lose our life in this world in order to gain eternal life because I don't want to do that, so perhaps I can use clever intellectual tricks regarding interpretation to avoid that truth…"

The fact is that Joshua used simple and straightforward language to communicate his message. In fact he said:

I praise You, Father, Lord of heaven and earth, that You have hidden these things from the wise and intelligent and have revealed them to little children. (Matt. 11:25)

Truly I say to you, unless you are converted and become like children, you will not enter the kingdom of heaven. (Matt. 18:3)

As you might be able to see at this point, understanding Joshua is not so much a matter of the intellect as it is a matter of the heart. So, if our heart is not good, then we will use our intellect to ignore The Light of the world in favor of "the correct interpretation".

The truth is there are not many sayings or teachings of Joshua which are genuinely confusing from an intellectual standpoint. Certainly, his primary or core teachings are very clear and for someone to claim they are not and are "a matter of interpretation", betrays a strong bias in their heart.

So, we have seen a few of the means that religious leaders use to get people dependent upon them and thus keep people away from Joshua. We have also seen a main excuse people use to not actually listen to the real, historical Joshua of Nazareth.

In the next three chapters, we will look at how foolish it is for religious people like Christians to spend so much time on trying to find God's will for their lives.

Chapter Summary:

- Religious relativism is the belief promoted by many Christian leaders that virtually all of the teachings of Joshua of Nazareth cannot be easily understood or "taken at face value" due to the different culture(s) in which Joshua lived at the time the gospels were written;

- Religious relativism says that most things that a person said who existed in the distant past cannot apply to people today since ethical truth is relative and depends upon the culture in which it is believed, practiced or understood;

- Religious relativism is a primary way the Christian clergy keeps people dependent upon them and their "christ." Manipulating this dependency provides the Christian clergy with a "career" or "job" or means of income or material support in this life. The "laypeople" are taught that they need the religious leaders for the "correct interpretation" and most really run with that;

- Religious leader's claiming to be "original language experts" is another method they use to keep the people dependent upon them;

- The simple truth is that all of the ethical teachings and value teachings of Joshua of Nazareth apply to humans of all times and cultures. Furthermore, that all of the teachings of Joshua of Nazareth regarding God (the One whom he calls "my Father in heaven") are timeless and accomplish their purpose of revealing God the Creator and what He wants to all generations of humans on this earth.

30
WHY IS IT SO DIFFICULT TO FIND GOD AND HIS WILL?

Opening Questions:
- If God exists and He has a will for people's lives, why would He hide it?
- If the Creator cares about His creation (humankind) and wanted to communicate his will to people and had some ability to do so, would he use a more explicit form of communication that all people could have access to, or would he use an un-clearer form of communication that only a few people would have access to?
- If God has communicated His will and you can't find it, what does that say about you?

It is both fantastic and tragic how much time and effort is given to answering the question of this chapter title. The short answer to the chapter title question is because people are not listening to God. There are millions of Christian writings trying to address that question, from books to sermons to articles to films to everything in between. Most Christians spend their lives in a vain pursuit of "knowing God's will for my life"—they latch onto one thing after another, often things that have nothing at all to do with Joshua's teachings and everything to do with making money or perceived material security in the world. Or more clever Christians spend time in minimalist part-time or hobbyist "ministry". They are so certain that God would not ask them to actually love Him with all that is in them and thus give up their lives in this world and live for Him, so instead they start speculating about what God "really wants for my life."

They never stop to consider why a loving Father would hide or make it difficult to know His will for his children. If God knows best and has plans for people's lives, then surely he would communicate those plans. Imagine a wise and older dad who has a great plan for his children's lives - or at least for the beginning portion of their lives – yet he refuses to communicate those plans to his children!? It is one thing for the children to be able to consider whether they want to accept the dad's plan…it is another thing altogether for the dad to not communicate the plan. And yet, this is one of the many delusions Christians engage in instead of DOING what God's Messenger teaches!

Let's address this topic. Finding God's will for *how* we are to live our lives is not found through some personal mystical or mysterious "spiritual" process or prayer. Rather, it was given to humankind about 2,000 years ago by God's only pure Messenger, Joshua of Nazareth and is freely available to all who are willing to listen to Joshua. Sadly, few people are listening.

In short, *God's will for HOW we are to live our lives is to be caring for each other (this is what loving each other means) on a daily basis and not working for money or other material securities as our primary pursuit.*

For people who have faith in Joshua and the Creator/Father he reveals, the *how* we are to live our lives is given in his teachings—there is **no** need to "find God's will" for **how** we are to live our lives. He leaves the *where* to live our lives up to us; and He leaves the lesser work (which work is how we provide food, shelter, and clothing four ourselves and others, or our artistic or creative expressions, etc.) we do in our lives up to us. The "how we live our lives" choice, along with whether we engage in the higher work (bringing people to our Father), are the most basic of faith choices – God's will revealed - and those faith choices will set our eternal destiny.

Does God Hide His Will from People?

Trying to find God's will for their life is of primary importance to many hundreds of millions of people. Perhaps billions of people think it is essential to know God's will for their lives. All those people have many different ways to try and achieve this, but there are some commonalities across religions.

Most religions have their "holy scripture" or sacred writings of people who claim God communicated with them, or they knew God, or had experiences with God, and wrote those communications, thoughts or experiences down. Those writings were passed down from generation to generation in written form and are now many people's "holy scripture" or "sacred writings." So for hundreds of millions of people, reading their holy scripture is their primary way of hearing from, and knowing about God.

Another favorite way people use to try and know God or to hear from God is from other living people. Thus, each religion or sect has its leaders - men or women who supposedly know God well (or have figured him/her out better than others) and tell or teach other people about God. Many religions have their holy men, priests, religious gurus, enlightened one(s), anointed leader(s), prophet(s), popes, patriarchs, or most popular Bible teacher, preacher, pastor, elder, etc. These people are looked up to as a person who is closer to God than the person looking to them as their spiritual leader and thus they are sought to understand God and His will for their life. This method appeals to those people who are not reading oriented and who prefer to listen to other people tell them how to know God or God's will for their lives. Of course, many religious leaders point to the scripture and use the scripture and say the scripture is the best way to know God, but they usually also teach that you need them to understand the scripture.

Perhaps the third most popular way for people to seek to know God or his/her will for their lives is by personal experiential "revelations." This method can take many forms. From three or four experiences (or "coincidences") taking place in a short period of time, and trying to piece together the "message" of those experiences; to having a dream; to seeing a vision; to seeking how a piece of toast took the form of "the Virgin Mary" and what that sign means to them. Many people use various methods to receive "revelations" from God. These methods include prayer, meditation, drug use, food and water fasting, hypnotic chanting or other means.

Finally, some believe a combination of the above methods will yield the best results for knowing God or His will for one's life.

The primary focus of the following three chapters will be the third method mentioned above, to see what Joshua teaches about "revelations, visions, and dreams" - in other words, does Joshua of Nazareth state that one way he or his Father will use to communicate to people is through visions, dreams or revelations. There are *many* Christian and religious people who say, "the Spirit revealed this to me"; or, "the Holy Spirit came upon me and showed me"; or, "I went through the refining fire with the Spirit, and he showed me"; or, "God showed me in these dreams"; or, "God whispers this in my ear", etc. However sincere these statements might be, or however real those experiences are for an individual, the question must still be asked, are those communications from God? Can a person know for sure if they are or are not?

Joshua does address all three of the ways listed above which people use to try and hear from God or to know God's will for their life. In this chapter, we will look at the "Holy Scripture" way to try and know God's will.

The Scripture or Sacred Writings:

There are many millions of people who look to their scripture to know God or to hear from God. The Muslims have the Quran and a few other books. The Jews have the Tanakh. The Christians have the Bible. The Buddhists have the Sutras (Sanskrit) or Sutras (Pali). Just those groups alone account for several billion people, and there are dozens more religions each with their "sacred scripture." Each religion has their leaders whose job often includes studying the scripture to pass what they learn onto people less concerned about reading the scriptures themselves. The basis for believing (or trusting) the scripture in each religion is essentially the same. That basis is the belief that people who lived in the past, often long ago, were somehow fundamentally different than contemporary people - usually more morally pure or "holy" and thus closer to God. Or, that God somehow worked differently in the past than today concerning how he communicates with people.

Thus, many believe the people who lived long ago received communications from God or thought they heard from God or had experiences with God, which they wrote down. There is no objective basis for concluding that "scripture" contains authentic communications from God (except perhaps fulfilled prophesy, and then only prophetic scripture). It is merely people choosing to believe or trust what their scripture says for various reasons, usually because their religious leaders tell them they ought to, or because they find some truth in the scripture that is meaningful to them and then wrongly assume all scripture is truthful.

While Joshua's words are found in what many people call "the scripture" or "the Christian scripture" or the Bible or the New Testament - his words are only a small part of that "scripture." This author would estimate that out of the entire protestant Bible, Joshua's words probably make up less than five percent of that scripture. For the disciples of Joshua, we are only interested in the words of Joshua for he is our Master and the only one we listen to and follow. We don't revere "the scripture or believe that "the scripture" can lead us to God or God's will. Rather, we have our Leader - please listen to him:

If you continue in my word (*not "the Bible" or Moses" or Paul's, etc.*)**, then you are truly disciples of mine; and you will know the truth, and the truth will make you free.** (John 8:31-32)

Please note he says, "my word," not "the scripture" or any other source of spiritual truth. Here is a saying to help you understand this important distinction. All of Joshua" Words are found in what Bible believing people call "the scripture," but not all of the scripture is Joshua" Word. Joshua"

Words are preserved in the first four books of what people label the New Testament - those four books are often called "the gospels." Now, the Biblians will claim that the entire Bible is "God's Word," and thus, they deduce that the entire Bible is Joshua's word. This is a widespread claim and belief these days, but it is false.

For the disciple of Joshua, "the scripture" is only the place where Joshua's words are found *since it is NOT the book or the classification of content ("scripture") we care about, but rather the Person who spoke what was recorded!*

Joshua mentions "the scripture" a few dozen times in his teachings, but the context is almost always to get the Jews to listen to their scripture (see John 8:17 and 10:34 for his references to "your law") in order to know that he is/was the promised Messiah of Israel. In other words, Joshua used the Jewish scripture to assist in his trying to get the people living in Israel to see that he is/was their Messiah and thus they should listen to *him!*

Please understand another critical distinction in this regard. Joshua did *not* teach that his followers ought to study/read the scripture to hear from or know God. Instead, he explained that those people who were hearing *him* ought to believe what HE said about *himself*, his Father (the true and living God) and God's purpose for their lives.

Yes, Joshua did say that the scripture contained some important truths from God, and thus some sayings in the old testament to the descendants of Jacob were the Word of God. Yes, Joshua did fulfill a few of the Jewish scripture's Messianic prophesies. However, he also taught that the most critical truth from God is that *a person listens to God's Son, who is himself.* It is vital that the reader understand that while Joshua's words are found in what people call "the scripture" or "the Bible," he does not say that reading people's words in that scripture, other than his own, will help them hear from God or know God. In fact, Joshua says regarding the scripture:

> You search the scriptures because you think that in them you have eternal life; it is these that testify about me; and yet you are unwilling to come to me so that you may have life. (John 5:39-40)

> All things have been handed over to me by my Father, and no one knows the Son except the Father; nor does anyone know the Father except the Son, and anyone to whom the Son wills to reveal Him. (Matthew 11:27)

> This is eternal life, that they may know You, the only true God, and Messiah Joshua whom You have sent. (John 17:3)

These three sayings lay out one of the most important truth's that Joshua teaches regarding knowing, and hearing from, God. First, he says that people would "search the scriptures" because they think they will find eternal life through knowledge of the scriptures. He says this practice would be error in as much as they would not turn in faith to the Person of Joshua as their new Truth above the scriptures. He says the scriptures "testify about me," NOT, "they are to be used to know God." Furthermore, he says the scriptures (old covenant) testifying of his being God's Anointed One should cause a person to "come to ME" (*not "remain in the scripture"*) to have "life."

Please reread the above paragraph, slowly, and seek to understand it thoroughly, for what it says is critical.

It is essential to understand that Joshua never says that a book would be compiled after he left, that would contain His Father's Words. Instead, he said that he was the Father's perfect Word to men. Please listen to him:

> And Joshua cried out and said, "He who believes in me, does not believe in me but in Him who sent me. He who sees me sees the One who sent me. I have come as Light into the world, so that everyone who believes in me will not remain in darkness. If anyone hears my sayings and does not keep them, I do not judge him; for I did not come to judge the world, but to save the world. He who rejects me and does not receive my sayings, has one who judges him; the word I spoke is what will judge him at the last day. For I did not speak on my own initiative, but the Father Himself who sent me has given me a commandment as to what to say and what to speak. I know that His commandment is eternal life; therefore the things I speak, I speak just as the Father has told me. (John 12:44-50)

Why, dear reader, would you listen to other people try and tell you about God when the Light says what was just quoted? He says that all who do not "believe in me" are in darkness. That includes people who wholeheartedly believe the old testament scriptures are the Word of God. Thus, we can conclude that the old testament scriptures cannot take a person out of the darkness— that they offer so little light that a person who looks to them will be in darkness.

So why would a person who knows the Light want to go to the darkness and shadows to understand the Light?

Joshua said much about the future as it pertains to the kingdom of God, and to provide his disciples a framework for understanding future events. Again, he never mentioned anything about a book being compiled, nor did he say that other people after him would reveal his Father more thoroughly than he did, let alone write down his Father's will/thoughts in writings. In fact, Joshua says that he alone is the perfect revelation of the

Father and that his Words alone should be fully trusted to know God and
His will (see Matt. 11:27 above).

Joshua very clearly warned his disciples that many would come in his
name and deceive many.

What more could he say?

And yet, his teachings remain largely ignored by those claiming he is
important to them, while those same people spend much time trying to find
God's will "in the scripture."

Therefore, while Joshua" Words were preserved and placed in "the
Bible" or the "Christian scripture," he says that he alone - not the other
people's words or thoughts in the scripture - is the one sure Way to hear
from, and know, the Father.

This is eternal life, that they may know You, the only true God, and
Messiah Joshua whom You have sent. (John 17:3)

The Main Objection to this Simple Truth

Many people are exposed to, and subsequently believe the falsehood,
that the Bible or the scripture (other than Joshua" teachings) is the best way
to hear from God and know God. When they hear that Joshua and his
teachings only is the best way to know God, they object to the simple truth
that the one who calls himself the Truth is to be the only authoritative and
sure way to know God and his will for a person's life. The most effective
argument against this truth is to claim that Joshua himself teaches that his
followers are to look to the scripture to know God and his will for a
person's life. Joshua does not teach this. What he does teach is:

- Some sayings and writings in the Jewish scripture (old covenant)
  contain truth;
- Some sayings and writings in the Jewish scripture contains his
  Father's thoughts and thus are his Word;
- He implies that many, perhaps most events recorded in the Jewish
  scripture were accurate historical accounts of events, although he
  often does not directly address the cause of the event. If you know
  the Father by the Son, then one would know that the Father did
  not cause certain events;
- He, in his role as the Messiah of Israel, fulfilled prophecies
  recorded in the Jewish scripture thus validating his Messiah-ship
  for those needing that type of validation to believe.

Sadly, so many cannot see the simple truth that while the above four
points are valid; they **do not** say that the follower of Joshua needs the
Jewish scripture to follow him successfully. Joshua does *not* say, "read the

Jewish scripture (or old covenant scripture) to know God and his will for your life," nor anything to that effect. Rather and in rebuke, he plainly says:

> If you continue in *my word* (not Paul's or "the Bible's" or anyone else's), then you are indeed disciples of mine; and you will know the truth, and the truth will make you free. (John 8:31-32)

The real Joshua wants us to be free:
- Free from the bondage of our nature of fear and self-pride and selfishness and the wrongness (sin) that nature produces;
- Free from the darkness of religion, religion being the things people believe and do which have NO BASIS in the teachings of Joshua of Nazareth;
- Free from the mostly loveless life that fear and self-pride and selfishness produces.

Joshua does say that the "law" recorded in the Jewish scripture was good and binding on the Jewish people, but he also says that the law while good, *is imperfect*, and that to treat others the way you want to be treated "is the law and the prophets."

Next, we will take a look at how people look to other people and to personal experiences to try and find God's will.

Chapter Summary:
- People of all religions and by the billions are searching for God's will for their life;
- God does *not* hide His will; instead, He gave His will for people's lives concerning **how** to live one's life and what is valuable versus what is not valuable to pursue in life;
- Many people erroneously believe that the Creator has hidden His will from we His created beings and they do so because they refuse to look to The Light;
- While all religions have truth in them about human nature and human relationships, there is only One Messenger who most clearly conveys God's will to humanity and that Messenger's life, a record of his words and deeds are in the four gospel books;
- While The Messenger's teachings are considered part of "Holy Scripture" by the religionists, his words are Life everlasting.

31

LOOKING TO PEOPLE AND PERSONAL
EXPERIENCE INSTEAD OF TO GOD

Opening Questions:
- If God sent one perfect Messenger to convey His will and He succeeded, why would He send more imperfect messengers?
- If The Messenger said, "Many will come in my name and mislead/deceive many," why would you listen to other supposed messengers who come in his name?
- Why would God supernaturally communicate to one person and not another? Doesn't He love and care about every person?
- If many people have hallucinations about spiritual things, why would you think that those hallucinations are from God?

Spiritual Leaders, Prophets, Oracles, etc.:

Looking to other living people is perhaps the second most popular way that people use to hear from God and to know things about God. (It is often closely tied to the first way, the scripture, since most of the people who claim to be hearing directly or clearly from God reference the scripture to some degree to bolster their authority.) There is no shortage of people who claim to hear directly from God or to be some spiritual leader or who claim to know God and are willing to share that with others - usually for something in return, even if just to be recognized as someone hearing from God. From the pope in the Vatican to the village shaman to the local pastor, people are quick to claim to represent God, and the masses are quick to look to other people to hear from God. There is a tendency in us to look to others for help, and spiritual guidance is indeed not exempt from this tendency. In fact, it is widespread.

There are hundreds of thousands of books written by Christian authors, leaders, authorities, ministers, preachers, pastors, scholars; and at least as many Bible-based leaders on the earth today. From the hugely popular television evangelist who speaks to millions at a time, to the president of some influential Christian "ministry," to the local pastor at the small religious organization in the country - each of these people has one thing in common. They are claiming to represent God - or know some critical communication from God - and thus people ought to listen to them to know God and His will for their life.

However, there is a significant flaw in this method. That flaw is that all people are imperfect and have faults, including those who claim to have some specialized knowledge of God that they want to impart to others. *Thus, it seems unreasonable that a perfect God could communicate flawlessly through imperfect people.*

What does Joshua say to his followers about this? Does he address who his disciples are to look to, and listen to, in order to hear from God and know God? Yes, he does very clearly. Please listen to him:

All things have been handed over to me by my Father; and no one knows the Son except the Father; nor does anyone know the Father except the Son, and anyone to whom the Son wills to reveal Him. (Matthew 11:27)

For not even the Father judges anyone, but He has given all judgment to the Son, so that all will honor the Son even as they honor the Father. He who does not honor the Son does not honor the Father who sent him. (John 5:22-23)

But do not be called Master; for One is your Teacher, and you are all brothers. Do not call anyone on earth your father; for One is your Father, He who is in heaven. Do not be called leaders; for One is your Leader, that is, Messiah. (Matthew 23:8-10)

You call me Teacher and Lord; and you are right, for so I am. (John 13:13)

No one can serve two masters; for either he will hate the one and love the other, or he will be devoted to one and despise the other. You cannot serve God and wealth. *[Or God and any other master]* (Matthew 6:24)

I have other sheep, which are not of this fold; I must bring them also, and they will hear my voice; and they will become one flock with one shepherd/pastor. (John 10:16)

Calling them to himself, Joshua said to them, "You know that those who are recognized as rulers of those who have no knowledge of my Father (Gentiles) lord it over them; and their great men exercise authority over them. But it is not this way among you, but whoever wishes to become great among you shall be your servant; and whoever wishes to be first among you shall be slave of all. (Mark 10:42-44)

Joshua of Nazareth leaves no doubt as to whom his followers are to listen to in order to know God and His will for their lives. Let us review his words above again in a summary format:

- Joshua's Father, the true and living God, is only known perfectly by Joshua and whomever Joshua wills to reveals his Father to;
- The Father has given Joshua all judgment, and thus all people will stand before Joshua as the sole judge of the life they lived on earth;
- Joshua tells his followers that he is to be their only Master, Teacher, Shepherd/Pastor, Leader;
- To make it abundantly clear regarding how his followers/disciples are to view other disciples of his, he says that we are to consider each other as equal brothers who have no authority over one another but instead seek to be each other's servants.

Are you, dear reader, unclear as to what Joshua teaches concerning the source of knowledge and understanding of his Father? If you are confused or unclear, it is because you are not listening carefully to him:

Therefore Pilate said to Him, "So you are a king?" Joshua answered, "You say correctly that I am a king. For this I have been born, and for this I have come into the world, to testify to the truth. Everyone who is of the truth hears **my** voice". (John 18:37)

Can YOU hear HIS voice, dear reader, truly? Or is your spirit dead to the Word of Life? Or are you listening to many other voices who say they represent his voice? Have you been deceived into believing that Paul's voice or Moses" voice or Preacher Popular's voice or Bible scholar so-and-so is the same as HIS voice? Or are you listening to the many "christs" created by the thousands of Bible believing leaders or even your imagination? Have you rejected all "jesus" religion based on the *Hasty Generalization* fallacy?

Some write to this author and say, "well, why should we listen to you? Aren't you asking people to listen to you, and thus making the same error you are accusing others of making?" My reply is, "don't listen to me unless I accurately repeat Joshua's truths, and better still, listen *first* to the One I am pointing you to". That should be the reply of every true disciple of the Light. Again, please listen to him, for he claims that he is the perfect manifestation of the true and living God:

> Joshua said to him, "Have I been so long with you, and yet you have not come to know me, Philip? He who has seen me has seen the Father; how can you say, 'Show us the Father'"? (John 14:9)

> I have many things to speak and to judge concerning you, but He who sent me is true; and the things which I heard from Him, these I speak to the world. (John 8:26)

> So Joshua said, "When you lift up the Son of Man, then you will know that I am he, and I do nothing on my own initiative, but I speak these things as the Father taught me. And He who sent me is with me; He has not left me alone, for I always do the things that are pleasing to Him". (John 8:28-29)

> I speak the things which I have seen with my Father; therefore you also do the things which you heard from your father. (John 8:36)

> For I did not speak on my own initiative, but the Father Himself who sent me has given me a commandment as to what to say and what to speak. I know that His commandment is eternal life; therefore the things I speak, I speak just as the Father has told me. (John 12:49-50)

> Do you not believe that I am in the Father, and the Father is in me? The words that I say to you I do not speak on my own initiative, but the Father abiding in me does His works. (John 14:10)

> This is eternal life, that they may know You, the only true God, and Messiah Joshua whom You have sent. (John 17:3)

So, for the disciple of Joshua, we have one person we look to in order to both know God and to hear from God. And we have a perfect person through whom a perfect God can speak through, and thus we can be assured that there is no human flaw corruption in the words of the one who calls himself the Light of the world. Please listen to him:

But because I speak the truth, you do not believe me. Which one of you convicts me of sin? If I speak truth, why do you not believe me? He who is of God hears the words of God; for this reason you do not hear them, because you are not of God. (John 8:45-47)

When a Bible believing person hears these truths, they often respond with, "well, your position is contradictory or self-defeating because imperfect people wrote down Joshua's words. While it is true that imperfect people wrote down the Perfect One's Words, the issue is did the Perfect One's perfect words/teachings/concepts get recorded accurately - is it possible that imperfect people could accurately write down what they saw and heard? Stated another way, could imperfect people (people with character flaws and moral faults) hear a perfect person's words and accurately record them? *The answer is yes, it certainly is possible.* And if the imperfect ones did accurately capture the Perfect One's Words and deeds, then we have a reliable standard. (Please note, what is it about Bible people that they resist listening only to Joshua who they claim is their god? Why is it that they are largely ignorant of Joshua" core teachings?)

To illustrate this important point from a different perspective, please consider this question. Is it possible for a young or immature mathematician to write down the basic teachings of Einstein which they heard him teach, even if they had personal faults and weaknesses? The answer is yes. So, while only Einstein may have had perfect understanding of a particular mathematical concept, others who knew very little about his advanced math could successfully record what he said if he used terms they could understand. The same is true of the Light of the world. Joshua of Nazareth used simple, understandable terms/words to tell the world who he is, why he came, and what he wants, and imperfect men were able to capture and preserve his perfect teachings/concepts/truths in what people call the four gospels.

Revelations, Visions, and Dreams

The third primary way people claim to hear from God is directly through visions, revelations or dreams. This method is prevalent, and in fact, many religions are built on this method. A person, the founder of the religion, supposedly has a vision/revelation/dream from God, and then either shares it with others verbally, and/or writes down their vision/revelation/dream, and that vision becomes their future follower's holy scripture or sacred writings and thus the basis of another religion or sect within a religious system. Examples would include the Mormons with Joseph Smith's writings; Paulians (those who look to Paul to know God) due to his Damascus road experience; or those who focus on the book of

Revelation in the Bible. Those are all examples within Christianity. Outside of Christianity, Islam would be an example of the former (Mohammed's writings).

Perhaps the main reason this method of trying to hear from God, and thus know God, is so popular is that it cannot be proved to be wrong - unless a person has a standard against which to judge its content/message as true or false. Unfortunately, when a person is in the realm of "only-I-experienced-it," typically the only standard that person will submit to is "I" - they are the only standard to judge the message or the experience (vision, revelation, or dream) as true or false. And of course, this is also true of those who listen to them or follow them. This method/claim of hearing from God has always been popular but is particularly popular in this age of relativism and emotionalism, where each person makes up their reality. The other side of that coin - that which is very unpopular - is believing that absolute truth exists (has been given to humanity) to which all people will be held accountable - the very claim of the one who calls himself "the truth" against which all human beings will be judged.

Perhaps the second most popular reason for believing that God communicates directly to individuals through means other than prayer is because it removes faith from a relationship with God. You see, if God communicates directly with me, I don't need any faith to believe and trust in Him. By definition, faith requires a person to trust in God with no direct or personal evidence to validate that God exists.

For the follower of Joshua, the only exception to this was when Joshua visited the earth the first time and performed miracles to prove who he was. Those who saw/experienced his miracles had evidence on which to base their faith. However, concerning signs from God, Joshua said:

> This generation is a wicked generation; it seeks for a sign, and yet no sign will be given to it but the sign of Jonah. (Luke 11:29)

And;

> We must work the works of Him who sent me as long as it is day; night is coming when no one can work. While I am in the world, I am the Light of the world. (John 9:4-5)

Therefore, once the Light left the world and went back to the Father, no more signs would be given. We will look at this more closely in the upcoming chapter *The Comforting Christian Delusions*.

He concluded this line of thought by saying:

Joshua said to him, "Because you have seen me, have you believed? Blessed are they who did not see, and yet believed". (John 20:29)

In other words, those who have a faith that trusts with no evidence are in a better potential place of blessing than those who had evidence.

Please don't confuse prayer and a vision. Prayer, as Joshua of Nazareth teaches, is merely a person speaking to/communicating with God with no physical evidence that God is listening. Prayer involves a personal communication with God, NOT new information (revelation) from God or who God is, or what He is like, or how He worked or is going to work - prayer has no such "new information" aspect in this regard - it is purely present tense relational.

A vision, revelation or dream, on the other hand, is a real or perceived real spiritual/mental event where new information or insight is received or understood (or perceived as "given by God") by the person experiencing the event. They claim new information or insight regarding who God is, what He is like, or how He worked (past) or is going to work (future). While the information created or understood in the event is metaphysical (no physical evidence can be offered to support it), it is none-the-less perceived and understood by the person as "evidence" to them of the genuineness of the new information - in other words, the experience itself validates the content of the new information. Of course, this is circular (and thus erroneous) reasoning to use the event to validate itself - in other words, "because I had a vision, revelation or dream about the kingdom of God, it must be true." Not so - this is a false statement. In contrast, if you come to believe something that the Light of the world validates as correct through his recorded teachings then it is from God.

Finally, this method is prevalent because it is easy to get other people to listen to YOU, perhaps the Only Person in your area who is having such communications from God. This reason is closely associated with the first reason, as it is virtually impossible for other people to discern whether the claim is valid or not because they often have no standard to judge claims as true or false. They must rely solely on the word or testimony of the person who claimed to have the vision, revelation or dreams. And if they are drifting about spiritually - if they have no standard to judge such claims - then they are very open to believing such claims. I hope the reader can see the effectiveness and popularity of this method of trying to hear from God, from those who want other people relying upon (or even just listening to) *them* to hear from God.

This author would suggest that listening to the one who defeated death and showed us what real love is would be the best One choice.

Does Joshua address visions, revelations, and dreams? Yes, he does, sometimes directly, but mostly indirectly. You see, Joshua could not address every possible spiritual claim that people in the future would make. But he did leave his followers principles and teachings that address people claiming to have unique insight into God by whatever means, including visions, revelations, and dreams. Here are the relevant instructions of the Light in this respect. After each teaching, I will make a brief comment about the teaching and the underlined section as it relates to the topic of visions, revelations, and dreams.

Addressing the "New Information from God" claim

All things have been handed over to me by my Father; and no one knows the Son except the Father; nor does anyone know the Father except the Son, and anyone to whom the Son wills to reveal Him. (Matthew 11:27)

The saying, "nor does anyone know the Father except the Son" makes Joshua of Nazareth the only reliable source of knowing God, period. He does say further that he will reveal his Father to whom he chooses, and he makes it clear in other teachings that he can only reveal his Father to his disciples due to their faith (see John 15:15; Matt. 13:10-12 where he says regarding non-disciples, "to them, it has not been granted to know the mysteries of the kingdom of heaven"). Unlike their Master, however, Joshua's disciples are imperfect, and thus they cannot do better than their Master. Therefore, only the Son can accurately reveal the Father, and thus no accurate new information is possible unless he said that he would appear to people after his ascension, in visions or dreams.

No longer do I call you slaves, for the slave does not know what his master is doing; but I have called you friends, for all things that I have heard from My Father I have made known to you. (John 15:15)

Joshua plainly says, "all things," and so we understand that he revealed everything about the Father that he heard from the Father. One could argue that the Father would tell more things to others who came after Joshua. However, someone claiming they had new information from God should be very suspect given that Joshua said that no one perfectly knows the Father except himself (Matt. 11:27; John 3:13); and that many would come in his name after him, and would deceive many.

It is a true statement that a perfect God could not reveal his truths more accurately and clearly through an imperfect person than He could reveal through his only Perfect Son. God did speak through His Son, and that Son spoke much about the future. Therefore, since the Son heard directly from the Father, and he taught his followers what the Father said, we can conclude that the Son conveyed all the critical things that his Father wanted Joshua and his followers to know, including future events. It is possible that those who wrote down Joshua" Words did omit some of his teachings regarding future events. However, there would be no way to verify that and thus that speculation leads nowhere. In conclusion, no new information would be necessary for the follower of Joshua of Nazareth regarding the fundamental teachings of the Kingdom of God, since the Son/King perfectly revealed the Father and His will.

> For false Christ's and false prophets will arise, and will show signs and wonders, to lead astray, if possible, the elect. But take heed; behold, I have told you everything in advance. (Mark 13:22-23)

This teaching and warning from the Light provide two points which directly speak to the "new information" aspect of communication from God by personal visions, revelations, and dreams. First, he warns that people will make claims about personal knowledge they have about or from God and will perform fake miracles to deceive people into listening to their message. This point is dire, but sadly is mostly ignored as people are lining up by the millions to listen to people claiming to speak new truths from God, but who are not. And what defense does the real Messiah give his followers against such powerful deceptions? Simple -"I have told you everything in advance." So, the Light of the world told his first followers all the information they needed to know so that they would not be led astray by others claiming to speak for God. If he told them everything in advance, and the gospel writers included all the salient points he gave them, then no new information would be forthcoming regarding the kingdom of God.

> All who came before me are thieves and robbers, but the sheep did not hear them. (John 10:8)

This saying eliminates all people who came before Joshua and who claimed to be God's spokesperson to humanity - who claimed to be God's anointed bearer of Truth.

Next, we will take a look at the topic of the Holy Spirit and the primary false claims associated with that topic.

Chapter Summary:
- Listening to people *other* than The Messenger is **the** mistake which causes human beings to be lost;
- God does *not* send dreams, visions or "revelations" to people;

- God does *not* send new information about Himself – what He is like, what He did, is doing or will do;
- There is One perfect revelation of God, Joshua of Nazareth, and by listening to him alone, a person cannot go astray.

32
THE HOLY SPIRIT OR A SILLY SPIRIT?

Opening Questions:

- Does Joshua of Nazareth provide clear teachings about the role and function of the Holy Spirit?
- Why is there so much strange behavior attributed to the "holy spirit"?
- Does the turning away from reason to emotionalism play into the popularity of "holy spirit" religious movements?
- Without some objective standard to understand the Holy Spirit, would that not leave the door wide open to all kinds of claims about the Holy Spirit?
- Does the Holy Spirit somehow communicate new or unique God knowledge to individuals?

The Holy Spirit is referred to by the vast majority of Christian/Biblian people claiming to have revelations from God. From famous Christian leaders who have millions of people listening to them to the individual who has few people listening to her, to say "the Holy Spirit revealed this to me" is one of the most popular validation claims used to get people to believe that they are getting special communications from God. But is the claim, "the Holy Spirit showed me" a true claim? How can we know? Fortunately, Joshua of Nazareth does give us some guidelines to judge people's claims regarding things they supposedly received from God or the Holy Spirit. Let us take a look at the Son's Words in this respect.

But the Helper, the Holy Spirit, whom the Father will send in My name, He will teach you all things, and bring to your remembrance all that *I said to you*. (John 14:26)

This teaching says that the role of the Holy Spirit will be to be the enabling teacher of the disciple, enabling them to receive the *teachings of* Joshua, "all that I said to you." This would have a vital function for the first disciples as they remembered Joshua" Words and wrote them down. It would also have application to later disciples as we hear Joshua" Words (that which was written down in the four gospels) and need to remember them. In the context of this chapter, please note that the Holy Spirit will bring Joshua's words and teachings to the followers of Joshua, and *no other* person's words.

I will ask the Father, and He will give you another Helper, that He may be with you forever; that is the Spirit of truth, whom the world cannot receive, because it does not see Him or know Him, but you know Him because He abides with you and will be in you. (John 14:16-17)

Here Joshua calls the Spirit, the "Spirit of truth." Thus, anything attributed to the Spirit would be true, and thus would not contradict what Joshua says in the four gospels (nor would it contradict itself). Therefore, if any person says, "well, the spirit revealed this to me" and it runs contrary to what Joshua teaches, or the message contains contradictory statements, or the message can be validated as false by observation; then it is false and not from God.

I am the way, and the truth, and the life; no one comes to the Father but through Me. (John 14:6)

When the Helper comes, whom I will send to you from the Father, that is the Spirit of truth who proceeds from the Father, He will testify *about me*. (John 15:26)

Joshua again calls the Spirit, "the Spirit of truth" and says that the Spirit will "testify about ME" - which makes perfect sense since Joshua called himself "the Truth." *Please note that the Spirit will not testify about any other person other than Joshua.* So, for all those people looking for some "testimony from the Spirit" about some person, they will be waiting a long time since the Spirit will only "testify about (Joshua)."

But I tell you the truth, it is to your advantage that I go away; for if I do not go away, the Helper will not come to you; but if I go, I will send

Him to you. And He, when He comes, will convict the world concerning sin and righteousness and judgment; concerning sin, because they do not believe in me; and concerning righteousness, because I go to the Father and you no longer see me; and concerning judgment, because the ruler of this world has been judged.

I have many more things to say to you, but you cannot bear them now. But when He, the Spirit of truth, comes, He will guide you into all the truth; for He will not speak on His own initiative, but whatever He hears, He will speak; and He will disclose to you what is to come. He will glorify me, for He will take of mine and will disclose it to you. All things that the Father has are mine; therefore I said that He takes of mine and will disclose it to you. (John 16:7-15)

Joshua provides more of the role of the Holy Spirit here in this passage. He says the Spirit will do one primary thing regarding people who do not believe the real Joshua (the world). He will "convict the world," meaning he will use men's conscience to show men that they are guilty regarding:

"**Sin**, because they do not believe in me" - the one sin that people condemn themselves with is of hearing of Joshua of Nazareth and his truths, and not submitting to him for who he says he is, or stated another way, of rejecting him;

"**Righteousness**, because I go to the Father and you no longer see me." While Joshua was on the earth, he was the perfect example of righteousness - the perfect Man without sin - in truth, the Light of the world; but since he left to go back to the Father, the Father now chooses to use His Spirit (perhaps through disciples of Joshua) to show men their unrighteousness, and thus what true righteousness really is;

"**Judgment**, because the ruler of the world has been judged" - the one who rules the world has been judged as wanting, guilty, self-doomed. Joshua teaches that men have two choices concerning whom they will listen to for ordering their lives -either himself or the prince of the world. The King says that he defeated the ruler of the world, and so now each person must decide who they will submit to, either the King (of the Kingdom of Heaven) or the prince (of the world). Sadly, the people (the world) submit to the prince for the truth is that as long as a person submits to anyone but the King, they are in some measure submitting to the prince.

This role of the Holy Spirit is very clear and yet most "Holy Spirit" oriented Christian sect members (like the Pentecostals) are ignorant of those teachings or just pass them over.

The latter part of the passage quoted above starting with, "I have many more things to say to you", is a more difficult saying which does appear to open the door to new communications from God. Let us look carefully at what he says.

As always, context is the most critical factor in understanding the Master's teachings. Please pay particular attention to the first sentence in that latter paragraph, which says, "I have many more things to say to you, but you cannot bear them now." Joshua knew that his first followers at that time could not bear some of the truths he would like to have told them, and so he graciously decided to reveal those things to them later. In this author's opinion, that "later" was after his resurrection during the forty days he came to them after his resurrection and before his ascension.

Joshua says in the previous chapter:

> No longer do I call you servants, for the servant does not know what his master is doing; but I have called you friends, for all things that I have heard from My Father I have made known to you. (John 15:15)

First, the "all things that I have heard from My Father I have made known to you" statement would contradict the contention that John 16:12-15 says that we now need additional or new information (perhaps his sent ones (apostles) words as well) because Joshua failed to make all things known to them. Second, the context of this statement is Joshua teachings and commandments and how they need to keep his commandments and teachings. Thus, it would mean that the "all things" that Joshua heard from his Father was all the important teachings of the kingdom of God as given by the King - all the commands and teachings that his followers need to keep in order to fulfill the "if you keep my commandments, you will abide in my love" teaching in verse 10. There is no temporal context in John 15 about the future - instead, the setting is pure relationship with the King and the King's Father.

Even about end time events, Joshua says, "Behold, I have told you in advance." (Matthew 24:25); and so Joshua" Words in Matt. 24-25 contains all this author needs to know about end time events.

Then, in John 16, Joshua turns to specific future events they will personally experience. And in verses 5-6, Joshua says something that fills their hearts with sorrow - he tells them he is going to leave them. They can't understand that, and it leaves them sorrowing.

But because I have said these things to you, sorrow has filled your heart. (John 16:6)

Then in verses 7-11, Joshua tells them why it is to their advantage that he goes, and he explains the role of the Spirit's work.

Then, he returns to the same train of thought he left off at in verse 6, when he says, "I have many more things to say to you, but you cannot bear them now." Remember, their hearts were sorrowing at that point, so what more could they receive about what was about to happen? They already were not accepting that Messiah had to physically die and go back to the Father somehow, so how could they understand anything else about that event or the teachings of the kingdom of God? All they could do at that point was to sorrow and reject the concept of the Messiah dying, leaving them alone on the earth and not restoring the kingdom to Israel.

Even after his resurrection, they were asking, "Lord, is it at this time you are restoring the kingdom to Israel?" (Acts 1:6) Even after his resurrection, they were not receiving Joshua's teachings (which he had given them entirely as he said in John 15:15) on how the kingdom of God was going to manifest itself on the earth for a time before his second return. Their religious baggage was in the way, just as for billions today, our religious baggage can interfere or prevent our receiving the truths of the Truth.

However, the Spirit was about to come and start his role of "guiding them into all the truth" that *Joshua had already spoken to them.*

Yes, the Spirit can tell us what is to come for our individual lives if we are willing to hear him. Joshua already gave them the picture of what was going to happen in John 16:2, and the Spirit can help us know what lies ahead of the fork in our road as we walk after the Master. But the Spirit's primary role from their perspective would be to bring to their remembrance all that the King had already spoken to them, for they had not received much of what he said - it bounced off their hearts!

But when He, the Spirit of truth, comes, He will guide you into all the truth; for He will not speak on His own initiative, but whatever He hears, He will speak; and He will disclose to you what is to come. He will glorify me, for He will take *of mine* and will disclose it to you. (John 16:12-14)

But the Helper, the Holy Spirit, whom the Father will send in my name, He will teach you all things, and bring to your remembrance all that *I said to you.* (John 14:26)

If you say that "He will disclose to you what is to come" means some important end-time truths that Joshua wanted us to know, then you again have a contradiction when Joshua says, "Behold, I have told you in advance." (Matthew 24:25) Thus, it appears the best understanding of the "He will disclose to you what is to come" saying is that it addressed the personal realm of each disciple's experiences. In other words, the Spirit can show us what is to come regarding an experience we are going to go through.

For example, Joshua elsewhere says, "*When they bring you before the synagogues and the rulers and the authorities, do not worry about how or what you are to speak in your defense, or what you are to say; for the Holy Spirit will teach you in that very hour what you ought to say.*" (Luke 12:11-12) Here Joshua says that the Holy Spirit will lead the disciples in what they ought to speak at the moment they need it most. Thus, the Holy Spirit will assist them in the future when they are in a situation of duress and possible persecution. Similarly, the Spirit can work to disclose to the disciple what lies ahead on their journey following the Light.

Please note dear reader (especially if you are a person exposed to Pentecostal Bible religion) that Joshua nowhere says that the Spirit will cause people to do most of the things that Paul attributes to "the Spirit" in his letters, especially his letters to the Corinthians. Joshua tells us much about the Holy Spirit and his role in the disciples" life, and yet the Master never even comes close to attributing to the Holy Spirit all the "manifestations" that Paul says the Spirit will cause. Please seriously ponder this dear reader. One of the most fundamental mistakes people make is listening to Paul rather than to Joshua. See *Appendix 11, The Stranger Paul.*

Besides, the Master never says that his Father will communicate to people through dreams. If that were going to be a mode of communication that God would use with His children, then surely His Son would have mentioned it in his many dozens of teachings regarding God's communications with His children. The Father does give explicit instruction on how to hear from Him, but few are listening:

> While he was still speaking, a bright cloud overshadowed them, and behold, a voice out of the cloud said, "This is my beloved Son, with whom I am well-pleased; listen **to him**! (Matthew 17:5)

For those not wanting to "listen to him," telling people about their dreams and revelations from "God" is a way to draw attention to you and make yourself seem more important to God than those not getting dreams and revelations.

Next, we will conclude the theme of finding God's will with the most important fact to take away from the whole "finding God's will" thing.

Chapter Summary:

- Joshua of Nazareth gives plain teachings about the role and function of the Holy Spirit, which lessons are almost universally ignored;
- The Holy Spirit does not override our will or directly cause behavior like many Christians claim based on Paul's teachings or some other religious leader's emotional manipulation;
- The Holy Spirit – who is the Father's Spirit – has two primary roles:
  - o For those with no faith, to work with their conscience to bring conviction of sin/wrongness, righteousness, and judgment;
  - o For those with faith, as our comforter and enabling teacher, bringing to our remembrance Joshua's Life-giving truths recorded in the four gospel books.
- The Creator, our Father, does not reveal himself or new information about Himself to "special individuals," rather, he revealed Himself to us through His Son – through Joshua's life, words and deeds recorded in the four gospel books. I suggest if you want to look to anyone else to know God, that whom you look to first defeat(ed) death to validate their claims;
- Holy Spirit religion will grow as it appeals to one's emotions instead of to truth. It also is an easy way to get people listening to *you* since all it takes is a clever manipulator who can play to people's emotional sentiments.

33
GOD AND HIS WILL FOUND – HOW TO LIVE OUR LIVES

Opening Questions:
- Is there a difference between being instructed how to climb a mountain, for example, versus deciding which mountain to climb?
- Did God give us a clear and certain standard for the basic "how" we human beings ought to live the lives He gave us?
- How many sermons, books, seminars, study series, or other such things – usually income generators - are created or held to help people "find God's will for their lives"?
- If the Creator sent a how-to-live-our-lives pattern-Giver, should we not do what he says?

After just reviewing how the Spirit can guide us in certain circumstances, it is essential to distinguish again between that guidance versus the plain teachings of Joshua on how we ought to be living our lives. Perhaps the most vital matter to consider is *how I should live my life to please God?* This question is closely related to the question, "how do I know God's will for my life?" The answer is amazingly simple - listen to Joshua of Nazareth, and he will tell you. Sadly, very few people do this. Over two billion Christians are claiming some association with "Jesus Christ," but out of those billions, very few are taking seriously the reading, understanding, and doing of the teachings of Joshua. Joshua himself predicted this sad fact:

Enter through the narrow gate; for the gate is wide and the way is broad that leads to destruction, and there are many who enter through it. For the gate is small and the way is narrow that leads to life, and there are few who find it. (Matthew 7:13-14)

Few find the narrow way or gate as Joshua says, "I am the Way"; and "I am the gate." It is much easier to hide in Bible religion or "church" traditions and thinking having Bible knowledge or holding the right "church" doctrine or getting "revelations from the holy spirit" is the way to heaven.

A critical point the reader must understand is the difference between knowing the basics of how we should be living our lives, versus God's guidance for an individual in various circumstances. Sadly, since most Bible people are not listening carefully to Joshua, they are like lost sheep without the Shepherd guiding them on the basics of how they ought to be living their lives. Instead of listening carefully to the Shepherd and living according to his teachings, they look to all the other voices telling them how to find God's will for their lives! So, they reject the Light's teachings on the basics on how they ought to be living their lives and yet expect God to guide them in various circumstances in which they find themselves?!

They will read some of the thousands of books on the theme of "finding God's will for their lives," all the while ignoring the teachings of the Light who tells them how they ought to be living their lives. Dear reader, please don't make the mistake of confusing the real guidance of the Holy Spirit regarding circumstances we might find ourselves encountering, versus Joshua of Nazareth telling his disciples the basic daily pattern of how we ought to be living our lives. Again, if we are not willing to listen to and obey the only good Shepherd, why should we expect God to guide us in various circumstances? When God says:

While he was still speaking, a bright cloud overshadowed them, and behold, a voice out of the cloud said, "This is My beloved Son, with whom I am well-pleased; listen to him! (Matthew 17:5)

And we don't "listen to him," on what basis do we expect him to guide us on lesser matters?

Let us make this last point clear, as it is imperative. We must distinguish the difference between the basics of HOW we ought to be living our lives VERSUS getting guidance from the Father through the Spirit on the forks in the road we encounter while living according to the teachings of Joshua. The heavenly Father has given us all we need for understanding the basics of how we ought to be living our lives through his Son's teachings for us in the four gospel accounts.

In those teachings of the Light, we ought to understand the basics of how we ought to be living our lives, which fundamentals are built on the foundational teaching of looking to lose our lives in this world to gain Life Everlasting. Once we grasp the basics of how we ought to be living our lives AND start applying them to our life, THEN we should expect our Father to give us guidance on which fork to take in the road we encounter. In the upcoming *The Solution* section, we will learn what Joshua teaches is the HOW we ought to be living our life and WHAT we should value in this life.

As an example, let's say my passion is to be a mountain climber - I consider mountain climbing the most important thing in my life. There are many techniques mountain climbers need to learn to climb a mountain successfully.

- They must learn about proper climbing equipment and how to use it;
- They must learn different climbing and hold techniques for certain types of mountain surfaces;
- They must learn how to handle changes in weather conditions;
- They must learn how to train for the rigors of climbing mountains, so they are physically fit;
- They must learn to evaluate and manage the risks they take and how to minimize them;
- They must learn to work as a unified team with other climbers;
- They must learn how to climb on rock versus soil versus snow or ice;
- They must learn how to communicate if in distress, etc.

To learn all this, a person who wanted to be a successful mountain climber would need to learn all the "how to's" to have a good chance of successfully climbing mountains. There would be a good deal of discipline involved in educating, preparing, and training oneself actually to climb mountains, and probably the best way to do so would be to be taught by an expert, experienced mountain climber.

To sum up, there are necessary skills that a mountain climber would need to learn to actually, successfully climb mountains. *After* a mountain climber was duly trained and *practicing* climbing mountains, *only then* would they be in a position to look for guidance on WHICH mountain to climb or which way to get to the top of the peak.

In like manner, only after a person is understanding the "how to live one's life" teachings of Joshua of Nazareth, **and practicing** *those teachings by living according to them, should a person expect to be able to see which path to take when encountering forks in the road, or in the example above, which mountain to climb.*

Sadly, today's Biblians/Christians largely skip over the "how to live one's life" teachings of Joshua and just look for guidance in decisions they face, and sadly many of those decisions that are faced are contrary to the "how to live one's life" teachings of Joshua. In other words, since religious people are not looking to lose their lives in the world (a basic "how to live" teaching of Joshua), the decisions they ask God for help on, are decisions of one desire of the flesh versus another. To put it another way, we need to make sure we are on the narrow road before the Way can show us how to navigate the narrow road.

As a real-world example of this, this author recently saw a communication from Christians asking people to pray over whether the husband ought to go back into the U.S. Army or work at some other job - they were "seeking God's will for their life." The basic "how to live one's life" teaching of Joshua of "love your enemy" would prevent a disciple from joining a world's military. Thus, there is no need to "seek God's will" on the matter of joining a world's military since God's will is revealed in Joshua's teachings.

Another real example to illustrate the point happens countless times each day, as people in the religious buildings (people call "the church") hear a message from a preacher and respond in some way indicating they "want to follow christ." Perhaps most are sincere in their expressed desire to "follow christ" yet do they diligently study the teachings of Joshua of Nazareth? Not typically. Usually, they use one of the three methods addressed in this chapter to try and "follow christ" - they read their scripture, they listen to the preachers and Christian authors, and for many sects, they starting looking for signs from "the Spirit" to guide them into "the spiritual life"—all sad but clever ways to reject the Light.

Therefore, these people are not significantly different from the mountain climbing example above. These people are like a mountain climber who only reads about how beautiful the top of a mountain is, yet never actually prepares to climb a mountain by learning all the how to's of mountain climbing and then putting the principles into practice by training and practicing. The Christians, having seldom, if ever, trained/practiced what Joshua teaches (because they are listening to other voices, and doing things *other than* what Joshua of Nazareth says), expect some direction from God on the life decisions they face, and that, dear reader is very unreasonable.

> For which one of you, when he wants to build a tower, does not first sit down and calculate the cost to see if he has enough to complete it? *(Which one? The Christians caught up in the grace teaching who would complain, "there is work involved in building the tower!")* Otherwise, when he has laid a foundation and is not able to finish, all who observe it begin to ridicule him, saying, "This man began to build and was not able to finish." Or what king, when he sets out to meet another king in battle, will not first sit down and consider whether he is strong enough with ten thousand

men to encounter the one coming against him with twenty thousand? Or else, while the other is still far away, he sends a delegation and asks for terms of peace. So likewise, whoever of you does not forsake all that he has cannot be my disciple. (Luke 14:28-33)

Conclusions from Previous Three Chapters

The primary purpose of the previous three chapters is to turn people to Joshua of Nazareth so that they can know God's will for their life. Sadly, the vast majority of people who are involved in the Bible and the Christian religious system have very little knowledge of Joshua" teachings, and thus little knowledge of his person and his Father. The Bible religious system's purpose is to keep people in the shadows and darkness by shielding them from the true Light. And one of the favorite ways to do that (especially among the sects influenced by Pentecostal teachings) is to teach the people that they don't really need Joshua to hear from God. Instead, they have "the Spirit" who will guide them in their "walk with God." This is just another way for people not to take seriously the teachings (and thus the person) of Joshua of Nazareth. It is another distraction and excuse for a person not diligently being a student/disciple of the Light.

The purpose of this author is not to dampen or hinder a genuine person of faith's relationship with the heavenly Father - quite the opposite. The author contends that *if a person, who claims to be somehow following Joshua is ignorant of his teachings and thus not living them out, then they are in fact not a disciple of Joshua as he defines it.* Therefore, what I am doing is blowing on whatever embers might exist out there.

Joshua makes it clear what a Master - student/disciple relationship is, and unfortunately this relationship is what is attacked most diligently by those who oppose the Light. What better way to assail this relationship than by getting those who might be willing to "follow Joshua" to listen to people other than Joshua himself?

The previous three chapters have endeavored to examine and point out the most popular religious things which people use to *replace* making Joshua of Nazareth, their Master. To recap, they are the scriptures, favorite Bible/spiritual teachers, and personal experiences or "insight from the Holy Spirit." People use all three to keep away from the Light of the world.

As this author pointed out in this chapter, the teachings of Joshua looked at in these chapters do not make a perfect logical case for the Holy Spirit *never* communicating something other than Joshua's teachings to a disciple. Unfortunately, for many, this little crack in the door will justify all the rubbish they claim comes from the Spirit. As we have seen, the Holy Spirit can give guidance for a disciple's circumstances. Equally, perhaps, more importantly, we also have seen that the Holy Spirit will *not* provide new information regarding who God is or how he wants His children to live their lives while on the earth. The Father's Son has given all that is necessary for a person to know God's general (the basics on how to live one's life) will for their life, which is to *do* what Joshua *teaches*.

For the person reading these preceding three chapters who is concerned about truth, I hope you will agree that Joshua does put parameters on what the Spirit will communicate. And if you are looking to visions, dreams, revelations or "the Spirit" for the basics on how to live your life, you are guilty of ignoring the Light. In fact, even if you are not looking to visions, dreams, revelations or "the Spirit" for your life's decisions, yet are not listening carefully to Joshua and living according to his teachings, you are also guilty of ignoring the Light. As was addressed earlier, Joshua teaches his disciples quite plainly how we ought to be living/ordering our lives. Yet it is much easier to ignore him (and his core teaching of losing our life in this world to find Life everlasting) and instead look to "the Spirit" to "guide us" in the things of the world which we love!

In the past few chapters, we have looked at the primary claims of many Christians regarding God's will and how to find God's will. The next chapter will take a brief look at some Christian/Biblian theology which is widely considered essential, which does not pass the test of logic, and keeps people in a delusional state regarding reality.

Chapter Summary:
- Finding God's "will for my life" is a major endeavor for most religious people, including Christians;
- The simple truth is that God has revealed very clearly **how** he wants people to live. There is no mystery to be uncovered there – no will to be found - since The Light revealed that some two thousand years ago!;
- Since people don't want to listen to God about how to live their lives, they spend much time and energy trying to find the mysterious God's will for what to do with their lives;
- If Christians started to live according to the revealed will of God through Joshua of Nazareth, their lives would be drastically different for the better. Most would not be looking for "God's will for their lives" since they would be living it out in the most critical way and would naturally be directed regarding the where and with whom!
- The Creator gave his model for humankind, the Son of Man. The vast majority of people's would receive a clear answer to their wonderings about what God's will or primary purpose is for their

284

lives if they just chose to have faith in and listen to the Son of Man or Model for humankind.

34
THE COMFORTING DELUSIONS

Opening Questions:

- Is it wrong to apply logic to God belief claims? (Please remember the proper definition of "faith")
- Is it right to believe something that is false?
- Is it okay to have faith in something that is false?
- Is it healthy or in a person's best interest to be delusional?
- Why does God have to be "all-powerful" to save an individual from him/her self?
- Is it wrong to expect the reality that we experience each day to line up with God claims that would manifest in that reality?

Most religious people who take the label Christian, Muslin or Jew or other such theists state that God is all-powerful or all-mighty. Anyone who thinks a bit about this claim can see the attraction of this claim. Wouldn't it be great to have "Superman" protecting your back at all times? Who would not want that? Thus, human beings created a god that assuages their fears of being hurt or killed. Also, you have the competitive tribal mentality of "our God is greater than your god." Thus each group's god is "more powerful" than the others!

The thinking goes like this, "if God is for me, who can be against me" to quote the Christians beloved Paul. That saying of Paul is wrong from two perspectives. First, it completely contradicts Joshua of Nazareth's experience and teachings. Was God for Joshua? Yes. Were people against him? Yes, most, that is why they publically killed him. Thus Paul's statement is proved false. Furthermore, Joshua teaches that "If you were of the world, the world would love its own; but because you are not of the world, but I chose you out of the world, because of this the world hates you." John 15:18ff. Thus the people of the world are very much against the followers of The Light.

Second, even Paul's saying does not address physical protection. But religious people often don't let facts or sound reason get in the way of their imaginary comfort blanket! So, most Christians and Muslims and Jews go about quoting their beloved scripture which assures them that their God – being all-powerful – will protect them in this world even with evidence and proof countering that claim coming in daily by the hundreds of millions of times!

My question, as a disciple, is where does Joshua say that his Father is all-powerful?

Another objection to the fact that God is not all-powerful is, "well, if God is not all-powerful, then he is not worthy of placing my faith in." In other words, "if God is not the way I want him to be, then I will not place my faith in him." *That is a statement that supports the point in this book that most religious people make up a god who serves them instead of letting the teachings of Joshua, sound reason and observations guide them to know God.* What the religious person is saying or objecting to if they are to believe that God is not all-powerful, is their erroneous belief that "IF God is not all-powerful, He cannot save me (or those I believe I need in my life)." Two questions to that objection are:

1. Save you from what?
2. Why does he have to be all powerful to save you?

Regarding the first question, most Christians would say, "save me from hell" or "save me from horrible things happening to me in this life" or "save my loved ones from harm." The "save me from hell" fear is irrational if you know the teachings of Joshua of Nazareth regarding the Father's character as we saw in an earlier chapter. Our Father does not send us to hell (a place of destruction, not of eternal torment), rather, we send ourselves either to Life or justice and destruction – it is completely up to us. God does not force us to love Him or each other. Therefore, it is irrational to fear God not being all-powerful regarding "going to hell" since He does not send us there. So, in truth, we should be afraid of ourselves if we are going to be fearful of hell at all!

Regarding the, "save me from horrible things happening to me in this life" or "save my loved ones from harm" fear, *God cannot intervene in this realm or He would.* His power is constrained to His realm unless He has an agent like Joshua of Nazareth to work in this realm and then it is localized to that agent. There are no guarantees in this life regarding what will happen to our bodies. Thankfully, as followers of the Light, we do have his promises that our Father will receive us when our body dies.

Do not let your heart be troubled; believe in God, believe also in Me. In my Father's house are many dwelling places; if it were not so, I would have told you; for I go to prepare a place for you. If I go and prepare a place for you, I will come again and receive you to myself, that where I am, there you may be also. And you know the way where I am going. (John 14)

The "I will come again and receive you to myself" does not necessarily refer to a physical coming.

Truly, truly, I say to you, he who hears my word, and believes Him who sent me, has eternal life, and does not come into judgment, but has passed out of death into life. (John 5)

Please note he says, "my word," *not*, "the Bible," or Paul's or Moses's or popular preacher or author or Bible scholar or Greek expert, etc.

What we can know for sure, without error, is that there are thousands of people – from small children to people of faith to the relatively innocent (those who are not doing something wrong to other people) – who are both treated unjustly each day, and who are suffering from various things in this world each day. And yet, God is not intervening to help them. To conclude otherwise is to be deluded.

Here are the dictionary definitions of "delusion":

"Something a person believes and wants to be true, when it is actually not true." [51]

"a: Something that is falsely or erroneously believed or propagated." [52]

"b: A persistent false psychotic belief regarding the self or persons or objects outside the self that is maintained despite indisputable evidence to the contrary." [52]

Such delusionary religious beliefs are yet another reason why non-theist people reject believing that God exists, let alone trying to get to know God or placing their faith in him. The average person reasons that since religious people have some delusional beliefs, that all their beliefs are questionable if not delusional. That is faulty reasoning, but you should be able to see how the delusional beliefs of religious people make an easy excuse for people who don't believe God exists to throw the baby (Joshua of Nazareth) away with the dirty bathwater (Christian/Bible religion and its false beliefs in his name).

Unfortunately, a primary purpose of religion is to put so many false and silly and wrong and foolish and harmful and delusional beliefs about God

---

[51] Cambridge Dictionary, www.dictionary.cambridge.org, May 2018

[52] Merriam-Webster Dictionary, www.merriam-webster.com, May 2018

out amongst the human race that people who are willing to use their mind and thus reason well, will reject God's existence. (Really the one Joshua calls the father of lies assists in propagating those falsehoods among religious people.)

Of course, the religious people don't believe they are doing that, but that is precisely the nature of deception or of being deluded. Religious people are deceived and deluded on some essential things regarding God. In their delusion, they mislead others and ask them to join them in their delusion. Finally, this delusion work serves to keep non-religious people away from God. They have a powerful natural motivation to assist with this process since people want to feel secure and want to believe that a god will save them – will preserve their life in this world - when they need it. And this, in spite of Joshua saying:

> He who loves his life (in this world) loses it, and he who hates his life in this world will keep it to life eternal. (John 12:25)

Let us review this widely held religious belief about God in more detail. Here are some key claims/doctrine of the Christians regarding the nature and character of God.

- God is all–knowing or omniscient;
- God is all-seeing or everywhere at once or omnipresent;
- God is all-powerful or omnipotent;
- God is all-loving and cares about each person on the earth;

OK, let's use reason and logic well here to evaluate these claims, for these claims are in the realm of precepts or beliefs, not faith (faith means extending trust to something not physically verifiable) and thus tested by observation and logic.

If God can see all things (omnipresent), then he can see all the evil acts that are committed each day on this planet against children and innocent people. Is this not correct?

Those who are offended at the possibility that God is not all-powerful will sometimes offer the argument, "What does "innocent" really mean?" What they are getting at is their belief that all people are guilty of sin - there are no innocent adults - thus all people deserve punishment for their sins.

Let us respond to this argument by first defining the term/concept of "innocent."

Cambridge dictionary says, "not guilty of a particular crime, or having no knowledge of the unpleasant and evil things in life, or (of words or action) not intended to cause harm." [53]

---

[53] Cambridge Dictionary, www.dictionary.cambridge.org, May 2018

If you search the other dictionaries, you should agree this is a pretty good, comprehensive definition of the term/concept.

Please note that there are three definitions of "innocent" in Cambridge's single definition. Here they are separated.

1. Not guilty of a particular crime;
2. Not knowing the unpleasant and evil things in life;
3. (of words or action) not intended to cause harm.

So, let us take a look at my statement that uses the concept of "innocent."

I said, "If God can see all things (omnipresent), then he can see all the evil acts that are committed each day on this planet against children and innocent people."

Placing children aside for a moment, clearly many adults exist who meet definitions one and three above. These people are not guilty of crimes nor are they walking around looking to harm people. When those people are treated unjustly, cruelly or are wrongly-harmed, are they deserving of that treatment? I would ask for a teaching from the Light of the world to back up those who claim they are worthy of that treatment. Since God teaches us to even, "love our enemies" even as He does, they will come up empty.

Even as adults, if we have lost our internal, pure, spiritual innocence due to our experiencing or understanding evil or that which is wrong, how would that make us deserving of unjust treatment? Only a very distorted view of God would have a person answer that due to our understandings (lack of innocence) in our minds, we deserve unjust treatment by evil people while on this earth.

Finally, let's look at the children. There are many, many young children – as well as older disabled people like Downs Syndrome people – who are innocent by all three definitions, and yet are unjustly treated and wrongfully suffering each day. In fact, young children and disabled people like Down's Syndrome people are disproportionately treated unjustly, wrongly, abused, neglected and harmed each day on this planet. The weaker and innocent are shamefully treated and preyed upon regularly each day by the millions. To deny this is irrational.

So, now that we have shown the error of trying to use the concept of "innocence" to justify an all-knowing and all-loving and all-powerful God *not* intervening in this realm let's take a closer look at this delusional belief.

Here is the "trilemma" or argument or syllogism that Christian's attempt to reconcile as stated earlier in the book:

Premise 1:   God is All-Powerful (meaning he can do anything he wants in any realm…nothing or nobody can stop his will and work)

Premise 2:   God is All-Loving (meaning he cares deeply about the
                 welfare of people and would not want them to come to –
                 at a minimum – unjust harm or suffering)
Conclusion: God prevents unjust harm and suffering in this world.

Let us now test this argument using reason, logic, and observation.

Verifiable, Undeniable Facts:

Fact 1: Many thousands of relatively innocent people are unjustly
harmed or treated wrongly each day on this planet, including Christians and
others who say they believe in God. From emotional pain to being treated
wrongfully or shamefully, to physical death and everything in between -
harm, pain, and suffering happen each day on this planet countless times.
The reader should know the causes by now! In fact and ironically, the real
and historical person of Joshua of Nazareth was tortured and killed, and he
was genuinely innocent! Yes, he said he could have saved himself, but that
is not the point. The point is that it is usual in this world for innocent
people to be harmed, mistreated, abused and used *and* it is normal for God
not to intervene.

Fact 2: Most of the innocent people harmed (used, abused, mistreated,
hurt, injured or killed) are women, children, and the different or disabled—
the weak and vulnerable.

Fact 3: Of the many thousands of people harmed each day on this
planet, there are no reliable, verifiable reports of miracles delivering people
from harm or death. There are billions of cell phones spread across the
earth at this point, most of which have cameras and yet nothing – no
evidence that an all-powerful God is saving or protecting innocent children
or people from harm.

No, the testimony of religious people claiming that God does miracles
(acts that defy physical laws) does not change the facts. If God did
miracles, there would be evidence of that work.

So, those are the facts that observation and reason provide. Many
thousands of vulnerable or weaker people are unjustly treated, harmed,
killed, or left to die each day. So the question is where is the all-powerful
God to intervene and protect them?

And yet the religious people continue in their delusional chant, "God is
in control—God is in control". Well, logic tells us that if God is in control
of a world filled with evil, then God is responsible for that evil. See any
problems with that reasoning? If not, why not submit to the truth of it and
start down the road of finding real freedom instead of staying in religious
delusion?

People should value reason for it is the means to determine what is real from what is false. When religious people proclaim false beliefs – beliefs which do not meet the test of observation, reason or logic – they do great harm, not the least of which is encouraging people to believe that **all** God-beliefs are false. In so doing, they turn people away from the One who can indeed save us from ourselves and spiritual death.

The "God is in control" belief is very popular and powerful because it provides two things. First, it provides a false sense of security by believing that God is going to help me physically in my hour of need. Second, it alleviates or removes the personal responsibility to take any action associated with god-beliefs. Why? Well, if God is in control…if god is running things and orchestrating all the events around me, then I cannot change anything, therefore, why try? Or, "if I try to change something it might go against what God is doing, and I don't want to go against what God is doing." As we have seen, since religious people don't claim to know God's will, they might offer a slightly different version of excuse like, "I am not going to mess with God's will even though I don't understand that person's suffering."

This belief does an outstanding job at justifying religious people's lack of behavior that would otherwise be consistent with their god claims. Along with Paul's grace doctrine, this belief works very well in preventing religious people from working to try and fix the problems they encounter each day…it provides an excellent justification for being cowards and ignoring all the wrong around them. Instead of rolling up their sleeves and addressing the wrongs and evils, many hide in their god beliefs and in their "sanctuaries" and do nothing or very little.

If God, in fact, is all-powerful and all-knowing and can see all things that happen on this earth;

And he acted based on love for people (and a person who loves another person certainly acts to protect them from unjust harm);

Then surely he would intervene to prevent the unjust-caused pain and suffering of innocent people.

Again, does the reader find fault with my reason or logic? Finding fault does not mean quoting some "scripture" to contradict that argument. Instead, it means using reason and logic to point out an error in the discussion.

No, the objection to the above facts of, "but God's ways are higher than our ways" does not make the truth go away…it is merely a parroted religious response which seeks to avoid or deny what is true. And the religious people respond, "No, that saying about God's ways is Scripture, the Word of God!" Yes that is "scripture", but no, scripture is not the word of God, and if it was, why do you look to a God who has the power to stop children's suffering and abuse yet does not? Back to the delusional denial, "oh, but God's ways are not our ways." Well, THAT god's ways are cowardly and evil, dear person. How would you describe the three-hundred pound strongman watching a sniveling one-hundred fifty pound pervert abuse a young child and do nothing about it?

Some religious people will argue that God purposely hides His deeds from people and that is why there is no evidence. The reasonable question to that assertion is why? Why would this all-powerful God conceal his kind acts and thus select one suffering child to save (who was hidden) over another, who was not? An omnipotent being who also cared about His creations and that could keep, for example, young children from unjust suffering would do so because his love would drive him to do that.

Furthermore, didn't the real God say?

Let your light shine before men in such a way that they may see your good works, and glorify your Father who is in heaven. (Matt. 6)

Would God not be a hypocrite to teach us not to hide our good works, but He would?

The truth is that no such help is forthcoming as the factual evidence of each day proves. God does **not** intervene in the affairs of humankind as any non-deluded individual can easily judge. So, why not consider coming out from the delusion and instead listening to the One who says, "I am the truth"? Why not give up your Bible religion and reliance on contradictory "scripture" and instead put your faith in the Light of the world? Why not put away what *you* want God to be, and instead accept who He is as revealed by The Light and truth?

The same objection repeated many times does not mean it is a valid objection, "but we cannot know God or his ways..." The Light says, "And this is eternal Life, that you may know God."! In fact, it is critical that we "know God" as best as possible because God created us to love others including Him and He does love us and does *not* want us to destroy ourselves. The best way to know God is to study and know the teachings of His Messenger, the One about who God said, "This is my beloved Son in whom I am well pleased – listen to *him*!"

As previously discussed, religious people hanging onto the "God is all powerful" belief generally do so because they are afraid that if God is not all-powerful, then He will not be able to "save" them from difficulties in this life, or at the end of their lives. The question is, is that fear reasonable? As we have seen, fear and reason are enemies, and when fear influences a person's heart, they cannot usually reason well. My question in return is to ask, "do you have god beliefs just so you can get something from God?" If you do, then you are not listening to the greatest commandment that The Light validated.

And this is the first and greatest commandment, that you love the Lord your God with all your heart, with all your soul, with all your mind, and with all your strength. (Matt. 22:36-38)

Love does not act on "what do I get out of it." Rather, love is a metaphysical "attitude" which includes, valuing someone or something higher than I value myself. I don't deny that wanting to continue one's existence after physical death is a reasonable desire for all those who believe that our life does not end after our body dies. However, if our motivation is purely selfish because we never entered into a faith relationship with our Father and our Master, then a strictly selfish motive will not prevent us from destroying our souls.

If we have even a little bit of real faith, then our love for our Father will be our principal motivation and self-preservation will be secondary. Joshua addressed this motivation in part when he taught:

All those who seek to keep their life will lose it; while those who seek to lose their life for my sake, shall find life. (Luke 9:24)

Therefore, if we have a little bit of faith, we will not need some false security blanket belief about God being "all-powerful" so that He can physically save us in this life. If we truly love our Father with all that is in us, then we will very much look forward to being with Him in fullness once we leave our bodies when we physically die. We are grieved, angry and frustrated at how the people of this world run the world and all the injustice and suffering and wrongness in this world, and we would rather be away from such darkness. We know that God does not have to be "all powerful" to save us from destroying ourselves, nor does He have to be all powerful to receive us to Himself when our bodies die.

The Creator set things up so that when all people physically die, they transition to his realm/dimension to receive the consequences of their life choices. This process is not an "all-powerful" issue, any more than whether gravity exists or will work the next moment. God is powerful enough to have set the rules up and to maintain the rules system, which "system" rewards those who love and who care about what is true and right, and which rules brings consequences to those who refuse to love and who care primarily for themselves instead of others.

Miraculous Healing

The above truth, that God does not intervene in the affairs of people, addresses this sub-category as well. God does NOT heal one person and leave others suffering. He is not a respecter of persons and loves ALL people, not just some. Yes, He is pleased more by the children who listen to Him and endeavor to do what He says is right; and yes, those who are more faithful to Him in this life will gain greater things in the Life to come; *but*, that does not change his love for all. For God so loved all the people of the earth that He gave His Special Messenger, yes, His very Son...

Yes, the Light did heal people – both physically and spiritually – but he did so to reveal his and his Father's character and primarily as a witness to his message. If he did not do the works of healing, then people would not have paid any attention to him – he would have been just another of the many thousands of people in history-making fantastic God-claims - and the Creator's Message would not have been preserved and propagated. Joshua of Nazareth, the Light of the world, had greater faith than any person in history AND the window for miraculous works closed after his return to the Father. Please listen to him in that respect:

> As he passed by, he saw a man blind from birth. And his disciples asked him, "Teacher, who sinned, this man or his parents, that he would be born blind?" Joshua answered, "It was neither that this man sinned, nor his parents; but it was so that the works of God might be displayed in him. We must work the works of Him who sent me as long as it is day; *night is coming when no one can work*. While I am in the world, I am the Light of the world. (John 9:1-5)

Are you willing to receive this truth? The Light left this world and night came, dear reader, and thus *"no one can work"* miracles.

The simple truth, dear reader, is that God – the Creator of the human race – is not all-powerful in this realm of the face of the earth or the third dimension in which we exist. He is all-powerful in his realm/dimension of existence, but not ours. The Creator has limitations, and He needed what Joshua of Nazareth - His Son - had to accomplish those miracles. So, when Joshua left, the window was closed and "no one can work" wonders. It is that clear and straightforward, and that also best fits our factual observations and experience in this world.

Some non-theists and agnostics state that both premises are false – that God is neither all-powerful nor a Being whose core characteristic is love. The reason this author rejects the dismissal of the proposition that God is not a being of love is twofold. First, the first cause argument. The Designer made human beings capable of love; thus, the Designer must at a minimum known what love is to have created human beings to be capable of expressing love. Second, the Messenger of God was very clear about the importance of love as well having lived love out well to validate his teachings on love.

Don't be afraid, dear reader, God is real, and He does love you, but you only have one thing to concern yourself with...and that is to love your Father back, and thus get to know Him and start doing what His appointed Messenger said, the primary of which is love one another. We are given a body for a short time; our body is merely our means to express ourselves while we exist in this realm of the surface of the earth. But our bodies will inevitably fail and die, and then *our window* of choices will close.

Those who make Joshua their Leader are not afraid to lose our bodies because we know who we are and where we are going. We know that we only have these bodies for a relatively short time and that where we send our spirit/soul is *far more important* than what happens to our bodies while on this earth.

Therefore, listen to the Light as he says:

> Those who seek to keep their life in this world will lose Life, while those who seek to lose their lives in this world for my sake will find Life everlasting! (Luke 9:24)

Don't let fear run your life. Don't allow self-pride prevent you from learning. Don't have false views of God—don't make Him into a selfish "security blanket" for that is not what He is and that is not what He wants to be to you. Trust that he will receive your soul/spirit when your body dies IF you have placed your faith IN HIM and His Messenger, Joshua of Nazareth and thus have committed to living for love, truth, and rightness. Let go of the silly false religious beliefs which bind you and are entirely selfish, and will cause the opposite behavior from what God wants. Find the freedom not to be afraid to have your body die because you will come to know your Father in fullness and thus you will truly know where you are going and that to be with Him is FAR better than what this world has to offer. Find the freedom that only comes from the Father's Freedom Giver:

> If you continue in **my** words/teachings/truths (*not* Moses" or Paul's or Isaiah's or John's or preacher so-and-so or "the Bible," etc.) *then* you are MY disciple/pupil/student; and *then* you shall know the truth, and the truth will set you **free**! (John 8)

...the freedom to become part of the solution instead of remaining part of the problem. The freedom that comes when we walk out of our cage after we asked the Freedom Giver to unlock it for us!

Prayer

Joshua teaches his disciples to pray. He even provides an example prayer. Prayer is the child of God's way of talking to our Father, expressing our thoughts to Him, perhaps of our seeking to understand Him, and asking him to help us with the things we think we need. Prayer is good and necessary. However, like most God-things, religious people fail to recognize some critical ways that prayer is both misunderstood and abused.

Many religious people use prayer like the guy in the genie story who rubs the genie bottle to get what he wants. How many people each day pray a prayer in the form of, "Oh, God, please give me these material things so my life will be better" or "God, please bless me"? Billions? Asking for daily bread – sustenance for this day – is far different than asking for more than what I truly need.

This topic is also the best example of misrepresented teachings of Joshua in the four gospels. For example, the gospel author of John has Joshua saying, "In that day you will not question me about anything. Truly, truly, I say to you, if you ask the Father for anything in my name, He will give it to you. Until now you have asked for nothing in my name; ask, and you will receive, so that your joy may be made full."

The unqualified "anything in my name" clause is at best, difficult to process. Stated another way, it simply does not come to pass in people's lives; therefore, something about it is false. The possibilities are that Joshua did not say it at all. Or, he said something about prayer, but it was twisted into "anything in my name."

Some people will say that "if you just have enough faith, God will grant you your wishes." Let's look at the problem with that reasoning. First, Joshua says that if you have faith as great as a mustard seed, you will be able to do amazing things. He also said that people's faith played an important role in their receiving God's miraculous healing that Joshua performed while he was here on the earth. As we have seen, however, those miraculous powers were limited to when Joshua was here on the earth, and their primary function was to validate Joshua's Person and his Message about the Creator as well as reveal God's character.

So, the religious person who hears that a person is not having their prayers answered might say, "You are not getting from God what you want because you don't have enough faith"; or, "you must have sin in your life, and that is why God is not answering your prayers".

So, let's say I had a young niece, six years old, who was suffering from cancer and was in great pain. If I pray for her healing and she is not healed, according to the religious person who says, "oh, you don't have enough faith to get what you want" or "your sin is why God is not answering your prayer"; *God will not intervene because of something wrong with me.* In other words, because I have something wrong with me – perhaps my faith is not great enough, or I have a sin I am struggling with – he will not grant my prayer, and thus He will not bring healing or pain reduction to that suffering six-year-old. Do you see the problem?

Again, the Christians will say that God is both all-powerful and all-loving, and *he could* intervene and heal my six-year-old niece's cancer, but He does not. Furthermore, when I ask Him in prayer to please have mercy on my six-year-old niece and stop her suffering, he will refuse to grant my request because he sees a fault in me. In other words, he refuses to heal a suffering child's cancer because He does not like something about **me**. That dear reader is messed up.

So, let's use another example to make this point clear. Let's say I have an uncle who is an excellent surgeon and he could operate on my six-year-old niece to possibly cure her cancer. I go over to his house one evening to beg for him to please perform surgery on my niece, but he says, "Me help you after the thing you did to me seven years ago? Hah, no way, you operate on her yourself!" Thus, my uncle throws me out. I ask the reader, what kind of a person would you say that surgeon is?

That dear reader is essentially the answer that most Christians give to the circumstance that happens probably millions of times each day. The Christian's say, "well, God will not help your daughter because of something wrong with *you*"; or "God will not help those people because of something wrong with *you*"; or, "God will not help *you* because of something wrong with YOU," etc.

The simple truth is that it is love-less and utterly lacking compassion to be able to help a needy person but to refuse to do so because you find fault with the person requesting help for the needy person!

Of course, most Christians will respond with something like, "God can do what God wants" or "God's ways are higher than our ways" or "who are we to question God and his ways" or "how dare you question our most tightly held religious beliefs." In other words, "shut up and go away with your reasoning—you offend us with your logic." Or worse, they will attack the messenger just like the religious people some 2,000 years ago attacked The Messenger. Instead of fighting against truth, I ask you to consider embracing it, moving on and possibly finding more freedom in your life.

Next, we will look at the contrast between the average easy, American Christian's life and the sayings of Joshua about how it will be difficult to following him.

Chapter Summary:
- Reason, logic, and observation tell us that a being does not exist who is all-powerful, all-knowing and all-loving. In particular, he cannot be both all-powerful and all-loving. The Messenger tells us

298

He is all-loving and he does not teach that He is omnipotent. Therefore, we throw out all-powerful;

- Just because the Creator is not all-powerful does not mean he did not create us; nor does it mean he cannot provide a superior existence for us once we leave our bodies; nor does it mean that God cannot provide new bodies for us in the future (the resurrection);

- God does not intervene in the affairs of men today from the perspective that He does not cause physical things to happen or not happen. Therefore, He does not physically heal today nor do other physical miracles;

- Prayer is good, but its primary purpose is to encourage us to know God and to act as God wants. We certainly can ask for physical things from God, but He is not going to perform a miracle to get us what we ask. He gave us a fantastic earth from which we can produce our food, clothing, and shelter, and He expects us to work together to meet our physical needs;

- Having delusional beliefs about God is detrimental to all involved, particularly those who don't believe God exists. Holding or promoting delusional beliefs only strengthens the unbelief of those with no faith in the Father Joshua reveals.

35

THE EASY LIFE VERSUS "DIFFICULT IS THE WAY THAT LEADS TO LIFE"

Opening Questions:

- If you claim to follow Joshua of Nazareth, and yet your life does not match up with his teachings, what should that tell you?
- If religious people "do life" in a way that is indistinguishable from non-religious people, what does that say about the religious people?
- Does getting cancer, for example, somehow count as some difficulty that came due to faith in God?
- If a Christian is persecuted for their clothes or their religious meeting attendance or their holiday observances, is that persecution due to faith in Joshua of Nazareth if he does not teach that people ought to do those things?
- What is the difference between one religious person (say a Christian) being persecuted for their religious beliefs or practices and another religious person (say a Buddhist) being persecuted for their beliefs and practices?

Look at the lives of the average Christian in the U.S.A. Would you describe their lives as any more difficult than the non-Christian? In fact, most Christian's partake in a comfortable life in the U.S. They have their money making jobs and careers in the world which they spend the majority of time serving with very little if any serious thought to "ministry." With some smaller percentage of their disposable time and income, they build their religious buildings and have the programs – most of which appeal to entertainment desires – and live just like the agnostics and atheists next door or across town. They have many they call their "friends" and work hard at being popular with as many people as they can. What sacrifices are they making for their supposed faith? What work or "jobs" have they lost because they spoke a bit of Joshua's truth or any truth? How could that in any way be described as "the difficult way" that the Light states will be the norm for his followers?

When confronted with this truth, Christians in nations with Christian majorities will often respond with, "well, my mom and dad just died in a car accident"; or, "my sister just got diagnosed with cancer." I don't deny those are difficult trials that deserve compassion, but they are *not* trials caused by their faith nor do those trials have anything to do with God! Instead, they are the difficulties and trials and sufferings ALL human beings face each day (Illness, injury, disease, loss, etc.) and those are **not** what the Light had in mind when he said it would be difficult to follow him.

Contrast this life of the average Christian with what Joshua of Nazareth says will characterize his follower's lives and experiences:

> Enter through the narrow gate; for the gate is wide and the way is broad that leads to destruction, and there are many who enter through it. For the gate is small and the way is narrow (or difficult) that leads to life, and there are *few who find it.* (Matt. 7:13-14)

> If the world *(the people of the earth who don't have Joshua as their leader)* hates you, you know that it has hated me before it hated you. If you were of the world, the world would love its own; but *because you are not of the world, but I chose you out of the world, because of this the world hates you.* Remember the word that I said to you, "A servant is not greater than his master." If they persecuted *(sought to harm)* me, they will also persecute you; if they kept my word, they will keep yours also. (John 15:18-20)

> Strive (or agonize) to enter through the narrow door; for many, I tell you, will seek to enter (through religion) and will not be able. (Luke 13:24)

> Blessed are you when people insult you and persecute you, and falsely say all kinds of evil against you *because of me.* Rejoice and be glad, for your reward in heaven is great; for in the same way they persecuted the prophets (those who spoke God's truth) who were before you. (Matt. 5:11)

> A disciple is not above his teacher, nor a slave above his master. It is enough for the disciple that he become like his teacher, and the slave like his master. If they have called the head of the house Beelzebul,

how much more will they malign the members of his household!
(Matt. 10:24-25)

These things I have spoken to you, so that in me you may have peace.
In the world you have difficult troubles, but take courage; I have
overcome the world. (John 16:33)

Those are just a few of many sayings that convey the same truth, that
the followers of The Light of the world will have a difficult time while
living our lives out in this world *due to our faith in the light and speaking and
living out his truths.* This makes perfect sense since we believe the Light and
speak his unpopular truths like:

- God exists and we will be held accountable for how we live our
  lives;
- We can know God and He wants us to know Him and He made it
  simple to know Him;
- God expects us to live out of love for Him and others and not for
  money or other things;
- Absolute truth exists and can be known – all things are not relative;
- Joshua of Nazareth teaches that human being will be held
  accountable for their thoughts and behavior in this life;
- Joshua of Nazareth teaches that people love darkness rather than
  light because people are evil;
- Joshua of Nazareth teaches that HE is the only sure Way to
  Eternal Life;
- Religion (including Christian or Bible religion) is wrong, misguided
  and has its primary purpose to hide the Messenger to mankind;
- We cannot live with – or be at peace with - our natural or legal
  relatives if they refuse to follow the Light;
  - We will live with other followers of the Light – our true
    brothers and sisters - instead of with others who don't love
    him and thus who refuse to follow him;
- We are in bondage to fear, self-pride and selfishness if we don't
  allow Joshua to take us out of our cage;
- God wants us to practice true love towards one another which we
  are unwilling to do;
- Seeking a materially secure life in this world (refusing to truly share
  what we have with other disciples) runs contrary to the Life and his
  teachings;
- There is right behavior and wrong behavior, a right way and wrong
  way to live one's life;

- You cannot live like everybody else and try and be accepted by everyone if you are going to truly follow Joshua - you *must* be different, and thus...
    o We will be rejected, persecuted, reviled, mocked, slandered, harmed and killed in *all cultures at all times* for repeating and living out Joshua's truths;

That is not an easy life, and that difficult life is totally foreign to the vast majority of Christians in the U.S. and around the earth in western nations especially at this time. Go ahead and ask a Christian, "what persecutions or hardships have you had to endure due to your faith in God?" Most will look at you with a blank stare and ask what you mean.

This author has lived in the U.S. for his whole life, and I have experienced persecution due to my faith. I have had children I love wrongly taken from me due to the corrupt people who run the legal system, and I was not even granted visitation rights unless I didn't talk about Jesus! Just so you are clear, murderers in prison get visitation rights with their children, but I was not even allowed to speak to my children due to my faith. I was told by the legal people running the system that I was not allowed to talk about Jesus to my children or else I would not be able to see nor communicate with them. The Christians I was seeking support from during that time turned away from me and treated me like I had leprosy. They just assumed my then assistant district attorney wife was correct because of her position in the world and I had something wrong with me.

I have lost work multiple times because I spoke unpopular truths or because I refused to ignore Joshua or because I would not affirm people in the wrong things in which they wanted affirmation. The Christians have rejected me, and when I went into their religious buildings, I didn't last long because I consistently communicated that some of the things they were believed or were doing were wrong. In my efforts to preach the gospel to people publically, I have had stones and bricks thrown at me some ripping my clothes. I have been thrown off of public property (where in the U.S. you are supposed to have a right to peacefully assemble and speak) just for trying to tell people about the real Joshua of Nazareth. I have had my natural Christian family cut me off totally, and my dad even testified against me at the divorce trial that my ex-wife initiated due to my faith. And guess who the majority of that persecution has come through – Christians and Biblians!

So, I don't speak from an ivory tower or inexperience when I say that disciples of Joshua of Nazareth are persecuted. Disciples" being persecuted and rejected and slandered and mocked is the normal experience in every nation and culture and during all history. The only things that vary are the disciple's faith and courage and the level of hostility of the people of the world. The more faith and courage a disciple has, the more harshly and quickly they will be persecuted.

In addition to pointing to natural problems that affect everyone, many Christians respond with something like, "well, we are in a Christian nation and that is why we have it easy." That excuse and the false things behind it are becoming more and more difficult to defend even for the confused. The U.S. is a Christian nation, but as this book reveals, the description "Christian nation" is a relatively meaningless label. As we have seen, "Christian" is merely a religious label and it is *not* synonymous with being a follower/disciple of Joshua of Nazareth. And even the ethical beliefs that Christians once held based on their religious beliefs are going away so that lawlessness and evil are growing exponentially.

The simple truth is that Christians do NOT follow nor represent Joshua of Nazareth and THAT is why they have an easy life in the U.S. or anywhere else they don't faithfully repeat his truths and attempt to live them out. The Christians are the ultimate examples of the "have your cake and eat it too" principle. Meaning, they love their life in this world, and thus they live no differently than the people they claim "need to be saved"; and yet they think that their religion will "get them into heaven."

Joshua of Nazareth's truths have been unpopular ever since he came some two thousand years ago and in all places. No "culture" is conducive to his truths on how we are supposed to live our lives because human nature is the same no matter what nation, culture or century in which we live. *People create cultures, and those cultures reflect their thoughts and ways apart from the Light of the world.* Human nature has not changed, and thus people's reactions to the truths of the Light of the world have not changed. That is why he prepared us with timeless sayings like:

> If the world *(the people of the earth who don't have Joshua as their leader)* hates you, you know that it has hated me before it hated you. "If you were of the world, the world would love its own; but because you are not of the world, but I chose you out of the world, because of this the world hates you. "Remember the word that I said to you, "A servant is not greater than his master." If they persecuted (sought to harm) me, they will also persecute you; if they kept my word, they will keep yours also. John 15:18-20

They indeed did persecute Joshua, so, reason that out…

His word was to make him your leader and to follow him. Disciples repeat his words/teachings/truths today and get the same response from the vast majority of people - they did not keep his word, they do not keep our word.

Saying there is a right way and a wrong way to live one's life has always been unpopular due to our nature of wanting to do whatever we want irrespective of its impact on others. People have always been bound in the cage of self-pride and fear and selfishness. When we disciples come along and say, "Hey, did you know you are bound in a cage created by your self-pride and fear and selfishness," the reaction is almost always the same...ridicule, offense, and attack. Ironically, it is self-pride that causes that reaction. We all want to believe we are "free," and we insist on defining "freedom" from merely a physical or outward perspective. As we shall see in the next chapter, this is a great error.

Increasingly, the citizens of the U.S. are some of the most enslaved people of the earth due to their turning away from even a vague God belief and associated ethical standard on which to order rules. While the U.S. is a nation founded on Christian religious beliefs, the simple truth is that not only have the majority of its people abandoned faith in the Bible-god, but they are abandoning even a moral ethic derived from the Bible or their religious sects.

How does the average Christian's live their life? It is indistinguishable from any other person's life, whether people of other religions or non-theists or agnostics. "Earning a good living," code for storing up treasures on earth, is how Christians live.

'So You Deny Christian Persecution?'

Many Christians will respond to the prior truths by pointing out the Christian persecution around the world and saying this somehow disproves my point.

Joshua teaches two types of persecution will gain reward from God:

Blessed are those who have been persecuted for the sake of righteousness, for theirs is the kingdom of heaven. (Matt. 5)

Blessed are you when people insult you and persecute you, and falsely say all kinds of evil against you because of Me. Rejoice and be glad, for your reward in heaven is great; for in the same way they persecuted the prophets who were before you." (Matt. 5)

As you can see, he says that first, those persecuted for speaking out against that which is wrong or immoral or trying to stop that which is wrong or immoral peaceably will gain the kingdom of heaven. This applies to any person, not just disciples. Any person who listens to their conscience and thus practices fighting non-violently against that which is wrong or immoral is worthy of the kingdom of heaven.

Second, he says that when disciples are persecuted because of our love for, faith in and obedience to Joshua – persecuted for being his follower— for our speaking *his truths and expressing our faith in him* - our reward will be great.

Please note he does not say, "blessed are those who are persecuted for being different" or "blessed are those who are persecuted because of their religion."

The fact is that many different groups are persecuted around the world. *Almost all religious minorities are persecuted to some degree.* The Jews were persecuted by certain German people not too long ago, and are persecuted today in many places. Buddhists persecute Muslims and vice versa depending on where they live and who is the majority. Hindu, Muslims, and Christians regularly persecute one another, and they regularly persecute people of different sects within their religions. There are many dozens of examples of large-scale religious persecution happening today even as there are millions of daily instances or expressions of fear, dislike or hatred towards religious people of all stripes.

It is merely a minority dynamic where the majority persecutes the minority for not conforming to the majority and not taking the majority's religious label or engaging in the "right" rituals or not using the correct "God vocabulary" or beliefs. Religious and racial and nationalistic and tribal persecution has existed for as long as humankind has existed. It is one of the base wrongs of people that self-pride and fear generates. Call it what you will, tribalism, nationalism – the dynamic is the same – "we hate you because you are not like us (different skin color, language, clothing, ways of doing things, etc.) and you refuse to believe like us (religion) or to submit to our great political ruler(s) or our God".

Dear reader, the kind of religious persecution just described has little or nothing to do with being persecuted for speaking and living out Joshua's teachings. Christians - known through clothing styles or religious organization membership or labels (Catholic, Protestant, Pentecostal, etc.) or holiday celebrations - are persecuted *just because of their religious self-identification*, just like Jews or non-violent Muslims or Hindus or Buddhists, etc. are persecuted just because of their identification with those religions. They are generally **not** persecuted for speaking or living out the truths of Joshua of Nazareth.

So, for example, if a Christian, who is living in a Muslim majority area, is leaving their place of gathering and some Muslims see them walking down the street after leaving their "church", that Christian might be beaten or threatened just because they are a Christian, *not* because they speak the Light's truths or live his teachings out! I hope this book is making clear the difference between a Christian and a follower/disciple of the historical Joshua of Nazareth. Again, in that example, that man is harmed simply because of a religious label or affiliation or self-identification, *not* because he is speaking the Light's truths or living them out.

I don't minimize the courage that it takes for a Christian to live in areas where they are persecuted due to other religious people being hostile towards them. Although, Joshua of Nazareth does address that if you had faith instead of religion:

> But whenever they persecute you in one city, flee to the next... (Matt. 10:23)

If Christians are being persecuted because they are staying where they are and fighting for what is perceived as theirs ("my parents had this house/property, and it is mine..."), then they are partly to blame for whatever harm they might suffer due to their persecution. Of course the other Christians are to blame for not welcoming the persecuted Christians into their communities, but of course, you need to love one another to have and live in communities! Since the Christians do not love one another and thus stay apart from one another, there are virtually no "communities" to which one could bring persecuted Christians. We will see why in the upcoming chapter, *I love Ice Cream, I love You.*

I also don't judge persecuted Christian's faith one way or another. If they are being courageous due to faith and acting out of love and their behavior is consistent with Joshua's teachings, then good for them, they are doing well, and I commend them! However, and as we have seen, it is *far better to know* the God you have placed your faith in because we lose much through ignorance.

> This is eternal life, that they may know you, the only true God, and me (*Joshua of Nazareth*, **not** *"the Bible"*) whom you have sent. (John 17:3)

When we do something right by chance or in ignorance or without the right motivation, what reward do we deserve? Or if we do something out of ignorance or without the right motive, will that please the person that hopes we would serve them out of love?

Lastly, it is a fact that Christians persecute other non-Christians as well as Christians who belong to a different sect. In contrast, disciples of Joshua persecute no one because we have overcome the self-pride or fear or selfishness that drive most persecution.

Christianity in a Nut Shell

So, this section has described the sad state of the successful failure that is called "Christianity" and those people who make up the religious system and its organizations in the name of "jesus christ." The success in drawing people in and collecting money from them to build their fiefdoms – their buildings and programs and "ministries" – all the while failing at carrying out what their proclaimed God says!

This is the successful failure.

Now, there are many well-intentioned and decent people who take some Christian label and participate in Christianity and its local organizational expression they call "the church." Many are sincere in what they believe and are decent moral people - that is they don't intend to harm people. Some spend some time doing useful stuff like giving poor people money or traveling to other countries for a week to help some materially poor people build housing. Unfortunately, those things, while good, are the minor things that God wants and expects of ALL human beings. In other words, there are Muslims and Jews and Hindus and Buddhists and Agnostics and Atheists, etc. who do the same things the Christians do, and it is NOT because they all have a right understanding of God, but rather that *we all have a conscience given by our Creator.* That conscience encourages us, pushes us, chides us, reminds us, whispers to us, and points us to do good instead of evil.

Here is the problem stated from another perspective. If you don't know the directions to get somewhere, you are highly unlikely ever to get there. If you do know the directions, you have a good chance of getting to the destination, even if you make a few mistakes. Well, the vast majority of Christians and Biblians do not know the Messenger's teachings because they are not listening to him, and thus they don't know the directions! This is what it means to be lost, and yes, it is true, many are lost in their sincere Bible and Christian religion.

So, what is the simple, undeniable truth regarding the human race and love as defined by the Standard given by the Creator? Please hear his words:

This is the judgment, that the Light has come into the world, and men loved the darkness rather than the Light, for their deeds were evil. (John 3:19)

That the people of the earth – *especially Christians who use the Bible to hide the Light* - love the darkness rather than the Light and their loveless-ness and all it manifests is a great evil!

What is the first reaction from those with no faith or humility? "Oh, I am not evil—my deeds are not evil—I love jesus…" Unfortunately for many who utter such things, they are merely self-deluded falsehoods based on the *wrong standard* to judge what is evil. The self-deceived religious people say, "I don't murder, and I don't" purposely harm others, and I don't smoke or drink, and I don't use drugs, and I don't..." And the list of "do not's" goes on and on, but they have the wrong standard to judge whether they are evil or not!

The Light says "love one another," and Christians are **not** doing this and yet they believe that abstaining from overt acts of harming others or one's self is what makes a person acceptable to God or a "good person." They could not be more wrong, for *what makes a person evil is rejecting our Father's love and truth and therefore refusing to love others!* What is the greatest evil above all others? *The lack of love for our Father and others is the greatest evil!* And what makes a "good person" is a person who cares about what is true and right and tries to help people see they need Joshua as their Leader. People need more than just good moral behavior – more than just abstaining from wrong-doing and doing a bit of "convenience good works" as it fits into my overall selfish life-style.

The sad truth is that the average Christian lives no differently than the average Muslim or Jew or Hindu or Buddhist or Atheist or Agnostic, etc. You will know the Christians only by their love for their book, the Bible, and their traditions; their attendance at their religious entertainment meetings in the buildings they call "the church"; their self-righteousness; and their loveless-ness. Sadly, you will also know the Christians by their ignorance of the teachings of the one they call their God!

If you care about what is true, then you will listen to the Light and believe what he says.

> This is the judgment, that the Light has come into the world, and men loved the darkness rather than the Light, for their deeds were evil. For everyone who does evil hates the Light, and does not come to the Light for fear that his deeds will be exposed. But he who practices the truth comes to the Light, so that his deeds may be manifested as having been wrought in God. (John 3)

If you care more about yourself and your life in this world, then you will not listen to the Light.

The religious people are the "try and have your cake and eat it too" crowd. They are quite a bit less honest than the non-religious crowd. They are like the most adept tap-dancing lawyer that can turn "yes" into "no" or black into white with a mere few flicks of his/her tongue. They have built up for themselves a self-serving delusion that they are not soon going to give up the house they have built for themselves with its multi-colored, flashing lights.

This is the current sad state – the successful failure – that is Christianity.

In the next section, we will move onto describing the solution to the successful failure. Or stated another way, how we could minimize failure and maximize success according to the One who gets to define those things.

Chapter Summary:
- Joshua of Nazareth teaches that those who choose to follow him will suffer in this world. We will be rejected, persecuted, reviled, misunderstood, mocked, slandered, etc. There are no time or cultural exceptions to that truth—the Way is challenging in all times and cultures because truth about human nature and our ways is an offensive in all times and cultures;
- Christians in the U.S. and many other nations live lives that are indistinguishable from the very people they say "need to be saved";
- Normal difficulties like illness or accident or loss that all people experience do *not* amount to being persecuted for faith in Joshua;
- Christians are persecuted in various places on the earth, but they are generally persecuted for their religion, *not* necessarily for their faith in Joshua, just like many other religious or political or tribal minorities are persecuted in many parts of the earth;
- Christians persecute other non-Christians and even Christians who belong to a different sects/divisions;
- Christianity, while a success in the world's eyes, is a failure in the eyes of the One who said, "Come, follow me." Christians, in general, do not know nor speak the Light's truths – at least his unpopular ones - and they do not live according to his teachings. If they did, they would be persecuted in all nations, particularly in Christian countries.

Section Summary:
- Christianity is a religion, it is not faith in Joshua and it does not lead to Life;
- Religious people have hidden The Light in the big book they call the Bible. If you surround the truth with enough falsehoods and lies, most people will never find the truth;
- Most of the beliefs about God the Christians consider "essential" or "foundational" are false when compared with Joshua's teachings, and no sects I am aware of have "love" as their most important belief/concept let alone attempt to practice it;

- The Christian gospel is an admixture of Hebrew religious beliefs and popular beliefs and it presents a "heaven can be gained for free if you just believe this God-stuff" gospel. Christianity's gospel is significantly different than the good news that Joshua of Nazareth brought to mankind;

- "Going to church" has wrongly become the main Christian work they do to try and be accepted by God, just like "observing the Sabbath" was for the religious people of Joshua's day;

- Christian leaders attempt to hide the contradictions, falsehood and problems with their religious beliefs using complicated theology or concepts. They nullify The Light's teachings using various forms of religious relativism and alleged language expertise;

- Christian religion is essentially a hobby for most – albeit a fear or guilt driven one for many – and one of the favorite "chasing unicorn" practices is to "find God's will for my life". They do this to avoid actually living according to Joshua's teachings;

- One reason many people reject God is due to Christianity's claim that God is all powerful and all loving. They know - since reason, logic and observation inform them as such – that that claim is false. Christians are no different than other religious people in this respect in that they often don't care about what is true and instead go with their religious dogma;

- Most things that are really worthwhile or memorable or character building in life are difficult. This is very evident in athletics, or where people were injured or disabled and had to work very hard to accomplish something. Being Christian is in no reasonable way difficult for the vast majority of Christians all over the earth, but particularly in the U.S. and Europe at this time. In contrast, following Joshua is difficult in all times and cultures, but it is also the most worthwhile and noble thing a person can do with the life they are given.

SECTION 5:
THE SOLUTION: FINDING FAITH IN A AGE OF FEAR AND FALSEHOOD

Theme:

- The Freedom Giver can enable and lead us to have meaningful, purposeful, impactful, beautiful lives characterized by sharing true love with others;
  - o Hope Rekindled;
  - o Purpose Gained;
  - o Love Found;
  - o A Call for Desperately Needed Change

Section Introduction

As we have seen, Joshua of Nazareth defines "religion" as a creation of men, *not* facts about or from God. In fact, that is the reason why Joshua came to the earth. He came to reveal his Father, God, the Creator and Designer of the human race, because people needed a lot of help and had got a lot wrong about their Creator and did not have the will to treat one another well. He did not come to create a religion or be a religious figurehead! Rather, he came to be a Model and a Leader for the people of the earth—he came to show us the Way.

Joshua of Nazareth said that *he* represented his Father, God the Creator, perfectly, like no one in history ever had. He said this:

All things have been handed over to me by my Father; and no one knows the Son except the Father; nor does anyone know the Father except the Son, and anyone to whom the Son wills to reveal Him. (Matt. 11:27)

So Jesus said to them again, "Truly, truly, I say to you, I am the door of the sheep. All who came before Me are thieves and robbers, but the sheep did not hear them. I am the door; if anyone enters through Me, he will be saved, and will go in and out and find pasture. The thief comes only to steal and kill and destroy; I came that they may have life, and have it abundantly". (John10:8-10)

Many who claim to speak for God but do not will arise and will mislead many. (Matt. 24)

Simply put, only the Son can accurately reveal the Father, and thus a person can only know God properly through the Son. A very simple truth which he conveyed many times from different perspectives to make sure it was communicated well. To repeat and paraphrase these teachings, Joshua taught that *he and he alone was the most perfect revelation of God to humanity and no one else before or after him would be able to duplicate his revelation.*

Thus, the One True Messenger of the Creator came and delivered the Solution to mankind's problems.

So, what are the components to the solution to help people see that living a life like the one Joshua calls people to will both lead to a badly needed change and rightness as well as eternal life? How can one escape the successful failure or never enter into it to begin with? Let us take a look at some important concepts in order to fully develop the answers to those questions.

36
HOW IMPORTANT IS FREEDOM?

Opening Questions:
- Are their different forms or types or qualities of freedom?
- Can a person be free in a prison cell?
- Can we have a "successful American life" and not be free?
- Are their some choices that take away our freedom even while we are free to go and do anything we like?
- What is the purest and most valuable form of freedom?

What is freedom? Here is the ordinary dictionary definition of freedom. "The condition or right of being able or allowed to do whatever you want to, without being controlled or limited." [54]

This is a good and proper definition of "freedom" as it is commonly understood, however, is it flawed? Yes, it certainly is. The flaw exists in the phrase, "whatever you want to." If we human beings were beings of love, truth, and rightness, then freedom would result from our being able to do "whatever we want to" because we would want to love others and deal with them in truth and rightness. However, one only needs to look around the world a bit to see that we are not beings which consistently nor regularly behave based on love, truth, and rightness.

In fact, we only need to look in the mirror and objectively examine our daily words, motivations, and deeds to come to the same conclusion that we do not act in perfect love, truth, and rightness all the time, even as disciples. However, as disciples of the Light, we have the power to live by love, truth, and rightness in a very high percentage of our daily lives. This example is

---

[54] Cambridge Dictionary, www.dictionary.cambridge.org, April 2018

what the Master called for when he said, "Therefore, be perfect as your heavenly Father is perfect."

As we have seen - and made what I hope is a compelling case for - the fact is that we are bound in a cage of self-pride and fear and selfishness. This state will NEVER produce true freedom or stated another way we will never be free while in our cage.

There are two aspects to true freedom that ought to be understood. *First, an individual is not free who treats other people wrong.*

They may believe they are free as they act wrongly towards others – hurt, use, take from, abuse, neglect, disrespect them with either wrongful words or behavior – but they, in fact, are in a cage of their own making – if they have not killed their conscience, their conscience will condemn their wrongful words or behavior and that is not real freedom. If they have destroyed their conscience, then they have little hope of escaping the cage.

It is a fact that a person can act shamefully and wrongly towards other people hundreds of times each day and NEVER break the laws of the nation in which they live. A person can complain against others and curse others and treat other's harshly and without patience or compassion...and never break the law. Furthermore, the law can easily provide a way to justify ourselves wrongly. I will say again, law/rules can restrain behavior; they cannot motivate love and the fruit of love.

There is an outer element to freedom and an inner element to freedom. Like most things, people look primarily to the outward and physical to understand their life in this world. So "freedom" for most people means not being in a prison cell or a wheelchair or some other such movement or location or function restriction or constraint.

However, it is a fact that a wealthy person living in a multi-million dollar mansion with several "beautiful" women and driving around an expensive sports car can be in more of a cage (less free) than the man living in a prison cell. These illustrations reveal the second fact.

The most valuable and meaningful freedom is internal, not external. This fact is yet another proof of the spiritual or metaphysical nature of human beings and thus evidence against the physicalist view.

Real freedom exists in inner peace and contentment. Real freedom is gained through living out true love, which gives instead of takes. Those people who are the freest are those who don't hold onto their lives in this world any longer, but instead live to love/help other people, and to give their lives away to bring the freedom and love they have found in their Father to others.

Can you, dear reader, accept these simple truths about "freedom"?

- Freedom is gained through truth, not falsehood.
- Freedom is gained through rightness, not wrongness.
- Freedom is gained through humility, not self-pride.

- Freedom is gained through faith, not fear.
- Freedom is gained through love (selflessness), not selfishness.
- Freedom is found in giving our lives away to help others, not in taking from others to "better" our lives in this world.

This high form of freedom is gained through faith in the right thing/noun. The best, highest freedom is found through faith in the correct person and identifying that correct person is accomplished by reason/truth.

Therefore, we should expose that which gets in the way of a person finding freedom and love so people can see their choices—these basic life choices:

- Liberty or bondage (remain in the cage).
- Faith or fear.
- Compassion or hard-heartedness.
- Humility or self-pride.
- Love or selfishness.
- Truth or falsehood.
- Reason or emotions.
- Rightness or wrongness.
- Reality or delusion.

Those are the most basic and essential and meaningful choices we make as human beings.

If we make right choices, then we enter into the Life we were created to live. If we make wrong decisions, then we will stay out of the Life our Creator wants for us and remain in our half-life in our self-made cage.

The Freedom Giver put it this way:

> The Spirit of the Lord is upon me,
> Because He anointed me to preach the gospel to the poor.
> He has sent me to proclaim *release to the captives*,
> And recovery of sight to the blind,
> *To set free* those who are oppressed,
> To proclaim the favorable year of the Lord. (Luke 4)

And:

> So Joshua was saying to those people who had believed Him, "*If you continue in my word, then you are truly disciples of mine; and you will know the truth, and the truth will make you free.*" They answered Him, "We are Abraham's descendants and have never yet been enslaved to anyone; how is it that you say, "You will become free'?" Jesus answered them,

"Truly, truly, I say to you, everyone who does/practices what is wrong is the slave of wrongness. The slave does not remain in the house forever; the son does remain forever. *So if the Son makes you free, you will be free indeed.* (John 8)

The Son is the best and surest way to set us free, for he is The Freedom Giver and Messenger from the Creator/Father and thus he can free us from our wrongness. If our cage of self-pride and fear and selfishness is the wrongness that we need to be set free from, then the Son is the best and surest way that we can be free from the cage in which we placed ourselves.

For the religious folks, please try and see that "the Bible" or "going to church" or "*being a good person by not doing wrong*" or many of the other things you believe you find freedom in are wrong! Only faith in the Son – the person of Joshua of Nazareth and only *his* truths and teachings as spoken by *him* and located in the four gospel books – can set you truly free if the deepest, ultimate sense. And we are only truly a "good person" if we care about what is true and right and try and help others see they need Joshua as their Leader.

For the religious person to think that your religious teachings somehow make you free is to be badly self-deceived. Believing false things does not enable us to be free. We looked at Christianity's teachings in the prior section. If you are willing to make Joshua your Standard of truth and you are eager to strive for objectivity, then you ought to conclude that Christianity is a successful failure.

For the non-theist, to think that your rejection of God makes you free is to be badly self-deceived. Believing false things does not enable us to be free. As we have seen, assuming that no designer is needed to reasonably account for human beings is a mistaken view. And to deny a metaphysical reality is also irrational.

Please understand, we, dear reader, choose and shape our destiny. *There is no deity planning our lives or directing our lives or controlling our lives or the lives of others*—God did *not* make our cage nor put us in it. That is part of the delusion revealed in this book. We are entirely in control of what we do with our lives and whether or not we will enter into the Life freely offered, or stay in our self-made cage and thus out of the Life. Typically when we reject the freedom offered we look to justify our Life-less-ness through all kinds of clever justifications, excuses, and delusion, religion being a primary one.

So, once a person comes to the understanding that freedom can only be found through faith in the Freedom Giver and thus knowing how to live rightly; having the power to live rightly; and then living rightly - where does that leave a person? It leaves a person needing a Leader!

To find what is true and right you must decide to allow reason, logic, and observation (where possible) to inform you in all domains in your life. Learn to use reason and logic well, the tools that allow us to identify and put forth true things. Care genuinely about what is true, and if you do that with all your heart and determination, then you will do well, and you will find the truth.

Do not believe the false claim that "science" is The Truth that will set you free or that makes sense of everything. Science rightly done is merely a tool and method, all the philosophical claims by its adherents notwithstanding. Science is the best tool to understand the physical world in which we live. Truth from Joshua is the best source to understand our nature, the metaphysical aspects of human life, our purpose as human beings and why and how we should live our lives.

Finally, caring about what is right is critical. Truth is higher than "rightness" and encompasses thoughts and beliefs, whereas "rightness" has to do with human behavior and *how* we are to live our lives, not *why* we are to live our lives. There is a right way and a wrong way for us to live and behave. Or, stated another way, people can behave wrongly, or they can behave rightly. To deny this is irrational. When we live rightly, mainly when we act with love towards others, the conscience we have will reward us with internal peace.

The world makes a big deal about leadership, and they are right to do so. In the next chapter, we will take a look at the vital concept of leadership and see how one particular leader is badly needed.

Chapter Summary:
- Freedom is a critical concept to self-aware, sentient, free will beings. When we perceive that we do not have freedom, our spirit usually is downcast, depressed or discouraged;
- The highest form of liberty is not external or physical or circumstantial, but rather internal. The enjoyment of external freedom will change depending upon circumstances. Inner freedom will result in peace that no one can take away;
- The choices we make affect our freedom and our lives. For example, choosing to serve money instead of people puts people into bondage and takes away their liberty;
- Human beings need the Freedom Giver sent by the Creator to set them free, and they need the Freedom Giver to keep them free.

37
WE NEED LEADERSHIP

Opening Questions:

- What makes someone a good leader?
- If there were many good leaders, would not the world be a better place?
- In general, are Christian leaders any different than business leaders, for example?
- If I am a weak leader and I have easy access to gain the knowledge I need to be a good leader, and yet I don't search that out, am I not more accountable for my poor leadership?
- If I am a lesser leader and I am following the best leader, am I not doing well and should not my leadership and life reflect it?

Everyone needs leadership, even leaders!

What percentage of the world's leaders are good leaders? Given how the people of the world are doing, the answer to that question should be self-evident. Good leadership at all levels of – government, societal, private industry, religious organizations, other organizations - would mean that there would be far less conflict and injustice and wrong and suffering that exists in the world.

Let's start by taking a brief look at some vital leadership concepts. Below is a continuum of leadership qualities and values.

Bad, Mediocre, Good, Better, Best

There are seven critical elements to ethical leadership in this world:

- Leader's motivation
- Leadership by principle or by feelings
- Personnel decisions objectively or subjectively
- Commitment to training or not
- Real, just, fair or generous reward/compensation or not
- View of personnel – inherent value
- View of personnel – unity
- View of personnel – idea value

Bad Leadership

- Bad leaders care only for themselves and what they can get out of their leadership position;
- Bad leaders don't lead or organize by principles, policies or rules but rather by their personal opinions or moods or "gut instincts";
- Bad leaders make personnel decisions by favoritism and make organizational decisions based on who they believe will kiss their butt the most fervently, what they often label "loyalty";
- Bad leaders spend little time training members/employees and expect them to "get it" or else;
- Bad leaders pay their employees based on some rigid structure that does not reflect how the organization operates and does not reward truly productive or creative employees. They don't even bother having symbolic or non-monetary "rewards" like "best employee of the month" type events;
- Bad leaders use people in their organization like they would use non-human assets with no real concern for the people's well-being;
- Bad leaders don't care about contention or wrong treatment among the people of their organization as long as they believe it will not adversely affect them or what they want;
- Bad leaders don't want to hear any ideas from their "employees/slaves," for their arrogance makes them believe that people "lower than themselves" cannot possibly have better ideas than they do;

Mediocre Leadership

- Mediocre leaders say they care about something more than themselves, and they pick one or a few relatively minor things to demonstrate this, but in general "self" is still number one;
- Mediocre leaders say they run thing by principles or rules or core values and other such concepts, but in reality, they do that only some of the time and instead go by "their instinct" or "their gut" – in reality, their emotions, moods, and feelings just like bad leaders;
- Mediocre leaders make most personnel decisions based on personal favoritism even while they profess to be objective and impartial. They only seek to appear objective and impartial if they believe the decisions will somehow benefit themselves or allow their work to continue;
- Mediocre leaders only pay lip service to member training but don't seriously carry it out nor hold people accountable for learning or implementing the training;
- Mediocre leaders only reward members or employees if those rewards are trivial or mainly ceremonial—they do not give them significant monetary rewards because they are afraid they will have to do that with more and more people which will mean they will have less for themselves or their masters;
- Mediocre leaders say they care about their members or employees and they make some minimal effort to attempt to convince people that they do, but in reality, if it means better money success or power success for the leader if the leader uses and/or abuses some or many employees, then "so be it";
- Mediocre leaders make minimal efforts to bring unity among their personnel. Typically they address staff who are disruptive or bringing open contention;
- Mediocre leaders have some mechanism or process or forum for employees to submit their ideas, but generally speaking, they do not seriously consider those ideas;

Good Leadership

- Good leaders mostly get past themselves and a purely selfish motivation;
- Good leaders lead by principles they create or adopt that will lead to accomplishing the work they are conducting and are relatively consistent in their decisions, which decisions conform to the principles;

- Good leaders rarely show favoritism, but generally are impartial to individuals in their personnel decisions;
- Good leaders spend a good bit of time educating members on the fundamental operating principles and the importance of working by them and have effective training programs and ensure most are adequately trained;
- Good leaders acknowledge and appreciate knowledge, ability, and experience and reward those who solve problems or advance the work;
- Good leaders have some genuine level of concern for the members of the organization;
- Good leaders recognize beneficial and helpful attitudes as well as harmful and destructive attitudes and reward and correct respectively and thus put significant effort into unity;
- Good leaders are not so proud as to dismiss employees suggestions on improving the organization or its operations;

Better Leadership:

- Better leaders have all the attributes of Good leaders above, plus:
  - o Better leaders care more for people than for money or power;
  - o Better leaders lead by example first, not by authority only, and they earn that authority through behavior, not assumed by position;
  - o Better leaders look to solve significant problems even if the problems they encounter are not a part of their usual domain of responsibility;
  - o Better leaders promote the most skilled and those with superior attitudes even if they are unpopular due to reasons that are not valid (for example, if someone holds an unpopular "religion" or political views);
  - o Better leaders recognize constraints to success and seek to change them, even if they know it might upset those in higher authority;
  - o Better leaders listen to suggestions, correction, and criticism and take action if the suggestions, correction or criticism are right;
  - o Better leaders are willing to step aside and let someone else they believe would be a better leader, lead.

Best Leadership

Please note that the transition in leadership character and concerns is moving from ethical to this last category which represents an ethic, not from this world.

- The Best Leader care's nothing for money or power unless it can be used in a genuinely selfless manner to help others gain what is truly valuable;
- The Best Leader lead's only by truth and example and never uses his authority to get his Way;
- The Best Leader never gets offended or upset when someone does what is foolish or wrong;
- The Best Leader continues to care about the member who is entirely against him;
- The Best Leader has the solution to all of our most significant needs;
- The Best Leader doesn't make mistakes and is one hundred percent reliable concerning his character and consistency of nature in his understanding of our needs;
- The Best Leader always wants what is best for us and is always willing to give it to us even if we hate him or ignore him;
- The Best Leader keeps all of his promises and never breaks his word.

Care to guess who qualifies for the Best Leader!

Of course, those categories of leadership above are a continuum, and it is unlikely that a single leader will fit cleanly into one of those categories. It is more likely that they will have characteristics from two sequential types meaning attributes from Bad and Mediocre or from Mediocre and Good. It is less likely that they will span a category and have characteristics from Mediocre and Better. However, and in general, most leaders will have a majority of attributes of one type, because one's character would make it so. *Not only does one's character matter, but it is also the primary characteristic which affects whether someone will be a good leader or not.* The world foolishly does not recognize this truth and instead values educational achievements or reference accolades.

Many leaders are in their positions for the wrong reasons. How many people are put in positions of power or leadership over others due to butt-kissing, brown-nosing, cronyism, sexual favors/interest, seniority, etc.? How many leaders are in their positions because they paid money to gain some degree from a particular school, which intellectual effort and subsequent knowledge has little or no bearing on the quality of their character? How many leaders are in their position because their dad owned the business before them? How many people are in positions of power or leadership due to their bloodline (England's Kings and Queens, for example) or whom they know or to whom they are related? How many leaders in democracies say what they believe the people want to hear to get elected and then break the promises with sayings like, "Oh, my position on that matter has evolved since the campaign'? In other words, how many leaders are where they are due to the *wrong* reasons—perhaps the vast majority? Is it possible that in all of human history, there have been only a very few people who could be characterized as a "better" leader as defined previously?

Of course, it is possible to be a good leader and to have received your appointment to that leadership position for reasons other than being a good leader (like your dad owned the company before you), but that would be the exception rather than the rule.

Most leaders have most of their leadership characteristics from the Bad or Mediocre categories, and thus the work they lead fails or merely survives or hobbles along in spite of the leadership (due to better people in the organization working hard and keeping things going) with minimal growth and the morale of the members is generally poor. I would estimate this accounts for about seventy-five percent of the world's leadership.

Few leaders are Good leaders, and the work they lead has steady growth, and the members of the organization are not significantly discontent, and some are content. I would estimate that good leaders account for about twenty-five percent of the world's leadership.

Very few are Better leaders, who continue or improve or grow the work they are leading and the vast majority of the members' morale is excellent. I would estimate that better leaders account for less than one percent of the world's leadership. Better leaders are often constrained by legal or cultural traditions or by what people expect or by poor principles or corrupt ethics of those that surround them or are "over them."

There is only One Best Leader.

If my view is correct, poor leadership is the execution level reason *why* the world is the way the world is. The existential reason of why there are so few good leaders is because leaders are in the same cage as everyone else. If the blind follow the blind, both will fall into a pit. The people of the world are regularly falling into pits over and over again as they follow the *wrong* leaders-spiritual, political, business, etc.

However, we can all agree the vast majority of people need some leadership.

The Christian religious system – the people who take some Christian label and "go to church" – is no different than the world regarding the quality of its leaders—most are in the Bad to Mediocre range.

The Christian religious system is a mutually beneficial system that has many millions of leaders. *The people hire (assign, receive, appoint) leaders who will bless them and tell them what they already believe about God, and the clergyman/religious leaders get money and power to do so.* Both parties are very content with this system, and this dynamic is a big part of the successful failure.

Many Biblians and Christians are taught to deny that their religious leader is their leader and teacher because their spiritual leader trains them to pay lip service to the delusion that "christ" is their leader or "God is leading us." Thus, when a disciple of Joshua suggests to the Christian that they are indeed following their religious leader and not Joshua of Nazareth, most will deny this claim. However, because a claim is rejected does not mean it is not true.

The simple truth is that God is not leading Christian sects through the Christian leaders; instead, the Christian leaders are leading the people. That Joshua is not Christian's leader is easily proved by the fact that Christians are, in no small measure, ignorant of the teachings of Joshua of Nazareth. Said another way, I could easily develop a quiz on the teachings of Joshua of Nazareth that the vast majority of Christians of all stripes – including their leaders - would fail. Therefore, if a person is ignorant of a leader's ways, how can they possibly follow that leader?

Furthermore, it is true that the vast majority of Biblians and Christians look to their religious leaders to understand God and know what God wants. And, of course, the religious leaders desire that for that enables them to have a job/career/'ministry'…in other words, that enables them to take money from people for their "work" of telling people about the god of their sect/division/denomination; and to perform the rituals that people believe they need in life (weddings, funerals, etc.); and to ensure they will go to heaven.

Christian leaders versus The Leader

Joshua said the following some two thousand years ago, and like almost all of his teachings, they still hit the bullseye some two thousand years later.

Then Jesus spoke to the crowds and His disciples, saying: "The theologians, Bible scholars, and religious leaders have seated themselves in the chair of Moses (now, the chair of "Christ"); therefore all that they tell you, do and observe, but do not do according to their deeds; for they say things and do not do them. They tie up heavy burdens and lay them on men's shoulders, but they are unwilling to move them with so much as a finger. But they do all their deeds to be noticed by men; for they wear their clerical collars and hats and wear fancy clothes. They love the place of honor at weddings and banquets and the chief seats in the religious organizations, and respectful greetings in the marketplaces, and being called Bible Teacher, Pastor or Reverend by men. But do not be called Pastor/Teacher; for One is your Pastor/Teacher, and you are all brothers. Do not call anyone on earth your father; for One is your Father, He who is in heaven. Do not be called leaders; for One is your Leader, that is, me. But the greatest among you shall be your servant. Whoever exalts himself shall be humbled; and whoever humbles himself shall be exalted. (Matt. 23:1-12)

If you have eyes to see, you can see nothing has significantly changed.

In this passage, Joshua reviews some of the behaviors of the religious leaders of his day. His main points are quite clear.

First, they say they represent God, just as Moses did, but they do not. They very much like to claim and exercise authority over people due to their claiming to serve God.

Second, most practice hypocrisy—that is they tell people to do things they are unwilling to do, and they instruct people not to do things that they regularly do. For example, they teach people they need to "tithe" – religious language to get the people to give money to leaders of the organization – or God will be angry at them (the burden) while not helping anyone in their organization with real, daily work or struggles.

Third, their self-pride and selfishness cause them to do things primarily to be noticed by people as "a godly man" or whatever. They wear unique religious clothing or fancy business suits to appear better than other people, or closer to God or other such silly things. They like to be called by their silly religious titles like pastor or reverend or minister or priest or elder or the hundreds of other titles they have invented for themselves over the years. This title-taking reinforces their desired authority over the people and the people looking to them instead of to Joshua.

They like presiding over prominent social events and ceremonies (like weddings and funerals) thus further solidifying their money earning vocation among the people, as people come to wrongly believe they need these guys and gals to make their traditions, rituals, and ceremonies officially accepted or approved by God.

Then Joshua says plainly, "*don't be this way—don't do these things, for I am the people's Teacher and Leader and my Father is their only spiritual Father*".

What more could he say?

Yes, dear reader, he means what he says in that passage, and yes, he does rebuke religious leaders who do those things and who seek to replace him as his people's leader. And if we are truly honest, probably well over 99% of all Christian religious leaders are guilty of practicing in some way, and some degree what Joshua says is wrong in that passage cited above. Remember the definition of religious? By definition, religious leaders do not listen to Joshua of Nazareth, and they instead substituted their own self-made (and Bible justified) god stuff and religious stuff to have the people turn to them and rely on them for their perceived God-needs. Furthermore, almost all Christian leaders refuse to live a life of love for the people they say they care about or they claim to "shepherd."

Of course, there have always been a very few true servant-models who follow Joshua and encourage and help others to do the same—to follow him *with* them. But it is *not* some organizational joining thing with leaders and authority, etc. Instead, it is sharing his Life together based on his top principle, the new command as we will see in the chapter on love.

Furthermore, The Light says this in John 10:

Truly, truly, I say to you, he who does not enter by the door into the fold of the sheep, but climbs up some other way, he is a thief and a robber. But he who enters by the door is a shepherd of the sheep. To him the doorkeeper opens, and the sheep hear his voice, and he calls his own sheep by name and leads them out. When he puts forth all his own, he goes ahead of them, and the sheep follow him because they know his voice. A stranger they simply will not follow, but will flee from him, because they do not know the voice of strangers." This figure of speech Jesus spoke to them, but they did not understand what those things were which He had been saying to them.

So Jesus said to them again, "Truly, truly, I say to you, *I am the door of the sheep*. All who came before me are thieves and robbers, but the sheep did not hear them. I am the door; if anyone enters through me, he will be saved, and will go in and out and find pasture. The thief comes only to steal and kill and destroy; I came that they may have life, and have it abundantly.

I am the good shepherd; the good shepherd lays down His life for the sheep. He who is a hired hand, and not a shepherd, who is not the owner of the sheep, sees the wolf coming, and leaves the sheep and flees, and the wolf snatches them and scatters them. He flees because he is a hired hand and is not concerned about the sheep. I am the good shepherd, and I know My own and My own know Me, even as the

Father knows Me and I know the Father; and I lay down My life for the sheep. I have other sheep, which are not of this fold; I must bring them also, and they will hear My voice; and *they will become one flock with one shepherd."* (John 10)

In this passage, Joshua says that he is both *the only good Shepherd/Pastor as well as the door of entry itself.*

Yes, the same term that is translated "shepherd" (poimen is the Greek transliteration) here in John 10 is translated as "pastor" in Paul's letter of Ephesians chapter four. In that chapter in Ephesians, Paul says, "And He (God) gave some as apostles, and some as prophets, and some as evangelists, and some as shepherds/pastors and teachers, for the equipping of the saints for the work of service, to the building up of the body of Christ..." The English term "pastor" is essentially the Spanish version of "shepherd." In this saying, Paul directly contradicts Joshua by saying God gave many – millions! – of leaders to "build up the body of christ," whatever that is, for Joshua did *not* teach the concept of "the body of christ."

This passage of Paul in Ephesians chapter four is more-or-less the foundation of the people and their organizations which call themselves "The Church" with its leaders and their authority and all the other things that the religious people use to represent the kingdom of God falsely. As we have seen, it is a false, empty substitute for actually following The Light of the world. The simple truth is that Paul is the Leader of most Christians.

For more on Pauls' role in the successful failure, see *Appendix 11, The Stranger Paul.*

Another critical thing to notice in the quote of Joshua is in the last verse which says, "they will become one flock with one shepherd." How many "flocks"/churches with how many "shepherds"/pastors?

One.

Not thousands or millions. Rather, One.

This saying perfectly reflects Joshua's words in John 17 where he says:

The glory which You have given me I have given to them, that they may be one, just as we are one; I in them and You in me, that they may be perfected in unity, so that the world may know that You sent me, and loved them, even as You have loved me. (John 17:22-23)

Joshua teaches that the glory of God is manifest through Joshua's follower's unity. Furthermore, he explains that his follower's unity will be the witness to the world that God sent Joshua and that God loves everyone but especially those who follow His Son.

How is that unity working out among Christians and Biblians?

Is God glorified with the thousands of divided Christian sects? To claim there is unity among the loveless divided Christian sects is to be deluded. Sadly, delusion is a staple of religious people all over the world as they mouth their religious doctrine and platitudes even while what they state does not exist.

(For more detail about Christian leadership, see *Appendix 10, Christian Church Doctrine Debunked.*)

So, what does it mean to actually, really "follow Joshua", or stated another way, to have **him** *as our Leader?*

As is often helpful, let us start answering that question with a contrast of what it is *not* to follow Joshua.

- "Going to church" is not following Joshua and has no part in following Joshua;
- Supporting religious organizations is not following Joshua and has no part in following Joshua;
- Reading the Bible (teachings and thoughts other than Joshua's) is not following Joshua and has no part in following Joshua;
- Praying may or may not be part of following Joshua; *if* you are praying to the Father *only Joshua* reveals by his own words and deeds as recorded in the four gospel books;
- "Doing ministry" is not following Joshua and only has a part in following Joshua if "ministry" is properly defined. If by "ministry" you mean helping and serving other people in real, daily life through sharing Life with them in the Family, then yes - if you mean some occasional organizational meetings, then no.

I hope the reader has a good idea as to what it means to follow Joshua at this point in the book! Here are some answers regarding what someone who has their Leader as Joshua "looks like":

- It means we will be different and thus we will disturb other people with our difference. Not because we are obnoxious or rude or because we have different clothing or other superficial things, but because we don't affirm people the way they want to be affirmed in all the things they say or do—we don't affirm their love of the things of this world;
- We will speak truth to people and thus will offend most;
- We will desire to harm no one. We do not use threats or force or violence to accomplish our Work;
- We will be kind to people when they don't deserve it and bring compassion to people to show our Father's heart;

- We will not live for money and power and entertainment, and self-pleasure like the rest of the people of the earth do;
- We will hold the concept of love as Joshua defines that as the highest truth/principle by which we will seek to live. This love – along with our rejection from the people of the world - will bring disciples together to live in groups/Families/communities and share his Life together and do his work together, the Greater work;
- Our unity comes from our Leader, the person of Joshua of Nazareth and the Father he reveals. That unity is manifest by the love we share with one another, and the Family Life we model before the world. That unity will be what makes us the light of the world and which makes us both desperately needed as well as hated and persecuted. Why? Needed because the Leader of Joshua of Nazareth is what the people of the earth need as The Solution to their worst problems. Persecuted, "because the people of the earth love the darkness rather than the Light because their ways/deeds are evil," and we point out the evil of their deeds.

It is that simple.

Some might ask, "does that mean that there are no human leaders among the disciples of Joshua?" The answer is yes and no. There are no spiritual teachers or leaders among the disciples of Joshua, meaning there is no person who is looked to as "the teacher" or "the leader" because Joshua is that to every disciple. *Said another way, there are no spiritual leaders or teachers who wield authority over others.* However, that does not mean that there are not more mature, experienced or knowledgeable disciples that others would do well to listen to and learn from as they live and speak the Master's truths. It also does not mean that disciples do not have different talents. Joshua said this in this regard:

Therefore, behold, I am sending you prophets and wise men and scribes; some of them you will kill and crucify, and some of them you will scourge in your religious buildings, and persecute from city to city… (Matt. 23:34)

So, some disciples will see what is happening in the world around them, gain useful insight, and be able to speak The Light's truths in a strong, convicting manner (prophets). Some will be able to help other people with things they don't understand or decisions they are facing (wise men). Some will be good writers who will proclaim The Light's truths with their writing skills (scribes). Disciples value each disciple in a Family for whatever talents or skills they bring to the Family, remembering that "the greatest among you shall be the lowest servant of all."

What About Solving All the World's Problems?

You might ask, "how will relatively small groups of people living the way that Joshua prescribes solve all the problems in the world? You have been saying a solution to the world's problems is forthcoming, and now you tell us they cannot be solved?!"

Understandable question...not a fair question, but an understandable one.

If you can receive it, I have provided the solution to all the world's problems!

All the world's problems regarding human-caused conflict, lack of love and neglect, can be solved IF people will make Joshua their true Leader! Because people choose *not* to make Joshua their true leader does not mean the solution has not been identified and given, nor does it mean it will not work. To say, "making Joshua of Nazareth one's Leader will not solve the problems", is a false claim. When the people who say that refuse to give Joshua of Nazareth a chance to lead them, it is like the soccer player who says, "we will never win the world cup without a good coach," but refuses to listen to the new coach and thus will not do what he says!

Or, as another illustration, not making Joshua their leader and saying he can't fix the problem is like the alcoholic asking the question, "what is the cure for alcoholism if I continue to drink alcohol"! Or like saying the solution can be known and realized at the top of the mountain but refusing to make an effort to climb the mountain.

The simple truth is that for every person that participates in one of Joshua's Families/Flocks, *the problems are solved for that group of people.* And for every successful group of people living the way the Way wants, you will have a model for other people to learn from, emulate and mimic. Seeing truth and love lived out is a powerful thing and it is desperately needed-not seeing it is a horrific omission that those who claim to "follow Jesus" are responsible for and which they will be held accountable. It is truly horrible to take people's only true Hope and hide him beneath an empty and shallow counterfeit—the successful failure.

These groups of Joshua followers are not constrained to any particular nation or continent or culture. Joshua's followers and thus his Families (groups of people living as we should) can be manifest anywhere at any time. It just takes a few people with faith and courage and love as *he* defines those things.

The world will never solve the most critical human-caused problems that plague humankind, for the simple reason that the people of the earth refuse to listen to Joshua—the world – those who reject the Light - are the ones who killed him some 2,000 years ago and nothing has changed regarding human nature. If he came again, they would kill him again. And when his disciples speak, they are marginalized, ostracized, labeled "extremists," slandered, ignored or killed by the religious ruling class and their politician friends or corporation buddies. That is not his fault, but the people of the world's fault.

Nor will the disciples of Joshua solve all the people of the world's problems for the simple reason that their Leader must be obeyed to solve the problems! We cannot force anyone to listen to the Light, nor live the way he says we ought to live. *People who create and live in cages cannot be expected to free others!* The fact is that for a group of people following Joshua of Nazareth, the problems described in chapter two are solved…those problems will not characterize, nor be an influence among those people!

We know the solution to our problems, and we follow the One who solves them. If we do that well, we will be the city on the hill shining a desperately needed Light in this dark world so that others can come out of the darkness of their cages and into the Light and Life. If we do that well, we will lead people out of the multi-colored house and out of the dark, cold, empty lot, and into the house with the warm, bright, life-giving Light.

Joshua of Nazareth provides a framework in his recorded teachings that gives an ethic for human relationships that would change radically the group of people practicing it. Getting free from the cage of fear, self-pride, and selfishness is what faith in Joshua can do. Making Joshua or Life Leader and thus living according to his teachings – teachings like "love one another" and "treat others the way you want to be treated" for example – *is transformative and revolutionary but only IF people would listen to him and do it.* Think about it!

In the remaining chapters of this "The Solution" section, we will look at some critical issues that must be understood in light of The Light's teachings to grasp how the practical solution manifests itself.

The next chapter will address what you must do to enter into Life and become a person who can be part of the solution. Or, stated another way, what you must do to make it out of your cage and thus enter into Life so that you can help others do the same and thus start living Life as we ought.

Chapter Summary:
- Very few leaders are Good leaders, and even fewer are Better leaders due primarily to the cage of fear and self-pride and selfishness and that which flows from those things like the desire to serve money and to wield power/authority;
- Christian leaders are no different than leaders in other world domains like government or business. However, since they claim

to represent The Light even while they fail to live by his teachings, they are in a very unfavorable position of accountability;

- Christian leaders are more accountable when they claim to follow The Light of the world, and this should concern them;
- Christian leaders neglect the essential teachings of the Light, and thus they generally do not truly love the people that are part of their organizations;
- The Best Leader is Joshua of Nazareth, and he does solve the most profound and most significant problems of those who through faith and love follow him.

38
CHANGE AND HARD WORK

Opening Questions:

- Can we become better human beings if we don't change?
- Is it not true that the hardest things in life are often the most valuable experiences?
- Did Joshua say that following him would be easy?
- If I am unwilling to undergo difficult change or engage in hard work, can I be a successful follower of Joshua of Nazareth?
- Who is genuinely our model for change?

The heart of the solution has been given. Make Joshua of Nazareth, your Leader and live by truth and rightness for love. Making him your leader is not easy and will require a change in views, beliefs, perspectives, behavior, and lifestyle, contrary to the false "gospel" of Christianity. In fact, the "grace" Paulians will be especially offended by this chapter.

When people hear that Joshua wants people to change their lives to live according to his principles, they get offended. This is especially true of Christians and Biblians because they have been taught and believe that "believing in christ" and "receiving God's grace" is all that is necessary to "go to heaven". Most also believe that partaking in some religious rituals like "going to church", or merely trying to be a "good person" according to the world's standards which means primarily abstaining from doing wrong, is what will "get them to heaven". Unfortunately, they are only too happy with that false "gospel."

Sadly, non-theist and agnostics seldom get this far, as they typically have thrown the baby (Joshua of Nazareth) out with the bathwater (Christianity) long ago and will not consider the fact that most of what they have heard and experienced regarding "jesus christ" from Christians is inaccurate or wrong. It is also much more difficult for a non-theist or a relativist to examine their own lives since they have no standard to do so except their conscience or some arbitrary and deficient standard.

Non-theists have to push past the false beliefs and fallacies of their circles – as well as having rejected the falsehoods of Christianity - and get back to the reasonable life questions such as:

- Is it reasonable that human beings – very complex organic machines with a spiritual component – just happened by natural forces?
- How is it possible to know right from wrong?
- If forgiveness, for example, is real and yet it is not physical, doesn't that mean a non-physical reality exists?
- Do I have a soul and if I do, what happens to me when my body dies?
- Do I get to choose my state/place/condition after I die?
- If I choose to live by love as defined by Joshua of Nazareth, why would that be bad, wrong or harmful – would the quality of my life be better or worse?

After they arrive at the place reason will lead them after answering those questions, the most critical question becomes, what is wrong with the Real Joshua of Nazareth's core teachings as revealed in the four gospels or this book? What is wrong with true love, sharing, caring about what is true and right? Doesn't everyone need a leader? Shouldn't people choose the best leader possible? On what objective basis should I believe that I am the best leader for my life? Doesn't fear, self-pride and selfishness pretty much make it impossible to be a best-type leader? Is there anyone who can love me more than my Father-Creator and His Son?

If those who hear Joshua's truths about love and life and get it to some extent but are not willing to do it, they use various ploys to avoid the truth or explain it away. For those who are offended, the end of the communication will often end with some statement like, "we are not willing to change our way of life—we have been living this way for these hundreds of years…" In other words, defending their "way of life" is a very high priority—so high, wars regularly start over that. Stated yet another way, not being willing to change due to selfish reasons *is* the way things are—that *is* the status quo of humanity and "the world" Joshua entered into, describes and rebukes.

Change is difficult, especially personal characteristic change. *Changing ourselves is one of the most challenging endeavors of life, and yet it is perhaps the most valuable and meaningful endeavor of life…without change we cannot become better human beings.* Setting our goals high is what makes an opportunity for an exceptional life. Striving after those goals and accomplishing them – if they are genuinely noble - makes for an outstanding life—a life well lived.

Hard work is not something most people look forward to but is often a matter of perspective. Some people's physically hard and unenjoyable work is another person's comfortable and enjoyable work. Are we talking about effort regarding "hard work" or some other characteristic? I think for most people when they speak of "hard work" they are speaking about something *they don't want to do.* It could be easy physically or mentally, but if they don't like the work, it is considered "hard." So, really, "hard work" for most people equals work I don't want to do, or I don't like to do.

In this case, there is no way of getting around the hard work of self-change. The reason self-change is so tough is due to our self-pride and lack of humility. Since many walk around in the delusion that they are the cat's meow (yeah, I know, old saying) or that they are God's gift to the world, they see no reason to change anything about themselves. The self-focused, narcissistic society of selfishness and self-esteem encourages this in those leaning towards humility and cements it for the arrogant. However, if you want to follow Joshua and BE part of the solution instead of part of the problem, you are going to have to change. For that matter, if we want to be a better human being, we are going to have to change.

The solution as stated in this book is straightforward to understand. Make the historical person of Joshua of Nazareth – the one who defeated death to prove all he said and did was true and right – your Leader. If and when you do that, the first thing he will ask of you is for you to change—to give up a life lived out of fear, self-pride, and selfishness—of taking from, taking advantage of, hurting and neglecting others—to give up living for or working for money and material things and instead start working for Joshua and the kingdom of God. We must be willing to sincerely look in the mirror without rose-colored glasses and honestly see. And then we must start practicing a life of love with others.

That dear reader will involve change—significant change and that change all starts with our seeing our guilt and shame and then having our spirit re-born from above.

Joshua answered and said to him, "Truly, truly, I say to you, unless one is born from above he cannot see the kingdom of God. Nicodemus said to Him, "How can a man be born when he is old? He cannot enter a second time into his mother's womb and be born, can he?" 5 Joshua answered, "Truly, truly, I say to you, unless one is born of water *(the natural birth marked by the breaking of the mother's water)* and the Spirit *(the spiritual birth)* he cannot enter into the kingdom of God. 6 That which is born of the flesh is flesh, and that which is born of the Spirit is spirit. Do not be amazed that I said to you, "You must be born from above." (John 3)

Sadly and tragically, many Christians have been taught to believe they were "born again," due to some ritual (usually baptism) they partook in as a child or adult or due to some merely emotional experience they had in the past. The truth is that being born from above will involve significant change, and it needs to happen after we are adults. No children need to be born from above, for their relative innocence keeps their spirit alive, and it keeps them open to considering truth. It is once we pass into adulthood that our spirit dies, we stop listening well to our conscience or justify our bad behavior and thus embrace the world, and we enter into the darkness of the walking dead.

Ultimately, the solution begins with *you*, dear reader. If *you* don't allow the Creator to take you out of the cage you are in individually, then you will always be part of the collective problem. If you refuse His invitation to bring you to a higher level of existence, then you will remain in the cage, and you will continue to be part of the problem despite all your religion or protestations or denials to the contrary.

Here is what the Creator's Messenger said regarding getting out of the cage of self-pride and fear and selfishness.

Truly, truly, I say to you, he who hears my word, and believes Him who sent me, has eternal life, and does not come into judgment, but has passed out of death into life. (John 5:24)

How does a person pass from death into life? Joshua was talking to living people when he made that statement, so he was not talking about physical life - please read the teaching in context to confirm this. He answers plainly. One passes from spiritual death (a person with a dead spirit) to spiritual life (one's spirit made alive) by *hearing **his** word - which is to listen to and receive what **he** (not "the Bible") says as true because the person hearing believes that God sent Joshua.* Being born from above is the only sure way to avoid condemning one's self through a life lived in bondage to self-pride, fear, and selfishness - and instead, entering into eternal Life!

The Light provides another view of the same event—the event of a person passing from death to life, in these sayings:

Truly, truly, I say to you, unless one is born again (from above) he cannot see the kingdom of God—I say to you, unless one is born of water and the Spirit he cannot enter into the kingdom of God. (John 3:3, 5)

These two sayings have the same thing in view—a human being passing from an existence with a dead spirit - a spirit that died at some point after childhood. To a reality with a living spirit, a reborn spirit—that is with the ability to know, commune with, and love our Creator and Father as Joshua reveals Him.

The New Birth Analogy: Being Born Out of This World

Each human being must pass through a second birth experience if they wish to enter eternal Life. The first is the natural birth which all people experience and which birth is universally marked by the breaking of the water of the woman giving birth. The second is the spiritual birth where a person's dead spirit is made alive by the Father's Spirit—the living water to which Joshua refers. Joshua uses simple and universally known concepts and imagery to convey essential truths. In this case, he used the birth experience. A baby in her/her mother's womb is essentially asleep - completely unaware of life outside the womb. It is in a dark, virtually silent place, asleep, being fed and provided oxygen without any effort of his/her own. It is in a state of existence that, while real and true, is very different than life outside the womb.

When the baby is born, he/she enters into a whole new realm of existence. Sound and sight and taste and smell are now actively used to understand his/her new domain. He/she must now choose to eat food and drink water to sustain the body. He/she now uses their spiritual components to navigate the new realm. The heart is used to make choices about what to think and how to behave. The soul is used to express emotions associated with thoughts and experiences and nudge us with our conscience. The mind is used to understand the new realm, both physical and metaphysical components of the new realm outside the womb.

The same is true of the new spiritual birth. A person moves from one realm of existence to another - from no faith at all or faith in the wrong thing(s) (in the womb or the world) to new faith or faith in the right Person (out of the womb or into the kingdom of God). Just like a baby in the womb, the person who has reached adulthood - but has not been born again or born from above - exists in a spiritual realm of darkness where the use of their heart, soul, and mind are dysfunctional or misguided. They live in spiritual darkness with the manifestations of hopelessness, despair, depression, anger, frustration, loveless-ness, internal pain or suffering, lost-ness, confusion, etc. The person whose spirit has not been made alive by the new birth is ruled by a dark nature of self-pride and fear and selfishness—they exist to "better" and protect their lives in the world at all costs. They are spiritually asleep in the darkness just like the baby in the womb or a person in the world.

The person who has been born from above or gain, in contrast, have "come out" of the darkness of the "womb" / world and have entered into a new realm (the kingdom of God). They did what was required to be free from the cage of self-pride and fear and selfishness. They have left the darkness and have come into the Light. They now have a new understanding of life and now live to help others out of the darkness. They are not despairing or depressed or loveless or hopeless or lost or confused about essential life matters and life in this world. In short, they have had their spirit made alive due to their seeing their need to get out of the darkness, and have placed their faith in the Light of the world to remove them from the darkness of this world and its ways. They have become a new person with a different life perspective and purpose and a new understanding of how to live the new Life they have been given through their faith in Joshua and the Father HE reveals.

If a person has not experienced these things - if they are not born from above - then "they cannot enter the kingdom of God," or stated another way, they will condemn themselves and terminate their existence one day.

One experiences these things by first seeing their need to be made alive. In other words, a person must see or sense at some level that they are living a life of spiritual death:

- A life not knowing or caring about what is right or wrong, true or false;
- A life of ignoring their Father and His Messenger and Leader;
- A life of living by their self-pride, fear, and selfishness and all the wrong and hurtful things said and done as a result;
- A life of living for money or material thin;
- A life of hopelessness regarding death.

Once a person sees that is *true of them*, they will sense great remorse over that wasted, empty, loveless, hurt-and-take-from-others life and turn to the Father to make them alive to a life of caring about what is true and right and living by love. A person deserving death being offered Life freely; from being guilty of ignoring the Life and hurting other people; will be most thankful for the forgiveness offered by the Father—they will be as a flutterby having changed from a caterpillar—they will be a new person! Not a perfect person for that will be striven for by hard work, but rather a new person—a new perspective, purpose, motivation, etc.

What are the primary manifestations of passing from death to life—from having one's spirit made alive by God's Spirit and thus entering into an existence of faith in one's heavenly Father and Joshua? The primary manifestations are a dramatic change in one's life perspective; a new found love for their heavenly Father as revealed by Joshua and a desire to know the One's who made me alive:

> This is eternal life that they may know You, the only true God, and Joshua of Nazareth whom You have sent. (John 17:3)

How do you get to know God and Joshua His Son? Stated another way, how do you get to know the Creator of life on the earth and His Messenger? By reading Joshua's words - *not* anyone else's - as a child would, and believing what he says. How do you know you believe what he says? How do you know if you love him?

> If you love me, you will do as I say. (John 14:15)

The primary manifestation of loving someone in authority over us is to be eager to do what they want.

The Change: From Child to Adult and the Death and Rebirth of Our Spirit

As we saw back in chapter three, all people (except severely disabled people) are born with all three metaphysical components (heart, soul, and mind) and their spirit. Those components develop over time as we grow. Children are known for their innocence and their willingness to accept what is told to them as true. Innocence is defined as "freedom from guilt or sin through being unacquainted with evil," or, "not knowing what wrong is, accepting things at face value, and having an intuitive predisposition to do right, trusting people."

As children, we know that we exist due to something outside ourselves, even though we cannot understand that Source—we have an innate trust in that which created us, even if told that falsehood that our parent's created us. (The truth is, our parents just brought together the raw materials of sperm and egg and the Creator's miracle of genetics took over to create our bodies (the "hardware') while the Creator Himself continues to be the Source of existence of our spiritual or metaphysical components (the "software")).

To use the other metaphor, as children, we exist outside of the cage of fear, self-pride, and selfishness even while we still are influenced by those weaknesses. In other words, if children have both light (truth based knowledge, a functioning mind, and a working conscience) and darkness (self-pride and fear and selfishness) – the light in children is greater than the darkness.

However, something happens as we human beings start reaching adulthood—as we enter into our teenage years. We transition from the innocence of childhood and its fundamental outlook and relational dynamic of trusting others; to the non-innocence of understanding what is wrong and wanting what is wrong to some degree, and to *not trusting others* because of the wrong-ness we experience with ourselves and the people we encounter or with whom we have relationships. This lack of trust extends to all beings, including the *One who designed and created us*. We impugn human characteristics or wrong attributes on the Creator and thus decide he is not worthy of our trust/faith; or that he will condemn us for our wrongs; or worse that He does not exist; or worst of all that HE is the reason for our faults and wrong-wanting. Religion plays the primary role in this wrong understanding of our Creator/Father.

When we leave innocence and a simple trust/faith in our Source, our spirit "dies" in a sense, or we become spiritually blind, deaf and dumb—we *fall into darkness*. We enter into this darkness when we turn away from simple faith/trust in our Creator to trusting only in ourselves or to a limited extent in others we deem worthy. We also leave reason as the primary way to understand the reality in which we find ourselves. This does not mean we don't use reason at all, instead, that we primarily use reason well only when we stay away from life's most essential "why" questions.

So, there we are, "walking dead" as teenagers. We have our hearts, souls, and minds, but our spirit dies as we walk away from innocence and *start living some version of, "everyone has to do it to survive in this world" or "everyone does it, therefore so will I" or "I need to do this to get what I want"*. We enter into the darkness of a life now *guided by fear, self-pride, and selfishness*. We walk into the cage of self-pride and fear and selfishness and close and lock the door. We put ourselves in a prison of our own making.

We live to preserve our life in this world, often at any cost as we value our body and partake of the delusion that our body *is* who we are. We reject faith in anything we cannot prove by physical means or validate with our senses. We reject sound reason and objective evaluation when it points to "places where we don't want to go."

However, even in this self-inflicted state of darkness, our Creator provided a sign or manifestation of being in this state of soul/spirit, and that sign or indication is emptiness in our soul...at some level, we sense an incompleteness, longing or emptiness within ourselves. Our being able to detect this emptiness can range from shutting it down altogether and thus not sensing it at all; to only sensing it during specific experiences or thoughts; to obvious and even continuous pain. We have some level of understanding that we are missing something important.

Then, what is most common is people try very hard to fill that emptiness with something other than our Father and His love.

- Money
- Education
- Careers
- Drugs
- Alcohol
- Sex
- Another person (boyfriend, girlfriend, spouse)
- Vicarious "relationships" (e.g., Facebook, etc.)
- Thrill-seeking
- Entertainment, etc.

There are many ways that people seek to fill the emptiness they experience in their soul. But those ways *never* satisfy. Oh, we can hide the void for a time with these things, but it will always come back IF we are listening. Many people try very hard not to listen, and consumer electronics have made that quite easy. How many people are bound to their smartphone and are always looking to electronically delivered content to avoid quiet times of self-reflection?

Just like a lock can only be opened by the right key; like only the correct password can gain one access. The only Person that can fill the emptiness of our soul; that can bring our dead spirit back alive; is our loving Father the Son of Man reveals!

For this reason, the Creator sent His Life—to bring us, our spirits - back alive and to set us free from the cage we place ourselves in! For this reason, the Creator, our Father, sent his Light—to bring us out of the darkness. For this reason the Life and Light said this:

> I have come as Light into the world, so that everyone who believes in me will not remain in darkness. (John 12:46)

> Truly, truly, I say to you, unless one is born from above (or again) he cannot see the kingdom of God; I say to you, unless one is born both naturally and of the Spirit he cannot enter into the kingdom of God. (John 3:3, 5)

> If you continue in my word (NOT "the Bible'), then you are truly disciples of mine; and you will know the truth, and the truth will make you free! If the Son sets you free, you will be free indeed! (John 8)

This necessary experience/event that Joshua speaks of above is required to bring our dead spirit back to life; he does not want us to "remain in darkness"—he does not want us to remain bound in our prison. If a person has not been born from above, then they cannot see - nor enter

- the kingdom of God. Sadly, when many people get a slight understanding of what the Light is saying here, they will immediately claim they have been "born again" even when they have not. These are the religious crowd of some particular sects.

How can a person know if they have been born from above? That is like asking a man who has been in prison and tortured for years if he knew when his rescuer got him out of that prison! You will know! That is like asking a woman blind from birth when her eyes are healed, and she opens them and sees a most beautiful sunset if she knew when her eyes were opened! She will know!

Many will claim that they love the Lord our God with all our hearts, soul, mind and strength, but claiming something does not necessarily make it true. We can only love a Person if we truly believe they exist; and in respect to Joshua and our Father, if we have genuinely transferred our faith/trust/confidence to those Persons and thus gotten to know them. We also cannot place our faith in something or someone who frightens us. Religion makes our Father frightening.

How can a person know if they have indeed been born from above? How can a person know if they genuinely love their heavenly Father with all that is in them? That is like asking a child who loves her parents - and those parents are taken away when she is ten years old - if she will know when she is reunited with them six months later! You will know!

How can a person know they have indeed been born from above? That is like asking a genuinely remorseful prisoner who is heading for the electric chair if they will remember when the prison warden came and stopped the execution to tell him he was pardoned due to the victims believing he was genuinely remorseful and that a pardon is granted.

Here are some objective signs of that new birth or of entering the kingdom of God or eternal life:

- If we have changed significantly from a person who was primarily guided by self-pride and fear and selfishness, to a person who lives and fights for what is true, for what is right, and who desires to love Joshua, our Father and others above all things;
- If we now think about and want to talk about our Father and Joshua, our new first loves, most of the time;
- If we see our sin and our wrongness and are moved to change;
- If we hate the wrong in this world and will do what is required to bring change, no matter what;
- If we are truly willing to lay down our lives (physically die) out of love for our friends;

- If we don't live for money and material security and entertainment and pleasure and for those from whom we get something back, and the other things the people of the world live for;

Now would be a perfect time for self-reflection from the reader.

This change is a requirement to set a new destiny for ourselves. The kingdom of God is all about internal change first and then followed by external manifestations of that internal change. This chapter provided what is required for the inward or inner transformation. The following chapters will make clear the life changes or external changes that will occur if we have entered Eternal Life.

Chapter Summary:
- Allowing ourselves to be changed, and then working to improve ourselves is required if we are going to live an exceptional life and be an exceptional human being. While personal change is difficult, it is also the most rewarding experience we can have in this life;
- Hard work is part of following Joshua. The easy way that Christianity presents is a false, empty, bankrupt and shallow substitute to the real life of caring about what is true and right, seeking to live out love, and thus being a real change agent in this world;
- If we will not change ourselves nor be willing to work hard, then we will never be in a place to change others or have a significant beneficial impact on others—we don't want to be a disciple/disciplined;
- The most critical internal change that can occur in a human being is to have our spirit made alive and thus move from death/darkness into Life/light and begin our journey through faith in our new found Father and Master;
- The most important external change for a human being is committing to change ourselves to be more like The Light of the world—to behave and live differently as he instructs.

39
I HAVE CHOSEN YOU OUT OF THE WORLD

Opening Questions:

- When Joshua speaks of "the world" of what exactly is he talking?
- What does it mean to "not love God back"?
- What does it mean to be out of the world?
- How do we support ourselves when we are chosen out of the world?
- Do politics solve problems like greed, loveless-ness, loneliness, drug addiction, etc.?
- Is education "good" if the content is false, harmful, has no practical value or encourages wrongness or confusion?
- Why would someone not want to be part of a group of people who care about each other?

If we don't let our supposed leader lead us, then he is not our leader.

If we will not even bother to listen to our supposed leader (very few people read and know Joshua's teachings), then how can he lead us? Furthermore, if we will not believe nor do what he says, then in what way is he/she our "leader"?

Following Joshua well – actually having him as your Leader - means you must let him pull you out of your cage of self-pride and fear and selfishness, and then out of the world which opposes him.

Will you let him? It is not easy to essentially learn to die to our selfish nature, but again, that which is difficult is valuable.

Many people, perhaps most, do not want to take what they describe as "extreme measures" to try and fix a wrong. They usually describe it as "extreme" to make a choice look less rational or less "normal." When we are comfortable and believe we are secure, we don't want to change things that impact our comfort or perceived security. In other words, we will work very hard to preserve our life in this world any way we can instead of being willing to lose our life in this world for the Life's sake.

The Light of the world does not give us that option...we cannot remain comfortable and abide in a delusion of security and at the same time follow him nor reap the benefits of following him.

For example, if something is corrupt - like say the people who control a legal system and their self-serving rules – it is extremely difficult if not impossible to change that system from the inside. In other words, as soon as you enter the system and don't play by their rules, you will be cast out. That is the nature of systems made up of and controlled by people.

For example, if you are a lawyer – a new, young, very naïve, lawyer – and you accept a client who at some point confesses they are guilty of murder, you could not tell the court that your client is guilty—you are obligated to defend them or to reject them as a client but not tell anyone they are guilty. That way of doing things, dear reader, is not only corrupt but evil. Would the lawyer defending that murderer hold to the rules if they murdered their child, for example? I could cite many other examples of the corrupt nature of the U.S. legal system and the people who make it up, but if that one example cannot demonstrate its corruptness, then 100 more are unlikely to cause you to see the truth.

The same is true of any system controlled by people. From legal to medical to business to financial to military to governmental to religious, etc. The following logic is undeniable - since human beings are lost, in darkness, corrupt, any system they form will be affected by that darkness. See Chapter 2, *The State of Humankind* for the manifestations of that darkness if you have forgotten or want to try and deny that statement.

So, our Creator gave us a Way out of participating, supporting, being part of the dark thing that the *light of the world* came to reveal. You see Light exposes things, and when people and their dark ways are exposed, they don't typically react by saying, "I am truly sorry" and then change. No, rather they seek to silence the person exposing the darkness—they seek to destroy the light. That is exactly what happened with The Light of the world. The Light consistently communicated this:

> *For God so loved the world, that He gave His only begotten Son,* that whoever believes in Him shall not perish, but have eternal life. For God did not send the Son into the world to judge the world, but that the world might be saved through Him. He who believes in Him is not judged; he who does not believe has been judged already, because he has not believed in the name of the only begotten Son of God. *This is the judgment, that the Light has come into the world, and men loved the darkness rather*

than the Light, for their deeds were evil. For everyone who does evil hates the Light, and does not come to the Light for fear that his deeds will be exposed. But he who practices the truth comes to the Light, so that his deeds may be manifested as having been wrought in God. (John 3)

He came and exposed the darkness that human beings abide in, and the people responded as they almost always do:

Pilate said to them, "Then what shall I do with Jesus who is called Christ?" They all said, *"Crucify Him!"* And he said, "Why, what evil has He done?" But they kept shouting all the more, saying, *"Crucify Him!"* When Pilate saw that he was accomplishing nothing, but rather that a riot was starting, he took water and washed his hands in front of the crowd, saying, "I am innocent of this Man's blood; see to that yourselves." And all the people said, "His blood shall be on us and on our children!" Then he released Barabbas for them; but after having Jesus scourged, he handed Him over to be crucified. (Matt. 27)

Joshua speaks of "the world" many dozens of times in the four gospels and uses the phrase in very important contexts. The term could mean "the earth" or it could mean *the people of the earth who do not listen to him or who don't do what his Father wants.* The quotes above are of the latter meaning, and are the topic of this chapter.

In John chapter 3 quoted above, Joshua provides some fundamental teachings about the world. Joshua makes two critical points in his instructions about "the world."

First, that his Father, the Creator God, *loves the people of the earth.* That is, He very much cares about us and wants what is best for us. God does not want unjust suffering and wrongly caused pain and conflict. Being the Creator, he does know what is best for us, and he knows why he created us. In short, the main thing he wants for human beings is that *we take care of each another with love as the basis for that caring.* He is compassionate towards us and wants us to show compassion and forgiveness to one another with no qualifications of "us" versus "them." We are all human beings, and there are *no significant outward, physical, natural or demographic differences between us about which God cares.*

- What nation or state we live in or were born in;
- Our physical appearance like skin or hair color or body shape;
- Our intellectual abilities or lack thereof;
- Our physical abilities or lack thereof;
- Our languages;
- Our sex/gender;

- Our clothing styles or clothing traditions (unless we dress to promote ourselves sexually, which is wrong);
- The food we eat.

Or any of the other things that people can't change about themselves or which don't matter and which they divide over and for which they end up treating each other wrongly.

After we are in the primary mode of caring for one another – which of course would mean there is little conflict (some will exist due to our mistakes, weaknesses, and failures) and no harmful or violent conflict – we can use the talents he has given us to create and do good and beautiful things. It is that simple.

His second point is this – which we as human beings have a *badly corrupted nature* that *we* choose, adopt or assimilate as we become adults. Joshua says, "And this is the condemnation, that the people of the earth who refuse to listen to me, love the darkness rather than the light as evidenced by the evil things they do." What he means is we human beings have a severe problem that we need to overcome to live out the first point above about love and caring and creating. We saw how to fix that problem in the prior chapter.

Dear reader, the simple truth in the prior paragraph about humans having a corrupt nature is undeniable if you have the correct standard against which to evaluate that saying. The correct standard is Joshua and this command he gives: "be perfect, as your heavenly Father is perfect." And what does "perfect" mean when Joshua uses the term?

The core of perfection is that we care about what is true and right as the Standard Joshua teaches and thus execute/do/live out/practice "love" towards other people – *love* properly defined!

Again, the Creator and His Messenger define *what "love" is*, and they define it as *valuing other people manifest through selfless behavior towards them motivated by compassion and wanting to share Life with them.*

So, how is humanity doing with living out the desire of the Creator of the human race - that we love one another? Do you deny the darkness in which "the world" abides? Do you deny that self-pride, fear, and selfishness bind the people who don't listen to Joshua, and that is the cause of most of the human conflict and lovelessness? Do you deny that people are not practicing love in their lives?

Please review Chapter 2 for the answer to that question. Then, examine your own life.

Do I need to list more facts? Do you, dear reader, deny these simple facts about human life on this planet each day? Do you deny the facts about your own life and choices each day? To believe, "oh, people are essentially good" is to have a very low standard to measure what is "good"; it is, in fact, to justify evil—and the only reason we would justify evil is because, well, we are part of it and at some level approve of it or are too selfish to care.

That is one of the purposes of why Joshua came. When he says, "I am the Light of the world" and "He who rejects me and does not receive my sayings, has one who judges him; the word I spoke is what will judge him at the last day."; what he is saying is, "I am the standard by which each human being will be held accountable and judged." The Creator leaves it up to us what we will choose. Joshua's role as the judge is to review the facts with the person being judged and affirm or reveal the true nature and motivation of the choices we made in this life. We choose our after-death destiny. We choose either Life or death. Most people un-knowingly select death due to self-pride, fear, and selfishness which prevents us from seeing our need and finding and putting our faith in the Light. Most use their minds to deceive themselves and exist in a self-created and self-justifying delusion either religious or non-religious.

So, to sum up, at this point, Joshua of Nazareth teaches the concept of "the world." In many instances (and you can know by context), he is referring to the people of the planet who reject him and his Way of Life - truth, love, and rightness.

If you ask one-thousand Christians about "the world" concept, most will be clueless...meaning they will be ignorant of what Joshua means when he talks about "the world" because they are ignorant of Joshua and his teachings. If they know anything about the concept, and you ask them, "in what way are you not part of the world," they will generally look at you with a blank stare—in other words, they have no idea. Or they will start telling you how they are better than other people from a moral standpoint. What they will NOT say is some version of, "I live differently than the people of the earth who reject Joshua and his love teachings – I share my life with others who also are of the Light, and together, we model the Light's Solution." Or, they will not say, "We try our best to not participate in the loveless-ness and falsehoods and lies, and we try our best not to affirm those who do engage in and approve of them. Thus, we are different and set apart".

One thing is for sure, if Christians know anything about "the world" concept, and you ask them if they are of the world, most will say, "no, of course not", even though they have no idea of how they are not part of the world and their lives give no indication that they are not of the world! There is a knowing in the human conscience regarding this topic, and it is an aspect of this truth:

"...that the people love the darkness rather than the light..." (John 3:19)

Dear reader, we each have to ask ourselves, "am I still part of this world'? We can only answer that "no" with assurance *if* we have allowed ourselves to be chosen out of the world by Joshua...

If you were of the world, the world would love its own; but because you are not of the world, ***but I chose you out of the world***, because of this the world hates you. (John 15:19)

Please ask yourself, "In what way have I been chosen out of the world—what are the living manifestations of that choice?" If you have no clear answer to that; no manifestations; then you are still part of "the world," and thus *you* are still part of the problem.

If you saw the Lord of the Rings movies, remember that line when Meriadoc asks Treebeard about his decision to fight against Saruman, and Treebeard answers that they will not fight. Do you remember Meriadoc's response? To paraphrase, he said, "how can that be your answer? You are part of this world?" In other words, you need to pick a side and fight – you need to kill to solve this problem. That is the core statement of evil. It comes from the belief that as a being on this planet, you *must* participate in killing other people to do what is right to stop evil.

The Light of the world states in stark contrast, "love your enemies." But he did not only state it, he lived it out and allowed the world to kill him out of their hatred of his Light, and it's exposing the darkness they abide in. While the Light was very bright, it perhaps was at its brightest when, while the men of the world were driving the spikes through his hands and feet and mocking him, he looked up to our Father and said, "Father, forgive them, because they do not know what they are doing." It is similar to the righteous man of faith who stands up for what is right and good against evil men, and the evil men point a gun at his head before they murder him, and he says, "Father, forgive them because they do not know what they are doing."

For those who are part of religions or religious sects who have remote places like monasteries, where a very few of their people go to live "out of the world," you are badly deceived. Physically removing yourself from people God wants us to love is *not* what it means to be chosen out of the world. Joshua did not do it, and neither should we. Instead, it means to turn away from pursuing that which the world considers valuable—to not participate, endorse, support, or be part of the evil deeds associated with caring more about myself or money (or other material things or even animals) than about people. When we do this among people with the motivation to show them truth and love and introduce them to our Father, they will – in general – be offended and persecute us, thus giving evidence of the metaphysical or spiritual reality described in this book. There is no reasonable merely physical cause to account for people persecuting those who do or say what is true or right and thus it is yet another proof of the spiritual or metaphysical reality.

Finally, we have to ask ourselves, "What am I doing to help fight the darkness?" God expects people to listen to His Son and to do what *he* says and to repeat his teachings to others. *that* is the primary way we can fight the darkness—not fight other people, but fight against the lies, the falsehood and lovelessness of the people of "the world"—fight not with violence but with truth and love!

Our on-going revolution started by the truth and love Revolutionary is one of leadership, belief, and behavior, and it is one of priorities.

So, for example, when a person says, "I am going to set my life to have a successful career as a businessman, artist, athlete, engineer, etc.", what they are saying is that *following Joshua is not the will of their heart*—that pursuing that which the world considers valuable is more important than what Joshua considers valuable. What Joshua asks us to do with our lives is to build the Father's Family which will represent and manifest the kingdom of God. That endeavor has as its focus loving each other, which is behavior focused on giving more than on taking, sharing more than keeping, helping others more than myself. You could pursue some of those other things but only if you are part of a Family thus demonstrating that they are less important than following Joshua

If they are primary and not secondary - if you spend most of your time pursuing your dreams in this world and thinking about those things instead of Joshua, his teachings and doing what he says - *then you forfeit eternal life.* Why? We give up eternal life because the Light says that love is the most vital concept by which the Creator wants us to order our lives. When that is not the case, you get what you see, experience and for most, participate in each day in this world—lives guided by self-pride and fear and selfishness and all the conflict and misery and loneliness that brings. Stated another way, we are either using our will to follow the Light of the world and live according to his Way and promote his Way; or we are choosing to support the world and what they say is essential. There are only two fundamental ways - the broad way or the narrow way - the easy way or the hard way. Our will usually is misguided and desperately needs proper guidance and strength which only faith in Joshua can provide.

A Word About Politics

Many well-intentioned people including Christians have turned to involvement in politics to try and change things for what they believe will be the better. Ironically, many religious people do this because they know at some level the social club they call "the church" is powerless and thus is not having a significant impact on the lives of people.

I understand this choice, but it is a mistake. It is a mistake because politics, politicians, and government do not have the right Leader and thus cannot solve the most critical problems that affect people each day. Said another way, there are two kingdoms, and politicians are of the kingdoms of this world, *not* the kingdom of God. Joshua said this:

> *My kingdom is not of this world.* If my kingdom were of this world, then my servants would be fighting so that I would not be handed over to the Jews; but as it is, my kingdom is not of this realm. (John 18:36)

The King clearly says that his kingdom is **not** of this world or realm; therefore, we who have entered into the Light's kingdom do not go back to the old kingdom of darkness and try and fix it.

To believe that the political kingdoms of this world and the people who play that game in the world (politicians) will solve fundamental problems of people is naïve at best. You should know what the fundamental problems of humanity are at this point! Self-pride and fear and selfishness lead to most of the difficulties every nation or society experience. Government policies and laws cannot fix the underlying problems! Since most Christians, in general, cannot see the King and his kingdom, they spend time and energy supporting and promoting the king's and kingdoms of this world.

To recap, self-pride leads to people wanting power over others thinking they can solve people's problems, primarily through money or material means. Self-pride also prevents people from learning and finding truth in any domain. Fear causes people to stay in little boxes…it takes away any freedom that might be available to them and causes them to abide in darkness and is used to justify many wrongs done. Fear works hard against courage and thus prevents positive change. Both self-pride and fear work together to harden selfishness. Selfishness works hard against love, and love *is the solution* that is so desperately needed by all people.

Politicians – the agents who create and promote political ideology and who form governments – are human beings with the same flaws and weaknesses as anybody else. If an individual does not have a strong character (ethical view of human life); when that person gets a position of power, things don't work out so well. Don't believe me? Just look at the state of the world! Just look at the state of the U.S. government and its Christian politicians for example. If politicians don't have the selflessness or courage to do what is right regarding simple matters like, for example, balancing a budget, why would you expect them to solve more important problems?

People turn to politics because they don't see any other way to try and change things. *They commit this error because they don't have faith in Joshua of Nazareth and thus he is not their Leader.* For religious people, their "church" is a powerless thing which does not truly improve the lives of its members or bring needed change to those in the community. It is exceptionally irrational to continue placing one's hope in politicians when in the vast majority they have proven themselves over and over again not worthy of keeping their promises let alone acting selflessly and genuinely fixing even minor matters that government could fix.

People turn to politics because they want someone else to fix their problems, and they view their problems from a worldview of primarily money and material problems. Due to the relative material abundance that the U.S. people enjoy, this view is irrational, but then people without any higher purpose in life and even a standard of right or wrong often think and behave irrationally.

People turn to politics because it avoids having to work closely with others to try and make things better. The average U.S. citizen is only too happy to move from some workplace to their house and in front of their screen—visit a polling booth on election day and then complain about things. They don't want to share Life with others because the love of most has grown cold, just as The Light predicted. The people of the U.S. have, in general, perfected the selfish, materialistic, independent, autonomous lifestyle. They see no need to love other people outside of the natural family relationships from whom they get something back. And so, they have and are making their bed.

> For if you love those who love you, what reward do you have? Do not even those you consider the worst kind of people do the same? If you greet only those in your group, what more are you doing than others? (Matt. 5)

Politics, politicians, and government cannot cause love to be manifest in and among people. Politics, politicians, and government cannot solve greed or hopelessness or hatred or confusion or suicide or drug addiction or entertainment addiction or hundreds of other manifestations of those in their cage of self-pride and fear and selfishness.

Therefore, to look to politicians or governmental systems to bring the most critical change to you and your life is wrong and foolish. You must find the love and courage to bring change yourself and with others who are following The Light. Indeed, the saying, "be the change you want to see" must not just be a slogan you post on your door, but rather the way you live your life. Remember not to deceive yourself thinking you are doing well living your life if you are only being moral and abstaining from wrong things. To follow the Light means you will get to know him by reading his words and then living and speaking HIS truths to people and that Life is difficult and takes courage.

A Word about Education

Let us start by defining "education."

"The process of teaching or learning in a school, or the knowledge that you get from this." [55]

"The process of receiving or giving systematic instruction, especially at a school or university." [56]

"The act or process of imparting or acquiring particular knowledge or skills, as for a profession." [57]

It would be irrational to claim that "education" in and of itself is wrong. There is nothing wrong with learning itself, and even the precise *how* education is delivered is not that important. However, it does make a considerable difference concerning *what* you are learning. For example, one could learn to hate people different than themselves or how to steal automobiles or how to cheat and lie or how to "successfully" rob stores or how to torture people or how to deceive old people over the phone to wrongly take their money, etc.

That we learn is very important, but *what* we learn - meaning the content of our education - is much more critical.

A sad fact of reality is that someone who graduates at the top of their Harvard class is in fact considered a more valuable human being than the person who does not graduate from High School even if the person did not graduate due to sound, selfless reasons. The people of the world believe that education is an essential part of becoming a "valuable, enlightened and productive member of society." For many, education is one of the things that are worshipped (considered highest in worth) in the world. Thus, those who graduate from the most esteemed schools are valued the highest regarding human worth and potential.

Is this high valuing of "education" warranted is the crucial question? Or, stated another way, do those people who graduate from these esteemed educational institutions consistently change the world for the better? The truth is no they do not – look at the world! They have been graduating from these esteemed educational institutions for millennia and yet, business as usual. Graduating from those esteemed institutions does not fix the world, but it does provide the graduates with power and money.

---

[55] Cambridge Dictionary, www.dictionary.cambridge.org, May 2018

[56] Oxford Living Dictionary, www.en.oxforddictionaries.com, May 2018

[57] www.dictionary.com, May 2018

As we saw in the "Leadership" chapter, it does not require much education to be a good leader, only good character. The fact is that graduating from Harvard or Yale or Oxford, etc. is NO indication of a person's character. In fact, people graduating from those schools often end up becoming the world's leaders, and as we have seen, the state of the world is sorely lacking!

The simple truth is that, in the U.S., a person who does well in their primary education – first through about eighth grade – has learned all they need to be successful according to the world's definition of success. In other words, *what is far more vital than the content of the education a person receives is the quality of their character and the motivation they have for doing good.* If a person is going through a college or university program to graduate with a "promising career" (code speak for making lots of money in their life or gaining power over others), then they will *not* be a significant change agent for good.

That fact is that private colleges and universities are very profitable businesses. And as for state colleges and universities, they are very comfortable "non-profits," meaning while they are not allowed to make a "profit," their expenses are very high on the taxpayers and those associated with operating the non-profit make high wages and live very comfortably. Simply put, there is a *lot* of money in the education business. Therefore, to pretend that being "an educator" or those who support them is somehow a noble profession is false. It is no more virtuous than the fellow putting groceries in your bag or the girl handing you your receipt at the bank IF what you teach omits a regular and robust explanation and promotion of good character.

What is noble is selfless, sacrificial behavior to help other people with the *right content* if you are an educator. Collecting your paycheck to teach students about things that have little or no relevance to real life or actual practical matters is *not noble.* In fact and in general, it is not only a waste of time and money but harmful to the students IF your ideologies are wrong. Sadly, most colleges and universities in the U.S. at this time indoctrinate the students into their political and ethical ideologies, and many of those ideologies are sorely lacking and lead to immoral or wrongful behavior or conflict. Add to that the fact that most young people graduating from college or university don't get an appropriate job upon graduation, and you have a failed educational system in the U.S.

For a person who is a follower of Joshua, it would be radically inconsistent to "go to college/university." A disciple would not pay money to sit in some class to hear a teacher indoctrinate their students into their ideologies which ideologies ignore the Light of the world and teach ethics contrary to his teachings.

The only education in the U.S. that has any real value after High School would be trade schools which specifically train students to be proficient at skills and trades that have practical value. Of course, you don't need those schools; you need people who are selfless enough to apprentice young people into a given trade/skill.

In short, non-religious schools make it very clear that Joshua of Nazareth is entirely irrelevant to life if he even exists at all. Ignoring Joshua in all their ways and teaching things which contradict him is hardly an education worth receiving...just look at the fruit of that education as you look at how the world is doing. The college and university education system is all about the same thing the rest of the world is all about – money. They are very profitable businesses, and they will teach whatever people want to hear.

Religious schools are just as bad if not worse because they ignore Joshua and teach things that contradict him in his "name'! Religious schools are just like their counterpart, religious organizations – they often and unfortunately produce hypocrisy in people.

While most religious schools do generally teach a "God-based ethic," that ethic has very little power to change people who do not ascribe to the god the school teaches. Just like their religious organization brethren, these religious schools cannot help with what is most important and sadly serve as a substitute for the King and his Kingdom.

Here is one more aspect of education we must address. One of the ways we deceive ourselves is this, "oh, well I need a degree in such and such to be able to do that work." The truth is that an average person could learn the vast majority of "jobs" or work that people do within a relatively short period of time. Instead of tens of thousands of dollars paid to a university or college to learn some skill all that is required is an apprenticeship. For example, most people think that people in the medical services industry need an extensive education to practice some medical service competently. That is a false belief whose purpose is to earn money for the people running the educational institutions.

The fact is that even to become a general surgeon, for example, all that would be required is a competent young person apprenticed by a skilled surgeon. So, instead of many years of expensive "education" and hundreds of thousands of dollars paid to trainers, all that would be required is a surgeon willing to apprentice a young man or woman over a few years along with probably one-quarter of the book study that the educational system forces on people. You could have competent young surgeons able to perform basic surgery in about two to three years (depending upon the person) instead of the money making system that currently exists.

This same thinking that a person "needs a degree in such and such" to perform some work is very often used as an excuse not to serve our heavenly Father. Since the world – particularly the western world – has successfully gotten people to believe the falsehood that they need extensive education and training to accomplish some work task, people now use that as an excuse not to follow or serve Joshua. The religious organizations are just like their non-religious brethren in this respect. They insist that a person have some degree from some school to be competent to "perform ministry" whatever the heck that means.

So, for example, if you ask a person who claims to be "following Jesus" to come, serve Joshua with you, they will often respond with some version of the excuse of "well, I don't think I am qualified." They so deeply misunderstand what it means to follow and serve Joshua, *and* in reality, they don't want to follow and serve the Real Light, they use an excuse, "but I am not qualified." The truth is a young teenager can meaningfully contribute to the Greater work. The whole "I need education" is merely yet another excuse to not follow the real, historical Person of Joshua of Nazareth.

In summary, we must allow the King to take us out of the world and into the Kingdom, and this transference has real, rubber-meets-the-road manifestations in life. Perhaps the biggest challenge we will face in being chosen out of the world is the fear associated with giving up what most of the world considers valuable and thus pursues. The next chapter will address perhaps the greatest obstacle for people following the real, historical Person of Joshua of Nazareth.

Chapter Summary:
- While God loves all the people of the earth, only some choose to love Him back by putting their faith in and listening to His Messenger;
- The Messenger defines "the world" as the people of the earth who will not listen to him, or who are ignorant of him and won't listen to the lesser light of their conscience either;
- The Light calls his followers out of the world, and this is an essential part of following Joshua. Being out of the world does not mean we run to the forest or jungle or mountains and live apart from other human beings, nor does it mean to build castles and religious fortresses and cloister ourselves in them;
- What being called out of the world does mean is that we will not fit into the worlds governments, businesses, educational institutions, organizations or other groups of people who reject Joshua as their Leader. As we speak his truths and try and live them out, we are rejected by the world, and at the same time we are the light he calls us to be;

- If we refuse to allow him to call us out of the world, we will never be a part of the Family he invites us into, and thus we will never actually follow him, all our objections notwithstanding;

- Getting involved in politics will not bring significant and meaningful individual change to people's lives. Therefore it is foolish to spend substantial time trying to bring change in that domain/kingdom for political kingdoms are of this world;

- Receiving an "education" in the world (secular or religious) when it is not teaching a person useful things or when it includes teaching a person false views of reality (like Joshua is irrelevant) or immoral or unethical principles, is harmful.

40
"I DON'T LIVE FOR MONEY..." REALLY?

Opening Questions:

- If I spend the majority of my time pursuing money or material things for myself, then am I not living for money?
- Is living for money and material things genuinely satisfying?
- Is there any significant difference between Christians and non-Christians in the U.S. when it comes to "careers" and making money?
- Can someone follow Joshua and still spend the majority of their time working for money or material things for themselves?
- What does Joshua mean when he says we must forsake all to follow him?

The simple truth is that the vast majority of Christians live for money, just like the rest of the world. Their educations – including religious – and "careers" are all about making enough money to live "the good life," just like the rest of the people on the planet. Their currency bills might say, "In God We Trust," but that is a lie just like most things in the world. The currency should say, "In This We Trust." Said another way, Christians worship money and the material life just like non-theists who, while they don't claim to "worship" anything, yet never-the-less worship money and the material life—they just deny it a bit less than Christians and choke on a term that doesn't fit their worldview, i.e. "worship."

What is Wrong with Earning Money?

Money, or currency or the currency notes and coins themselves are not evil. There is nothing inherently wrong with paper or ink or metal.

Furthermore, if by "earning money" you mean receiving payment for honest, ethical work done, then "earning money" is not the problem. Whether you earn/receive/take a lot of money or whether you earn/receive/take very little money, how much you earn/receive/take is not the primary problem either.

Instead, living for money and the things it buys is evil and is the problem:

- Not sharing money and material things is the problem;
- Only sharing non-tax money with blood and legal relatives is the problem;
- Spending the majority of our time working FOR money is the problem;
- Not working for Joshua the majority of the time is the problem;

Finally, and most important in this context, an unwillingness to share one's money and other material things with other disciples is **the problem,** *for it is a manifestation and evidence of a lack of the most important thing – love.* People's love of money and perceived material security takes the place of loving one another.

Many Christians and Biblians are wealthy and who spend their lives seeking to build their material wealth. There are many contemporary Biblians and Christians who preach a very popular "prosperity gospel" whose basic message is "God wants to bless you to be materially wealthy!" The people of the world chasing after material wealth - money, wealth and the perceived material security it buys - is undoubtedly one of the things that most human beings spend their lives doing.

The term "worship" is derived from the straightforward English concept of "worth" or "worth-ship," thus, that which is worth the most to an individual is that which he/she "worships." So, if you are spending the majority of your time working for the food which perishes (money/material things), then you ought to use logic to conclude that you are worshipping money, all your objections notwithstanding. One does not need to bow down to an image or statue of a dollar bill to be worshipping money. In fact, the whole bowing down thing is just another outward act that does not mean the person worships the thing/person to which they bow. The proof of what we value – what we worth-ship – is proven in our daily lives...how we spend our time, how we behave, what we think about and what comes out of our mouths from our hearts.

For where your treasure is, there will your heart be also. (Matt. 6:21)

In other words, that which you value the most will take the majority of your heart's focus/attention.

Due to Christianity's errors, what is not widely known is Jesus/Joshua's position on his followers and how they should treat money and material things. The Real Light of the world's view is not widely known because it is very unpopular and goes against our natural inclination to store up wealth for ourselves or for others who we believe we might get something back from or whom we think we're obligated. Simply put, the disciples of Joshua will live a very different life regarding how they view and manage money and material things and how they live their lives with those views at heart.

The Primary Principles of Disciples Regarding Handling of Money and Material Things

Here are the primary principles he teaches regarding money and material wealth for his followers:

Principle 1. We share what we have with others, especially disciples.
Thus, we are complying with two principles Joshua provides regarding this matter:
> a. "A new command I give to you, that you love one another as I have loved you; for this is how the people of the earth will know that you are my disciples IF you love/care for one another." (John 13:34-35);
> b. "So then, none of you can be my disciple who does not give up all his own possessions."

As we have observed, material things and currency are not evil, but they do provide a strong temptation to worship them or be in bondage to them (or to serve them), which temptation we overcome by our sharing with others, particularly other disciples. The sharing Joshua is talking about in the new command above *has nothing to do with the natural family*. People assume that a husband will provide for his wife and children when they are young. When an individual becomes a disciple and joins other disciples to share Joshua's Life together, the larger Family becomes the priority, not the "nuclear or natural" family. The natural family will become part of the Supernatural Family and find strength and encouragement there.

The world primarily shares only among natural or legal family members. In fact, there are Christian ministries that promote and defend focusing on the natural family and are clueless about the Supernatural Family.

The disciples share first amongst themselves and then to their "neighbors" at large, for Joshua made it very clear that the natural family is intended to mean virtually nothing from a Kingdom of God perspective. Of course, God wants people to love one another, including natural family members, but when that love rises above the spiritual family members, it becomes just another expression of selfishness. The true test of real love is if we are willing to share with those to whom we have NO natural or legal connection to, and thus don't have the perception that we "owe" each other something.

It is effortless to deceive ourselves and say, "I am not ruled/controlled/influenced by money," but the proof, so to speak, is "in the pudding" which pudding is *sharing*—and not just "convenience sharing," but everything we have got sharing—Life sharing. Sharing with others is a significant part of what it means to love other people, and the lack of sharing with one another among the Christians is both proof and a manifestation of their not listening to Joshua of Nazareth and thus their lack of love for one another.

As disciples, what we control materially comes and goes, ebbs and flow, but our practice is to share and give, not to be selfish which would mean to take and store "for me." Since this is true, a disciple will not store up large amounts of material things for themselves.

We do not live a life characterized by having better material things than the average person around where we live—we seek to live simply - not "materially above" our neighbors - and to use the material things we have in a non-wasteful, wise, selfless manner.

The following illustrations will help you understand the principles above.

Illustration: Part 1
Two men are sitting around a campfire in the woods – John and Bob. They have left living in areas with other people to "get away from the wickedness of the world to serve God." They believe that they have "forsaken all to follow Jesus'. John has only the clothes on his back and two cans of beans. Bob has only the clothes on his back and three cans of beans. Both John and Bob are Biblians and claim some Christian label. Since they won't "work for money" or do "secular work" since that is "not what God wants," they ask others to give them things in trade for their religious materials, or they scavenge from what other's throw away, thus their cans of beans. Their "gospel" is primarily one of hell avoidance and fear. John resents that Bob has one more can of beans than he has and Bob resents John's resentment.

Illustration Part 2:
Two neighbors live next to each other in an average "middle class" neighborhood in the U.S. Each have about the same amount of material

things like their house and car etc. Rachel and Ryan are disciples of Joshua, and they share their house with other disciples and sometimes with other neighbors in need. They have a "three bedroom, single-family house," but they have four other disciples living with them, and they use their only other bedroom for the occasional down-and-out young women they find in the city who needs help. They try to work as little as possible to provide food, clothing, and shelter (the lesser work) for themselves and the others they help; since they spend the majority of their time proclaiming Joshua to the people they encounter (the Greater work).

Ryan and Rachel share everything they have with the four other disciples because they consider them good friends and actual brothers and sisters. Furthermore, Ryan and Rachel are doing well trying to love their neighbor as they love themselves - thus they are living out the "new command" as well as the second greatest command. Furthermore, since they are living selflessly like that due to their faith in Joshua and his Father, they are also fulfilling the greatest command.

Next door to Rachel and Ryan are Bonnie and Harry. Bonnie and Harry are "church-going Christians" – in fact, Harry is an "elder" of the religious organization and is president of the church board - and they don't share anything they have like most other Americans, and if they do any significant sharing, it is only with blood or legal relatives. They live a life indistinguishable from the "atheists" next door and the "agnostics" across the street. They are not living out the new command, nor are they living out the first or second greatest commands even though they regularly profess to "love God", and sing the loudest during "worship service."

Rachel and Ryan are disliked by their neighbors for the "unconventional', "weird', "strange", "religious" way they are living and sharing their material things with non-relatives, but they are most disliked by the Christians who consider and treat Ryan and Rachel like "religious fanatics" and "cultists".

In contrast, Bonnie and Harry are well liked by their neighbors, held up as "model citizens" and "good church going people" since their selfish lifestyle affirms their neighbor's selfish lifestyles and they almost never talk about anything but the things of the world!

Question: Who is doing better listening to Joshua - John or Bob, who have "given everything up for the lord'; the "cultists" Ryan and Rachel; or the godly churchgoers and good citizens Bonny and Harry?

Principle 2. We don't "work for money," which is to say that we are not working for the money itself or for the non-essential things that money can buy—we don't serve money. We work for our Father and Joshua, the Greater work, while we seek to minimize the lesser work of providing food, clothing, and shelter for ourselves and others, thus we comply with what Joshua means when he says:

> No one can serve two masters; for either he will hate the one and love the other, or he will be devoted to one and despise the other. You cannot serve God and wealth. (Matt. 6:24), and;

> Do not work for the food which perishes, but for the food which endures to eternal life, which the Son of Man will give to you, for on him the Father, God, has set His seal. (John 6:27), and;

> Do not store up for yourselves treasures on earth, where moth and rust destroy, and where thieves break in and steal. But store up for yourselves treasures in heaven, where neither moth nor rust destroys, and where thieves do not break in or steal; for where your treasure is, there your heart will be also. (Matt. 6:19-21), and;

> It is easier for a camel to go through the eye of a needle than for a rich man to enter the kingdom of God. (Mark 10:25), and;

> Blessed are you who are poor, for yours is the Kingdom of God & Woe to you who are rich, for you are receiving your comfort in full." (Luke 6:20, 24).

Before we met Joshua, we were most likely working for money to secure and multiply our material possessions. This effort is a big part of loving our lives in this world. When we "meet" Joshua, everything changes, and one of the biggest changes is that we stop working for money and the unnecessary possessions that the money buys and supports. Thus, when we first come into Joshua's Life, we must stop living for, or hang onto, our possessions—we must forsake them. What this means for some people is that we must walk away from our belongings to start following Joshua.

After we have forsaken that which was holding us back from following Joshua, we must now adjust to the new way of Life. This adjustment does *not* mean we don't accept money or material compensation the lesser work we do. This does not mean we don't plant our gardens for food to eat or build or maintain structures to live in or do work for someone and receive payment for our work to buy something we need. Instead, it means our motivation for the lesser work we do is to provide necessary material things for ourselves and to help support others and thus support the Greater work—it means we do not store up for ourselves material possessions.

Just like a martial arts pupil has a master in the martial arts domain does not mean that the pupil never eats or drinks or maintains a shelter or works for food. Instead, it means that for what that pupil cares about – in this example learning the ways of the martial art they are studying – that domain will be primary and will shape the other non-primary domain things in his/her life even while the pupil does spend time and energy doing work not directly related to the primary domain. Or, just like the woman hired to sew garments yet who does some things above and beyond sewing garments to help others with whom she works.

Our motivation is not to become wealthy or to store up wealth or to be materially secure. Instead, we do the greater work to serve our Father and our Master and the lesser work to:

a. Provide the things we need for life on this earth for ourselves and *thus try not to be a burden to others*;

b. Provide for those we share his Life with;

c. Help needy people around us.

What the Above Principles Mean Regarding How Followers of Joshua Cannot Live

The primary manifestation of this truth is that we cannot have work or "a job" or a "career" apart from a Joshua Family that regularly takes up the majority of our day and yet has nothing to do with doing Joshua's work—that situation is normally called "my career', "my job" or "my vocation". If we are not participating in, nor being part of, nor actively looking to become part of a group of disciples (or Family of Joshua) and instead are living the "regular American life," then we are not submitting to God's Leader (His Son) and are likely serving money.

Not to be part of a group of people who are sharing Joshua's Life and thus sharing their material things and doing his work, is to disobey his new command:

A new command I give you, that you love/care for/share with one another as I have loved/cared for/shared with you; for this is how the people of the earth will know that you are my disciples, IF you love/care for/share with one another. (John 13:34-35)

The new command is the most important principle that is to be lived out, so we can call ourselves whatever we want, but if we are not obeying his new command out of love for our Master and Father and other people, then we are not following the Real, historical person of Joshua of Nazareth.

Contrast the above truth to "Christian ministry" and "church" where such a concept is completely foreign and very much rejected and despised. Trying actually to love other people is anathema to the comfortable (selfish) American Christians who love their life in this world and will only consider sharing with their blood or legal relatives. Those who try and live out the new command will be labeled by the religious people as "cultists" and "heretics" out of the fear the religious folks have for the Light and his Way.

Furthermore, if we are not serving God through our Greater work of bringing our Father and Joshua to others, then we are not submitting to God's Leader (His Son) and are likely serving money or some other thing. Please listen to him in that regard:

> Those who ignore me, I will ignore before my Father who is in heaven, while those who acknowledge me as their Master, I will confess before my Father who is in heaven. (Matt. 10:31-33)

The Real U.S. Currency Motto, "In Money We Trust"

This author has traveled some and has seen how the United States is held up by many people in "non-industrialized" nations as the best nation to live in due primarily to the material abundance that U.S. citizens possess. The U.S. government turns down millions of requests by people to live here and become citizens, even while hundreds of thousands seek to enter the nation illegally to partake in the material security and abundance the U.S. provides.

The U.S. does have some things about it that are favorable and preferable to other alternatives. It remains one of the most politically and governmentally free places to live on the earth. The rule of law, meaning people agreeing to live by rules, remains but is fading quickly due to a relativistic worldview and the associated turning away from the moral principles that a majority of "God-fearing" religious people once held.

The capitalistic system, while generally greed motivated, can work well when there is abundance and when the people are less greedy and are instead generous and looking to help others—this too is fading quickly due to the people's selfishness.

(As an aside, different forms of human government have strengths and weaknesses, but any version of government and economic system – from democracy to monarchy, from capitalism to communism – will either thrive or fail due to the people's character, especially the leaders. If people are generous and motivated, capitalism works well. If people are greedy and motivated, capitalism does not work well but will create rich and poor social classes. Greed – that a person desires more for me and not caring about how much others have – is synonymous with selfishness, and when greed rules people's hearts, some socialistic principles provide better solutions.)

For those who don't have Joshua as their Leader, the democratic political system does still allow some degree of freedom to choose one's government leaders, although that too is fading quickly due to the corruption of the people turning away from even sound moral principles. All one has to do is to look at other "democratic nations," especially in Africa, to learn that the political solution of "democracy" does not solve the basic problems. Africa is full of "democratic nations" even while those nation's people are struggling for basic material necessities primarily due to the greed and corruption of the leaders of those nations. Sad that people cannot see that the U.S. is headed right down that hole due to the people turning away from even a sound and shared moral standard. Turning away from a shared moral standard and a shared belief in some kind of God-accountability will lead to destruction due to the darkness of human nature.

But I digress a bit. While this chapter is about "money" and how disciples handle it, evidently it has broader implications. We disciples were never intended to be part of the nations of the earth. Yes, we would live in them, and yes, we should be grateful for every good thing those nations provide. But we are to be *first*, the model for humanity to see—groups of people living as human beings are supposed to live! **Love** is to be the difference between us disciples and the sad, dark world in which we find ourselves. How we handle the money and material things we get to control for a short time has everything to do with whether we actually "follow Joshua," or not—whether we genuinely love God or not.

If we cannot love our friends, we surely will never be able to love our enemies. If we will not share our stuff with other disciples/friends and thus fulfill a vital element of the new command, then what makes us believe we will lay our lives down for them?

The Solution to Greed

Here is Merriam-Webster's definition of greed:

"A selfish and excessive desire for more of something (such as money) than is needed." [58]

I hope the reader can see that greed is one of the motivations that rule the hearts of many, many people and which strongly influences many if not most. I hope you can also see that greed is the cause of Problem #1 identified in chapter two, "The State of Human Kind." Here is a description of that problem again in case you forgot:

"Nearly 1/2 of the world's population — more than 3 billion people — live on less than $2.50 a day. More than 1.3 billion live in extreme poverty — less than $1.25 a day. One billion children worldwide are living in poverty. According to UNICEF, about 22,000 children die each day due to poverty."[59]

---

[58] Merriam-Webster Dictionary, www.merriam-webster.com, April 2018

[59] Source: https://www.dosomething.org/us/facts/11-facts-about-global-poverty

Thousands of children are dying from preventable disease and starvation, while the number of billionaires has risen to over 1,800 and the number of millionaires has risen to about 16 million. What does that mean from a wealth distribution standpoint?

- Half of the world's wealth belongs to the top 1% of the wealthiest people;
- The top 10% of adults hold 85% of the world's wealth, while the bottom 90% hold the remaining 15% of the world's total wealth;
- The top 30% of adults hold 97% of the total wealth.

"According to the Organization for Economic Co-Operation and Development (OECD) in 2012 the top 0.6% of world population (consisting of adults with more than 1 million USD in assets) or the 42 million richest people in the world held 39.3% of world wealth. The next 4.4% (311 million people) held 32.3% of world wealth. The bottom 95% held 28.4% of world wealth." [60]

So, let's get a simple fact straight. Tens of thousands of children are outright dying each day, and millions more are suffering, neglected and abused, and billions of people are scraping by to survive each day, while a few hundred million people who could easily help them, *don't, and instead ignore them and justify their lack of help.* Clear enough?

The simple truth is that there are more than enough resources on this planet for all human beings. Furthermore, with our improved technology, it would be a simple matter to develop, manage and distribute those resources fairly.

I would argue that greed is one level up from the root problem which is fear. For example, let's say you have three people who are in a situation where they believe they may not have enough food to "make it." Due to the circumstances, one person must get and divide up the food into three equal rations for each person and then serve it to the other two people. They rotate who goes to get and divide up the food. If two people divide the food 33% for each, but the third gives herself 50% and the other two 25%, how would you describe that third's person's behavior? I think greedy would be a fair description of the third person's motivation, although in this case, it is not "more of something than is needed" so much as it is more of something than is fair or right.

I would venture to say that most greed is motivated by wanting to somehow insulate or protect one's self from harm or death. The thinking

---

[60] The World Fact Book – Central Intelligence Agency. Distribution of Family Income – GINI Index. https://www.cia.gov/library/publications/the-world-factbook/fields/2172.html

OECD DATA. Income Inequality. https://data.oecd.org/inequality/income-inequality.htm

goes, the more I have the the less likely I am to die. As one looks around our communities or the world at large, I believe the evidence bears that out. How many problems does greed generate?

So, I would say that fear of death is a primary problem in the world. How many people harm or take from or kill other people to, from their perspective, save themselves from harm or death? How many take more resources to themselves than they need because of the fear of, "I may not have enough..."?

So, what if the fear of death could be removed? How much greed-generated injustice, abuse, neglect, and conflict would go away on the earth each day?

Well, the Creator provided a solution to that problem, but to receive the answer, you must have faith in the One who said it:

> I am the resurrection and the life; he who has faith in me will live even if he dies, and everyone who lives and has faith in me will never die. Do you believe this? (John 11)

Why not leave your greed behind and become a generous one—one that genuinely shares with at least your friends?

In the next chapter, we will take a close look at The Primary manifestation of having The Light of the world as one's Master and thus what real love looks like lived out. For if we don't live out love the way The Light says, we are not his followers.

Chapter Summary:
- Living for money and the things it buys is evil and is a significant problem for all human beings of all times and all cultures;
- We cannot serve God and money/material things. If we are spending the majority of our time working for money or doing anything other than bringing Joshua and his Life to others, then we are not serving God and are likely serving money or material things;
- The average Christian works for money just like the agnostic or atheist or new age person or Jew or Muslim or whatever- label person they work with;
- Not sharing one's material things with other disciples is a manifestation of loving money and living for it instead of for people. It is effortless to deceive ourselves while we give some of our money away yet refuse actually to share daily Life with other followers;
- If disciples of Joshua are not living a truly shared Life with other disciples – meaning we are not treating each other like Family and

thus sharing our money and other stuff with each other – then we are failing badly and have no witness to this dark world;

- Following Joshua has a beginning, and when we start following Joshua, we must give up the selfish life and walk away from holding onto material things and working for material things, and instead begin to work for Joshua;

- Greed is a tremendous problem for perhaps most people, but our Creator and Father provided a solution to greed and a primary underlying cause of greed, which is fear of death.

For more detail on how disciples of Joshua should forsake all and thus view the handling of money and material things, see *Appendix 12, Zealousness but not for Love.*

41
I LOVE ICE CREAM, I LOVE YOU!?

Opening Questions:
- If people did not want to love other people (and yet at some level they know they should), would defining love as something(s) that it is not, help accomplish that?
- Is the highest, purest form of love an emotion towards others?
- If true love needs to be practiced and you are not practicing it, are you a good person?
- If people who know each other and live near each other really understand love, will they be apart or together?
- If a person claims that love is the most critical concept God gave to human beings, and yet that person does not practice love, what does that say about that person?

Ah, now we get to the second most crucial aspect of the solution. It is second because you cannot know what love is unless you use truth to do so and we need the right Leader to define love properly for us.

This matter gets to the crux of the successful failure that is Christianity and the Christians who practice their religion. They are successful from the world's perspective of material abundance and influencing or controlling people, but failures from the perspective of refusing to DO the most critical thing that the one they call "their god" asks—love one another.

Remember how we defined love in this book according to Joshua's definition instead of the world's definition. Love is the manifestation – the practical outworking – of the solution!

Almost everyone if asked the question, "are you a loving person," will answer, "yes." They do this because our Creator gave us a conscience and we "know" that that is how we ought to be.

But the fact that most people believe something about them does not make their claim authentic does it? It is similar to asking people, "are you a good person"? How many will answer, "no, I am not"? Very few due to our self-filters and rose-colored glasses we wear especially when looking into the mirror!

Listen to the average person as they say, "Oh, I love ice cream; I love my dog; I love that TV show; I love pizza; I love that park; I love those shoes; I love that movie." And then they say to someone, "I love you." A little bell should ring or a little red flag ought to go up for that person and they ought to ask, "so what is the difference between me and the pizza?"! Sadly and frequently, there is very little difference.

There is no better way to destroy the meaning of a word than to broaden or re-define its meaning until it loses all clarity and becomes virtually meaningless. For example, the saying, "everyone is special" nullifies the plain meaning of "special" and does, in fact, result in the belief that therefore "no one person is special" - and so it is with "love." By the way, the "everyone is special" saying is usually misused because of *people not making the distinction between the value of a person versus their ability to do certain things.* So, for example, all the little girls on the soccer/football team are equally valuable as human beings, but not all are good soccer players—a few are exceptional or unique soccer players.

So, what "love" has come to mean in the general culture is "I really like" or "that thing really pleases me." Love has become for many, merely a strong emotional liking for something and synonymous with "really like."

It is Not "unloving" to Correct Another Person

Before we look at what love is, it is important to address the usually wrong concept of "unloving." Many Christians wrongly believe that to love others includes accepting what is wrong. They are like the wrongly weak mother who "just knows little Jonnie is a good kid," even while he bullies, threatens and assaults other children on a regular basis. As another example, many Christians say "loves does not cause a person to condemn homosexuals," but what they really mean by that is that the beliefs behind homosexual marriage or homosexual child raising are good and right. They refuse to distinguish between individuals and principles or between wrong and right, often because they are no longer capable due to their relativism.

As another example, many Christians oppose child discipline on the basis that "it is not loving," even as their child is practicing wrong behavior or language towards other people on a regular basis because their lack of consequences is encouraging that. The simple truth is that true love does not exist in a vacuum – it exists between people - and it is expressed while observing, acknowledging or promoting what is right. From another perspective, love is not represented by wrong behavior or by endorsing or ignoring wrong beliefs or behavior. *It is imperative to understand that love between two or more people cannot work or flourish if there is something false or wrong in the relationship(s).*

In conclusion, it is NOT *"unloving" to correct another person's false beliefs or wrong behavior, and in fact, and ignoring harmful behavior is truly un-loving.* It is unloving to want to harm another person or to harm another person – harm meaning physically or materially. To call the verbal correction of a person "unloving" for telling them that, for example, it is wrong for two men to marry is both false and VERY destructive. As we saw in the relativism chapters, it will be the end to all commonly held ethical standards. And this is in fact what is happening in the U.S. at this time.

What is the Standard to Know What "Love" Means?

To know if something is true or false, you need a standard against which to judge, evaluate or measure. For example, if I say, "I am over 6 feet tall", and you say, "no you are not," we need to agree on the length of a "foot" and then measure it correctly to determine who is right. So, before we can determine my actual height, we need to first agree on the unit of measure, in this case, a "foot" of the English system.

As another example, you can say, "Suzy is a giving person," but what is the standard to determine that? Well, one would need to start by agreeing that "giving" means to give good things to other people, whether material or relational. Then, we could talk to all the people Suzy interacts with on a regular basis, and ask them if Suzy "gives good things to them" on a regular basis. If the majority said, "yes," then your statement is validated as true. If the majority says, "no," then your claim - on an objective basis - is wrong, even if a few individuals that Suzy favors disagree.

As you can see, while non-physical things like human motivations, thoughts, words and subsequent behavior are more difficult to measure if no standard is known or agreed upon (in the example above "giving" has no precise standard), it is still possible if people can agree to a standard.

The excellent news is that the Creator of humankind gave the universal standard for human behavior! The Creator sent His Messenger and Representative to show us and tell us the rules for human motivation and behavior—for what is right versus what is wrong human behavior. The Messenger's name is Joshua or Jesus of Nazareth.

The people of the earth, in general, have not done very well over the millennia—conflict, abuse of power, neglecting one another, harming one another and the pain and suffering have been the usual order for thousands of years. Oh, yes, every once in a while there is an exception with people participating in the exception and doing much better than the norm. Those exceptions have sadly been few and far in-between and relatively small in scale.

As was stated previously and validated by the One who defeated death, the Creator of the human race sent a Messenger to mankind about two millennia ago, and he made it *very clear* what the Creator wants of His created race of humanity—he wants this all-important concept called "love" to be known and practiced by the human race. Sadly and tragically, the human race has, for the most part, ignored the Messenger and has gone on its usual way of being bound by self-pride and fear and selfishness, thus continuing the established order of conflict, abuse of power, neglecting one another, harming one another and the pain and suffering it brings.

There has always been some - very few in proportion to the general population of the earth - who have listened to the Creator's Messenger (or the conscience given to them by the Creator) and thus have endeavored to live by this all-important concept of "love."

What Love Is and Is Not

Let us first clarify what love is *not*, for many are self-deceived thinking they are "loving" people because they have the wrong definition or understanding of what real love is.

- *Love is not an emotion or feeling.*
    - o While emotions and feeling can result from the expression of love, those emotions or feelings is not how Joshua defines love. This error is one of the most significant mistakes that is currently believed by people;
- *Love is not a feeling of (or emotion based) attraction to another person.*
    - o The attraction to the other person is usually a strong self-desire to, in some way, "have" that other person - often for sexual reasons, frequently to try and fill insecurity we have, sometimes for control reasons;
    - o The strong emotional desire for a person of the opposite gender is widespread in the teenage years and is often called, "first love," while an accurate description would be, "first emotional infatuation." This infatuation often has the boy's or girl's insecurity as a substantial factor in the "crush."
- Love is not merely friendship, although the best friendships will practice love. Two people who are companions and thus good friends usually practice love in that relationship;

374

- Love is not "liking" another person because they affirm you or because you have similar interests and thus enjoy spending some time together—that is friendship;
- Love is not civility, politeness, being considerate of others, graciousness, being merciful, patient or maintaining self-control - *although all of those things are good.*
    - o So, if you practice those things, then you are a better person than most, but practicing those things still does not make you a person exercising "love" according to the Light.

Here is the Christian's leader Paul's take on love: "Love is patient, love is kind and is not jealous; love does not brag and is not arrogant, does not act unbecomingly; it does not seek its own, is not provoked, does not take into account a wrong suffered, does not rejoice in unrighteousness, but rejoices with the truth; bears all things, believes all things, hopes all things, endures all things. Love never fails."

Paul says many good things about how we ought to be - he lists many good character traits or human virtues - but he also makes the terrible mistake of re-defining love. Paul re-defines love so broadly to mean several things (or nothing, just like the term "special" example given previously in this chapter!), and thus, the pure definition of love is lost or hidden in his confusion. In other words, a person reading Paul's understanding of love could be very patient and kind but refuse not to seek their own and deceive themselves into thinking because they have two characteristics of love, they are a person of love. As another example, I can be a non-jealous person or humble person or a calm person or a forgiving person, but still be unwilling to share my life with other disciples which is what love does.

An excellent way to test the meaning of love is to plug the supposed "things" that someone says love is into John 3:16, perhaps the best definitional statement of what love is from Joshua. For example, that saying of Joshua is, "For God so loved the world that he sent His only beloved Son...." So, to test Paul's definition of love, let's plug in a few of the many characteristics he claimed were part of "love" into the saying of Joshua. "For God so not-jealous-ed the world that he sent..."; or, "For God so displayed patience that he sent..."; or, "For God so not provoked the world that he sent..." As you can see, many of the good things that Paul lists do not fit in with what is perhaps the best definitional statement of "love" given by Joshua.

Just like the Bible hides the Light by burying his Voice amidst many other voices, so Paul surrounds the core of love - "does not seek its own" - with many things love is not. Thus, he provides the example - and for many, the authority - to redefine the most critical concept given by the Creator, and which concept was *clearly* defined by the Creator's Messenger.

So, let us take a brief look at this all-important concept to gain clarity on it.

We must first find the authority or standard to know what "love" is. Since the dictionaries didn't exist at the time and since the Model for humanity defined love, we would do well to listen to him. In short, Joshua defines love as, "To value someone and have compassion for them and to behave selflessly towards them (help them) and to want to be with them." Please read that again and think about it for that is the core or "heart" of the "love" that the Light of the world teaches.

Now, ask yourself in a real, honest way, towards whom in your life are you practicing love?

Here are a few relevant facts to consider about "love":

Fact 1: The Light speaks to the concept of "love" about sixty times in the four gospel books, so it is *the* primary topic and concern of his.

Fact 2: The Light says the three greatest commandments are about "love."

> One of them, a lawyer, asked Him a question, testing Him, "Teacher, which is the great commandment in the law?" And he said to him, "You shall love the Lord your God with all your heart, and with all your soul, and with all your mind." This is the great and foremost commandment. The second is like it, "You shall love your neighbor as yourself." On these two commandments depend the whole Law and the Prophets. (Matt. 22:37-40)

> A new commandment I give to you (my disciples), that you love one another, even as I have loved you, that you also love one another. By this, all men will know that you are my disciples if you have love for one another. (John 13:34-35)

Fact 3: The Light affirms and clarifies the two greatest commandments and says we are to love everyone we encounter or know in as much as they will let us, even those who make themselves "our enemies."

> (In contrast, Moses and thus the Hebrew scripture taught/teaches, hate and kill your enemies: "You shall not hate your fellow countryman in your heart..." (Lev. 19:17) & "Take full vengeance for the sons of Israel on the Midianites (not your fellow countryman)...Now therefore, kill every boy and male child, and kill every woman who is not a virgin..." (Num. 31:1-18). Therefore, you make a great error if you try to understand God through the Hebrew scripture.)

Fact 4: The "new command" is not negotiable, nor would someone want it to be if they have the heart to receive it. For the disciples love for one another will be the *only* way for "all men" to know that we are followers of the Life. And yes, love will be "seen" by other people as we live together in unity and peace and care for each other and do the Master's work together.

Fact 5: The Light says that if those who say they follow him do not live "love" out, then they do not, in reality, represent him. So, if you claim to be a "follower of Jesus Christ", and you are not sharing your life (really his Life) with them - that is living with other followers as actual "brothers" and "sisters" and truly good friends - then you are deceived and living a religious lie that will only serve as self-condemnation.

Fact 6: The Light says that no greater love can be demonstrated than to lay our lives down for our friends. So, if we are unwilling to live for and with our friends, what would make us think we would be willing to die for them other than the delusion self-pride would generate?

If you can accede to the above truths about "love," *and* you want to live by "love," *and* you can see that you have *not* been living by love, then you are on the brink of a very different life than the one you have been living.

The simple truth is that the manifestations of love cannot exist by one person willing to live by love. It takes at least two people who are ready to love each other for the manifestations of the love that Joshua talks about to exist. Furthermore, if you claim to be a disciple of Joshua, the new command cannot be lived out among mere blood or legal relatives. Nor can it be lived out amongst a religious group of people who do not love each other as Joshua defines it.

It is important to note before we take a closer look at love, that love does not exist in isolation of other important aspects of human life, or stated another way, love exists within - or is "subservient to" - only one constraint—truth. We could not even know what love is without truth because using reason and logic to know truth is how we understand what metaphysical things are. In short, we cannot be practicing something wrong against another person and love them.

Joshua teaches those wrongs and rights clearly, but IF we are living by love, we really won't need to "refrain from the wrongs" since we will naturally be doing what is right. Said another way, love causes us to do what is right without having to concern ourselves with abstaining from what is wrong. Love is active and reaching out, or "other's" focused (what can I do to help that person), whereas "rule" or "law" is passive and preventative and self-focused (what will happen to me if I do that wrong thing).

The Creator has given human beings the spiritual aspect of our nature called a conscience. The conscience is the "rule" or "law" of knowing wrong human behavior programmed into our nature—it "informs us" when we are thinking about doing something wrong, or doing something wrong; or after we do something wrong. But our conscience does NOT motivate us to love—something more is required for that. The conscience is largely reactive, not proactive. For people of faith, we must first experience our Father's love for us as expressed through His Son.

Manifestations of Those Living by Love

Here are some characteristics or "manifestations" of people who are living by the "love" that Joshua of Nazareth teaches—manifestations of those living out the "new command":

- *We are together, not apart.* Love brings people together; it does not separate them or drive them apart. To follow the Light and live by his love will lead to being in one of his Families. Thus, if we are alone or only living with our natural family members (the easiest way for Christians to deceive themselves and avoid trying to live out the new command), then we are not loving well or perhaps not at all, and we are certainly *not* living out Joshua's new command;

- *We are not afraid to discuss important things with others due to the love we receive from our Father*—we are secure in Him (therefore not ruled by fear) and in what we believe because we have placed our faith in His Son as our Teacher, and he says he is all the truth that really matters!;

- *We point others to the One's (our Father and Master) who gave us this love, showed us this love and empower us with love,* because we want them to experience them too, and we want them to experience life everlasting instead of destroying themselves for the worthless things of the world;

- *We reach out to others to try and get them to see how special this faith-given love is and to participate in it* for we know that it is *the solution* to all of humanity's problems;

Most Christians, when they hear these simple truths, respond with self-pride or fear and say something like this, "Oh, what are you saying, that we need to be part of a commune; that we need to be part of a cult; that we need to live like socialists, groupies or hippies." or a myriad of other *fear-based defensive responses*. My response is, "no, I am just repeating what Joshua of Nazareth teaches."

Or they will say, "show me a verse in the Bible that supports your view of love", and I quote Acts 2:44-45, "And all those who had believed were together and had all things in common; and they began selling their property and possessions and were sharing them with all, as anyone might have need."; but those who don't have ears to hear and who do not want to live by love will not listen even to their beloved Bible if it says something they don't want to hear, and will find every excuse or "theological" trick to make the words of no effect.

Those who fight against his simple truths and his definition of love are those where the seed falls on the bad soil—where holding onto this world and their lives in this world have domination over listening to the Light and his Way of love despite the Life saying:

> For whoever wishes to save his life will lose it; but whoever loses his life for my sake will find it. (Matt. 16:25)

Dear reader, if you are looking to save or preserve your life in this world, then you will lose eternal life, which is real Life.

A Word to non-Theists and Agnostics about Love

This author believes that the Creator gave love and thus He knows what it means and how important it is. The Creator's Messenger affirmed just that. We who listen to The Light have the privilege of knowing what love is and have a real opportunity to live love out among others who are not in a destructive mode due to being trapped in their cage of self-pride and fear and selfishness.

If you cannot correctly define love, you cannot understand it. And if you cannot understand love, you have very little chance of living it out or practicing it. Most people don't know what love is. Many can recognize it when they see it in action, but it is like a mysterious firework that burns in front of them for a brief moment and then is gone. The conscience God gave all people enables the recognition of true love, but not the understanding. If we are in a cage of self-pride and fear and selfishness, we cannot know, understand nor practice true love well if at all.

We need The Light to give us understanding about true love. In fact, the apex of The Light's story was the most potent manifestation of true love the people of the earth have had an opportunity to witness. Friends forsook him, mocked, beaten, tortured, and then publically nailed to a cross – all wrongfully. He did not deserve that treatment – it was entirely and thoroughly unjust. And yet at the end of all that wrongful treatment, he said to the men doing that to him, "Father, forgive them because they don't know what they are doing."

That dear reader is true love.

That is the expression of compassion without bounds; it is arguably the most exceptional example of selflessness ever expressed. He did not care about what was happening to him. Instead, he cared about the fate of those men who were – at that time –his enemies and thus were set on a course of self-destruction. As the expression of the Creator, The Light did not want them to destroy themselves. At that moment, Joshua of Nazareth consummated all his teachings on what real love was all about. He demonstrated *the* concept that could change human kind's course:

> "Love your enemies" or "love those who choose to make themselves your enemies"

This author argues that until a person can contemplate what The Light did, and the love the Father/Creator demonstrated to all people through His Son, we cannot know true love at its deepest level. Furthermore, unless we experience the Father's love – receiving his merciful forgiveness for all our wrongdoings - we don't have much of a chance of living true love out.

Atheists and agnostics will typically vehemently disagree with those statements. I ask in return, what is your standard to know what true love is? In other words, if I poll one-thousand agnostics, for example, and ask, "What is love," I think it is fair to say that you will get many different answers and the most popular will be some version of, "it is how I feel for certain people." In fact, most of the seven billion human beings currently on the earth would not get that right no matter what labels they take for themselves. Genuinely loving other people is not easy (that is part of the reason why it is so valuable) and thus it is not consistently practiced.

Furthermore, I ask in return to non-theists and agnostics, what is your motivation for living true love out? True love gives, it does not take. True love suffers without complaining and looks to help those who cause the suffering. A more anti-evolutionary view you will not find—a stronger antonym to the "survival of the fittest" doctrine is hard to imagine. Animals don't help their competitors; animals don't sacrifice themselves to protect the weak. And no, dear reader, finding a few exceptions to the general truths I just stated does not nullify the realities I just said! Remember your logical fallacies!

Finally, and as stated earlier in the book, when a person truly loves other people, that spiritual connection for those who return true love is powerful. True love expressed and understood between two people is arguably the most valuable experience this life can provide. The Creator did not set things up so that the most valuable thing human beings can experience in this life is destroyed upon death. In fact, that is one of the aspects of Hope that The Light provides us. If we are willing to love other people truly, that love and relationship will be preserved and made more beautiful and real post-physical death.

What about those people who don't believe in life after death? If you are a parent who loves your child, the last thing you want is to lose that child. If you lose them, it will cause a whole lot of suffering. The pain of "heartbreak" is real and is worse than physical pain. (Yet another proof of the metaphysical or spiritual reality we exist in.)

For the few left who truly love their spouses, the thought of being without them is harrowing. The fact is that many older people, who lose spouses they love through physical death, give up on life and die shortly after that. Many people labor under the falsehood that physicalists put forth that when we die, we cease to exist. That is one way to view reality, and I would say a horribly inferior or deficient way and denying some essential facts. Those who truly love another person will *not* want to leave them...will not want to see them destroyed, annihilated. And yet, this is the belief that non-theists labor under and surely only selfishness enable them to "move on."

The excellent news is that followers of The Light have a Person who defeated death who says, "*He who lives in and believes in (places their faith in) me will never (spiritually) die.*" How much is that worth? You don't have to labor under the falsehood and hopelessness that you are nothing more than molecules and that you are annihilated when you physically die!

Of course, physicalists will say that view is delusional. They say this despite the clear evidence and proof of a designer and a spiritual/metaphysical component to human nature and reality. I would counter that physicalism is delusional...just as delusional as a person insisting that computers and their functioning are merely a function of hardware.

They say the disciple's view is delusional despite four corroborating books which books document the life of an extraordinary Person – a materially poor, politically unconnected, religiously offensive, misunderstood Man - who changed the lives of countless individuals for better by his words and deeds.

I digress a bit. Many non-theists and agnostics will say because we are annihilated when we physically die, we are more motivated to love in this life. I don't think there is any evidence of that. What I know and experience is that people are somewhat delusional about death—they are basically in denial about death for their entire life. I understand this because most people believe that their existence will end upon physical death, so they push it off and understandably refuse to contemplate it honestly. Therefore, to think that the average person lives their life consciously aware of their death is unreasonable and not supported by evidence.

What I have experienced and what I have observed is that human nature is fundamentally selfish, and therefore, if the average person believes their life is going to end in say the next week, it will not necessarily motivate them to all of a sudden live selflessly. Instead, it is likely to bring additional fear and anxiety and the desire to experience the few things they value highest in this life.

Ultimately I posit that those who believe that we are annihilated upon physical death, will not likely love as frequently and cannot love as deeply as those who know we will not lose the love we expressed in this life. The simple truth is that those who know we are heading Home to a Father who loves us and that we will continue to experience the love we encountered while on the earth, are empowered to love...to give...to be selfless and live for what is truly valuable. Those who believe their physical life on this earth is all they will experience are not likely to give their lives away in love for others.

Back to the Christians

If you continue in all the self-delusion about how you are a person of God's love when you are not, you are destroying yourself and forfeiting Life.

If you think you can live the selfish, independent, proud American way—the way of "this is mine, and that is yours, and you stay over there except when it is convenient for us to get together for a few meetings"—then you are on the broad way of destruction.

If you think attending a religious service is somehow fulfilling a life of love, you are badly deceived and are both working against the Light and are very much part of the problem.

If you are a Christian or Biblian who thinks having some ideology that is different than "the mainstream," or that not being part of the dead Christian system is noble - yet you are not living out the new command - you too are badly deceived and falling short.

There is no greater love than this, that we lay down our lives for our friends. (John 15:13)

Lay down our life means to die for our friend. I say again if we are not willing to *live with* our friends and help them and care for them each day, then what makes us think we will die for them other than the delusion produced by self-pride???

Here come the lame excuses:

"Oh, I would *but* my religious leader says; *but* my wife; *but* my parents; *but* my husband; *but* my job; *but* my children; *but* my situation; *but* I have this problem; *but* my career; *but* my work..." and on and on the loveless-ness goes, growing colder and colder as each year passes. For the record, none of those excuses will bring Life nor will they prevent you from sending yourself to destruction—but then, that is the nature of delusion and deception isn't it?

The love of most will grow cold, but he who endures (continues by faith to love) *to the end* (even when love has been redefined, and the people grow content in their selfish, materialistic lifestyle) *will be saved* (from the emptiness and self-condemnation and destruction that faithlessness and loveless-ness brings). (Matt. 24:12-13)

Following The Leader and his teachings on love in a context of truth and rightness is the "meat" of the solution, dear reader. So, what do we do about the truth and rightness framework of understanding? Or stated another way, what are the fundamental realities we must agree on to be the city on a hill of which The Light speaks—to be a unified people?

We will look for answers to that question in the next chapter.

Chapter Summary:
- The most important concept of "love" has been redefined into many things, thus destroying any objective understanding of the concept. Without the right understanding of the concept, who can practice it or encourage others to practice it?
- The world does not practice love and has redefined/reduced love to emotions associated with particular circumstances or feelings for others, usually romantic or wanting another person often for selfish reasons;
- The Creator's Messenger defines the core of love as selfless behavior motivated by compassion and valuing others at least as much as we value ourselves. When we practice love (or see it practiced), we usually are blessed by our emotions validating that practice;
- Those who understand love and who want to practice love will live with others of the same understanding—love will bring people together and have them share life together;
- Disciples of The Light must live out the new command if there is any chance of having an impact on the increasingly cold and dark world in which we live—in this age of darkness.

42
HOW TO ACCOMPLISH UNITY

Opening Questions:
- How essential is unity for any group of people trying to accomplish something?
- What is the best source to understand Joshua of Nazareth - himself or others?
- Would it help develop unity if disciples could agree on a way to prioritize Joshua's teachings?
- Did Joshua provide the priority or relative importance of his teachings?
- If disciples don't have unity, what are we saying to the world?

As we have seen, the Bible is an extensive book that contains many thousands of supposed teachings from God.

Please consider this example. Twenty city people with no experience in being out of a city environment were kidnapped and blindfolded and transported to the center of the Canadian wilderness. They were told before they were left that they would be given instructions that would allow them to survive and escape the wilderness.

Ten were in one group, and another ten were in the second group. Group one was given a piece of paper with three instructions. Those three instructions were the keys to successfully getting out of the wilderness.

Group two was given a piece of paper with one-hundred instructions. These hundred instructions were all true but included many less essential and relatively trivial solutions to the things the people would face in trying to escape the wilderness. Things like the best way to boil water and optimal sleeping configurations given the temperature. The instructions included the three critical truths needed to escape the wilderness, but they were buried in the other one-hundred directions.

I ask the reader, which group will more likely find unity in the purpose of escaping the wilderness? Once a leader, leaders or a leadership method occurred, it would then come down to the ten people evaluation the instructions. The group with a hundred directions will have almost ten times the opportunity for disunity as they argue over what is essential or not. The group with only three instructions will have much lower chance for disunity.

In the same way, what should be the baseline common ground of disciples of Joshua to be with one another and work together? This critical question needs addressing. Listen to the importance of unity in this statement of the Light:

> The glory which You have given Me I have given to them, that they may be one, just as We are one; I in them and You in Me, that they may be perfected in unity, so that the world may know that You sent Me, and loved them, even as You have loved Me. (John 17)

This unity can only have a reasonably good chance of being attained if it is clear and straightforward. As we previously saw in the complexity chapter, each sect making their "statement of faith" (really statement of belief) slightly different than the thousands of others is part of the mechanism that produces the splintered, shattered glass bowl that is the successful failure. It is also extremely noteworthy that virtually none of those statements of belief have "love one another" included in them.

The Bible is a vast book, and it is only too easy to select a set of doctrine or beliefs from the scripture and make a sect/division out of it. Add to that the additional sources of God or spiritual belief looked to in addition to the Bible, for example:

- The writings of the many "prophets" of Christianity like Joseph Smith and the book of Mormon;
- The Vatican's Catchecism;
- Menno Simmon's writings;
- Charles Taze Russel of the Jehovah's witnesses;
- The latest Urantia Book, etc.

And you have what you have on the earth – many thousands of divisions of Christianity. Ultimately, Christianity's lack of unity is due to a lack of faith in Joshua, not making him one's Master, and thus not having his love to empower people.

This author proposes something simple – *to have Joshua of Nazareth as our sole spiritual Leader and Teacher and to know God and Joshua and what they want only through the words and teachings of Joshua of Nazareth contained in the four gospel books*. That is common ground enough to seek very hard to unify with other disciples. And disciples *must* find unity IF we care about the Master's saying/prayer above regarding unity.

One would think this is entirely logical and reasonable. After all, Joshua did say to his followers:

You call me Lord and Master, and you are right, for so I am. (John 13)

How many "lords" and "masters" can a person have? Try to use reason and proper definitions when answering that question.

I am the good shepherd; the good shepherd lays down His life for the sheep; I am the good shepherd, and I know My own and My own know Me, even as the Father knows Me and I know the Father; and I lay down My life for the sheep. I have other sheep, which are not of this fold; I must bring them also, and they will hear *my voice; and they will become ONE flock with ONE shepherd*. (John 10:14-16)

How many flocks? How many Shepherds?

They (religious leaders) love the place of honor at banquets and the chief seats in the religious buildings (what people wrongly call "the churches'), and respectful greetings in the marketplaces, and being called "Pastor, Reverend, Minster, etc. ad nauseum by men. *But do not be called teacher; for One is your Teacher, and you are all brothers. Do not call anyone on earth your father; for One is your Father, He who is in heaven. Do not be called leaders; for One is your Leader, that is, me.* But the greatest among you shall be your servant. (Matt. 23)

How many spiritual/God/human relationship teachers can a follower of the Light have? How many spiritual Fathers can a person have (according to the large sect of Roman Catholicism, many thousands!)? How many spiritual leaders can a person have?

The simple truth has been available for two thousand years, but how many have listened? All it takes is a little bit of faith to hear his voice, so perhaps this is where we are:

When the Son of Man returns, will he find faith on the earth? (Luke 18:8)

The meaning and answer are apparent—probably not much at all. There will be tons of religion and billions of religious people, but very few with actual faith in the real, historical Son of Man.

Unfortunately, the saying, "that they may be perfected in unity," is one of the greatest mockeries of Christians. With four of their religious organization's building on each quadrant of two streets intersecting in a relatively small town – blessed Baptist, pretentious Pentecostal, everything Evangelical and cathartic Catholic – the lack of unity could not be more obvious. Of course, when confronted with this fact, they will stumble and bumble around with some words about "we are in spiritual unity" or the mysterious "unified body of christ," which goes to prove the delusional nature of many religious people. Paul's language about the mystical "body of christ" is all that is needed for Christians and Biblians to nullify the simple, evident truth about the *disunity* of Christians and their religion.

For disciples of Joshua, we desperately need to have him and him alone as our only standard to know God and to understand what God wants of us. Having the right standard for unity is critical. Without agreement on the measure, there can be no unity. Furthermore, the standard selected needs to be clear and ideally simple. This will minimize the potential lack of agreement. If a chosen standard is complex and thereby lacks clarity, it will be harder to find total unity.

Having the real, historical person of Joshua of Nazareth as THE standard to know God and to know how to treat other human beings is an excellent standard for it is The Standard given by our Creator. Compared to the large, complicated book that is the Bible, just having the teachings of Joshua in the four gospels is a far superior standard for several reasons, including the increased clarity and lack of complexity.

Furthermore, we must understand that there is a priority or difference of importance to Joshua's many teachings. For example, his instructions on "love" – what love is and what love means – are THE most critical teaching, far more important than his teachings on, say, how the "last supper remembrance" ought to be observed if at all or the importance of water baptism or the role of the Holy Spirit. *Therefore, if we find ourselves dividing over the lesser things, we are failing at the most important thing.*

Lastly, if we are not experiencing the persecution or rejection from the people of the world, we are unlikely doing well following Joshua, and thus we will not be in the right state of heart/mind to see our need for love and unity. In other words, following Joshua faithfully by ourselves for a time in the world will condition us well to be ready for the love and unity that glorifies God.

Clarification Guidelines for Understanding Joshua

If disciples or students or pupils or followers of the historical Joshua of Nazareth can agree to make him their sole/soul Leader for things about God and human relationships, that is a great place to start!

Back in chapter 28, *Religious Leaders Like Complexity*, I suggested the core beliefs of the followers of Joshua. I offer it again here:

1. Joshua of Nazareth is the unique Son of God (Luke 22:69-70; John 3:16,18; 5:25; 10:36; 11:4), the Messenger and Leader sent by God the Creator to humankind to save us from ourselves / our sins (John 3:16). You can best know Joshua of Nazareth and his Good News (or gospel) through his own words and teachings as preserved in the four gospel books. The Bible is not the word of God to humankind; instead the Person and teachings of Joshua of Nazareth in the four "gospel books" is the word of God to humankind. To look to "the Bible" or "the scripture" apart from Joshua's teachings is great error and thus we should look only to Joshua.

2. To begin following Joshua, we must:

   • Repent of our sins (see ourselves as guilty, stuck in our cage of self-pride and fear and selfishness, be remorseful and receive our Father's forgiveness for our wrongs, and stop practicing what is wrong)(Matt. 4:17);

   • Be born from above by placing our faith in Joshua and thus transition from spiritual death to eternal Life (John 3:3-7);

   • Turn away from or forsake all we have believed is valuable in this world, especially money, material things, and people who don't want us to follow Joshua (Luke 14:33; John 12:25; Matt. 10:34-39; 12:46-50);

   • Stop working for money as our primary pursuit in life, and start working for Joshua and his kingdom as our primary passion in Life (Matt. 6:24; 4:19; 9:9).

3. While there are many sins we can commit, there are three aspects of our nature of which we must be aware of and seek to be no longer controlled by - self-pride, fear, and selfishness. Self-pride prevents us from learning and having a critical character virtue that we desperately need to learn and be better people - humility (Luke 18:9-14). Fear not only prevents us from learning but also dramatically hinders us from using reason well in our decision making and in seeking what is true (Matt. 10:26, 31; Luke 5:10;

8:25). Selfishness works hard against love, and both self-pride and fear contribute to that as well (John 15:13; Matt. 6:19-21; Mark 8:35).

4. Joshua refers to this critical term - truth - over a dozen times in the four gospels. For example, he says, "I am the truth" and "all who are of the truth hear my voice" and "the truth will set you free." Furthermore, he says we are to "love the Lord our God with all our mind." Loving God with all our mind can only be reasonably understood to mean to use reason and logic well to find, know and understand God. Therefore, it is *critical* that we as disciples do our best to use reason and logic well and to be willing to "go" where ever those important tools lead us—even if reason or logic lead us to reject some of our most tightly held religious beliefs or practices that we picked up over the years. If someone uses reason or logic well to reveal that we believe something that is erroneous, we ought not to be offended and instead seriously consider if what the person is saying does in fact pass the test of reason as well as line up with all of Joshua's teachings (if he addresses it) in that area/topic/domain. Humility would also drive this reaction.

5. In Joshua's teachings, he does provide us with how we should treat each other as human beings. In fact, he gives the universal "ethic" in this saying, "Treat others the way you want to be treated" (Matt. 7:12). If we would keep this in heart/mind and act upon it, we would avoid MANY mistakes and wrongs done to other people. For people raised in religion and in light of that universal ethic, it is especially important to keep in mind things like "do you want to be condemned?"; "do you want to be judged harshly?"; "do you want to have others scouring for sin in your life?"; "do you want people pointing out your faults and weaknesses?"; "do you want people to be quick to forgive you when you do something wrong?", etc. Simply put, that ethic should drive us to concentrate on ourselves first, before we look to other to help in that way (Matt. 7:1-5).

6. To love Joshua means we will want to obey him (John 14:15). To know what to obey, we must first know *him* and *his* teachings and no one else's (John 8:12, 31-32; 12:48; 13:13; 14:6 Matt. 23:8-12; 24:35). His teachings are readily available to us in the four gospel books in any Bible.

7. In order to obey Joshua's new command of "love one another as I have loved you", we must join with other disciples and help them

in real, daily life as we all serve God together as manifestations of His Family (Love means to value someone highly and to treat them with compassion and with selfless behavior). Our neighbors often choose not to love us back. What is the disciple's excuse? (Mark 10:28-30) (See also Acts 2:44-45 as an example of the teachings of Joshua about love lived out);

8. Serving God means we follow Joshua our Leader and Master/Teacher together, and we do the Greater Work of proclaiming Joshua's gospel in all manner of ways, making disciples and forming little flocks and cities on hills (groups/Families of people) (Matt. 5:14; 28:18-20; Mark 8:35; Luke 12:32); and we do the lesser work of helping each other with what is needed to live on this earth (providing food, shelter, and clothing)(Matt. 20:8; Luke 3:14). By this Life, we will demonstrate his living Way so that the world may know that we are his followers due to our love for one another and the unity we manifest (John 13:34-35; 17:20-21).

9. Eternal life is a state of being or existence which a person enters into through faith in our Father as revealed by Joshua; and remains in through faithfulness to God as given by Joshua of Nazareth in the four gospel books. (John 3:3-4, 5:24, 8:12, 12:48, 16:6, 17:3, Luke 7:50, Matt. 11:27

I offer this as a suggestion as a set of core beliefs. I would be glad to communicate with other disciples to refine or adjust that set of core beliefs.

To further bring unity and reduce division and conflict, we need one other thing. We need to have some basic guidelines for understanding Joshua's teachings in those four gospels.

I suggest the following. There are six basic types of sayings of Joshua, and I will list them in priority order.

First are his statements about His Father, His Father's character, His Father's ways, and His Father's desires. These statements are of highest priority for they are the primary reason Joshua came...to reveal the Creator of human beings and His desire for them. Since the Creator is a perfect Being that does not change, these statements do not change with time or with circumstance. They are absolute for the Creator is a Perfect Being who does not change His character or His will. None of the sayings of Joshua regarding the Father's nature are affected by time or culture or circumstances or experience.

Second are his statements about himself – who he is/was. Perhaps the most significant statement in this regard is his statement, "I am the way, the truth and the life..."

Third are his "didactic teachings." "Didactic" means, "intended to teach, or to improve morals by teaching." Another way to describe these saying are general, objective teachings that convey principles or concepts that are not bound by time or circumstances but apply to all people in all times and all circumstances. For example, he says, "You have heard that it was said, 'You shall not commit adultery'; but I say to you that everyone who looks at a woman with lust for her has already committed adultery with her in his heart." In fact, all his teachings in the Matt. 5 and Luke 6 are didactic teachings and thus clearly do not have some circumstantial qualification to them as they are stating ethical rules or value observations for human beings that apply to all people, times and places.

The teachings about his Father and himself and the didactic teachings should be considered primary and of first importance. In other words, the didactic teachings as well as his teachings about the Father ought to be the foundation on which what disciples seek unity.

The other sayings of Joshua – those which do not reveal his Father's nature, who Joshua is nor are didactic teachings - are secondary or of a lower priority and should NOT be used as necessary for unity.

The following three types of sayings should be understood THROUGH the didactic teachings or statements he gave. We will look at some example of applying this guideline below.

Fourth are Instructions that are given in a circumstance but have plain qualifiers in them that what he is saying applies to more than just the specific situation in which they were spoken, or that the instructions or principles he is giving will be relevant in the future.

Fifth are instructions to his disciples to do certain things at the time Joshua was living in Judea in the first century A.D. These instructions do not have application outside of that time or place or circumstance.

Sixth are observations statements about things happened at the time he spoke them. These statements seldom have relevance to us today.

So, to summarize, here is the suggested order of priority for understanding Joshua and His teaching:

1. Statements about His Father – His Father's character or his Father's desires for humanity;
2. Comments about himself – who he was and what his purpose was;
3. Ethical or moral or guidance teachings or principles regarding God to human or human to human relationships. These teachings have no temporal or circumstantial or cultural constraints;
4. Instructions to his followers that are given in a circumstance but have plain qualifiers in them that what he is saying applies to more than just the specific situation or which will be relevant *in the future*;
5. Specific instructions given to his first disciples that are constrained to a time or place or situation, generally to that time and event;

6. Mere circumstantial observations or statements.

Anytime a lesser priority saying that contains an instruction, such as a four or five, is addressed by a priority one or two or three teaching, the priority one or two or three teaching wins. In like manner, anytime a type five saying has one or more type four sayings clarifying it, the type four wins.

Let us provide some examples to clarify this suggested method of having a unified understanding of how to understand Joshua and thus foster and accomplish unity among disciples.

Please consider these sayings:

When they had approached Jerusalem and had come to Bethpage, at the Mount of Olives, then Jesus sent two disciples, saying to them, "Go into the village opposite you, and immediately you will find a donkey tied there and a colt with her; untie them and bring them to Me. If anyone says anything to you, you shall say, "The Lord has need of them," and immediately he will send them. (Matt. 21)

Here, Joshua gave an explicit instruction to his followers when he said, "Go into the village opposite you, and immediately you will find a donkey tied there and a colt with her; untie them and bring them to Me." Since this instruction only applies to the first disciples who were hearing Joshua say it, it is a type four saying. In other words, while Joshua did give his disciples an explicit instruction, that instruction is not intended to be kept by disciples in the future since its relevance was constrained to that circumstance.

Here is another example:

Then He poured water into the basin and began to wash the disciple's feet and to wipe them with the towel with which He was girded. So He came to Simon Peter. He said to Him, "Lord, do You wash my feet?" Jesus answered and said to him, "What I do you do not realize now, but you will understand hereafter." Peter said to Him, "Never shall You wash my feet!" Jesus answered him, "If I do not wash you, you have no part with Me." (John 13)

Joshua here nowhere gives a specific didactic teaching like, "disciples should wash one another's feet." Furthermore, the primary reason he was washing their feet was because their feet were dirty and of course to demonstrate humility and love. This is a good example of a type five saying.

Therefore, to say, "oh, Jesus commands that we ought to wash one another's feet" is not reasonable. However, because it is not reasonable does not mean that religious people don't use it to divide from each other. Of course, it *is* reasonable to say, based on that foot washing *example*, disciples ought to help/care for/serve one another. The context of the passage makes that entirely clear. The foot washing experience was merely a practicing of the new command.

Here is another example:

> These twelve Jesus sent out after instructing them: "Do not go in the way of the Gentiles, and do not enter any city of the Samaritans; but rather go to the lost sheep of the house of Israel. And as you go, preach, saying, "The kingdom of heaven is at hand." Heal the sick, raise the dead, cleanse the lepers, cast out demons. (Matt. 10)

Many religious people would like this instruction of Joshua to apply to all times, but that desire is erroneous.

First of all, after Joshua went back to be with the Father, the racial or religious people group concepts of "Jews or Gentiles or Samaritans" are irrelevant to his followers and thus are no longer relevant in the kingdom of God. People are people and disciples do not view people from flesh perspectives.

Furthermore, he plainly said, "the kingdom of heaven is at hand," obviously meaning the King is physically here; so while the King is here, let's do these miraculous works so people can know he is the King!

Therefore, this looks like a good candidate for a type five saying.

Most importantly, Joshua gave a teaching explicitly addressing miraculous healing that clarifies any confusion on this issue. Here is the saying in context:

> As He (Joshua) passed by, He saw a man blind from birth. And His disciples asked Him, "Rabbi, who sinned, this man or his parents, that he would be born blind?" Jesus answered, "It was neither that this man sinned, nor his parents; but it was so that the works of God might be displayed in him. We must work the works of Him who sent me as long as it is day; night is coming when no one can work. While I am in the world, I am the Light of the world. (John 9)

Here, Joshua tells what will happen in the future when he says, "We must work the works of Him who sent me *as long as it is day; night is coming when no one can work. While I am in the world, I am the Light of the world.*" Thus, this is a type four saying. Therefore, the type four saying needs to take precedence over all the type-five sayings people want to use to justify miraculous healings today.

It is also imperative that the things disciples of the truth believe represent reality. In this case, it is quite apparent given observation of reality that people are not physically healed at this time by the God that Joshua reveals. That is not to say that some unexplained healings do not occur, but inexplicable healings do not equal a "God healed him/her" event. How can I know this for sure? I can recognize this due to all of the many thousands of young children needing physical healings each day who don't get any such healing. Or the many thousands of sincere Christian adults who need physical healing each day to don't get any such healing. In other words, if God could physically heal even one genuinely suffering child/person, then He would heal them all!

In summary, it is vital that disciples find and build unity on type one through four sayings, in that order. We have to be very careful to *not* get dogmatic on type five or six sayings. We indeed would be foolish for insisting that a type-five or six saying needs to be considered essential for unity.

If the disciples cannot agree on a type one through four saying, I would suggest that we be cautious before making it an essential belief. The one test that must be applied is to make sure it represents reality. For example, if a person says, "well, I believe Joshua when he says, "If you ask me anything in My name, I will do it", their needs be a reality check, and the person needs to demonstrate that saying is real.

To ignore these warnings is to head right down the same road that the successful failure has taken—a path of loveless division.

Topical Importance Recognized for Unity

In the previous section, I suggested a way to sort out Joshua's sayings so that disciples could be in unity. It is important also to note that some issues or topics or concepts are more important than others. For example, from our existential viewpoint, entering into eternal Life (and thus avoid destroying myself) would be a top priority if I wanted to preserve my existence after death, whereas exactly how to pray would be a lesser priority.

Joshua made this point about importance and priority here in this saying:

Woe to you, bible teachers and religious leaders, hypocrites! For you tithe mint and dill and cumin, and have neglected the weightier provisions of the law: justice and mercy and faithfulness; but these are the things you should have done without neglecting the others. (Matt. 23)

As you can see, he taught that some things were more important than others; in this case, essential concepts that very much affect how people treat each other – "justice and mercy" – are more important than religious practices that don't have – or have minimal – ethical relevance.

Furthermore, he teaches that love (self-less behavior motivated by compassion) is the most important thing/truth/concept with which human beings ought to be concerned. He says the two most important commands from God that the Jews of his time got right are about love. Also, he only labeled one teaching for his disciples a "command," and the new command he gives to his disciples is love one another. He addresses the most critical concept of love over fifty times in the four gospels. If we cannot understand anything else about Joshua, his Father and how we ought to treat one another, other than love, then we are doing well!

So, in addition to unity being based on the Person and teachings of Joshua of Nazareth, this unity must be based on two critical topical areas within Joshua's instructions – God's character and the nature of love.

One of the reasons – perhaps the primary one - there is so much division among Christians is because they do not know God nor do they prioritize love (in fact, most don't have a proper understanding of love due to their not wanting to know). They "know" the contradictory "wrath and love god of the Bible," but they don't know the Creator/Father who Joshua alone revealed.

As this book has laid out the case, God is a God of love and is *not* a God of vengeance, wrath, bloodthirstiness or other such things as those. The God of love is the character of God that was revealed by The Light of the world. And it is *that* character that will facilitate love among those with faith.

In the next chapter, we will take a look at the concept of "destiny" and how it applies to us. Our love expressed and unity practiced in this life have a significant impact on our eternal destiny.

Chapter Summary:
- For followers of Joshua of Nazareth, the unity *he* asks for must start with our having him as our *only standard* (truly our Master) for knowing God and what God wants for people;
- The words of Joshua in the four "gospel books" of Matthew, Mark, Luke, and John are the *best*, most objective sources for knowing the historical Person of Joshua of Nazareth. Using anything else will increase the likelihood of unnecessary division;
- Disciples should also have a way to prioritize the sayings of Joshua in the four gospel books to further help us find unity and thus avoid division. My suggestion in priority order is:

o Statements about His Father – His Father's character or his Father's desires for humanity;
o Statements about himself – who he was and what his purpose was;
o Ethical or moral teachings or principles given in a teaching mode (non-circumstantial like his teachings in Matt. 5) regarding God to human or human to human relationships;
o Instructions to his followers that are given in a circumstance but have plain qualifiers in them or the context that what he is saying applies to more than just the specific situation or which will be relevant *in the future*;
o Specific instructions given to his first disciples that are constrained to a time or place or circumstance, generally to that time and event;
o Mere circumstantial observations or statements.

- It is essential to recognize the relative importance of Joshua's teachings and what is entirely clear is that practicing love is the highest teaching he gives;
- Without love and the unity associated with that love among the disciples, we have no witness to the people of this world and we thus we are failing at the most critical aspect of being disciples.

43
SOME FINAL THOUGHTS

Opening Questions:
- What is the best worldview, or stated another way, what worldview best takes into account the reality we experience each day?
- Does to be a loving person mean not speaking truth that will offend some people?
- Doesn't "unloving" mean to refuse to try and love people?
- Doesn't each person have real needs and shouldn't pursuing the resolution to those needs be an essential motivation in our lives?
- Isn't it correct that self-pride and fear and selfishness guide most people?
- If the solution identified in this book is good and right, should he not be embraced and understanding him diligently pursued?

So, did we answer the questions posed at the beginning of the book?

Let's take a look.
- Is it reasonable to believe I evolved from hydrogen gas?
- Can mere physical chemicals reasonably account for my ability to know right from wrong, or to know and experience forgiveness?
- Is love merely an emotion?
- What is the purpose of human life?
- What is the purpose of my life?
- What is truly important in life?
- What am I as a human being?
- How do I value things and why?

- What am I truly living for and is it actually valuable?
- If there is a higher form of love and can I experience a life where I give and receive that love with others on a daily basis?
- Does Christianity genuinely represent God well?
- If Christianity is wrong, what do I do about my guilt?

Is it reasonable to believe I evolved from hydrogen gas?

    No, of course not.

Can mere physical chemicals reasonably account for my ability to know right from wrong, or to know and experience forgiveness?

    No, of course not.

Is love merely an emotion?

    As we have seen, no, it is much more.

What is the purpose of human life?

    The purpose of human life is to learn to love the One who gave us Life and to help other people find this Father who loves us and doesn't want us to destroy ourselves or others. Once we find Him and have taken care of all our primary and real needs through loving one another, we pursue the purpose of creating useful and helpful and beautiful things.

What is the purpose of my life?

    It is the same general purpose of any person's life as stated previously, but you get to choose all the details! The purpose of any disciple's life is to bring the Truth that matters to others; to care about what is true and right according to The Light and "fight" for it in this life, and to serve the One we love by loving and thus serving others.

What is truly important in life?

    People. Not money, but people. Not things, but people. Not "careers" but people. Not people's kingdoms, but people. Not education, but people. Not _____ , but people. Not self, but others.

What am I as a human being?

    We are beings with a metaphysical or spiritual component(s) (soul, mind, spirit) as well as a physical component (body) and we are beings created to love, to seek what is true, to do what is right and to create beautiful, good and helpful things.

How do I value things and why?

    Well, that depends upon what Standard you use to make such judgments. Whatever you do, be honest with yourself!

What am I truly living for and is it valuable?

    That, dear reader, only you can answer, but the chances are incredibly high that:

- You do not love your Father back;
- You are not listening to the One who wants to be your Master;
- You do not love other people except those from whom you get something back;

Instead, you are living a life bound in self-pride and fear and selfishness, and you are only willing to be civil and kind to those from whom you get what you want.

Is there is a higher form of love and can I experience a life where I give and receive that love with others on a daily basis?

Yes, there is, as we have seen. The only thing keeping you from experiencing that higher form of love with others on a daily basis is you and others.

Does Christianity genuinely represent God well?

No. The successful failure has been laid out before you. What are you going to do with the knowledge or understanding that you might have gained?

If Christianity is wrong, what do I do about my guilt?

The question is answered. Instead of asking for forgiveness from the love-wrath god or one of the many "christs" or "jesus" of Christianity, turn in genuine faith to your Father whom the Son reveals and sincerely ask for forgiveness.

This book is attempting to bring a sea change in many people's thinking. It is trying to make a paradigm shift away from people believing and practicing religion – or those who reject God's existence based on the Hasty Generalization fallacy applied to Christianity - *to people having faith in the historical person of Joshua of Nazareth and thus starting to live by love for truth and rightness.*

Many who read this book will claim that I the author am not acting in love by writing this book. Others will say the book is downright "hateful." Some will say this because their worldview is relativism and specifically they don't believe any truth can be known about God-things and thus "no one has a right" to make "negative" god statements or correct theological contradictions. Others will say this because I rebuke their cherished religious beliefs and practices. (Of course it is not me ultimately, but the One from whom I have learned.) Still, others will be deeply offended at some of the truths contained in this book due to personal conviction over wrongs committed or erroneous views held. I hope that some will accede to the realities in this book and start the new Life.

For most, they don't care about what is true—they have willingly or unknowingly committed to trying to live or understand life primarily through their emotions. Many labor under the belief that no creator exists to inform us about our existence. Still others are deceived in thinking their religion, and its doctrine represents the Creator.

Their reasoning (ironic that they use reason, but only when it serves to validate their emotional or arbitrary views) continues that since no truth exists about God stuff, a person who makes negative or corrective statements about God stuff is hateful. Of course, a slight mix of positive thinking philosophy to their relativism might contribute to that judgment as well.

Those who believe that are wrong.

I know that because "the Truth" tells me so, as does reason, logic, and observation. The religious folks might have bits and pieces of truth as part of their worldview, but it ultimately fails and leads them to darkness and self-condemnation and destruction since they reject the Life or insist on holding onto a "christ" of their own making, which "christ" does not bring Life, love or change. That is the clever sleight of hand the Christians use to make the successful failure.

We have looked at relativism in a previous section so we will not rehash it here. Suffice it to say that expressing different views on existential, spiritual, origin or other such beliefs is not "unloving." To be clear, *to be "unloving" means I refuse to love other people*—I refuse to value others and to act selflessly based on compassion towards other people.

To claim the book or author is "unloving" is irrational and redefining love to something it is not, as we have seen. Correcting what one believes is an erroneous view or belief is also not unloving as we saw in the tolerance chapter. To believe that correcting what one considers error is an "unloving act" is an erroneous belief. Profoundly deluded, dark and truthless people are taking it even farther and saying, "If you disagree with me and my views, then you are a racist or a bigot or an evil person." Sadly, many U.S. citizens at this point – of course including those who take some Christian label – abide in these false beliefs.

Thus, they are lost and in darkness.

The Big Picture: Needs and Change

Ultimately, this book is about changing people's lives. Taking on religion is not an easy task – I don't get a lot of "atta boy's"! As I have said several times in this book, there are many well-intentioned and relatively kind Christians. As I have also said, there are also well-intentioned and kind Muslims and Jews and Buddhists and Agnostics and Atheists, etc. But as we have seen, being a relatively kind and well-intentioned person is not what is involved in changing peoples" lives—not my life, not your life, not our neighbor's life, etc.

What changes people's lives is when an individual sees a need that penetrates into the fear, self-pride, selfish cage and has the power to make us want to get out. In other words, our correctly understanding reality and our needs has the potential to change our lives.

Whether we see how we are negatively impacting our children with certain behavior; or whether we lose someone we love; or whether we see something that is wrong due to it adversely affecting us or someone we care about; or whether we get a report from a physician saying we have cancer. Those are the types of things that generally have the potential to cause transformation in someone's life. We go with truth, and we see a need and start on the road to find the way out or to find the solution.

This book has revealed several vital needs, but it is up to the reader to choose to do something about them.

- A need revealed is the need to reject that which is false and commit to understanding reality through reason and logic and observation instead of emotions, or erroneous religious or scientific dogma, e.g., naturalistic evolution is true.

- Another need revealed is the need to overcome fear and self-pride and selfishness – to escape the cage - and thus truly love and help others.

- Another need revealed is the need to have the courage to leave self-serving groups of people (e.g. "the church') and instead start to make real changes in our lives and the lives of others and live a unified, collective life.

- Another need has been revealed to live differently than the masses – to practice love and thus live together as harmonious groups/communities of people, unified in their faith in Joshua of Nazareth.

The Need revealed in this book is to, by faith, love our Father back and get to honestly know Him through the real, historical Messenger He sent!

Do *you*, dear reader, see any of these needs in *you* or *your* life?

Joshua said it this way to the people of his day, "Repent, for the Kingdom of God is at hand." The concept of "repentance" has been pretty much hopelessly associated with wrong religion, but it is a useful and necessary concept. Here is what is required to repent:

- I see myself for what I am – a human being listening to the darkness that is in me much of the time, as well as the darkness of others;

- I see that I am in the cage of self-pride and fear and selfishness and how I have hurt, neglected, dishonored, used, abused and ignored people due to my self-made cage—how I have not even come close to living by love;

- I understand that I deserve consequences - condemnation and punishment (justice) - for all my wrongdoings and bad attitudes.

If I can come to that state of heart – knowing the above points to be true of myself – then I am in a position to repent. To repent means to feel genuine remorse as a result of seeing the things above, and to want to change as a result.

Repentance is the best time to transfer one's faith out of ourselves or false religious constructs (for example the many "christs" of Christian religion) or out of money or material security, and into Joshua of Nazareth and the Father HE reveals in order to accomplish the fruit of repentance. What is the fruit of repentance? It is a changed life—a truly changed life, not the religious version of giving up some "sin," only to remain in my cage of fear, self-pride, and selfishness and thus living no differently than people who don't know The Light.

The solution to the problems identified in this book is, like most things valuable, simple to understand IF you are looking to the right person to understand things and you really, genuinely want to know.

The solution is straightforward—choose the best leader for your life! And yes, "life" is higher and greater than "career", "job", "work", "religion", "church", etc. And no, you cannot remain part of this world – meaning you cannot remain in your cage of fear, self-pride, and selfishness and thus refuse to live by love and stay silent at all the wrong and ignore it – and at the same time follow The Light.

Joshua defines a successful follower of his as a person who listens' well to him and thus does what he teaches. Simple to understand, right? Remember the title of this book? Do you have more understanding now about the two standards to define and understand the terms "successful" and "failure"?

You can break that large success into different areas or domains that he covers in his teachings. Joshua has given his instructions priority through their repetitiveness and their emphasis in his recorded sayings. I propose only a few main areas of focus for success or failure.

First is how we do as human beings caring about what is true. After all, if we are following the One who said, "I am the truth," then surely we care about what is true! Truth would have to do primarily with beliefs and determining correct versus false beliefs and concepts. Caring about what is true is not restricted to the existential, ethical, metaphysical or spiritual realms, but to all areas or domains in life like politics or science or the lesser work we do. How well are we doing using observation, reason, and logic consistently and fearlessly to find truth? Once we see reality and we determine it will cost us something to proclaim it or reveal it or live by it, what do we do? Are we part of the multitudes of cowards unwilling to go where the truth leads them, or are we willing to become one of the few courageous change agents this world desperately needs?

Second, how we do as human beings living out the concept he taught and clarified called "love." That is to say, how well are we doing loving other people as Joshua defines love? If we are actually followers of the Light of the world, then we will love everyone, *and* we will be loved back by other true disciples. This sharing of true love will manifest itself in a collective-together Life – Families of his followers living together in peace and harmony - thus displaying the city on the hill and the little flocks of which he speaks.

Third, how we do as human beings caring about what is right. I am using "right" as primarily ethical and thus having to do with behavior—are we concerned with good versus bad behavior; are we personally trying to live rightly, and are we trying to help other's live rightly. Are we hungering and thirsting for that which is right? Or are we comfortable in our selfish cage? By the way, hungering and thirsting for what is right will *not* include violence as a means to achieve what is right.

Last is our eternal destiny—where do we send ourselves when our bodies die and do we get to retain the love we developed and experienced with others over this lifetime? Did we enter into what Joshua identified as Eternal Life and did we remain in that Life while we lived our lives in this world? Did we respond to our Creator/Father and His love for us? Did his love transform us and motivate us to love Him back and to love others? Did our faith and love bring us out of our cage so that we could work to change the wrong we experience along the Way? Simply put, did our faith enable us to improve and become better human beings and thus become change agents in this dark world?

One More Look: The Problem and the Solution...Family

Let us briefly paint the picture of the Solution one more time.

There is a Kingdom with a King, and that King wants his subjects to love one another. He said it this way:

A new command I give to you, that you *love one another as I have loved you*, for this is how the people of the earth will know that you are my followers, but only IF you love one another. (John 13:34-35)

Our Creator made us human beings as social beings, which is to say we like being around other people with whom we share views and interests. This social desire is right and natural, but for the followers of the Light, it is essential. Not by force or legal compulsion or guilt or wrongly motivated obedience, but by love.

The author of one of the gospels, Luke, recorded what he saw as the first disciples decided to do what Joshua said and love one another:

And all those who had believed were together and had all things in common; and they began selling their property and possessions and were sharing them with all, as anyone might have need. (Acts 2:44-45)

The behavior of those first disciples recorded in Acts 2:44-45 was merely a response to the King's new command to love one another. Due to faith and love, it was a fulfillment of this teaching of his:

Truly I say to you, there is no one who has left house or brothers or sisters or mother or father or children or farms, for My sake and the gospel's sake, but that he will receive a hundred times as much now in the present age, houses and brothers and sisters and mothers and children and farms, along with persecutions; and in the age to come, eternal life. (Mark 10)

Those described came into faith in The Light; they understood love in a way they never had before. They saw how empty and foolish it was to be selfish with material things; how empty it was to allow fear to destroy attempts to love others; and they responded accordingly. They chose to actually love one another thus it was in a "rubber-meets-the-road" fashion.

The same needs to happen today, as it has needed to happen in every generation in every culture on this earth since The Light went back Home.

Why isn't it?

This is the judgment, that the Light has come into the world, and men loved the darkness rather than the Light, for their deeds were evil. (John 3)

Because lawlessness is increased, most people's love will grow cold. (Matt. 24:12)

What Joshua mean's by "lawlessness" is simply another name for truth or ethical relativism or people having no standards of right or wrong, good or bad, true or false. As we have seen, this "lawlessness" is what is happening in the U.S., and around the world for that matter.

When human beings turn away from the Creator of their operating system (which operating system includes their mind and conscience), the primary effect is *fear*. Just like when a young child is lost, they experience fear—their parents provide them with security, and they get disconnected from their parents and don't know how to get back to them.

The same is true of adults; it is just that self-pride gets in the way of admitting one is lost and the fear associated with that lost-ness. The general flow of things is as follows:

1. People are getting more and more *disconnected from even their Father's ethical desires*;
2. This disconnection causes them *not to know what is right or wrong, good or bad, true or false*;
3. This causes them *not to know how to live life* – what is valuable, what decisions to make, how to view various things, how to behave, how to properly treat and relate to other people - and thus they sense (if they have not destroyed their conscience) they are getting *more and more lost*;
4. This understanding at some level that *they are getting lost causes fear to increase;*
5. *Fear causes love to decrease, diminish or stop – to "grow cold."*

This lost-ness and growing cold are what is happening and where the U.S. culture is at this time.

If those who claim to follow the One who defeated death to prove who he was do not live out the new command – if we refuse to love one another truly - then there is no hope left for people without faith. Without manifestations of the city on a hill and the little flock, there is *no true witness* to the reality of The Light and our Father.

Disciples of The Light *must* come together and **be** the Family that the world needs to see. If we call ourselves some follower of his, and yet we refuse to leave the things the world says are necessary or valuable and thus ignore the One who informs us clearly about what is important and valuable, then we have no reasonable basis to believe that we are actually his followers.

Families must start coming together, just as described in Acts 2 above, and just as it has happened through history. Here again are the fundamental dynamics of how it should be happening.

- Someone repents and places their faith in Joshua;
- That person starts to look for other disciples to join with and share his Life with;
- Disciples who connect agree to what the best situation will be regarding who leaves what and goes where concerning living with or in direct proximity to each other;
- Disciples use the resources they have to support one another and work together in all things;
- One disciple grows to two, then to three, etc. until Families are manifest;

- These groups of disciples live together daily as Family and support one another and care for one another as they do both the Greater work (bringing people to our Father and speaking the truth to all we encounter) and the Lesser work (supporting our physical needs in this world);
- The love that we have for one another will be our witness to this dark and dying world. People should look at us and say, "wow, as much as I disagree with their God beliefs, I cannot deny that they really and actually care for one another—they do exemplify how human beings ought to live."

It is that simple. Please note, I did not say "easy," but simple.

As I have been saying throughout this book, we are either part of the problem or part of the solution. We are either primarily givers or primarily takers. We either have the correct Leader, or we do not. We are either living by true love or merely expressing a lesser type of love occasionally when we "feel like it" or we get something or someone from it.

The fact is that Christians seek to get things from God. They want "blessings" from God, and they usually mean material things. They ask God for this and for that, never thinking about the fact that they ought to be seeking to give to God. Not material things, for He does not need that, but instead, our lives and our love-motivated service and devotion.

As we have seen, the successful failure has its leaders, and they tell the people, "we will do God's work for you, and all you need to do is support us (give us money and material things) to comply with what God wants of you." This "we follow God for you" view is both false as well as a critical part of the successful failure. The simple truth is that if a person love's God, they will be compelled by that love to serve God the way that Joshua teaches God's wants. And how does God want to be served? By first loving each other and being His called out people living for Him and not for the things the world considers valuable – to be part of a Joshua Family. Every person is an integral part of a Family of disciples of Joshua, and we each have our roles, talents, and responsibilities in making that expression of the Kingdom of God work.

So, why do Christians have so many things wrong about the One they proclaim as their God? It would be one thing to have a few relatively minor false understandings about Joshua of Nazareth, but this book documents that Christians have most of his most essential concepts wrong or they are not willing to do what he says. Oh, they are eager to sing about it and talk about it, but they are not willing to **do** it.

Joshua's life, words, and deeds are readily available in the four small books named after the assumed authors of Matthew, Mark, Luke, and John. His teachings in those small four books are much easier to understand than almost any of the Bible authors and the other sixty-two books in the protestant Bible. There can be only one reasonable answer as to why Christians get so much wrong about his Person and teachings, and that reason is that *they do not want to get to know him - they would much rather "do religion" in his name.* Why?

For whoever wishes to save his life will lose it, but whoever loses his life for My sake, he is the one who will save it. (Luke 9:24)

Here is the answer again:

1. The real, historical Joshua of Nazareth says that "people love the darkness rather than the light," and "narrow and difficult is the way," so few see their need to begin with. Instead, most are happy and comfortable in their cage of fear, self-pride, and selfishness. Most are content with their lives in this world, and their religion is merely a shallow social function or a form of spiritual life insurance - this describes the vast majority of Christians and Biblians.

2. Those who do make some sincere effort to get to know the real, historical Joshua of Nazareth will come to a point where they will sense, at some level, the truth of this saying/truth: "Those who want to keep their life will lose it, while those who seek to lose their life for my sake, shall find Life". The vast majority say "no, I am not going to go to that "extreme" to follow that Jesus'. So, they turn away from him and settle into a form of the successful failure and make up a "christ" or "jesus" to serve them. They join the others who never fully committed themselves to the real, historical Joshua of Nazareth and his teachings, and together, they make up Christian religion in his name.

That religion is the successful failure that now operates in some form in most of the earth.

Please recall the beginning of this book when I talked about houses with different lights. Here is that content again:

The purpose of my previous book was to take the lamp out of the closet and put the lamp on the table in the room so people could see by it. However, people are not making it into the room to see the lamp and the things in the room, but instead, are being kept in or led into the house next door because this house has a really cool light that is very attractive. The lamp in the first house – the life-giving one that can help people see clearly – is a pure, bright, clear, warm light. Also, the first house has many mirrors in it, and the bright, clear light helps people see what is in the mirrors. It can be a bit disconcerting since it shows things in the room – including the people - as we are. People who stay in this house grow and blossom just like plants and flowers exposed to the sun.

The light in the house next door, however, is made of many colors and flashes and pulses…a lot like the lights in Las Vegas! The house was built on purpose right next to the house with the bright, clear light.

Next to both houses is a lot of darkness…a cold, chilling darkness. Many are standing in that dark, cold lot because they went into the house with multi-colored lights and experienced the hypocrisy and lovelessness of those who dwell there rightfully ran out. Now they are justly frightened of houses with lights and so they are not willing to go into the house with the pure, bright, clear, warm light. So, they stay in the dark, cold lot which causes their spirits and hearts to get cold as well.

The purpose of the house with the many colored lights is to draw people away from the house with the bright clear, warm light. The lights in the Las Vegas house distorts things and makes things in the room somewhat difficult to see – fuzzy and unclear. There are very few mirrors in this house, and the ones there distort favorably the image of the people looking into it. This is very attractive to people, so as they journey towards the house with the bright, clear light – which light can help them, but which light shows them things they don't or may not want to see – they are easily distracted and drawn by the cool, multi-colored alternative. The vast majority end up on the house with the flashy light and stay there. Unfortunately, one of the effects of staying in this house is that people's spirits wither and die there.

This book is about the house with the flashy, cold lights and how it is different than the house with the bright, clear, warm Light. Thus, the purpose of the book is to describe the flashy-lighted house and to expose its true nature, and by revealing its nature and purpose, to encourage people to go over to the house with the bright clear, warm light.

For those with ears to hear and eyes to see, let them hear and see!

Chapter Summary:

- The opening questions in the preface of this book were satisfactorily answered;
- The real, historical person of Joshua of Nazareth offended people with the truths that he spoke. We who follow him will also offend people with the facts that we speak;
- It is not un-loving to speak what is true if it is done to sincerely enlighten or help people and not to humiliate or degrade them;
- We all have several essential needs that we should try, with all our heart, to find answers to and to change first ourselves;
- People are turning away from even ethical systems derived from - or contained in - religious beliefs. This turning away is and will continue to be very destructive;

- Families of the followers of Joshua of Nazareth are the most critical outward part of the solution – "your kingdom come, your will be done on earth as it is in heaven" - and must be engaged in to help other people avoid destroying themselves;
- The house with the flashy, cold lights and the cold dark lot must be forsaken/left/abandoned for the house with the bright, clear, warm Light.

44
OUR CHOSEN DESTINY

Opening Questions:

- If we have been given a choice regarding our after death destiny, and we refuse to consider the options seriously, are we not to blame if our after death experience does not go well?
- If a person is brought before a judge due to wrong-doing, should not the judge bring justice?
- Is the most critical concept of love about abstaining from doing bad or wrong things, or is it partaking in doing good and right things?
- If given this choice: "Come, enjoy Disney World today and for the next month"; or "come, work on your faults and weaknesses, speak truth that makes you unpopular, and actually love people you find hard to love, and you will get a reward in thirty years much more valuable than a Disney World experience". What choice is the vast majority going to choose?

As we noted earlier, it should greatly trouble a person's conscience to hear it stated that the after-death experience of Adolf Hitler and Mother Teresa will be the same, or said another way, that there will be no ultimate justice for Adolf Hitler and no ultimate reward for Mother Teresa. Even if that after death experience is the annihilation of their soul/conscience, it would be the same experience and thus equal or the same. Therefore, if that belief is correct, there is no life accountability for how human beings live their lives. One person could spend their life selflessly helping other people, while another could spend their life hurting other people and their end would be the same.

Indeed if you are prone to using and abusing other people, that view would be attractive and encourage you to go with the darkness that is in you. In like manner, if you have a predisposition to do good to other people, yet you believe that at the end of your life there will be no reward for all that effort that might well discourage you from doing the right things you are doing, especially if you struggle with the right motivation (love) while you are doing them. Either way, the belief that there is nothing after physical death but the annihilation of your soul will at a minimum reduce hope and motivation for good intentioned or behaving people, and at its worst, will enable and encourage those who like the evil they practice.

Of course, this view is not an argument for God's existence. However, it does address the human operating system that we have, and it does suggest that the One who designed and made our operating system is concerned about the attributes He created. In other words, why give people a conscience, for example, if not to use it? And why would our conscience inform us not to do what is wrong or bad if the Creator of that conscience was not concerned with wrong or bad behavior?

There are these concepts called sins of commission and sins of omission. They are valid concepts. Sins of commission are things we DO that we should not do. Examples are to cheat others and lie for selfish gain and take more than we should and DO various things caused by our fear and self-pride and selfishness that harms other people. The sins of commission are easy to see and are typically not a big control problem for most people. The law and rules are all about deterring sins of commission or restraining and punishing wrong behavior.

Sins of omission are the things we *don't do* that we ought to do. For example, if I see a person injured on the ground, I ought to help that person. Or, as another example, if I know someone is planning to do something wrong, I ought to attempt to stop them. Or, as an older person, I have a house with two or three empty bedrooms that would be a blessing to some needy souls, but I don't even think about that. Or, as a final example, if I know that a person believes something that is harmful – say they believe that using violence or force is a right or proper way to achieve a goal or objective – then I ought to try and have a discussion with that person to try and show them why that belief is wrong. The same is true with all beliefs, including God beliefs or existential beliefs or spiritual beliefs or religious beliefs or political beliefs. As a follower of the One who says, "I am the truth," we disciples address error that hides the Light or pushes people away from him. That is the purpose of this book.

The greatest sin is ignoring a Father who loves us. Here is a little story in that regard.

There once was a dad who truly loved his daughter. He decided to build her a beautiful play set outside in the backyard and to surprise her.

So, this dad carefully labored for two weeks to create this beautiful play set. He and his wife did not have much money, so this playset was the most costly gift they ever gave to their daughter. The day came when the dad and mom were going to show their daughter the playset. They put a blindfold on her and led her out the back door past the fence which usually hid the new play set. The dad took off the blindfold and said, "look, my beloved daughter, what I build for you." The daughter looked at the beautiful playset and said to her dad, "dad, I don't believe you built this for me—I wonder who put it there'. How do you think that made the dad feel? The dad put much effort into that gift only to have his daughter not believe he could do it nor believe it was from him. So it is with our heavenly Father and the children who refuse to believe He made them and all the capacities He gave us to have useful and meaningful lives and experiences.

At the end of the day – or at the end of this book's read – where do you the reader stand? Was this just an intellectual endeavor that will never get past your head to your heart? Will you fight against the truths clearly explained and documented in this book to justify your current beliefs, religion, traditions or lifestyle?

If you read or saw the Lord of the Rings series, remember Gandalf's saying to Frodo when, in the caverns of Moria, Frodo said, "I wish the Ring had never come to me. I wish none of this had happened." and Gandalf responded, "So do all who live to see such times, but that is not for them to decide. All we have to decide is what to do with the time that is given us." There is much truth in Gandalf's saying, and that saying applies to this book. You have been given the opportunity to "look" at something important and perhaps disturbing, and perhaps you are saying, "I wish I had never read this book." If that is your thought, I would respond, "So do most who have the courage to seek that which is most important, but what you must decide now is what you are going to do with the truth and time that is given to you?'

We are accountable to our Creator for what we choose to do with the life he gave us. He lets us freely choose what we do with that life and thus our destiny. We are accountable to the conscience He has given us. We are accountable to the truths that the Creator gave through His only begotten Son, and we are accountable to how well we used reason to find answers. In a sense, we are not accountable to Him, but instead accountable to our conscience and the truths He gave through His Messenger. Yes, He designed the system with its components in the two realms in which we currently live and will enter when we physically die. It is an automatic accountability system. We will stand before the Creator's appointed Judge, and the Judge will review our life choices - our thoughts, our decisions, and our behavior and show us the destiny we choose with those choices.

But since the truths were already given – and the programming of the human conscience was implemented and given to nearly every human being ever born – the Judge will merely point out the facts of the overall life choices we made and our associated behavior. Once we transition into the spirit realm when our bodies die – that dimension where the Creator and His Messenger/Judge exist - many will have a powerful urge to stay in the denial and delusion they choose during their life on the earth.

That will not be an option.

Nothing will be hidden from the Judge.

Self-justifications will not stand.

Excuses will be swept away in a torrent of clarity of truth.

Truth and reality will be perfect and clear at that time. That is why he said, "*there will be weeping and gnashing of teeth*" on the context of understanding reality and judgment. The weeping represents people who finally see what they traded for eternal Life. The gnashing of teeth represents the anger of those who still refuse to acknowledge reality and remain self-justified in defending their wrong life. Both represent those who choose Disney world (the equivalent of most religious organizations and their selfish, entertainment-oriented experience) over true Life.

In a nutshell, Christians do not listen to Joshua of Nazareth well if at all, so from that most critical perspective, they and the religious system they create, maintain and proclaim as a substitute for actually following The Light, are a failure. With all their success according to what the world considers valuable, Christianity and the Christians that make it up at this time in history are ultimately a failure. Without being the salt of the earth…without being a light for people to see by—by not caring about what is true and right according to the One they call "their god"—most importantly, by rejecting the correct definition and meaning of love and substituting empty, money-pursuing, shallow lives, they are sadly and in truth, a failure.

What might the final conversations "look like" for those who reject the Light and their conscience?

The Final Conversation: Christian or Religious Version

For most, they will not have a good answer to the primary question the Judge will ask, "Why did you ignore me, not care about what I said was true and right, and refuse to live a life characterized by love as I defined that most important concept"?

But Lord, I was deceived by religious leaders, and that is why I ignored you and did not live a life of love.

And he will say, "You had easy access to my words and teachings for many years, but you choose to listen to other voices so you could justify your life of bondage to self-pride and fear and selfishness, and thus your life of darkness and lovelessness."

But Lord, I had the Bible and tried to live by the Bible.

"Who asked you to look to this book to know me or follow me? I certainly did not. Instead, I said plainly and many times, "Follow *me*" and "*I am* the way, the truth and the life." That book recorded that my Father said, "This is my beloved Son in whom I am well pleased, listen to *him*," and "him" is *not* "the Bible." The Bible you had even had my words in red letters, thus setting them apart, but you ignored me just the same.

But Lord, I did a lot of good things in your name...

"Actually, you only spent seven percent of your waking hours of your life helping people and most of that in relatively shallow ways by giving them things instead of helping them in more meaningful ways. And even if you spent fifty-one percent of your life doing your religious good deeds, you still ignored me and refused to truly love others and refused to fight for what is true and right as I asked you to. You gave cheap, worthless things out of your abundance. You never even came close to thinking about laying down your life for your friends because you were too busy thinking about yourself and living for money, material things and pleasure and entertainment."

But lord...

"I am truly sorry for you, but you must experience the consequences of your life choices, even as you held others to accountability in the life you were given. Wouldn't you agree that is only just and fair?"

But I heard about your mercy, Lord, please grant me mercy now...

"You had my love, mercy, and forgiveness available to you for your whole life, and yet you rejected me and thus you did not show mercy, love or compassion to others except when you perceived you got something out of it. Do you want to see the video again?'

No...please, not again...please lord...

"Your destiny was always in your hands, and you could choose it all throughout the life you were given. You choose darkness and death instead of light and Life—you choose to reject reason and the truth it would have led you to unless it served your selfish purposes. You will now need to experience the consequences of your choices. I am truly sorry; I never knew you because you choose never to want to get to know me. You substituted that stupid book you called the Bible and many other voices for my Fathers words and truths as I spoke them."

But lord...(some angry yelling vulgarities and cursing, some weeping uncontrollably)

"I never knew you because you rejected my invitations to get to know me. Depart from me you who made up your own rules instead of listening to my voice and my Way—you who called evil "good" and good "evil'; you who redefined my most crucial concept given to humanity, love; you who would do anything except genuinely love other people as I asked."

Dear Christian or religious person, you have a choice. Continue in the darkness of loveless religion and the darkness of its confusion and hatred for that which is true. Or turn away from your loveless life and your hatred of the One who calls himself "the Truth," and instead, find Life! You can continue in the falsehoods of the successful failure, or you can start to love truth and listen to the One who says, "I am the truth." You can continue in the destiny of death and destruction you have chosen for yourself by virtue of your participating in the counterfeit and thus your rejection of the Light, OR you can enter into Life and love and start to follow the Light of the world—you can become part of the solution instead of being part of the problem!

The Final Conversation: Non-Theist Version

For most, they will not have a good answer to the primary question the Judge will ask, "Why did you ignore me, not care about what I said was true and right, and refuse to live a life characterized by love as I defined that most important concept"?

> But god, I saw what those people who said they represented you said and did, and it was wrong and they were hypocrites, and that is why I ignored you and did not live a life of love.

And he will say, "When others you encountered in life acted hypocritically you did not reject what their stated standard was. For example, do you remember when you were mistreated by a physician once, and as a result, you read the Hippocratic oath? Do you remember reading that oath? It said in part: "To hold my teacher in this art equal to my own parents; to make him partner in my livelihood; when he is in need of money to share mine with him; to consider his family as my own brothers, and to teach them this art, if they want to learn it, without fee or indenture..."? Do you remember realizing that physicians are practicing hypocrisy regarding the oath they took? You did not reject the author, Hippocrates, or his principles as false or as not worth listening to, did you?"

> No, God, but...

"Furthermore, you had easy access to my words and teachings for many years, but you choose to listen to other voices so you could justify your life of bondage to self-pride and fear and selfishness, and thus your life of darkness and lovelessness."

> But God, you did not provide any evidence as to your existence...

"How many times did you look in a mirror? When you were a child, you understood that machines needed a designer/creator—that they did

415

not just happen. You would never have believed that a computer's hardware created the software. When you were an adult, there were many times that you wondered about important concepts in your life like love, forgiveness, right and wrong and justice and at your deepest level you knew that those things needed a sufficient cause to account for their existence— you knew they were not physical, but you refused to "go there" because of the cage you choose to exist in."

But God…(a bunch of lame excuses)

"Remember that time you were in the car and your dad, the driver, had a heart attack and you were headed right for the train at the railroad crossing, and how you prayed, 'Oh, God, if you are real, please save us.' Why did you call out to me in that situation? If you were honest, it was because you didn't want to cease to exist. And yet after that, you ignored the obvious and made life's most important decisions with no thought to life consequences or your existence. I offered to you a way to not only continue to exist but to experience a much better existence, but you rejected my offer."

But God…(a bunch of lame excuses)

"I am truly sorry for you, but you must experience the consequences of your life choices, even as you held others to accountability in the life you were given. Wouldn't you agree that is only just and fair?"

But I heard about your mercy, Lord, please grant me mercy now…

"You had my love, mercy, and forgiveness available to you for your whole life, and yet you rejected it and thus you did not show mercy, love or compassion to others except when you perceived you got something out of it. Do you want to see the video again?"

No…please, not again…please God…

"Your destiny was always in your hands, and you could choose it all throughout the life you were given. You choose darkness and death instead of light and Life—you choose to reject reason and the truth it would have led you to unless it served your selfish or self-justification purposes. You will now need to experience the consequences of your choices. I am truly sorry; I never knew you because you choose to believe that which was unreasonable. You substituted science for the more important truths of human life like love, forgiveness, justice, and compassion, and thus you choose the path of self-deception—you learned to like it in your cage."

Dear non-theist. Just because at some point in history the people did not believe the earth was a sphere does not mean that it was not. In like manner, just because you think that the force of evolution has created all things you experience does not mean it is true. While I may not convince you that the facts and evidence all around us call for a designer sufficient to create human beings and all their aspects/qualities, I should be able to convince you of the non-physical reality and importance of reason and forgiveness, for example.

You have many legitimate grievances towards religious people and Christians and their beliefs and practices. In many cases, you have done well in pointing out their hypocrisy, contradictions, and wasteful practices. At some point, however, you would do well to make sure you are judging the religious people with the same diligence and standard that you judge yourself.

At the end of the day, we all are living for something—we all have some purpose that drives our behavior, decisions, and work. Some purposes are nobler than others. Most live for money, material things and themselves, and that is not a noble life. As we have seen, we are either part of the problem or part of the solution to the world's problems, of our neighbor's problems, and of our relationship problems. We are either living selflessly and helping others, or we are living selfishly and only assisting others from whom we get something in return.

We can know what a well-lived life looks like for we regularly make judgments about that matter. The question we must ask ourselves is what about me? Can I rise about the selfish life? Can I make a difference – a positive impact – on people's lives that I touch or influence? Can I help change people's existential destiny? Can I follow, and bring others to follow, the Perfect Leader? What motivates me to make such an effort? It is challenging to swim against popular sentiment, against our selfish nature, and against those who seek to keep an unjust status quo or to bring falsehood and wrongful contention.

For those who respond to The Light, who hear his voice, who make him their Leader and thus change and start to live according to HIS principles, there is one more conversation of note.

A Most Beautiful Conversation

Joshua: Hi Rianna, so good to see you in fullness! You have done well!

Disciple: But Master, I failed in so many ways...

Joshua: That is OK. What matters is your heart to try, and you did, consistently try due to your faith. I don't care about what you consider your failures; I care about your efforts, your commitment, your perseverance, your faithfulness.

Disciple: Really? (Rianna starts to brighten.) I don't think I had much faith—I often focused on the failures because I saw so much need and I wanted to help people, but despite my efforts, it seemed no one would listen.

Joshua: I understand. I see things, Rianna. I know how things are. If you recall, when our Father sent me, he sent me to millions of people and yet very few listened to me even though I did not sin and had the power to perform miracles to get people's attention. It doesn't matter how much failure you believe you had, rather, what matters is that you had faith in our Father and myself and you tried; you kept opening your mouth and communicating in other ways to try and turn people to me—you learned of my love and sought to practice it.

Disciple: I spent so many years trying to tell Christians about you, and as a result, I was hated, rejected and despised by them—I don't how many times I heard, "*you are wrong.*" At times it was so hard to continue due to all those religious voices telling me I was wrong.

Joshua: I understand. It was the same for me when I was on the earth in your realm. The religious establishment and those who make it up or have allegiances to it have always been against me. As one of your songwriters once sang, "that's just the way it is, some things will never change." But you did well—you did not let their voices of faithlessness, doubt and error turn you away from me and my Way—you changed for the better!

Disciple: But Master, I don't think I loved as well as I should. I had this fault and this weakness, and so I don't know if I ever really understood your love well, nor am I sure I expressed it well.

Joshua: Dear Rianna, you understood my love well enough. If you recall, my love for you changed your life—you went from a taker to a giver, from a fearful person to a person of faith, from a proud person to a person of humility, from a selfish person to a selfless person. Just because you could not find many who were willing to love with you, does not change the fact that *you* choose to try and love me back, and to love others. I saw how many people you invited into my Way of Life and love. Just because they refused does not mean you failed. No, you were faithful with what you had.

Disciple: (Rianna is weeping now.) I don't know what to say…

Joshua: Remember all those times people rejected you due to your sincere faith in me? Do you remember the jobs you lost because you spoke what was true when people didn't want to hear it? Do you remember you're being forced to give up people who you cared about because you were only given two choices—go their way or follow me? Do you remember the ill will and harm intended for you because you stood for what was right and true? Do you remember how when they threatened to take your life, you stood your ground due to your faith in me and your love for us?" I know that those times don't seem like much time in your life, but those choices defined both your faith in us and the quality and importance and nobleness of the Life you choose.

Disciple: (Rianna can't speak through her tears…)

Joshua: You experienced so much rejection and heartache in your life – so much loneliness and unwanted separation - just because you choose to put your faith in me and our Father and you would not settle for anything else less than seeing true love lived out among people. People treated you wrongly and badly simply because you tried your best to speak what was true and you tried to help them even when they did not want help, which offended them.

Disciple: (Rianna's eyes are bright and filled with tears.)

Joshua: Well, Abba and I remember. In fact, we can review it any time we want! My friend and sister, you will be going to see our Father in a bit here, but I need to repeat this. Well done, Rianna! You were faithful in a little, and so you are going to be given much. I am proud to have you as my friend and sister, and I can speak for our Father in this— He is proud and grateful to have you as His daughter! Come, enter into the fullness of eternal life!

"I am the resurrection and the Life. Whoever has faith in me, though he/she dies, yet shall he/she live. And whoever has faith in me shall never die."

And he asks, "Where is your faith?"

The revolutionary of peace and rightness and Life invites us all to come, join his peaceful revolution!

Please see www.thepeacefulrevolution.info for more information on joining the peaceful revolution.

SECTION 6:
OBJECTIONS TO THE SOLUTION

Theme:
- Various Ways to Avoid The Light

Section Introduction

There are many objections to the fact that a historical person some two-thousand years ago came, gave a life-changing message and validated who he said he was – the Messenger of the Creator – through performing miracles, including defeating death.

The many objections are typically variations of these basic ones:

- You cannot prove God exists;
- You cannot prove that the gospels are reliable eyewitness accounts of the person of Joshua of Nazareth;
- The gospel accounts cannot be accurate accounts or reliable because they contain accounts of miracles;
- How could the Christian God exist if he is both all-powerful and all-loving? Really, why is there so much suffering in the world?
- Why doesn't God reveal himself if he/she exists?
- How could a loving God send people to hell?
- But all those religious people cannot believe something that is wrong!

In the next and last chapter, we will answer these questions and more.

45

OBJECTIONS ADDRESSED

Opening Questions: (Variations on the Section Questions)
- Are any books of antiquity accurate or reliable accounts of the past events which they chronicle?
- If metaphysical realities exist, why are miracles impossible?
- Is human suffering caused by God?
- Wasn't Joshua of Nazareth revealing in the clearest way possible that God does exist?
- Does God send people to hell?
- Doesn't history prove that vast majorities of people can and do believe things that are false?
- Can a person prove love exists?

The fundamental question, "Why do you state that it is reasonable to believe that the person of Joshua of Nazareth – his core teachings and major events in his life – were successfully recorded in the four gospel books?", must be addressed since *the person of Joshua of Nazareth is the primary standard which I use to demonstrate that Christianity is a successful failure.*

The Trustworthiness of the Gospel Books

It is interesting when talking to people who are skeptical about Jesus of Nazareth that they will often provide some specific claim justifying their doubt, and regarding that claim will state, "anything is possible" to justify the claim. For example, the skeptic might say, "oh, the manuscripts that they possess about the four gospels are far from infallible, and there are many possibilities regarding people tampering with them or just plain making stuff up—anything is possible."

In response to their, "anything is possible" statement, I often will respond with something like, "so, if anything is possible, then it is possible that the record of the four gospels is essentially accurate." Their reaction to that is often incredulity or offense, which reveals much.

If they were honest with themselves, their statement would be, "anything is possible except that the life and teachings and deeds of Jesus of Nazareth were accurately captured in those four gospel books." At least then they would be, and their bias would be laid bare. The simple fact is that not only is it possible that eyewitnesses successfully recorded the words and deeds of Jesus of Nazareth, but probable. There are no ancient texts that have four corroborating accounts by different authors about the same subject to prove their veracity.

This book is not some apologetic for manuscripts or texts. That type of work has been done, and the reader is free to research it. *This author's position is simple—it is possible that the four accounts of the life, teachings, and deeds of Jesus of Nazareth are generally accurate.* Please note I did not say "free from error" or the religious people's term, "inerrant"—I said generally accurate. Stated another way, the main events and fundamental or core teachings of Jesus of Nazareth were successfully preserved in the four gospels by the four gospel authors.

This position is no more unreasonable than trusting any other ancient historical texts of that period. And as already noted it is significantly more reasonable given the four accounts of the same subject and historical figure, Jesus or Joshua of Nazareth.

So, when someone makes some form of the statement, "we can't trust that the four gospels are accurate" a reasonable response is, "*Why not? Is it possible they are accurate?*" Again, the answer to that question will be revealing. If the answer is no, then that person has a bias so strong that they are not willing to consider things that might well be true on that topic.

Do people look to other writings and books of antiquity and believe they hold accurate accounts of historical events or people's thoughts? Yes, of course they do, and to some much older and less well attested than the four gospel books written in the first century.

The two most cited non-Christian sources of information that validate the existence of the historical Jesus of Nazareth are the works of ancient historians Josephus and Tacitus. The contemporary scholar Louis Feldman has stated that "few have doubted the genuineness" of Josephus" reference to Jesus of Nazareth in *book 20* of the *Antiquities of the Jews*, and that reference is only disputed by a few scholars. [61]

---

[61] Van Voorst, Robert E (2000). Jesus Outside the New Testament: An Introduction

A primary reason for discounting the authenticity of the four gospel books by non-theists is that they contain Joshua performing miracles. Of course, that demonstrates a bias against both the metaphysical as well as against a metaphysical or spiritual agent acting in this realm of the surface of the earth. Having a bias against spiritual things is not "open-minded" and like all bias, is not reasonable given the evidence that our human experience provides. Is it possible that a Being greater than humans and existing in a dimension beyond our third dimension did intervene through Joshua? Indeed that proposition is not logically impossible.

Given the favorite movies and books about the possibilities of aliens and super humans, their capabilities, and the people believing much of it is possible, it indeed is unreasonable to exclude the four gospel accounts as "fiction" due to the miracles documented in them. What would account for the acceptance by hundreds of millions of people of many unlikely things while rejecting a well attested historical document and its subject, Joshua of Nazareth? A plausible answer is fear, dislike or hatred of the concept of accountability or the agent of that accountability.

Let us take another look at this from a different view before we continue. I have met many Christians who say out of one side of their mouth, "Oh, I believe in Jesus" or "I believe everything he says." Out of the other side of their mouth, they say, "Oh, we can't be sure Jesus said that" regarding some actual teaching in the four gospel books that they don't like or with which they don't agree. You can't have it both ways and be an honest person operating by integrity. Either *the core, primary or essential events and teachings* of Jesus of Nazareth are successfully recorded in the four gospel books that we possess today, or they are not.

As soon as you start down the road of some form of a denial of that possibility – that the adult and public life of Jesus of Nazareth was successfully captured, recorded and preserved in the four books we possess today – then *you have no reasonable basis to say, "I believe in Jesus."* At least not the historical Joshua of Nazareth described in those four books. Sadly, most people don't care if they have a reasonable basis or not. Their made-up "christ" keeps them comfortable in this world, and in their beliefs, they are heading towards heaven, which is the placebo's (made up christ's) primary purpose.

If you reject the recorded sayings of the historical Jesus of Nazareth in the four gospel books- the historical person whose life was recorded by four separate authors (two of the books authored by eyewitnesses) in the four gospels - then what "jesus" do you believe? What "jesus" if you don't

to the Ancient Evidence. p. 83. Eerdmans Publishing. ISBN 978-0-8028-4368-5.

Maier, Paul L. (1995). Josephus, the essential works: a condensation of Jewish antiquities and The Jewish war. p. 285. ISBN 978-0-8254-3260-6.

even know his teachings because you never seriously read or studied them? What "jesus" if an actual disciple/follower of Joshua of Nazareth gives you a test containing his teachings and you fail the test? What "jesus" if you live contrary to the teachings of the real, historical person of Joshua of Nazareth?

The answer to "What jesus" is the imaginary "jesus christs" of the Christian religion. The ones people make up to "have their cake and eat it too"—to justify their lives in this world.

> Those who seek to keep their life will lose it; while those who seek to lose their life for my sake and the Gospels shall save it. (Mark 8:35)

It is irrational to claim to be a follower of the historical Jesus of Nazareth if you don't even know his teachings. It is doubly absurd to claim to be a follower of Jesus of Nazareth while at the same time stating or defending beliefs or behavior that run contrary to his teachings as contained in the four gospel books. And yet, that, in general, describes many of the people who make up the successful failure that is Christianity.

Of course, many religious people don't care about reason as they think that religious beliefs are somehow exempt from the test of logic. If they knew the One who says, "I am the truth"; and, "All who are of the truth hear my voice"; and "the truth will set you free"; then they would see the great error of their illogical way. Sadly, many religious people/Christians put reason aside when it leads them where they do not want to go. In a real and significant way, they are reason-phobic. Let us clarify some important distinctions in this regard.

We cannot validate metaphysical or spiritual realities with our senses. Stated another way, sensing spiritual things is not in the realm of reason or logic. For example, we cannot see an "angel," nor can we see our soul, nor can we hear an audible voice of God. If a person claims that they did hear an audible voice of God, for example, that cannot be validated using reason or logic unless their testimony about hearing God contained the content of that hearing. So, for example, if the person said, "I heard God, and She said that three equals one," then we can use logic to prove that the content allegedly communicated from God to that person is false. We cannot prove the experience was fake – that the person did not hear God – but we can prove that what was communicated in that alleged experience was false.

Furthermore, can we determine truth or falsehood about spiritual claims if we do not have a standard against which to judge the claim? For example, if someone says, "I believe Jesus visited the earth before he came to the people of Israel 2,000 years ago", that claim cannot be verified as true or false since Joshua does not address that in the four gospels nor do we have any eyewitness testimony writings stating that. Or, if another person says, "I believe God want's people to drink tea," that claim cannot be verified as true or false since Joshua does not address that in the four gospels. Please remember, dear reader, that the standard this author is using – since I am a disciple of Joshua of Nazareth and he is my Master – is Joshua of Nazareth, not "the Bible."

What can we conclude in this area of "can we trust the four gospels and how can we test stated God beliefs'? The answer to the first question is yes, of course, we can trust that the four gospel books contain the *core, primary or essential events and teachings* of the life of Jesus of Nazareth. If we question that four separate accounts of a subject who lived 2,000 years ago cannot be trusted as accurate, then we should say the same thing about all other writings during or before that time period which have the same or less manuscript support, especially if it only has one author/source and not four. Again, if you have a bias against metaphysical events, then you will reject that line of reasoning, but at least acknowledge you have a bias against the metaphysical even while you cannot prove the real and significant physical existence of numbers or forgiveness!

The answer to the second question is yes; we can evaluate God statements or proclamations or claims by using observation, reason, and logic to do so. Logic cannot prove or disprove the existence of the person of Joshua of Nazareth or any other person who lived in the past. Those who claim it can have a metaphysical bias which destroys any claim of objectivity. In fact, all God-claims ought to be rigorously tested using reason, logic, and observation. If they were – and people would accept the truth that reason and logic reveal regarding God claims - we would have far less religious conflict with which to deal. In fact, only One Man would be left standing at the end!

This chapter will not present a defense of, or the evidence for, the veracity of the gospels capturing and recording the three years of the life, deeds, and words of Joshua of Nazareth. With Google available, it is a simple matter to perform a search like, "manuscript evidence for the new testament," and to research the results yourself.

Bruce M. Metzger is widely considered to be one of the most respected and influential new testament scholars of the 20th century. In his works, *The New Testament: Its Background, Growth, and Content, 3rd ed.*, rev. and enlarged (Nashville: Abingdon Press, 2003), pgs. 317–8; *The Canon of the New Testament* (Oxford: Clarendon, 1997), pgs. 251–4 & 287-88; he makes a compelling case that the over 5,000 Greek manuscripts, about 10,000 Latin manuscripts, and over 9,000 manuscripts of the new testament in various languages that we possess leave little doubt that the new testament that we possess is accurate or faithful to the original writer's original manuscripts.

New Testament scholar Kurt Aland wrote a book giving reliable dates for the various new testament manuscripts that exist. The dates of these manuscripts range from c. 125 (the B52 papyrus, oldest copy of John fragments) to the introduction of printing in Germany in the 15th century.[62]

Again, I invite the reader to investigate these facts to verify my claim that it is reasonable and plausible to believe that the life, deeds, and teachings of the first-century figure of Joshua of Nazareth were successfully recorded and preserved in the four gospel books.

I recommend you read these articles on Wikipedia:

https://en.wikipedia.org/wiki/Jesus

https://en.wikipedia.org/wiki/Historicity_of_Jesus

Those articles contain many references that you can research. In short, the information in those articles/pages makes the case that it is entirely reasonable to believe that the four gospels books contain an accurate account of the public life and works of the first-century person of Jesus of Nazareth.

(For a response to typical objections to listening *only* to Joshua as The Standard for knowing God and how human beings ought to live, please see chapter 24, *Some Questions for Biblians and Christians.*

The Gospels Do Not Contain Truth Since They Contain Accounts of Miracles

This is an objection based on a bias against a metaphysical or spiritual reality. Or, stated another way, it is an objection that comes from a "scientific" (more precisely a physicalist) worldview. I have made a strong case in the book that there is a metaphysical or spiritual dimension to human existence. To deny the existence of spiritual or metaphysical things is irrational as we have seen. If there is a metaphysical realm or dimension that contains entities which do not conform to our physical models, then why is it a stretch to believe that those entities could intervene in our realm given the right conditions?

If we are bound only by the "laws of nature" (meaning the physicalist scientific view that all that exists are atoms and molecules, etc.), then how do you fit, for example, the real concept of forgiveness or reason or mathematics into that worldview?

One cannot prove that there is no metaphysical realm. Furthermore, a spiritual realm is the *best* conclusion given the deductive evidence and our human experience. Consider this argument once again.

Forgiveness is real.

---

[62] Aland, Kurt; Barbara Aland (1995). *The Text of The New Testament: An Introduction to the Critical Editions and to the Theory and Practice of Modern Textual Criticism.* Translated by Erroll F. Rhodes (2nd ed.). Grand Rapids, MI: Wm. B. Eerdmans Publishing Company. pp. 40f, 72f. ISBN 0-8028-4098-1.

Forgiveness is not physical.
Therefore, non-physical things are real.

If I don't love God, I will go to hell—Shouldn't love be a choice and not forced?

This is another popular false belief that prevents people from considering faith in their Father/Creator. It is often stated as, "So God wants to force me to love him, or else I am threatened with the possibility of going to hell." The false belief in the prior statement is the belief that God chooses where a person will spend their after physical death existence. It is also inaccurate to imply that God "forces" or uses threats to experience love.

The simple answer to the question is we can choose to love or not love whomever we wish, but if we decide not to place our faith in our Father nor love our Father / Creator and others, we forfeit eternal life. Eternal life is something that is earned. We can choose the sure way to Life by placing our faith in our Father and His Son and thus living for truth, rightness, and love; or we can try and earn it without His help by trying to help other people in this life through truth, rightness, and love. If we choose not to love our Father back and we don't do well with living for truth, rightness and by true love, then we send ourselves to the consequences that are just according to our choices. Hell is not a place of eternal torment, but rather a place of justice and termination.

Other than the plain answer that God doesn't choose your after physical life destiny, it can be revealing to ask these questions to those who offer that objection:

- Are you are required being? In other words, are you a necessary being, meaning some universal law exists that says, 'You must exist'?
- Did you have to exist or could you not have existed?
- Did you cause yourself to exist or was your existence given to you?
- How exactly are you causing your existence to continue right now?

The reasonable person will admit that their existence was given to them or at least they were not - nor currently are - the cause of their existence. (If they claim they are the cause of their existence, ask them to explain that to you with clarity. If they are a physicalist, they will argue that their existence is merely physical and thus you cannot productively move forward with deluded people who deny realities like the existence of reason and forgiveness). Every person has a cause of their existence, the Designer, and Creator of our souls. Existence is a privilege, not a right or a necessity. (Many newly forming human beings have their earthly existence taken away by having their bodies destroyed while being in their mother's womb.) We human beings are not necessary beings, which is to say we did not have to exist.

So, we should be grateful for our existence. Please consider this saying by Alfred Lord Tennyson - "it is better to have loved and lost than never to have loved at all." This statement about love is an important and profound truth which points out this critical fact about our human existence – to experience "love" is such a privilege and so special that it is worth the pain of having that love rejected or not returned then never to have experienced it before. Stated another way, to not "love" is not to experience the best of what human life is. Of course I would qualify Mr. Tennyson's "love" as a lesser love, yet still meaningful.

This same concept can be applied in this domain. It is better to have existed and lost my existence than never to have existed at all – this is particularly true when I get to choose if I want to continue to exist or not! Regarding love, not all of us experience the privilege of being loved back!

The next step in addressing this objection is to answer the question, "Is loving other people ever wrong"? In other words, is it wrong to love other people, or is it good and right to love other people? It is true that love is a choice of our free human will, but that does not eliminate the obligation that comes with this essential choice. (See the proper definition of love earlier in this book – love is to value someone at least as high as myself and to treat them selflessly due to compassion.) If a person loves us, are we not obligated to love them back? Or stated another way, if a person loves us, then should we not love them back? Wouldn't the world and our lives be much better if this happened? How would you describe the decision not to return love to someone?

Finally, if I love someone (an adult) and that person does not want to return my love, and that person chooses a destructive path in life even though I have warned them about that path, have I done anything wrong if I allow them to walk that destructive path? Would forcing them off that path honor their free will? Could I force them not to take that path? If I said to that person, "please just come over here and look and see how this path is better than the one you are choosing," but they refused to look, am I accountable for their self-destruction?

A final objection might be, "well, God did not have to set up a system where he allows us to choose our after physical death destiny-where we are held accountable for our actions-He could have just had us all go to heaven." Would that system be fair and just? In that system, Adolf Hitler would be in heaven with Mother Teresa.

No, the simple truth is that God has set up a perfect system where those who care about what is true and right and who want to love and give to others are rewarded; while those who choose not to love others and to primarily take from others, experience just consequences. Included in that system is the ability to choose to be exceptional; to live an exceptional life; to know and understand more and thus be a greater help to others and thus spread God's love, truth, and peace to others. That occurs – that exceptional life - when a person:

- Is grateful to their Father/Creator for being created and thus having life existence;
- Sees themselves for what they indeed are – a flawed, selfish, prideful and fearful being - and gladly takes the offer of forgiveness and freedom He continually extends to them; and
- Chooses, through faith, to love Him and His Son back and thus enter into Life—the exceptional Life that continues after physical death.

The person who turns their back on the One who loves them and who insists on living a selfish life:

- A life characterized by taking instead of giving;
- A life marked by caring more about one's self than others;
- A life characterized by living for material things and self-pleasures instead of trying to help others.

That person will "enjoy" the life given them by their Father, and when their body dies, they will experience fairness and justice, and by their wrong and willful choices, they forfeit Life everlasting—they turned down the exceptional Life and have no one to blame but themselves. Of course, people need to understand the decision of eternal life or not, and if they never heard of The Light nor understood the choice clearly, then God will sort that out.

Christian Responses to Disciples

Here are some examples of the Christian or Biblians response to the disciple of Joshua repeating Joshua's truths that the Christian does not agree with:

Example 1:

"You think you know more than leader /pastor /bishop /scholar /author so-and-so? Who do you think you are?"

This is an example of the logical fallacy of appeal to authority. It is a pride based objection not based on reason. The proper reaction to hearing something different would be, "Oh that is a real and interesting difference— I need to check that out".

Example 2:

"I've read the Bible many times; studied it for many years, and I know what it says, and you are wrong."

This is an example of the logical fallacy of appeal to expert opinion. It is a pride based objection not based on reason. The proper reaction would be to take one of the truths the disciple is stating, and provide reasons why it is wrong.

Example 3:

"Are you saying that all the leaders of the Christian religion are wrong?"

This is an example of the logical fallacy of argument from incredulity. It is a pride based objection not based on reason. The proper reaction would be to consider what Joshua of Nazareth said, find the quote to validate it is accurate and in context and research the claim to see if it is true.

Self-pride and fear and selfishness frequently work together to keep us blind, in darkness and unable to advance in becoming a better human being. For example, if I am afraid to go on a boat due to my fear of drowning, I might say to the person who is offering to take me on a boat, "well, I don't care for that type of boat." Self-pride prevents me from admitting my fear and causes me to provide an excuse rather than reveal the simple truth that I am afraid of drowning. The person might have a good reason to take me on the boat – perhaps to transfer me to an island where I could help people – but my fear causes my pride to provide an excuse for my selfishness!

Self-pride and fear and selfishness are "enemies" of two critical capabilities of people – love and reason. All three work against our ability to love other people. And all three work against reason to determine what is true and right. And without practicing love, knowing truth and acting rightly, we are truly falling short of being what we were intended to be as human beings…we are failing at life itself! (Of course, the materialistic lie comes along and whispers, "Oh, I am well of and comfortable, so I am not failing at anything…")

The simple truth is that people who live according to their natural nature of self-pride or fear or selfishness are the reason and cause for most of the suffering, coldness, injustice, pain, neglect, discord, conflict, abuse, and violence – in short, loveless-ness - that occurs in the world each day. I challenge the reader to think this through and consider the possibility that you are part of the problem rather than part of the solution…and then ask, "how can I overcome and be free of my nature of self-pride and fear and selfishness and the hurt that causes other people?"

Can you experience this world and watch the news and say, "Oh, people are doing well"? Is your standard so low (or in reality, you have no standard to judge such things), or are you in such a self-made bubble of self-pride or fear or selfishness that you refuse to see things how they are? Perhaps your standard to judge how YOUR life is going is, "If I am comfortable, well fed and entertained, all is well in the world." That kind of thinking is the epitome of a selfish life:

- A life with little or no consideration for others;
- A life lived in the darkness of self-pride and fear and selfishness;
- A life without any or very little true love;
- A "life" that will lead to self-condemnation and destruction;
- A "life" that forfeits Life everlasting.

Is that the kind of life you want to live? Do you want to miss the most beautiful aspect of human life? Are you sure no one will hold us accountable for how we live the life we have been given? Are you confident that by ignoring and denying the Standard given, you are exempt from being accountable? Do you want to reject reason and thus deny the simple truths in this section? I urge you not to do that and instead have a genuinely open mind, meaning you are not afraid to consider new things—meaning that you are not scared to look at the Light.

Why didn't Jesus stay on the earth?

Some skeptics ask, "how come Jesus of Nazareth did not stay on the earth to fix things?" The answer is simple and is addressed by the following simple question.

Did the people who were leaders or in authority where he came the first time he visited welcome him and listen to him and want him to stay?

If you know his story, he was killed by the people. It is not like he was welcomed and put on a throne then just decided to leave! What good would be done to stick around when people didn't want you around and were always trying to find ways to destroy you? If he stuck around after his resurrection, they would seek to kill him again and again and again…!

If you think Jesus would be welcomed today, then you have created a "jesus" of your own making and are ignoring the facts that the historical Jesus reveals. I can testify that as one of his followers, I am not welcomed by people, and I am only one of his students.

'Oh, You Are a Red Letter Christian'

Because many Bible publishers have printed Joshua's words in red ink instead of black ink to rightly set them apart from the other voices in the Bible, many Christians will put disciples in a box they call "red letter Christians." Sadly, these Christians or Biblians cannot distinguish between a Person and an ink color. Stated another way, since the Christians/Biblians have come to believe that a book (and by extension, its pages and letters and ink) represents God (due to listening to Paul more than Jesus), they cannot distinguish between the letters/words on the page and the subject the letters/words address. Therefore, when they hear a disciple articulate that we listen to and follow Jesus of Nazareth and not the Bible, they say, "oh, you are one of those red letter Christians."

No, we are disciples of the Person described by his own words in the four gospel books, and some Bible publishers have wisely chosen to print The Light's words in red ink to set them apart from the other author's opinions.

Answers to Section and Chapter Opening Questions:

Let us complete this chapter by directly answering the opening section and chapter questions. Here they are again:

- You cannot prove God exists;

A designer is required to account for the complex physical nature of our human bodies for example. A First Cause is required to account for the metaphysical realities like reason, forgiveness, and love. The evidence points to God existing, and the conclusions of mathematical probability science also support the existence of God. A Man some 2,000 years ago did some pretty amazing things to validate his Message, and part of his Message is that God exists!

- Why doesn't God reveal himself if he/she exists?

He did, and he does. He sent His Messenger some 2,000 years ago. He also reveals himself in a spiritual sense, to those who choose to believe Him and place their faith in him. God is revealed in His Creation, especially human beings. Wasn't Joshua of Nazareth revealing in the clearest way possible that God does exist? Joshua did say, "If you have seen me, you have seen the Father." Joshua's miracles validate that he did represent the Creator/Father and was uniquely connected to the Creator.

- How could the Christian God exist if he is both all-powerful and all-loving? Really, why is there so much suffering in the world?

That false belief has been answered and exposed as false. There is so much suffering in the world mostly because human beings refuse to love one another.

Human suffering is caused first by our perception of our lives. Pain – both physical and spiritual – is caused by people or natural events. There are no "acts of God" which bring destruction or suffering.

- How could a loving God send people to hell?

He could not and He does not. Rather, people send themselves to justice and destruction.

- You cannot prove that the gospels are reliable eyewitness accounts of the person of Joshua of Nazareth;

You cannot prove that any written works in that time frame or earlier are not contrived, so be consistent and throw out all those works as well. For that matter, throw out all the books up until several hundred years ago.

432

Having four written accounts by four separate authors of the same subject – which accounts mostly corroborate each other – is substantial evidence that the four accounts are authentic, accurate and reliable accounts. Having a bias against a metaphysical or spiritual reality when we have strong evidence that it exists is not a valid reason to dismiss the gospels.

- Version 2: Are any books of antiquity accurate or reliable accounts of events at the time the book was written?

Most reasonable people will answer yes. Therefore, if other books of antiquity are respected as being accurate accounts of events, then should not the four gospel book also be given that benefit of the doubt as well, especially since there are four accounts of the same subject?

- The gospel accounts cannot be accurate accounts or reliable because they contain accounts of miracles;

Having an anti-metaphysical bias is not an argument. Metaphysical things exist – like reason, logic, forgiveness, love, our soul or spirit – therefore it is reasonable to believe that there is more to that metaphysical realm which could include a Creator/Designer being who could act in this realm under certain conditions.

Miracles are not ordinary by definition, but it is unreasonable to discount that they could never have happened. The only people who can reasonably (within their wrong worldview) discount the possibility of miracles are those who are physicalists who also unreasonably deny the non-physical nature of things like reason, the human soul, and forgiveness. In other words, they are those who insist that a computer's hardware can account for its software applications and functions.

- But all those people cannot believe something that is wrong!

Yes, history does prove that vast majorities of people have believed wrong things. The earth being flat is one such example. Other examples include the belief that metaphysical causes caused the black plague. As science has advanced and revealed true causes behind physical events, it could be said that most people who lived in the distant past had wrong beliefs about many or even most physical causes. Thus, just because so many Christians (and people of other religions) have a wrong understanding about God and they misrepresent the living God by the one they claim as their triune god, does not mean God does not exist. Furthermore, just because people of the past had wrong/erroneous beliefs about metaphysical causes does not mean that a spiritual reality does not exist.

- Can a person prove love exists?

Yes, because it does occur on the earth between people *and* it is not physical but rather metaphysical or spiritual. The most important "thing" that exists regarding human beings is love, and it is not physical, and it must have a first cause. Or stated another way, whoever created human beings gave us the capacity to love and thus it must be relevant to that creator.

And no irrational physicalists, "love" properly defined is not produced by chemicals or animal instincts! (For that matter, what is the cause of "animal instincts"?)

What Exactly Is Wrong With Jesus' Teachings?

Many who oppose Joshua of Nazareth do so on false grounds. What I mean by that is they use the logical fallacies of the Straw Man or Hasty Generalization to apply criticism. Stated yet another way, they shoot down the false "christ" of Christianity to make their points, or they rightly reject wrong Christian theology/beliefs thinking those wrong Christian beliefs or practices represent the real, historical Joshua of Nazareth. What they don't typically do is to quote Joshua from the four gospels and criticize HIS teaching. And they indeed do not quote his sayings like, "love one another as I have loved you" or "Treat others the way you want to be treated."

This simple discussion below can get to the bottom of the issue IF the person who is a critic cares about truth and uses reason and logic well to find it.

1. What specific belief or practice of Christians do you think is wrong?
    o   When the person identifies something that has no basis in the real, historical Joshua of Nazareth's teachings, the following must be said.
2. "OK, you are right about that, but Jesus of Nazareth did not teach that nor did he set up nor endorse that practice. In other words, Jesus of Nazareth is not responsible for that silly thing or that wrong."

Once a disciple can work through two or three of these erroneous beliefs - and if the person is going to allow reason to guide them and they genuinely have an open mind - they ought to get to the place of actually listening to the real, historical Joshua of Nazareth.

So, I ask, what exactly is wrong with Joshua's teachings? *He made it clear that truth and rightness and love are the most important things we human beings ought to be concerned with, and so I ask again, what exactly is wrong with that?* A reasonable person with a working conscience will have no reply other than, "nothing."

Please consider that a moment.

If nothing wrong can be found in Jesus' primary teachings in the four gospels, why not listen to him? Or even if you find something you think is wrong, is it reasonable to dismiss all the right and good things he taught and lived out? Why reject him on the basis of all the wrong that people have created using his name/person? He is not to blame for the rubbish created and practiced in his name so why reject him on that basis? Nor is he responsible for his actual follower's failures or weaknesses—our failures and shortcomings do not nullify who he is or the truths that he spoke or the things that he did.

The only reasonable cause for the rejection of the real, historical Jesus of Nazareth would be his claims about who he is and what the One he claimed to represent wants. And, if it is accurate that the essentials that Jesus taught were *that truth and rightness and love are the most important things we human beings ought to be concerned with,* what does that mean for people who reject that?

Furthermore, if ultimately what the One he represents desires is that the highest form of love be lived out among people, what does that say about people who reject that desire? Perhaps the concept of accountability has a lot to do with the rejection of Joshua of Nazareth?

APPENDICES:

Appendix 1: The Christianity Conversation

Perhaps one of the better ways to show correct versus incorrect views is to have a dialog between two people who hold different views…

Please see the Christianity Conversation at http://thepeacefulrevolution.info/conversations.html#The_Christianity_D iscussion

Appendix 2: The Bible Conversation

Please see the Bible Conversation at http://thepeacefulrevolution.info/conversations.html#The_Bible_Discussi on

Appendix 3: Reference: Basic Teachings of The Light

- God exists, and that creator loves the people of the earth whom He created;
- Our creator is not a God of wrath or anger or vengeance but rather a God of love and compassion;
- Joshua of Nazareth was the unique Messenger of the creator to the point of calling himself the creator's Son and the Model for mankind i.e. "the Son of Man";
- Through faith in, and faithfulness to, Joshua and his Father, the Creator, a person can escape the cage of self-pride and fear and selfishness and enter into eternal life and thus preserve and enhance their existence after their body dies;

- Love is the most important "'thing" the creator gave humans the capacity to express, and He wants people to love each other more than anything else;

- Love does not exist or express itself in a vacuum, so truth and rightness are also extremely important "things" the creator wants us to pursue, know, value and practice;

- We are only to love God and other people, not things. We are to live to love others and thus we cannot work for money/material things and also live for, love and serve God and others; they are mutually exclusive—you cannot serve God and money or material things;

- The creator and His Messenger are against religion which destroys love and unity – "the traditions of men" and all God beliefs which have NO basis in the teachings of The Light of the world. Religion is a substitute for truth and love and rightness and works hard against the creator and his Son and their desire for love and unity among people;

- The primary belief traditions of men which keeps people away from the Light of the world is believing Paul's teaching about the scripture and by substituting "the bible" for the person of Joshua of Nazareth, thus nullifying Joshua's teachings with all the false statements about God and God's character that are contained in the other sixty-two books of the protestant bible;

- The primary behavior tradition of men to substitute for actually doing what Joshua wants is the tradition of "going to church" which means spending a lot of money to build a building to meet in, hear moral sermons in, sing songs in, and do other rituals in;

- Human beings are not neutral or good, rather we have a predisposition to not do what is right and good for others – we are locked in a cage of self-pride and fear and thus selfishness and darkness. Only faith in the God of love can effectively set us free from our self-made cage;

- Most human beings cannot see their need to overcome their self-pride and fear and selfishness, and thus ignore and reject the creator and His desire for people to love one another. This produces what Joshua calls "the world" in his teachings—people who live selfish lives not truly caring about other people;

- Followers of Joshua will share his Life together with other followers—we will be one another's true family and will live accordingly. We will be distinct groups of people living together and caring about and for each other and thus being the city on a hill and the little flocks;

- Joshua warned his first followers against "being deceived" or "being misled" several times and further warned that there will be many who come in his name and deceive many. There is only one Way to be sure to avoid that, and that is to make Joshua one's Master as he asks, which means a person will have no other authority regarding who God is and what God wants other than Joshua of Nazareth via HIS words/teachings/truths in the four gospel books.

Appendix 4: A Basic Framework for Human Sexuality

Please see the article at http://thepeacefulrevolution.info/sexuality.html

Appendix 5: The Trinity Trap

Please see the article at http://thepeacefulrevolution.info/trinity.html

Appendix 6: Islam

Please see the article at http://thepeacefulrevolution.info/NPT/islam.html

Appendix 7: Protestant Biblicism Debunked

Please see the article at http://thepeacefulrevolution.info/bible-scripture.html

Appendix 8: Forgiveness and Blood Sacrifice

Please see the article at http://thepeacefulrevolution.info/forgiveness.html

Appendix 9: Church Conversations

Please see these revealing conversations at http://thepeacefulrevolution.info/conversations.html

Appendix 10: Christian Church Doctrine Debunked

Please see the article at http://thepeacefulrevolution.info/church.html

Appendix 11: The Stranger Paul

Please see article at http://thepeacefulrevolution.info/apostle-paul.html

Appendix 12: Zealousness but not for Love

Please see article at http://thepeacefulrevolution.info/non-love-zealousness.html

OTHER BOOKS BY THIS AUTHOR

The Light of the World: The Life and Teachings of Jesus of Nazareth

Winner of the eLit Silver Award 2015! (See eLit reviewer notes below *)

A unique and fresh work that seeks to present Jesus of Nazareth by his own words as HE intended people to view him and hear him. There are many people who know some facts about "Jesus Christ", but there are very few people who have a good and solid understanding of his person and teachings. For example, did you know that Jesus did not teach that he was a sacrifice for people's sins?

As bible religion spreads across the earth like a cancer, fewer and fewer people understand the one who calls himself the Light of the world and the Son of Man.

What is Jesus' core message?

What claims does he make about himself, and can those claims be trusted?

Does Jesus give humanity answers to its problems?

You will never be able to know the answer to that question unless you read his words yourself.

This work contains his words in the four gospels alone with helpful notes to counter the many contemporary religious beliefs which seek to nullify his simple teachings.

If you are a skeptic, be a good skeptic and read his words to make a good judgment - don't rely on others. If it is possible his words and story could have been recorded accurately and preserved - and it is possible - what have you got to lose by listening to him?

If you are a physicalist - one who believes the human experience can be satisfactorily explained by atoms, molecules and proteins - are you 100% certain that belief best explains your personal human experience? To use a computer as an analogy, the hardware cannot account for, nor did it create, the software. In the same manner, the physical human body cannot account for our sentience, abstract reasoning, nor the moral compass that we possess.

If call yourself a Christian or believe you are somehow "his", this book might provide some critical information that will significantly change your perspective on his person and teachings.

As the 'church' experience gets more and more like regular western entertainment, perhaps you can see the negative trend there and search for answers as to how to escape. Tired of the fast food culture of the western world? Can you see the shallowness and emptiness of the "please myself as my top principle of life" philosophy? Tired of the un-reasoning culture of much of the eastern world? Hopefully, perhaps even tired of the world?

Out of all the "great works of literature", are not the words, teachings and story of the person who is arguably one of the most influential and controversial figures in history, worth reading and considering? There is a single great adventure that waits for those with eyes to see. Just know, it is not an easy adventure, but rather a very difficult one, but the journey and results are more meaningful and satisfying than the greatest adventures the earth can provide. It all starts with giving Jesus of Nazareth your sincere and undivided attention. May this work - which contains his words, story and teachings - be the beginning of that journey!

* eLit Reviewer Comments:

"A deep, well executed and thought out approach on the diversion of belief - mainstream Christian biblical sacred teachings versus the actions and words/teachings of the first hand Jesus of Nazareth. Mind bending insight that creates many questions (more than answers).

"By highlighting scriptures from the NASB, Spiess eats away through fads to get to facts to better understand true interpretation first hand.

o Interesting points
o Unique approach
o Well written and good examples
o Very in depth writing"

RESOURCES

The author's web site contains many insightful articles addressing many of the topics addressed or implied in the book, as well as:

- An audio version of this book;
- An audio version of my prior book;
- Commentary articles on most of the major social and moral issues causing conflict in the U.S.;
- Other audio messages addressing both the Kingdom of God and social moral or ethical issues.

Finally and perhaps most importantly, the web site provides the means to actually join the peaceful revolution and thus become part of the solution!

www.thepeacefulrevolution.info

ABOUT THE AUTHOR

Tim Spiess has been writing on spiritual, 'religious' and existential matters for about thirty years. He published the book - *The Light of the World: The Life and Teachings of Jesus of Nazareth* - in 2015 that **won the Silver Award from the national eLit Book Awards organization** (see http://www.elitawards.com/2015_results.php)

Mr. Spiess has engaged in paid work at various things over the years. Most of that work was in the Information Technology domain either performing project management or analyst work.

Mr. Spiess values reason and logic very highly, and spends much of his time trying to help others do the same. He sees religion as a major hindrance to solving people's problems. When defined properly, there is no contradiction or paradox or tension between "faith" and "fact". The problem is that people have the wrong standard…they listen to just about every voice other than Jesus'.

Mr. Spiess currently spends his time trying to help people to listen to Jesus of Nazareth, and thus to start living according to his teachings. He does this through his writings both in print, like the book, as well as articles and his primary web sites – www.JoshuaFamilies.info and www.ThePeacefulRevolution.info . He encourages people to come, join the peaceful revolution!

Earlier in his life Mr. Spiess earned a Bachelor's Degree in Environmental Science from the University of Vermont as well as a Master's Degree in Business from PACE University in New York. He designed and built his own 2,400 sq.ft. house; has developed software and created web sites; has traveled extensively around North America; has traveled to Africa and supported a non-profit fishing business in Lake Victoria, Uganda; and communicates regularly with people all around the world.

Mr. Spiess is an expert on Jesus of Nazareth, religion, ethics and existential beliefs. He is available for media interviews and speaking engagements and can provide solutions to the most vexing human problems.

He has a lovely wife he calls his "life companion" and four children. In his spare time he bicycles, skis, exercises and would like to wind surf and snorkel more! He lives in the country in the Midwest U.S. and enjoys the simple life it presents even while his vision and work is very much global in scope.

Made in the USA
Coppell, TX
17 October 2021